Jack Sheppard

William Harrison Ainsworth

Internationale Bibliothek G M B H Berlin
1922

Contents

JACK SHEPPARD
by
William Harrison Ainsworth

EPOCH THE FIRST. 1703.
JONATHAN WILD.

CHAPTER I.
The Widow and her Child.

ON the night of Friday, the 26th of November, 1703, and at the hour of eleven, the door of a miserable habitation, situated in an obscure quarter of the Borough of Southwark, known as the Old Mint, was opened; and a man, with a lantern in his hand, appeared at the threshold. This person, whose age might be about forty, was attired in a brown double-breasted frieze coat, with very wide skirts, and a very narrow collar; a light drugget waist-coat, with pockets reaching to the knees; black plush breeches; grey worsted hose; and shoes with round toes, wooden heels, and high quarters, fastened by small silver buckles. He wore a three-cornered hat, a sandy-coloured scratch wig, and had a thick woollen wrapper folded round his throat. His clothes had evidently seen some service, and were plentifully begrimed with the dust of the workshop. Still he had a decent look, and decidedly the air of one well-to-do in the world. In stature, he was short and stumpy; in person, corpulent; and in countenance, sleek, snub-nosed, and demure.

Immediately behind this individual, came a pale, poverty-stricken woman, whose forlorn aspect contrasted strongly with his plump and comfortable physiognomy. She was dressed in a tattered black stuff gown, discoloured by various stains, and intended, it would seem, from the remnants of rusty crape with which it was here and there tricked out, to represent the garb of widowhood, and held in her arms a sleeping infant, swathed in the folds of a linsey-woolsey shawl.

Notwithstanding her emaciation, her features still retained something of a pleasing expression, and might have been termed beautiful, had it not been for that repulsive freshness of lip denoting the habitual dram-drinker; a freshness in her case rendered the more shocking from the almost livid hue of the rest of her complexion. She could not be more than twenty; and though want and other suffering had done the work of time, had wasted her frame, and robbed her cheek of its bloom and roundness, they had not extinguished the lustre of her eyes, nor thinned her raven hair. Checking an ominous cough, that, ever and anon, convulsed her lungs, the poor woman addressed a few parting words to her companion, who lingered at the doorway as if he had something on his mind, which he did not very well know how to communicate.

"Well, good night, Mr. Wood," said she, in the deep, hoarse accents of consumption; "and may God Almighty bless and reward you for your kindness! You were always the best of masters to my poor husband; and now you've proved the best of friends to his widow and orphan boy."

"Poh! poh! say no more about it," rejoined the man hastily. "I've done no more than my duty, Mrs. Sheppard, and neither deserve nor desire your thanks. 'Whoso giveth to the poor lendeth to the Lord;' that's my comfort. And such slight relief as I can afford should have been offered earlier, if I'd known where you'd taken refuge after your unfortunate husband's--"

"Execution, you would say, Sir," added Mrs. Sheppard, with a deep sigh, perceiving that her benefactor hesitated to pronounce the word. "You show more consideration to the feelings of a hempen widow, than there is any need to show. I'm used to insult as I am to misfortune, and am grown callous to both; but I'm *not* used to compassion, and know not how to take it. My heart would speak if it could, for it is very full. There was a time, long, long ago, when the tears would have rushed to my eyes unbidden at the bare mention of generosity like yours, Mr. Wood; but they never come now. I have never wept since that day."

"And I trust you will never have occasion to weep again, my poor soul," replied

Wood, setting down his lantern, and brushing a few drops from his eyes, "unless it be tears of joy. Pshaw!" added he, making an effort to subdue his emotion, "I can't leave you in this way. I must stay a minute longer, if only to see you smile."

So saying, he re-entered the house, closed the door, and, followed by the widow, proceeded to the fire-place, where a handful of chips, apparently just lighted, crackled within the rusty grate.

The room in which this interview took place had a sordid and miserable look. Rotten, and covered with a thick coat of dirt, the boards of the floor presented a very insecure footing; the bare walls were scored all over with grotesque designs, the chief of which represented the punishment of Nebuchadnezzar. The rest were hieroglyphic characters, executed in red chalk and charcoal. The ceiling had, in many places, given way; the laths had been removed; and, where any plaster remained, it was either mapped and blistered with damps, or festooned with dusty cobwebs. Over an old crazy bedstead was thrown a squalid, patchwork counterpane; and upon the counterpane lay a black hood and scarf, a pair of bodice of the cumbrous form in vogue at the beginning of the last century, and some other articles of female attire. On a small shelf near the foot of the bed stood a couple of empty phials, a cracked ewer and basin, a brown jug without a handle, a small tin coffee-pot without a spout, a saucer of rouge, a fragment of looking-glass, and a flask, labelled "*Rosa Solis*." Broken pipes littered the floor, if that can be said to be littered, which, in the first instance, was a mass of squalor and filth.

Over the chimney-piece was pasted a handbill, purporting to be "*The last Dying Speech and Confession of* TOM SHEPPARD, *the Notorious Housebreaker, who suffered at Tyburn on the 25th of February,* 1703." This placard was adorned with a rude wood-cut, representing the unhappy malefactor at the place of execution. On one side of the handbill a print of the reigning sovereign, Anne, had been pinned over the portrait of William the Third, whose aquiline nose, keen eyes, and luxuriant wig, were just visible above the diadem of the queen. On the other a wretched engraving of the Chevalier de Saint George, or, as he was styled in the label attached to the portrait, James the Third, raised a suspicion that the inmate of the house was not altogether free from some tincture of Jacobitism.

Beneath these prints, a cluster of hobnails, driven into the wall, formed certain letters, which, if properly deciphered, produced the words, "Paul Groves, cobler;"

and under the name, traced in charcoal, appeared the following record of the poor fellow's fate, "Hung himsel in this rum for luv off licker;" accompanied by a graphic sketch of the unhappy suicide dangling from a beam. A farthing candle, stuck in a bottle neck, shed its feeble light upon the table, which, owing to the provident kindness of Mr. Wood, was much better furnished with eatables than might have been expected, and boasted a loaf, a knuckle of ham, a meat-pie, and a flask of wine.

"You've but a sorry lodging, Mrs. Sheppard," said Wood, glancing round the chamber, as he expanded his palms before the scanty flame.

"It's wretched enough, indeed, Sir," rejoined the widow; "but, poor as it is, it's better than the cold stones and open streets."

"Of course--of course," returned Wood, hastily; "anything's better than that. But take a drop of wine," urged he, filling a drinking-horn and presenting it to her; "it's choice canary, and'll do you good. And now, come and sit by me, my dear, and let's have a little quiet chat together. When things are at the worst, they'll mend. Take my word for it, your troubles are over."

"I hope they are, Sir," answered Mrs. Sheppard, with a faint smile and a doubtful shake of the head, as Wood drew her to a seat beside him, "for I've had my full share of misery. But I don't look for peace on this side the grave."

"Nonsense!" cried Wood; "while there's life there's hope. Never be downhearted. Besides," added he, opening the shawl in which the infant was wrapped, and throwing the light of the candle full upon its sickly, but placid features, "it's sinful to repine while you've a child like this to comfort you. Lord help him! he's the very image of his father. Like carpenter, like chips."

"That likeness is the chief cause of my misery," replied the widow, shuddering. "Were it not for that, he would indeed be a blessing and a comfort to me. He never cries nor frets, as children generally do, but lies at my bosom, or on my knee, as quiet and as gentle as you see him now. But, when I look upon his innocent face, and see how like he is to his father,--when I think of that father's shameful ending, and recollect how free from guilt *he* once was,--at such times, Mr. Wood, despair will come over me; and, dear as this babe is to me, far dearer than my own wretched life, which I would lay down for him any minute, I have prayed to Heaven to remove him, rather than he should grow up to be a man, and be exposed to his father's temptations--rather than he should live as wickedly and die as disgracefully as his father. And, when I have seen him pining away before my eyes, getting thinner and thinner every day, I have sometimes thought my prayers were heard."

"Marriage and hanging go by destiny," observed Wood, after a pause; "but I trust your child is reserved for a better fate than either, Mrs. Sheppard."

The latter part of this speech was delivered with so much significance of manner, that a bystander might have inferred that Mr. Wood was not particularly fortunate in his own matrimonial connections.

"Goodness only knows what he's reserved for," rejoined the widow in a desponding tone; "but if Mynheer Van Galgebrok, whom I met last night at the Cross Shovels, spoke the truth, little Jack will never die in his bed."

"Save us!" exclaimed Wood. "And who is this Van Gal--Gal--what's his outlandish name?"

"Van Galgebrok," replied the widow. "He's the famous Dutch conjuror who foretold King William's accident and death, last February but one, a month before either event happened, and gave out that another prince over the water would soon enjoy his own again; for which he was committed to Newgate, and whipped at the cart's tail. He went by another name then,--Rykhart Scherprechter I think he called himself. His fellow-prisoners nicknamed him the gallows-provider, from a habit he had of picking out all those who were destined to the gibbet. He was never known to err, and was as much dreaded as the jail-fever in consequence. He singled out my poor husband from a crowd of other felons; and you know how right he was in that case, Sir."

"Ay, marry," replied Wood, with a look that seemed to say that he did not think it required any surprising skill in the art of divination to predict the doom of the individual in question; but whatever opinion he might entertain, he contented himself with inquiring into the grounds of the conjuror's evil augury respecting the infant. "What did the old fellow judge from, eh, Joan?" asked he.

"From a black mole under the child's right ear, shaped like a coffin, which is a bad sign; and a deep line just above the middle of the left thumb, meeting round about in the form of a noose, which is a worse," replied Mrs. Sheppard. "To be sure, it's not surprising the poor little thing should be so marked; for, when I lay in the women-felons' ward in Newgate, where he first saw the light, or at least such light as ever finds entrance into that gloomy place, I had nothing, whether sleeping or waking, but halters, and gibbets, and coffins, and such like horrible visions, for ever dancing round me! And then, you know, Sir--but, perhaps, you don't know that little Jack was born, a month before his time, on the very day his poor father suffered."

"Lord bless us!" ejaculated Wood, "how shocking! No, I did *not* know that."

"You may see the marks on the child yourself, if you choose, Sir," urged the widow.

"See the devil!--not I," cried Wood impatiently. "I didn't think you'd been so easily fooled, Joan."

"Fooled or not," returned Mrs. Sheppard mysteriously, "old Van told me *one* thing which has come true already."

"What's that?" asked Wood with some curiosity.

"He said, by way of comfort, I suppose, after the fright he gave me at first, that the child would find a friend within twenty-four hours, who would stand by him through life."

"A friend is not so soon gained as lost," replied Wood; "but how has the prediction been fulfilled, Joan, eh?"

"I thought you would have guessed, Sir," replied the widow, timidly. "I'm sure little Jack has but one friend beside myself, in the world, and that's more than I would have ventured to say for him yesterday. However, I've not told you all; for old Van *did* say something about the child saving his new-found friend's life at the time of meeting; but how that's to happen, I'm sure I can't guess."

"Nor any one else in his senses," rejoined Wood, with a laugh. "It's not very likely that a babby of nine months old will save *my* life, if I'm to be his friend, as you seem to say, Mrs. Sheppard. But I've not promised to stand by him yet; nor will I, unless he turns out an honest lad,--mind that. Of all crafts,--and it was the only craft his poor father, who, to do him justice, was one of the best workmen that ever handled a saw or drove a nail, could never understand,--of all crafts, I say, to be an honest man is the master-craft. As long as your son observes that precept I'll befriend him, but no longer."

"I don't desire it, Sir," replied Mrs. Sheppard, meekly.

"There's an old proverb," continued Wood, rising and walking towards the fire, "which says,--'Put another man's child in your bosom, and he'll creep out at your elbow.' But I don't value that, because I think it applies to one who marries a widow with encumbrances; and that's not my case, you know."

"Well, Sir," gasped Mrs. Sheppard.

"Well, my dear, I've a proposal to make in regard to this babby of yours, which may, or may not, be agreeable. All I can say is, it's well meant; and I may add, I'd have made it five minutes ago, if you'd given me the opportunity."

"Pray come to the point, Sir," said Mrs. Sheppard, somewhat alarmed by this preamble.

"I *am* coming to the point, Joan. The more haste, the worse speed--better the feet slip than the tongue. However, to cut a long matter short, my proposal's this:--I've taken a fancy to your bantling, and, as I've no son of my own, if it meets with your concurrence and that of Mrs. Wood, (for I never do anything without consulting my better half,) I'll take the boy, educate him, and bring him up to my own business of a carpenter."

The poor widow hung her head, and pressed her child closer to her breast.

"Well, Joan," said the benevolent mechanic, after he had looked at her steadfastly for a few moments, "what say you?--silence gives consent, eh?"

Mrs. Sheppard made an effort to speak, but her voice was choked by emotion.

"Shall I take the babby home with me!" persisted Wood, in a tone between jest and earnest.

"I cannot part with him," replied the widow, bursting into tears; "indeed, indeed, I cannot."

"So I've found out the way to move her," thought the carpenter; "those tears will do her some good, at all events. Not part with him!" added he aloud. "Why you wouldn't stand in the way of his good fortune sure*ly*? I'll be a second father to him, I tell you. Remember what the conjuror said."

"I *do* remember it, Sir," replied Mrs. Sheppard, "and am most grateful for your offer. But I dare not accept it."

"Dare not!" echoed the carpenter; "I don't understand you, Joan."

"I mean to say, Sir," answered Mrs. Sheppard in a troubled voice, "that if I lost my child, I should lose all I have left in the world. I have neither father, mother, brother, sister, nor husband--I have only *him*."

"If I ask you to part with him, my good woman, it's to better his condition, I suppose, ain't it?" rejoined Wood angrily; for, though he had no serious intention of carrying his proposal into effect, he was rather offended at having it declined. "It's not an offer," continued he, "that I'm likely to make, or you're likely to receive every day in the year."

And muttering some remarks, which we do not care to repeat, reflecting upon the consistency of the sex, he was preparing once more to depart, when Mrs. Sheppard stopped him.

"Give me till to-morrow," implored she, "and if I *can* bring myself to part with him, you shall have him without another word."

"Take time to consider of it," replied Wood sulkily, "there's no hurry."

"Don't be angry with me, Sir," cried the widow, sobbing bitterly, "pray don't. I know I am undeserving of your bounty; but if I were to tell you what hardships I have undergone--to what frightful extremities I have been reduced--and to what infamy I have submitted, to earn a scanty subsistence for this child's sake,--if you could feel what it is to stand alone in the world as I do, bereft of all who have ever loved me, and shunned by all who have ever known me, except the worthless and the wretched,--if you knew (and Heaven grant you may be spared the knowledge!) how much affliction sharpens love, and how much more dear to me my child has become for every sacrifice I have made for him,--if you were told all this, you would, I am sure, pity rather than reproach me, because I cannot at once consent to a separation, which I feel would break my heart. But give me till to-morrow--only till to-morrow--I may be able to part with him then."

The worthy carpenter was now far more angry with himself than he had previously been with Mrs. Sheppard; and, as soon as he could command his feelings, which were considerably excited by the mention of her distresses, he squeezed her hand warmly, bestowed a hearty execration upon his own inhumanity, and swore he would neither separate her from her child, nor suffer any one else to separate them.

"Plague on't!" added he: "I never meant to take your babby from you. But I'd a mind to try whether you really loved him as much as you pretended. I was to blame to carry the matter so far. However, confession of a fault makes half amends for it. A time *may* come when this little chap will need my aid, and, depend upon it, he shall never want a friend in Owen Wood."

As he said this, the carpenter patted the cheek of the little object of his benevolent professions, and, in so doing, unintentionally aroused him from his slumbers. Opening a pair of large black eyes, the child fixed them for an instant upon Wood, and then, alarmed by the light, uttered a low and melancholy cry, which, however, was speedily stilled by the caresses of his mother, towards whom he extended his tiny arms, as if imploring protection.

"I don't think he would leave me, even if I could part with him," observed Mrs. Sheppard, smiling through her tears.

"I don't think he would," acquiesced the carpenter. "No friend like the mother, for the babby knows no other."

"And that's true," rejoined Mrs. Sheppard; "for if I had *not* been a mother, I would not have survived the day on which I became a widow."

"You mustn't think of that, Mrs. Sheppard," said Wood in a soothing tone.

"I can't help thinking of it, Sir," answered the widow. "I can never get poor Tom's last look out of my head, as he stood in the Stone-Hall at Newgate, after his irons had been knocked off, unless I manage to stupify myself somehow. The dismal tolling of St. Sepulchre's bell is for ever ringing in my ears--oh!"

"If that's the case," observed Wood, "I'm surprised you should like to have such a frightful picture constantly in view as that over the chimney-piece."

"I'd good reasons for placing it there, Sir; but don't question me about them now, or you'll drive me mad," returned Mrs. Sheppard wildly.

"Well, well, we'll say no more about it," replied Wood; "and, by way of changing the subject, let me advise you on no account to fly to strong waters for consolation, Joan. One nail drives out another, it's true; but the worst nail you can employ is a coffin-nail. Gin Lane's the nearest road to the churchyard."

"It may be; but if it shortens the distance and lightens the journey, I care not," retorted the widow, who seemed by this reproach to be roused into sudden eloquence. "To those who, like me, have never been able to get out of the dark and dreary paths of life, the grave is indeed a refuge, and the sooner they reach it the better. The spirit I drink may be poison,--it may kill me,--perhaps it *is* killing me:--but so would hunger, cold, misery,--so would my own thoughts. I should have gone mad without it. Gin is the poor man's friend,--his sole set-off against the rich man's luxury. It comforts him when he is most forlorn. It may be treacherous, it may lay up a store of future woe; but it insures present happiness, and that is sufficient. When I have traversed the streets a houseless wanderer, driven with curses from every door where I have solicited alms, and with blows from every gateway where I have sought shelter,--when I have crept into some deserted building, and stretched my wearied limbs upon a bulk, in the vain hope of repose,--or, worse than all, when, frenzied with want, I have yielded to horrible temptation, and earned a meal in the only way I could earn one,--when I have felt, at times like these, my heart sink within me, I have drank of this drink, and have at once forgotten my cares, my poverty, my guilt. Old thoughts, old feelings, old faces, and old scenes have returned to me, and I have fancied myself happy,--as happy as I am now." And she burst into a wild hysterical laugh.

"Poor creature!" ejaculated Wood. "Do you call this frantic glee happiness?"

"It's all the happiness I have known for years," returned the widow, becoming suddenly calm, "and it's short-lived enough, as you perceive. I tell you what, Mr. Wood," added she in a hollow voice, and with a ghastly look, "gin may bring ruin; but as long as poverty, vice, and ill-usage exist, it will be drunk."

"God forbid!" exclaimed Wood, fervently; and, as if afraid of prolonging the interview, he added, with some precipitation, "But I must be going: I've stayed here too long already. You shall hear from me to-morrow."

"Stay!" said Mrs. Sheppard, again arresting his departure. "I've just recollected that my husband left a key with me, which he charged me to give you when I could find an opportunity."

"A key!" exclaimed Wood eagerly. "I lost a very valuable one some time ago. What's it like, Joan?"

"It's a small key, with curiously-fashioned wards."

"It's mine, I'll be sworn," rejoined Wood. "Well, who'd have thought of finding it in this unexpected way!"

"Don't be too sure till you see it," said the widow. "Shall I fetch it for you, Sir?"

"By all means."

"I must trouble you to hold the child, then, for a minute, while I run up to the garret, where I've hidden it for safety," said Mrs. Sheppard. "I think I *may* trust him with you, Sir," added she, taking up the candle.

"Don't leave him, if you're at all fearful, my dear," replied Wood, receiving the little burthen with a laugh. "Poor thing!" muttered he, as the widow departed on her errand, "she's seen better days and better circumstances than she'll ever see again, I'm sure. Strange, I could never learn her history. Tom Sheppard was always a close file, and would never tell whom he married. Of this I'm certain, however, she was much too good for him, and was never meant to be a journeyman carpenter's wife, still less what is she now. Her heart's in the right place, at all events; and, since that's the case, the rest may perhaps come round,--that is, if she gets through her present illness. A dry cough's the trumpeter of death. If that's true, she's not long for this world. As to this little fellow, in spite of the Dutchman, who, in my opinion, is more of a Jacobite than a conjurer, and more of a knave than either, he shall never mount a horse foaled by an acorn, if I can help it."

The course of the carpenter's meditations was here interrupted by a loud note of lamentation from the child, who, disturbed by the transfer, and not receiving the gentle solace to which he was ordinarily accustomed, raised his voice to the utmost, and exerted his feeble strength to escape. For a few moments Mr. Wood dandled his little charge to and fro, after the most approved nursery fashion, essaying at the same time the soothing influence of an infantine melody proper to the occasion; but, failing in his design, he soon lost all patience, and being, as we have before hinted, rather irritable, though extremely well-meaning, he lifted the unhappy bantling in the air, and shook him with so much good will, that he had well-nigh silenced him most effectually. A brief calm succeeded. But with returning breath came returning vociferations; and the carpenter, with a faint hope of lessening the clamour by change of scene, took up his lantern, opened the door, and walked out.

CHAPTER II.
The Old Mint.

MRS. Sheppard's habitation terminated a row of old ruinous buildings, called Wheeler's Rents; a dirty thoroughfare, part street, and part lane, running from Mint Street, through a variety of turnings, and along the brink of a deep kennel, skirted by a number of petty and neglected gardens in the direction of Saint George's Fields. The neighbouring houses were tenanted by the lowest order of insolvent traders, thieves, mendicants, and other worthless and nefarious characters, who fled thither to escape from their creditors, or to avoid the punishment due to their different offenses; for we may observe that the Old Mint, although it had been divested of some of its privileges as a sanctuary by a recent statute passed in the reign of William the Third, still presented a safe asylum to the debtor, and even continued to do so until the middle of the reign of George the First, when the crying nature of the evil called loudly for a remedy, and another and more sweeping enactment entirely took away its immunities. In consequence of the encouragement thus offered to dishonesty, and the security afforded to crime, this quarter of the Borough of Southwark was accounted (at the period of our narrative) the grand receptacle of the superfluous villainy of the metropolis. Infested by every description of vagabond and miscreant, it was, perhaps, a few degrees worse than the rookery near Saint Giles's and the desperate neighbourhood of Saffron Hill in our own time. And yet, on the very site of the sordid tenements and squalid courts we have mentioned, where the felon openly made his dwelling, and the fraudulent debtor laughed the object of his knavery to scorn--on this spot, not two centuries ago, stood the princely residence of Charles Brandon, the chivalrous Duke of Suffolk, whose stout heart was a well of honour, and whose memory breathes of loyalty and valour. Suffolk House, as Brandon's palace was denominated, was subsequently converted into a mint by his royal brother-in-law, Henry the Eighth; and, after its demolition, and the removal of the place of coinage to the Tower, the name was still continued to the district in which it had been situated.

Old and dilapidated, the widow's domicile looked the very picture of desolation and misery. Nothing more forlorn could be conceived. The roof was partially untiled; the chimneys were tottering; the side-walls bulged, and were supported by a piece of timber propped against the opposite house; the glass in most of the windows was broken, and its place supplied with paper; while, in some cases, the very frames of the windows had been destroyed, and the apertures were left free to the airs of heaven. On the groundfloor the shutters were closed, or, to speak more correctly, altogether nailed up, and presented a very singular appearance, being patched all over with the soles of old shoes, rusty hobnails, and bits of iron hoops, the ingenious device of the former occupant of the apartment, Paul Groves, the cobbler, to whom we have before alluded.

It was owing to the untimely end of this poor fellow that Mrs. Sheppard was enabled to take possession of the premises. In a fit of despondency, superinduced by drunkenness, he made away with himself; and when the body was discovered, after a lapse of some months, such was the impression produced by the spectacle--such the alarm occasioned by the crazy state of the building, and, above all, by the terror inspired by strange and unearthly noises heard during the night, which were, of course, attributed to the spirit of the suicide, that the place speedily enjoyed the reputation of being haunted, and was, consequently, entirely abandoned. In this state Mrs. Sheppard found it; and, as no one opposed her, she at once took up her abode there; nor was she long in discovering that the dreaded sounds proceeded from the nocturnal gambols of a legion of rats.

A narrow entry, formed by two low walls, communicated with the main thoroughfare; and in this passage, under the cover of a penthouse, stood Wood, with his little burthen, to whom we shall now return.

As Mrs. Sheppard did not make her appearance quite so soon as he expected, the carpenter became a little fidgetty, and, having succeeded in tranquillizing the child, he thought proper to walk so far down the entry as would enable him to reconnoitre the upper windows of the house. A light was visible in the garret, feebly struggling through the damp atmosphere, for the night was raw and overcast. This light did not remain stationary, but could be seen at one moment glimmering through the rents in the roof, and at another shining through the cracks in the wall, or the broken panes of the casement. Wood was unable to discover the figure of the widow, but he recognised her dry, hacking cough, and was about to call her down, if she could not find the key, as he imagined must be the case, when a loud noise was heard, as though a chest, or some weighty substance, had fallen upon the floor.

Before Wood had time to inquire into the cause of this sound, his attention was diverted by a man, who rushed past the entry with the swiftness of desperation. This individual apparently met with some impediment to his further progress; for he had not proceeded many steps when he turned suddenly about, and darted up the passage in which Wood stood.

Uttering a few inarticulate ejaculations,--for he was completely out of breath,--the fugitive placed a bundle in the arms of the carpenter, and, regardless of the consternation he excited in the breast of that personage, who was almost stupified with astonishment, he began to divest himself of a heavy horseman's cloak, which he threw over Wood's shoulder, and, drawing his sword, seemed to listen intently for the approach of his pursuers.

The appearance of the new-comer was extremely prepossessing; and, after his trepidation had a little subsided, Wood began to regard him with some degree of interest. Evidently in the flower of his age, he was scarcely less remarkable for symmetry of person than for comeliness of feature; and, though his attire was plain and unpretending, it was such as could be worn only by one belonging to the higher ranks of society. His figure was tall and commanding, and the expression of his countenance (though somewhat disturbed by his recent exertion) was resolute and stern.

At this juncture, a cry burst from the child, who, nearly smothered by the weight imposed upon him, only recovered the use of his lungs as Wood altered the position of the bundle. The stranger turned his head at the sound.

"By Heaven!" cried he in a tone of surprise, "you have an infant there?"

"To be sure I have," replied Wood, angrily; for, finding that the intentions of the stranger were pacific, so far as he was concerned, he thought he might safely venture on a slight display of spirit. "It's very well you haven't crushed the poor little thing to death with this confounded clothes'-bag. But some people have no consideration."

"That child may be the means of saving me," muttered the stranger, as if struck by a new idea: "I shall gain time by the expedient. Do you live here?"

"Not exactly," answered the carpenter.

"No matter. The door is open, so it is needless to ask leave to enter. Ha!" exclaimed the stranger, as shouts and other vociferations resounded at no great distance along the thoroughfare, "not a moment is to be lost. Give me that precious charge," he added, snatching the bundle from Wood. "If I escape, I will reward you. Your name?"

"Owen Wood," replied the carpenter; "I've no reason to be ashamed of it. And now, a fair exchange, Sir. Yours?"

The stranger hesitated. The shouts drew nearer, and lights were seen flashing ruddily against the sides and gables of the neighbouring houses.

"My name is Darrell," said the fugitive hastily. "But, if you are discovered, answer no questions, as you value your life. Wrap yourself in my cloak, and keep it. Remember! not a word!"

So saying, he huddled the mantle over Wood's shoulders, dashed the lantern to the ground, and extinguished the light. A moment afterwards, the door was closed and bolted, and the carpenter found himself alone.

"Mercy on us!" cried he, as a thrill of apprehension ran through his frame. "The Dutchman was right, after all."

This exclamation had scarcely escaped him, when the discharge of a pistol was heard, and a bullet whizzed past his ears.

"I have him!" cried a voice in triumph.

A man, then, rushed up the entry, and, seizing the unlucky carpenter by the collar, presented a drawn sword to his throat. This person was speedily followed by half a dozen others, some of whom carried flambeaux.

"Mur--der!" roared Wood, struggling to free himself from his assailant, by whom he was half strangled.

"Damnation!" exclaimed one of the leaders of the party in a furious tone, snatching a torch from an attendant, and throwing its light full upon the face of the carpenter; "this is not the villain, Sir Cecil."

"So I find, Rowland," replied the other, in accents of deep disappointment, and at the same time relinquishing his grasp. "I could have sworn I saw him enter this passage. And how comes his cloak on this knave's shoulders?"

"It is his cloak, of a surety," returned Rowland "Harkye, sirrah," continued he, haughtily interrogating Wood; "where is the person from whom you received this mantle?"

"Throttling a man isn't the way to make him answer questions," replied the carpenter, doggedly. "You'll get nothing out of me, I can promise you, unless you show a little more civility."

"We waste time with this fellow," interposed Sir Cecil, "and may lose the object of our quest, who, beyond doubt, has taken refuge in this building. Let us search it."

Just then, the infant began to sob piteously.

"Hist!" cried Rowland, arresting his comrade. "Do you hear that! We are not wholly at fault. The dog-fox cannot be far off, since the cub is found."

With these words, he tore the mantle from Wood's back, and, perceiving the child, endeavoured to seize it. In this attempt he was, however, foiled by the agility of the carpenter, who managed to retreat to the door, against which he placed his back, kicking the boards vigorously with his heel.

"Joan! Joan!" vociferated he, "open the door, for God's sake, or I shall be murdered, and so will your babby! Open the door quickly, I say."

"Knock him on the head," thundered Sir Cecil, "or we shall have the watch upon us."

"No fear of that," rejoined Rowland: "such vermin never dare to show themselves in this privileged district. All we have to apprehend is a rescue."

The hint was not lost upon Wood. He tried to raise an outcry, but his throat was again forcibly griped by Rowland.

"Another such attempt," said the latter, "and you are a dead man. Yield up the babe, and I pledge my word you shall remain unmolested."

"I will yield it to no one but its mother," answered Wood.

"'Sdeath! do you trifle with me, sirrah?" cried Rowland fiercely. "Give me the child, or--"

As he spoke the door was thrown open, and Mrs. Sheppard staggered forward. She looked paler than ever; but her countenance, though bewildered, did not exhibit the alarm which might naturally have been anticipated from the strange and perplexing scene presented to her view.

"Take it," cried Wood, holding the infant towards her; "take it, and fly."

Mrs. Sheppard put out her arms mechanically. But before the child could be committed to her care, it was wrested from the carpenter by Rowland.

"These people are all in league with him," cried the latter. "But don't wait for me, Sir Cecil. Enter the house with your men. I'll dispose of the brat."

This injunction was instantly obeyed. The knight and his followers crossed the threshold, leaving one of the torch-bearers behind them.

"Davies," said Rowland, delivering the babe, with a meaning look, to his attendant.

"I understand, Sir," replied Davies, drawing a little aside. And, setting down the link, he proceeded deliberately to untie his cravat.

"My God! will you see your child strangled before your eyes, and not so much as scream for help?" said Wood, staring at the widow with a look of surprise and horror. "Woman, your wits are fled!"

And so it seemed; for all the answer she could make was to murmur distractedly, "I can't find the key."

"Devil take the key!" ejaculated Wood. "They're about to murder your child--*your* child, I tell you! Do you comprehend what I say, Joan?"

"I've hurt my head," replied Mrs. Sheppard, pressing her hand to her temples.

And then, for the first time, Wood noticed a small stream of blood coursing slowly down her cheek.

At this moment, Davies, who had completed his preparations, extinguished the torch.

"It's all over," groaned Wood, "and perhaps it's as well her senses are gone. However, I'll make a last effort to save the poor little creature, if it costs me my life."

And, with this generous resolve, he shouted at the top of his voice, "Arrest! arrest! help! help!" seconding the words with a shrill and peculiar cry, well known at the time to the inhabitants of the quarter in which it was uttered.

In reply to this summons a horn was instantly blown at the corner of the street.

"Arrest!" vociferated Wood. "Mint! Mint!"

"Death and hell!" cried Rowland, making a furious pass at the carpenter, who fortunately avoided the thrust in the darkness; "will nothing silence you?"

"Help!" ejaculated Wood, renewing his cries. "Arrest!"

"Jigger closed!" shouted a hoarse voice in reply. "All's bowman, my covey. Fear nothing. We'll be upon the ban-dogs before they can shake their trotters!"

And the alarm was sounded more loudly than ever.

Another horn now resounded from the further extremity of the thoroughfare; this was answered by a third; and presently a fourth, and more remote blast, took up the note of alarm. The whole neighbourhood was disturbed. A garrison called to arms at dead of night on the sudden approach of the enemy, could not have been more expeditiously, or effectually aroused. Rattles were sprung; lanterns lighted, and hoisted at the end of poles; windows thrown open; doors unbarred; and, as if by magic, the street was instantaneously filled with a crowd of persons of both sexes, armed with such weapons as came most readily to hand, and dressed in such garments as could be most easily slipped on. Hurrying in the direction of the supposed arrest, they encouraged each other with shouts, and threatened the offending parties with their vengeance.

Regardless as the gentry of the Mint usually were (for, indeed, they had become habituated from their frequent occurrence to such scenes,) of any outrages committed in their streets; deaf, as they had been, to the recent scuffle before Mrs. Sheppard's door, they were always sufficiently on the alert to maintain their privileges, and to assist each other against the attacks of their common enemy--the sheriff's officer. It was only by the adoption of such a course (especially since the late act of suppression, to which we have alluded,) that the inviolability of the asylum could be preserved. Incursions were often made upon its territories by the functionaries of the law; sometimes attended with success, but more frequently with discomfiture; and it rarely happened, unless by stratagem or bribery, that (in the language of the gentlemen of the short staff) an important caption could be effected. In order to guard against accidents or surprises, watchmen, or scouts, (as they were styled,) were stationed at the three main outlets of the sanctuary ready to give the signal in the manner just described: bars were erected, which, in case of emergency; could be immediately stretched across the streets: doors were attached to the alleys; and were never opened without due precautions; gates were affixed to the courts, wickets to the gates, and bolts to the wickets. The back windows of the houses (where any such existed) were strongly barricaded, and kept constantly shut; and the fortress was, furthermore, defended by high walls and deep ditches in those quarters where it appeared most exposed. There was also a Maze, (the name is still retained in the district,) into which the debtor could run, and through the intricacies of which it was impossible for an officer to follow him, without a clue. Whoever chose to incur the risk of so doing might enter the Mint at any hour; but no one was suffered to depart without giving a satisfactory account of himself, or producing a pass from the Master. In short, every contrivance that ingenuity could devise was resorted to by this horde of reprobates to secure themselves from danger or molestation. Whitefriars had lost its privileges; Salisbury Court and the Savoy no longer offered places of refuge to the debtor; and it was, therefore, doubly requisite that the Island of Bermuda (as the Mint was termed by its occupants) should uphold its rights, as long as it was able to do so.

Mr. Wood, meantime, had not remained idle. Aware that not a moment was to be lost, if he meant to render any effectual assistance to the child, he ceased shouting, and defending himself in the best way he could from the attacks of Rowland, by whom he was closely pressed, forced his way, in spite of all opposition, to Davies, and dealt him a blow on the head with such good will that, had it not been for the intervention of the wall, the ruffian must have been prostrated. Before he could recover from the stunning effects of the blow, Wood possessed himself of the child: and, untying the noose which had been slipped round its throat, had the satisfaction of hearing it cry lustily.

At this juncture, Sir Cecil and his followers appeared at the threshold.

"He has escaped!" exclaimed the knight; "we have searched every corner of the house without finding a trace of him."

"Back!" cried Rowland. "Don't you hear those shouts? Yon fellow's clamour has brought the whole horde of jail-birds and cut-throats that infest this place about our ears. We shall be torn in pieces if we are discovered. Davies!" he added, calling to the attendant, who was menacing Wood with a severe retaliation, "don't heed him; but, if you value a whole skin, come into the house, and bring that woman with you. She may afford us some necessary information."

Davies reluctantly complied. And, dragging Mrs. Sheppard, who made no resistance, along with him, entered the house, the door of which was instantly shut and barricaded.

A moment afterwards, the street was illumined by a blaze of torchlight, and a tumultuous uproar, mixed with the clashing of weapons, and the braying of horns, announced the arrival of the first detachment of Minters.

Mr. Wood rushed instantly to meet them.

"Hurrah!" shouted he, waving his hat triumphantly over his head. "Saved!"

"Ay, ay, it's all bob, my covey! You're safe enough, that's certain!" responded the Minters, baying, yelping, leaping, and howling around him like a pack of hounds when the huntsman is beating cover; "but, where are the lurchers?"

"Who?" asked Wood.

"The traps!" responded a bystander.

"The shoulder-clappers!" added a lady, who, in her anxiety to join the party, had unintentionally substituted her husband's nether habiliments for her own petticoats.

"The ban-dogs!" thundered a tall man, whose stature and former avocations had procured him the nickname of "The long drover of the Borough market." "Where are they?"

"Ay, where are they?" chorussed the mob, flourishing their various weapons, and flashing their torches in the air; "we'll starve 'em out."

Mr. Wood trembled. He felt he had raised a storm which it would be very difficult, if not impossible, to allay. He knew not what to say, or what to do; and his confusion was increased by the threatening gestures and furious looks of the ruffians in his immediate vicinity.

"I don't understand you, gentlemen," stammered he, at length.

"What does he say?" roared the long drover.

"He says he don't understand flash," replied the lady in gentleman's attire.

"Cease your confounded clutter!" said a young man, whose swarthy visage, seen in the torchlight, struck Wood as being that of a Mulatto. "You frighten the cull out of his senses. It's plain he don't understand our lingo; as, how should he?

Take pattern by me;" and as he said this he strode up to the carpenter, and, slapping him on the shoulder, propounded the following questions, accompanying each interrogation with a formidable contortion of countenance. "Curse you! Where are the bailiffs? Rot you! have you lost your tongue? Devil seize you! you could bawl loud enough a moment ago!"

"Silence, Blueskin!" interposed an authoritative voice, immediately behind the ruffian. "Let me have a word with the cull!"

"Ay! ay!" cried several of the bystanders, "let Jonathan kimbaw the cove. He's got the gift of the gab."

The crowd accordingly drew aside, and the individual, in whose behalf the movement had been made immediately stepped forward. He was a young man of about two-and-twenty, who, without having anything remarkable either in dress or appearance, was yet a noticeable person, if only for the indescribable expression of cunning pervading his countenance. His eyes were small and grey; as far apart and as sly-looking as those of a fox. A physiognomist, indeed, would have likened him to that crafty animal, and it must be owned the general formation of his features favoured such a comparison. The nose was long and sharp, the chin pointed, the forehead broad and flat, and connected, without any intervening hollow, with the eyelid; the teeth when displayed, seemed to reach from ear to ear. Then his beard was of a reddish hue, and his complexion warm and sanguine. Those who had seen him slumbering, averred that he slept with his eyes open. But this might be merely a figurative mode of describing his customary vigilance. Certain it was, that the slightest sound aroused him. This astute personage was somewhat under the middle size, but fairly proportioned, inclining rather to strength than symmetry, and abounding more in muscle than in flesh.

It would seem, from the attention which he evidently bestowed upon the hidden and complex machinery of the grand system of villany at work around him, that his chief object in taking up his quarters in the Mint, must have been to obtain some private information respecting the habits and practices of its inhabitants, to be turned to account hereafter.

Advancing towards Wood, Jonathan fixed his keen gray eyes upon him, and demanded, in a stern tone whether the persons who had taken refuge in the adjoining house, were bailiffs.

"Not that I know of," replied the carpenter, who had in some degree recovered his confidence.

"Then I presume you've not been arrested?"

"I have not," answered Wood firmly.

"I guessed as much. Perhaps you'll next inform us why you have occasioned this disturbance."

"Because this child's life was threatened by the persons you have mentioned," rejoined Wood.

"An excellent reason, i' faith!" exclaimed Blueskin, with a roar of surprise and indignation, which was echoed by the whole assemblage. "And so we're to be summoned from our beds and snug firesides, because a kid happens to squall, eh? By the soul of my grandmother, but this is too good!"

"Do you intend to claim the privileges of the Mint?" said Jonathan, calmly pursuing his interrogations amid the uproar. "Is your person in danger?"

"Not from my creditors," replied Wood, significantly.

"Will he post the cole? Will he come down with the dues? Ask him that?" cried Blueskin.

"You hear," pursued Jonathan; "my friend desires to know if you are willing to pay your footing as a member of the ancient and respectable fraternity of debtors?"

"I owe no man a farthing, and my name shall never appear in any such rascally list," replied Wood angrily. "I don't see why I should be obliged to pay for doing my duty. I tell you this child would have been strangled. The noose was at its throat when I called for help. I knew it was in vain to cry 'murder!' in the Mint, so I had recourse to stratagem."

"Well, Sir, I must say you deserve some credit for your ingenuity, at all events," replied Jonathan, repressing a smile; "but, before you put out your foot so far, it would have been quite as prudent to consider how you were to draw it back again. For my own part, I don't see in what way it is to be accomplished, except by the payment of our customary fees. Do not imagine you can at one moment avail yourself of our excellent regulations (with which you seem sufficiently well acquainted), and the next break them with impunity. If you assume the character of a debtor for your own convenience, you must be content to maintain it for ours. If you have not been arrested, we have been disturbed; and it is but just and reasonable you should pay for occasioning such disturbance. By your own showing you are in easy circumstances,--for it is only natural to presume that a man who owes nothing must be in a condition to pay liberally,--and you cannot therefore feel the loss of such a trifle as ten guineas."

However illogical and inconclusive these arguments might appear to Mr. Wood, and however he might dissent from the latter proposition, he did not deem it expedient to make any reply; and the orator proceeded with his harangue amid the general applause of the assemblage.

"I am perhaps exceeding my authority in demanding so slight a sum," continued Jonathan, modestly, "and the Master of the Mint may not be disposed to let you off so lightly. He will be here in a moment or so, and you will then learn his determination. In the mean time, let me advise you as a friend not to irritate him by a refusal, which would be as useless as vexatious. He has a very summary mode of dealing with refractory persons, I assure you. My best endeavours shall be used to bring you off, on the easy terms I have mentioned."

"Do you call ten guineas easy terms?" cried Wood, with a look of dismay. "Why, I should expect to purchase the entire freehold of the Mint for less money."

"Many a man has been glad to pay double the amount to get his head from under the Mint pump," observed Blueskin, gruffly.

"Let the gentleman take his own course," said Jonathan, mildly. "I should be sorry to persuade him to do anything his calmer judgment might disapprove."

"Exactly my sentiments," rejoined Blueskin. "I wouldn't force him for the world: but if he don't tip the stivers, may I be cursed if he don't get a taste of the *aqua pompaginis*. Let's have a look at the kinchen that *ought* to have been throttled," added he, snatching the child from Wood. "My stars! here's a pretty lullaby-cheat to make a fuss about--ho! ho!"

"Deal with me as you think proper, gentlemen," exclaimed Wood; "but, for mercy's sake don't harm the child! Let it be taken to its mother."

"And who is its mother?" asked Jonathan, in an eager whisper. "Tell me frankly, and speak under your breath. Your own safety--the child's safety--depends upon your candour."

While Mr. Wood underwent this examination, Blueskin felt a small and trembling hand placed upon his own, and, turning at the summons, beheld a young female, whose features were partially concealed by a loo, or half mask, standing beside him. Coarse as were the ruffian's notions of feminine beauty, he could not be insensible to the surpassing loveliness of the fair creature, who had thus solicited his attention. Her figure was, in some measure, hidden by a large scarf, and a deep hood drawn over the head contributed to her disguise; still it was evident, from her lofty bearing, that she had nothing in common, except an interest in their proceedings, with the crew by whom she was surrounded.

Whence she came,--who she was,--and what she wanted,--were questions which naturally suggested themselves to Blueskin, and he was about to seek for some explanation, when his curiosity was checked by a gesture of silence from the lady.

"Hush!" said she, in a low, but agitated voice; "would you earn this purse?"

"I've no objection," replied Blueskin, in a tone intended to be gentle, but which sounded like the murmuring whine of a playful bear. "How much is there in it!"

"It contains gold," replied the lady; "but I will add this ring."

"What am I to do to earn it?" asked Blueskin, with a disgusting leer,--"cut a throat--or throw myself at your feet--eh, my dear?"

"Give me that child," returned the lady, with difficulty overcoming the loathing inspired by the ruffian's familiarity.

"Oh! I see!" replied Blueskin, winking significantly, "Come nearer, or they'll observe us. Don't be afraid--I won't hurt you. I'm always agreeable to the women, bless their kind hearts! Now! slip the purse into my hand. Bravo!--the best cly-faker of 'em all couldn't have done it better. And now for the fawney--the ring I mean. I'm no great judge of these articles, Ma'am; but I trust to your honour not to palm off paste upon me."

"It is a diamond," said the lady, in an agony of distress,--"the child!"

"A diamond! Here, take the kid," cried Blueskin, slipping the infant adroitly under her scarf. "And so this is a diamond," added he, contemplating the brilliant from the hollow of his hand: "it does sparkle almost as brightly as your ogles. By the by, my dear, I forgot to ask your name--perhaps you'll oblige me with it now? Hell and the devil!--gone!"

He looked around in vain. The lady had disappeared.

CHAPTER III.
The Master of the Mint.

JONATHAN, meanwhile, having ascertained the parentage of the child from Wood, proceeded to question him in an under tone, as to the probable motives of the attempt upon its life; and, though he failed in obtaining any information on this point, he had little difficulty in eliciting such particulars of the mysterious transaction as have already been recounted. When the carpenter concluded his recital, Jonathan was for a moment lost in reflection.

"Devilish strange!" thought he, chuckling to himself; "queer business! Capital trick of the cull in the cloak to make another person's brat stand the brunt for his own--capital! ha! ha! Won't do, though. He must be a sly fox to get out of the Mint without my knowledge. I've a shrewd guess where he's taken refuge; but I'll ferret him out. These bloods will pay well for his capture; if not, he'll pay well to get out of their hands; so I'm safe either way--ha! ha! Blueskin," he added aloud, and motioning that worthy, "follow me."

Upon which, he set off in the direction of the entry. His progress, however, was checked by loud acclamations, announcing the arrival of the Master of the Mint and his train.

Baptist Kettleby (for so was the Master named) was a "goodly portly man, and a corpulent," whose fair round paunch bespoke the affection he entertained for good liquor and good living. He had a quick, shrewd, merry eye, and a look in which duplicity was agreeably veiled by good humour. It was easy to discover that he was a knave, but equally easy to perceive that he was a pleasant fellow; a combination of qualities by no means of rare occurrence. So far as regards his attire, Baptist was not seen to advantage. No great lover of state or state costume at any time, he was generally, towards the close of an evening, completely in dishabille, and in this condition he now presented himself to his subjects. His shirt was unfastened, his vest unbuttoned, his hose ungartered; his feet were stuck into a pair of pantoufles, his arms into a greasy flannel dressing-gown, his head into a thrum-cap, the cap into a tie-periwig, and the wig into a gold-edged hat. A white apron was tied round his waist, and into the apron was thrust a short thick truncheon, which looked very much like a rolling-pin.

The Master of the Mint was accompanied by another gentleman almost as portly as himself, and quite as deliberate in his movements. The costume of this personage was somewhat singular, and might have passed for a masquerading habit, had not the imperturbable gravity of his demeanour forbidden any such supposition. It consisted of a close jerkin of brown frieze, ornamented with a triple row of brass buttons; loose Dutch slops, made very wide in the seat and very tight at the knees; red stockings with black clocks, and a fur cap. The owner of this dress had a broad weather-beaten face, small twinkling eyes, and a bushy, grizzled beard. Though he walked by the side of the governor, he seldom exchanged a word with him, but appeared wholly absorbed in the contemplations inspired by a broadbowled Dutch pipe.

Behind the illustrious personages just described marched a troop of stalwart fellows, with white badges in their hats, quarterstaves, oaken cudgels, and links in their hands. These were the Master's body-guard.

Advancing towards the Master, and claiming an audience, which was instantly granted, Jonathan, without much circumlocution, related the sum of the strange story he had just learnt from Wood, omitting nothing except a few trifling particulars, which he thought it politic to keep back; and, with this view, he said not a word of there being any probability of capturing the fugitive, but, on the contrary, roundly asserted that his informant had witnessed that person's escape.

The Master listened, with becoming attention, to the narrative, and, at its conclusion, shook his head gravely, applied his thumb to the side of his nose, and, twirling his fingers significantly, winked at his phlegmatic companion. The gentleman appealed to shook his head in reply, coughed as only a Dutchman *can* cough, and raising his hand from the bowl of his pipe, went through precisely the same mysterious ceremonial as the Master.

Putting his own construction upon this mute interchange of opinions, Jonathan ventured to observe, that it certainly was a very perplexing case, but that he thought something *might* be made of it, and, if left to him, he would undertake to manage the matter to the Master's entire satisfaction.

"Ja, ja, Muntmeester," said the Dutchman, removing the pipe from his mouth, and speaking in a deep and guttural voice, "leave the affair to Johannes. He'll settle it bravely. And let ush go back to our brandewyn, and hollandsche genever. Dese ere not schouts, as you faind, but jonkers on a vrolyk; and if dey'd chanshed to keel de vrow Sheppard's pet lamb, dey'd have done her a servish, by shaving it from dat unpleasant complaint, de hempen fever, with which its laatter days are threatened, and of which its poor vader died. Myn Got! haanging runs in some families, Muntmeester. It's hereditary, like de jigt, vat you call it--gout--haw! haw!"

"If the child *is* destined to the gibbet, Van Galgebrok," replied the Master, joining in the laugh, "it'll never be choked by a footman's cravat, that's certain; but, in regard to going back empty-handed," continued he, altering his tone, and assuming a dignified air, "it's quite out of the question. With Baptist Kettleby, to engage in a matter is to go through with it. Besides, this is an affair which no one but myself can settle. Common offences may be decided upon by deputy; but outrages perpetrated by men of rank, as these appear to be, must be judged by the Master of the Mint in person. These are the decrees of the Island of Bermuda, and I will never suffer its excellent laws to be violated. Gentlemen of the Mint," added he, pointing with his truncheon towards Mrs. Sheppard's house, "forward!"

"Hurrah!" shouted the mob, and the whole phalanx was put in motion in that direction. At the same moment a martial flourish, proceeding from cow's horns, tin canisters filled with stones, bladders and cat-gut, with other sprightly, instruments, was struck up, and, enlivened by this harmonious accompaniment, the troop reached its destination in the best possible spirits for an encounter.

"Let us in," said the Master, rapping his truncheon authoritatively against the boards, "or we'll force an entrance."

But as no answer was returned to the summons, though it was again, and more peremptorily, repeated, Baptist seized a mallet from a bystander and burst open the door. Followed by Van Galgebrok and others of his retinue, he then rushed into the room, where Rowland, Sir Cecil, and their attendants, stood with drawn swords prepared to receive them.

"Beat down their blades," cried the Master; "no bloodshed."

"Beat out their brains, you mean," rejoined Blueskin with a tremendous imprecation; "no half measures now, Master."

"Hadn't you better hold a moment's parley with the gentlemen before proceeding to extremities?" suggested Jonathan.

"Agreed," responded the Master. "Surely," he added, staring at Rowland, "either I'm greatly mistaken, or it is--"

"You are not mistaken, Baptist," returned Rowland with a gesture of silence; "it is your old friend. I'm glad to recognise you."

"And I'm glad your worship's recognition doesn't come too late," observed the Master. "But why didn't you make yourself known at once?"

"I'd forgotten the office you hold in the Mint, Baptist," replied Rowland. "But clear the room of this rabble, if you have sufficient authority over them. I would speak with you."

"There's but one way of clearing it, your worship," said the Master, archly.

"I understand," replied Rowland. "Give them what you please. I'll repay you."

"It's all right, pals," cried Baptist, in a loud tone; "the gentlemen and I have settled matters. No more scuffling."

"What's the meaning of all this?" demanded Sir Cecil. "How have you contrived to still these troubled waters?"

"I've chanced upon an old ally in the Master of the Mint," answered Rowland. "We may trust him," he added in a whisper; "he is a staunch friend of the good cause."

"Blueskin, clear the room," cried the Master; "these gentlemen would be private. They've *paid* for their lodging. Where's Jonathan?"

Inquiries were instantly made after that individual, but he was nowhere to be found.

"Strange!" observed the Master; "I thought he'd been at my elbow all this time. But it don't much matter--though he's a devilish shrewd fellow, and might have helped me out of a difficulty, had any occurred. Hark ye, Blueskin," continued he, addressing that personage, who, in obedience to his commands, had, with great promptitude, driven out the rabble, and again secured the door, "a word in your ear.

What female entered the house with us?"

"Blood and thunder!" exclaimed Blueskin, afraid, if he admitted having seen the lady, of being compelled to divide the plunder he had obtained from her among his companions, "how should I know? D'ye suppose I'm always thinking of the petticoats? I observed no female; but if any one *did* join the assault, it must have been either Amazonian Kate, or Fighting Moll."

"The woman I mean did not join the assault," rejoined the Master, "but rather seemed to shun observation; and, from the hasty glimpse I caught of her, she appeared to have a child in her arms."

"Then, most probably, it was the widow Sheppard," answered Blueskin, sulkily.

"Right," said the Master, "I didn't think of her. And now I've another job for you."

"Propose it," returned Blueskin, inclining his head.

"Square accounts with the rascal who got up the sham arrest; and, if he don't tip the cole without more ado, give him a taste of the pump, that's all."

"He shall go through the whole course," replied Blueskin, with a ferocious grin, "unless he comes down to the last grig. We'll lather him with mud, shave him with a rusty razor, and drench him with *aqua pompaginis*. Master, your humble servant.--Gentlemen, your most obsequious trout."

Having effected his object, which was to get rid of Blueskin, Baptist turned to Rowland and Sir Cecil, who had watched his proceedings with much impatience, and remarked, "Now, gentlemen, the coast's clear; we've nothing to interrupt us. I'm entirely at your service."

CHAPTER IV.
The Roof and the Window.

L EAVING them to pursue their conference, we shall follow the footsteps of Jonathan, who, as the Master surmised, and, as we have intimated, had unquestionably entered the house. But at the beginning of the affray, when he thought every one was too much occupied with his own concerns to remark his absence, he slipped out of the room, not for the purpose of avoiding the engagement (for cowardice was not one of his failings), but because he had another object in view. Creeping stealthily up stairs, unmasking a dark lantern, and glancing into each room as he passed, he was startled in one of them by the appearance of Mrs. Sheppard, who seemed to be crouching upon the floor. Satisfied, however, that she did not notice him, Jonathan glided away as noiselessly as he came, and ascended another short flight of stairs leading to the garret. As he crossed this chamber, his foot struck against something on the floor, which nearly threw him down, and stooping to examine the object, he found it was a key. "Never throw away a chance," thought Jonathan. "Who knows but this key may open a golden lock one of these days?" And, picking it up, he thrust it into his pocket.

Arrived beneath an aperture in the broken roof, he was preparing to pass through it, when he observed a little heap of tiles upon the floor, which appeared to have been recently dislodged. "He *has* passed this way," cried Jonathan, exultingly; "I have him safe enough." He then closed the lantern, mounted without much difficulty upon the roof, and proceeded cautiously along the tiles.

The night was now profoundly dark. Jonathan had to feel his way. A single false step might have precipitated him into the street; or, if he had trodden upon an unsound part of the roof, he must have fallen through it. He had nothing to guide him; for though the torches were blazing ruddily below, their gleam fell only on the side of the building. The venturous climber gazed for a moment at the assemblage beneath, to ascertain that he was not discovered; and, having satisfied himself in this particular, he stepped out more boldly. On gaining a stack of chimneys at the back of the house, he came to a pause, and again unmasked his lantern. Nothing, however, could be discerned, except the crumbling brickwork. "Confusion!" ejaculated Jonathan: "can he have escaped? No. The walls are too high, and the windows too stoutly barricaded in this quarter, to admit such a supposition. He can't be far off. I shall find him yet. Ah! I have it," he added, after a moment's deliberation; "he's there, I'll be sworn." And, once more enveloping himself in darkness, he pursued his course.

He had now reached the adjoining house, and, scaling the roof, approached another building, which seemed to be, at least, one story loftier than its neighbours. Apparently, Jonathan was well acquainted with the premises; for, feeling about in the dark, he speedily discovered a ladder, up the steps of which he hurried. Drawing a pistol, and unclosing his lantern with the quickness of thought, he then burst through an open trap-door into a small loft.

The light fell upon the fugitive, who stood before him in an attitude of defence, with the child in his arms.

"Aha!" exclaimed Jonathan, acting upon the information he had obtained from Wood; "I have found you at last. Your servant, Mr. Darrell."

"Who are you!" demanded the fugitive, sternly.

"A friend," replied Jonathan, uncocking the pistol, and placing it in his pocket.

"How do I know you are a friend?" asked Darrell.

"What should I do here alone if I were an enemy? But, come, don't let us waste time in bandying words, when we might employ it so much more profitably. Your life, and that of your child, are in my power. What will you give me to save you from your pursuers?"

"*Can* you do so?" asked the other, doubtfully.

"I can, and will. Now, the reward?"

"I have but an ill-furnished purse. But if I escape, my gratitude--"

"Pshaw!" interrupted Jonathan, scornfully. "Your gratitude will vanish with your danger. Pay fools with promises. I must have something in hand."

"You shall have all I have about me," replied Darrell.

"Well--well," grumbled Jonathan, "I suppose I must be content. An ill-lined purse is a poor recompense for the risk I have run. However, come along. I needn't tell you to tread carefully. You know the danger of this breakneck road as well as I do. The light would betray us." So saying, he closed the lantern.

"Harkye, Sir," rejoined Darrell; "one word before I move. I know not who you are; and, as I cannot discern your face, I may be doing you an injustice. But there is something in your voice that makes me distrust you. If you attempt to play the traitor, you will do so at the hazard of your life."

"I have already hazarded my life in this attempt to save you," returned Jonathan boldly, and with apparent frankness; "this ought to be sufficient answer to your doubts. Your pursuers are below. What was to hinder me, if I had been so inclined, from directing them to your retreat?"

"Enough," replied Darrell. "Lead on!"

Followed by Darrell, Jonathan retraced his dangerous path. As he approached the gable of Mrs. Sheppard's house, loud yells and vociferations reached his ears; and, looking downwards, he perceived a great stir amid the mob. The cause of this uproar was soon manifest. Blueskin and the Minters were dragging Wood to the pump. The unfortunate carpenter struggled violently, but ineffectually. His hat was placed upon one pole, his wig on another. His shouts for help were answered by roars of mockery and laughter. He continued alternately to be tossed in the air, or rolled in the kennel until he was borne out of sight. The spectacle seemed to afford as much amusement to Jonathan as to the actors engaged in it. He could not contain his satisfaction, but chuckled, and rubbed his hands with delight.

"By Heaven!" cried Darrell, "it is the poor fellow whom I placed in such jeopardy a short time ago. I am the cause of his ill-usage."

"To be sure you are," replied Jonathan, laughing. "But, what of that? It'll be a lesson to him in future, and will show him the folly of doing a good-natured action!"

But perceiving that his companion did not relish his pleasantry and fearing that his sympathy for the carpenter's situation might betray him into some act of imprudence, Jonathan, without further remark, and by way of putting an end to the discussion, let himself drop through the roof. His example was followed by Darrell.

But, though the latter was somewhat embarrassed by his burthen, he peremptorily declined Jonathan's offer of assistance. Both, however, having safely landed, they cautiously crossed the room, and passed down the first flight of steps in silence. At this moment, a door was opened below; lights gleamed on the walls; and the figures of Rowland and Sir Cecil were distinguished at the foot of the stairs.

Darrell stopped, and drew his sword.

"You have betrayed me," said he, in a deep whisper, to his companion; "but you shall reap the reward of your treachery."

"Be still!" returned Jonathan, in the same under tone, and with great self-possession: "I can yet save you. And see!" he added, as the figures drew back, and the lights disappeared; "it's a false alarm. They have retired. However, not a moment is to be lost. Give me your hand."

He then hurried Darrell down another short flight of steps, and entered a small chamber at the back of the house. Closing the door, Jonathan next produced his lantern, and, hastening towards the window, undrew a bolt by which it was fastened. A stout wooden shutter, opening inwardly, being removed, disclosed a grating of iron bars. This obstacle, which appeared to preclude the possibility of egress in that quarter, was speedily got rid of. Withdrawing another bolt, and unhooking a chain suspended from the top of the casement, Jonathan pushed the iron framework outwards. The bars dropped noiselessly and slowly down, till the chain tightened at the staple.

"You are free," said he, "that grating forms a ladder, by which you may descend in safety. I learned the trick of the place from one Paul Groves, who used to live here, and who contrived the machine. He used to call it his fire-escape--ha! ha! I've often used the ladder for my own convenience, but I never expected to turn it to such good account. And now, Sir, have I kept faith with you?"

"You have," replied Darrell. "Here is my purse; and I trust you will let me know to whom I am indebted for this important service."

"It matters not who I am," replied Jonathan, taking the money. "As I said before, I have little reliance upon *professions* of gratitude."

"I know not how it is," sighed Darrell, "but I feel an unaccountable misgiving at quitting this place. Something tells me I am rushing on greater danger."

"You know best," replied Jonathan, sneeringly; "but if I were in your place I would take the chance of a future and uncertain risk to avoid a present and certain peril."

"You are right," replied Darrell; "the weakness is past. Which is the nearest way to the river?"

"Why, it's an awkward road to direct you," returned Jonathan. "But if you turn to the right when you reach the ground, and keep close to the Mint wall, you'll speedily arrive at White Cross Street; White Cross Street, if you turn again to the right, will bring you into Queen Street; Queen Street, bearing to the left, will conduct you to Deadman's Place; and Deadman's Place to the water-side, not fifty yards from Saint Saviour's stairs, where you're sure to get a boat."

"The very point I aim at," said Darrell as he passed through the outlet.

"Stay!" said Jonathan, aiding his descent; "you had better take my lantern. It may be useful to you. Perhaps you'll give me in return some token, by which I may remind you of this occurrence, in case we meet again. Your glove will suffice."

"There it is;" replied the other, tossing him the glove. "Are you sure these bars touch the ground?"

"They come within a yard of it," answered Jonathan.

"Safe!" shouted Darrell, as he effected a secure landing. "Good night!"

"So," muttered Jonathan, "having started the hare, I'll now unleash the hounds."

With this praiseworthy determination, he was hastening down stairs, with the utmost rapidity, when he encountered a female, whom he took, in the darkness, to be Mrs. Sheppard. The person caught hold of his arm, and, in spite of his efforts to disengage himself, detained him.

"Where is he?" asked she, in an agitated whisper. "I heard his voice; but I saw them on the stairs, and durst not approach him, for fear of giving the alarm."

"If you mean the fugitive, Darrell, he has escaped through the back window," replied Jonathan.

"Thank Heaven!" she gasped.

"Well, you women are forgiving creatures, I must say," observed Jonathan, sarcastically. "You thank Heaven for the escape of the man who did his best to get your child's neck twisted."

"What do you mean?" asked the female, in astonishment.

"I mean what I say," replied Jonathan. "Perhaps you don't know that this Darrell so contrived matters, that your child should be mistaken for his own; by which means it had a narrow escape from a tight cravat, I can assure you. However, the scheme answered well enough, for Darrell has got off with his own brat."

"Then this is not my child?" exclaimed she, with increased astonishment.

"If you have a child there, it certainly is not," answered Jonathan, a little surprised; "for I left your brat in the charge of Blueskin, who is still among the crowd in the street, unless, as is not unlikely, he's gone to see your other friend disciplined at the pump."

"Merciful providence!" exclaimed the female. "Whose child can this be?"

"How the devil should I know!" replied Jonathan gruffly. "I suppose it didn't drop through the ceiling, did it? Are you quite sure it's flesh and blood?" asked he, playfully pinching its arm till it cried out with pain.

"My child! my child!" exclaimed Mrs. Sheppard, rushing from the adjoining room. "Where is it?"

"Are you the mother of this child?" inquired the person who had first spoken, addressing Mrs. Sheppard.

"I am--I am!" cried the widow, snatching the babe, and pressing it to her breast with rapturous delight "God be thanked, I have found it!"

"We have both good reason to be grateful," added the lady, with great emotion.

"'Sblood!" cried Jonathan, who had listened to the foregoing conversation with angry wonder, "I've been nicely done here. Fool that I was to part with my lantern! But I'll soon set myself straight. What ho! lights! lights!"

And, shouting as he went, he flung himself down stairs.

"Where shall I fly?" exclaimed the lady, bewildered with terror. "They will kill me, if they find me, as they would have killed my husband and child. Oh God! my limbs fail me."

"Make an effort, Madam," cried Mrs. Sheppard, as a storm of furious voices resounded from below, and torches were seen mounting the stairs; "they are coming!--they are coming!--fly!--to the roof! to the roof."

"No," cried the lady, "this room--I recollect--it has a back window."

"It is shut," said Mrs. Sheppard.

"It is open," replied the lady, rushing towards it, and springing through the outlet.

"Where is she?" thundered Jonathan, who at this moment reached Mrs. Sheppard.

"She has flown up stairs," replied the widow.

"You lie, hussy!" replied Jonathan, rudely pushing her aside, as she vainly endeavoured to oppose his entrance into the room; "she is here. Hist!" cried he, as a scream was heard from without. "By G--! she has missed her footing."

There was a momentary and terrible silence, broken only by a few feeble groans.

Sir Cecil, who with Rowland and some others had entered the room rushed to the window with a torch.

He held down the light, and a moment afterwards beckoned, with a blanched cheek, to Rowland.

"Your sister is dead," said he, in a deep whisper.

"Her blood be upon her own head, then," replied Rowland, sternly. "Why came she here?"

"She could not resist the hand of fate which drew her hither," replied Sir Cecil, mournfully.

"Descend and take charge of the body," said Rowland, conquering his emotion by a great effort, "I will join you in a moment. This accident rather confirms than checks my purpose. The stain upon our family is only half effaced: I have sworn the death of the villain and his bastard, and I will keep my oath. Now, Sir," he added, turning to Jonathan, as Sir Cecil and his followers obeyed his injunctions, "you say you know the road which the person whom we seek has taken?"

"I do," replied Jonathan. "But I give no information gratis!"

"Speak, then," said Rowland, placing money in his hand.

"You'll find him at St. Saviours's stairs," answered Jonathan. "He's about to cross the river. You'd better lose no time. He has got five minutes' start of you. But I sent him the longest way about."

The words were scarcely pronounced, when Rowland disappeared.

"And now to see the end of it," said Jonathan, shortly afterwards passing through the window. "Good night, Master."

Three persons only were left in the room. These were the Master of the Mint, Van Galgebrok, and Mrs. Sheppard.

"A bad business this, Van," observed Baptist, with a prolonged shake of the head.

"Ja, ja, Muntmeester," said the Hollander, shaking his head in reply;--"very bad--very."

"But then they're staunch supporters of our friend over the water," continued Baptist, winking significantly; "so we must e'en hush it up in the best way we can."

"Ja," answered Van Galgebrok. "But--sapperment!--I wish they hadn't broken my pipe."

"JONATHAN WILD promises well," observed the Master, after a pause: "he'll become a great man. Mind, I, Baptist Kettleby, say so."

"He'll be hanged nevertheless," replied the Hollander, giving his collar an ugly jerk. "Mind, I, Rykhart Van Galgebrok predict it. And now let's go back to the Shovels, and finish our brandewyn and bier, Muntmeester."

"Alas!" cried Mrs. Sheppard, relieved by their departure, and giving way to a passionate flood of tears; "were it not for my child, I should wish to be in the place of that unfortunate lady."

CHAPTER V.
The Denunciation.

FOR a short space, Mrs. Sheppard remained dissolved in tears. She then dried her eyes, and laying her child gently upon the floor, knelt down beside him. "Open my heart, Father of Mercy!" she murmured, in a humble tone, and with downcast looks, "and make me sensible of the error of my ways. I have sinned deeply; but I have been sorely tried. Spare me yet a little while, Father! not for my own sake, but for the sake of this poor babe." Her utterance was here choked by sobs. "But if it is thy will to take me from him," she continued, as soon as her emotion permitted her,--"if he must be left an orphan amid strangers, implant, I beseech thee, a mother's feelings in some other bosom, and raise up a friend, who shall be to him what I would have been. Let him not bear the weight of my punishment. Spare him!--pity me!"

With this she arose, and, taking up the infant, was about to proceed down stairs, when she was alarmed by hearing the street-door opened, and the sound of heavy footsteps entering the house.

"Halloa, widow!" shouted a rough voice from below, "where the devil are you?"

Mrs. Sheppard returned no answer.

"I've got something to say to you," continued the speaker, rather less harshly; "something to your advantage; so come out o' your hiding-place, and let's have some supper, for I'm infernally hungry.--D'ye hear?"

Still the widow remained silent.

"Well, if you won't come, I shall help myself, and that's unsociable," pursued the speaker, evidently, from the noise he made, suiting the action to the word. "Devilish nice ham you've got here!--capital pie!--and, as I live, a flask of excellent canary. You're in luck to-night, widow. Here's your health in a bumper, and wishing you a better husband than your first. It'll be your own fault if you don't soon get another and a proper young man into the bargain. Here's his health likewise. What! mum still. You're the first widow I ever heard of who could withstand that lure. I'll try the effect of a jolly stave." And he struck up the following ballad:--

SAINT GILES'S BOWL.

I.

Where Saint-Giles' church stands, once a la-zar-house
stood; And, chain'd to its gates, was a ves-sel of wood; A
broad-bottom'd bowl, from which all the fine fellows, Who
pass'd by that spot, on their way to the gallows, Might
tipple strong beer, Their spirits to cheer, And drown, in a
sea of good li-quor, all fear! For nothing the
tran-sit to Ty-burn beguiles, So well as a
draught from the Bowl of Saint Giles!

II.

By many a highwayman many a draught
Of nutty-brown ale at Saint Giles's was quaft,
Until the old lazar-house chanced to fall down,
And the broad-bottom'd bowl was removed to the Crown.
  Where the robber may cheer
  His spirit with beer,
And drown in a sea of good liquor all fear!
For nothing the transit to Tyburn beguiles
So well as a draught from the Bowl of Saint Giles!

III.

There MULSACK and SWIFTNECK, both prigs from their birth,
OLD MOB and TOM COX took their last draught on earth:
There RANDAL, and SHORTER, and WHITNEY pulled up,
And jolly JACK JOYCE drank his finishing cup!
   For a can of ale calms,
   A highwayman's qualms,
  And makes him sing blithely his dolorous psalms
  And nothing the transit to Tyburn beguiles
  So well as a draught from the Bowl of Saint Giles!

"Singing's dry work," observed the stranger, pausing to take a pull at
the bottle. "And now, widow," he continued, "attend to the next verse,
for it consarns a friend o' yours."

IV.

When gallant TOM SHEPPARD to Tyburn was led,--
"Stop the cart at the Crown--stop a moment," he said.
He was offered the Bowl, but he left it and smiled,
Crying, "Keep it till call'd for by JONATHAN WILD!
  "The rascal one day,
  "Will pass by this way,
  "And drink a full measure to moisten his clay!
  "And never will Bowl of Saint Giles have beguiled
  "Such a thorough-paced scoundrel as JONATHAN WILD!"

V.

Should it e'er be my lot to ride backwards that way,

At the door of the Crown I will certainly stay;
I'll summon the landlord--I'll call for the Bowl,
And drink a deep draught to the health of my soul!
  Whatever may hap,
   I'll taste of the tap,
  To keep up my spirits when brought to the crap!
  For nothing the transit to Tyburn beguiles
  So well as a draught from the Bowl of St. Giles!

"Devil seize the woman!" growled the singer, as he brought his ditty to a close; "will nothing tempt her out? Widow Sheppard, I say," he added, rising, "don't be afraid. It's only a gentleman come to offer you his hand. 'He that woos a maid',--fol-de-rol--(hiccupping).--I'll soon find you out."

Mrs. Sheppard, whose distress at the consumption of the provisions had been somewhat allayed by the anticipation of the intruder's departure after he had satisfied his appetite, was now terrified in the extreme by seeing a light approach, and hearing footsteps on the stairs. Her first impulse was to fly to the window; and she was about to pass through it, at the risk of sharing the fate of the unfortunate lady, when her arm was grasped by some one in the act of ascending the ladder from without. Uttering a faint scream, she sank backwards, and would have fallen, if it had not been for the interposition of Blueskin, who, at that moment, staggered into the room with a candle in one hand, and the bottle in the other.

"Oh, you're here, are you?" said the ruffian, with an exulting laugh: "I've been looking for you everywhere."

"Let me go," implored Mrs. Sheppard,--"pray let me go. You hurt the child. Don't you hear how you've made it cry?"

"Throttle the kid!" rejoined Blueskin, fiercely. "If you don't stop its squalling, I will. I hate children. And, if I'd my own way, I'd drown 'em all like a litter o' puppies."

Well knowing the savage temper of the person she had to deal with, and how likely he was to put his threat into execution, Mrs. Sheppard did not dare to return any answer; but, disengaging herself from his embrace, endeavoured meekly to comply with his request.

"And now, widow," continued the ruffian, setting down the candle, and apply-ing his lips to the bottle neck as he flung his heavy frame upon a bench, "I've a piece o' good news for you."

"Good news will be news to me. What is it?"

"Guess," rejoined Blueskin, attempting to throw a gallant expression into his forbidding countenance.

Mrs. Sheppard trembled violently; and though she understood his meaning too well, she answered,--"I can't guess."

"Well, then," returned the ruffian, "to put you out o' suspense, as the topsman remarked to poor Tom Sheppard, afore he turned him off, I'm come to make you an honourable proposal o' marriage. You won't refuse me, I'm sure; so no more need be said about the matter. To-morrow, we'll go to the Fleet and get spliced. Don't shake so. What I said about your brat was all stuff. I didn't mean it. It's my way when I'm ruffled. I shall take to him as nat'ral as if he were my own flesh and blood afore long.--I'll give him the edication of a prig,--teach him the use of his forks betimes,--and make him, in the end, as clever a cracksman as his father."

"Never!" shrieked Mrs. Sheppard; "never! never!"

"Halloa! what's this?" demanded Blueskin, springing to his feet. "Do you mean to say that if I support your kid, I shan't bring him up how I please--eh?"

"Don't question me, but leave me," replied the widow wildly; "you had bet-ter."

"Leave you!" echoed the ruffian, with a contemptuous laugh; "--not just yet."

"I am not unprotected," rejoined the poor woman; "there's some one at the window. Help! help!"

But her cries were unheeded. And Blueskin, who, for a moment, had looked round distrustfully, concluding it was a feint, now laughed louder than ever.

"It won't do, widow," said he, drawing near her, while she shrank from his approach, "so you may spare your breath. Come, come, be reasonable, and listen to me. Your kid has already brought me good luck, and may bring me still more if his edication's attended to. This purse," he added, chinking it in the air, "and this ring, were given me for him just now by the lady, who made a false step on leaving your house. If I'd been in the way, instead of Jonathan Wild, that accident wouldn't have happened."

As he said this, a slight noise was heard without.

"What's that?" ejaculated the ruffian, glancing uneasily towards the window. "Who's there?--Pshaw! it's only the wind."

"It's Jonathan Wild," returned the widow, endeavouring to alarm him. "I told you I was not unprotected."

"*He protect you*," retorted Blueskin, maliciously; "you haven't a worse enemy on the face of the earth than Jonathan Wild. If you'd read your husband's dying speech, you'd know that he laid his death at Jonathan's door,--and with reason too, as I can testify."

"Man!" screamed Mrs. Sheppard, with a vehemence that shook even the hardened wretch beside her, "begone, and tempt me not."

"What should I tempt you to?" asked Blueskin, in surprise.

"To--to--no matter what," returned the widow distractedly. "Go--go!"

"I see what you mean," rejoined Blueskin, tossing a large case-knife, which he took from his pocket, in the air, and catching it dexterously by the haft as it fell; "you owe Jonathan a grudge;--so do I. He hanged your first husband. Just speak the word," he added, drawing the knife significantly across his throat, "and I'll put it out of his power to do the same by your second. But d--n him! let's talk o' something more agreeable. Look at this ring;--it's a diamond, and worth a mint o' money. It shall be your wedding ring. Look at it, I say. The lady's name's engraved inside, but so small I can scarcely read it. A-L-I-V-A--Aliva--T-R-E-N--Trenchard that's it. Aliva Trenchard."

"Aliva Trenchard!" exclaimed Mrs. Sheppard, hastily; "is that the name?"

"Ay, ay, now I look again it *is* Trenchard. How came you to know it? Have you heard the name before?"

"I think I have--long, long ago, when I was a child," replied Mrs. Sheppard, passing her hand across her brow; "but my memory is gone--quite gone. Where *can* I have heard it!"

"Devil knows," rejoined Blueskin. "Let it pass. The ring's yours, and you're mine. Here, put it on your finger."

Mrs. Sheppard snatched back her hand from his grasp, and exerted all her force to repel his advances.

"Set down the kid," roared Blueskin, savagely.

"Mercy!" screamed Mrs. Sheppard, struggling to escape, and holding the infant at arm's length; "have mercy on this helpless innocent!"

And the child, alarmed by the strife, added its feeble cries to its mother's shrieks.

"Set it down, I tell you," thundered Blueskin, "or I shall do it a mischief."

"Never!" cried Mrs. Sheppard.

Uttering a terrible imprecation, Blueskin placed the knife between his teeth, and endeavoured to seize the poor woman by the throat. In the struggle her cap fell off. The ruffian caught hold of her hair, and held her fast. The chamber rang with her shrieks. But her cries, instead of moving her assailant's compassion, only added to his fury. Planting his knee against her side, he pulled her towards him with one hand, while with the other he sought his knife. The child was now within reach; and, in another moment, he would have executed his deadly purpose, if an arm from behind had not felled him to the ground.

When Mrs. Sheppard, who had been stricken down by the blow that prostrated her assailant, looked up, she perceived Jonathan Wild kneeling beside the body of Blueskin. He was holding the ring to the light, and narrowly examining the inscription.

"Trenchard," he muttered; "Aliva Trenchard--they were right, then, as to the name. Well, if she survives the accident--as the blood, who styles himself Sir Cecil, fancies she may do--this ring will make my fortune by leading to the discovery of the chief parties concerned in this strange affair."

"Is the poor lady alive?" asked Mrs. Sheppard, eagerly.

"'Sblood!" exclaimed Jonathan, hastily thrusting the ring into his vest, and taking up a heavy horseman's pistol with which he had felled Blueskin,--"I thought you'd been senseless."

"Is she alive?" repeated the widow.

"What's that to you?" demanded Jonathan, gruffly.

"Oh, nothing--nothing," returned Mrs. Sheppard. "But pray tell me if her husband has escaped?"

"Her husband!" echoed Jonathan scornfully. "A *husband* has little to fear from his wife's kinsfolk. Her *lover*, Darrell, has embarked upon the Thames, where, if he's not capsized by the squall, (for it's blowing like the devil,) he stands a good chance of getting his throat cut by his pursuers--ha! ha! I tracked 'em to the banks of the river, and should have followed to see it out, if the watermen hadn't refused to take me. However, as things have turned up, it's fortunate that I came back."

"It is, indeed," replied Mrs. Sheppard; "most fortunate for me."

"For *you*!" exclaimed Jonathan; "don't flatter yourself that I'm thinking of you. Blueskin might have butchered you and your brat before I'd have lifted a finger to prevent him, if it hadn't suited my purposes to do so, and *he* hadn't incurred my displeasure. I never forgive an injury. Your husband could have told you that."

"How had he offended you?" inquired the widow.

"I'll tell you," answered Jonathan, sternly. "He thwarted my schemes twice. The first time, I overlooked the offence; but the second time, when I had planned to break open the house of his master, the fellow who visited you to-night,--Wood, the carpenter of Wych Street,--he betrayed me. I told him I would bring him to the gallows, and I was as good as my word."

"You were so," replied Mrs Sheppard; "and for that wicked deed you will one day be brought to the gallows yourself."

"Not before I have conducted your child thither," retorted Jonathan, with a withering look.

"Ah!" ejaculated Mrs. Sheppard, paralysed by the threat.

"If that sickly brat lives to be a man," continued Jonathan, rising, "I'll hang him upon the same tree as his father."

"Pity!" shrieked the widow.

"I'll be his evil genius!" vociferated Jonathan, who seemed to enjoy her torture.

"Begone, wretch!" cried the mother, stung beyond endurance by his taunts; "or I will drive you hence with my curses."

"Curse on, and welcome," jeered Wild.

Mrs. Sheppard raised her hand, and the malediction trembled upon her tongue. But ere the words could find utterance, her maternal tenderness overcame her indignation; and, sinking upon her knees, she extended her arms over her child.

"A mother's prayers--a mother's blessings," she cried, with the fervour almost of inspiration, "will avail against a fiend's malice."

"We shall see," rejoined Jonathan, turning carelessly upon his heel.

And, as he quitted the room, the poor widow fell with her face upon the floor.

CHAPTER VI.
The Storm.

A S soon as he was liberated by his persecutors, Mr. Wood set off at full speed from the Mint, and, hurrying he scarce knew whither (for there was such a continual buzzing in his ears and dancing in his eyes, as almost to take away the power of reflection), he held on at a brisk pace till his strength completely failed him.

On regaining his breath, he began to consider whither chance had led him; and, rubbing his eyes to clear his sight, he perceived a sombre pile, with a lofty tower and broad roof, immediately in front of him. This structure at once satisfied him as to where he stood. He knew it to be St. Saviour's Church. As he looked up at the massive tower, the clock tolled forth the hour of midnight. The solemn strokes were immediately answered by a multitude of chimes, sounding across the Thames, amongst which the deep note of Saint Paul's was plainly distinguishable. A feeling of inexplicable awe crept over the carpenter as the sounds died away. He trembled, not from any superstitious dread, but from an undefined sense of approaching danger. The peculiar appearance of the sky was not without some influence in awakening these terrors. Over one of the pinnacles of the tower a speck of pallid light marked the position of the moon, then newly born and newly risen. It was still profoundly dark; but the wind, which had begun to blow with some violence, chased the clouds rapidly across the heavens, and dispersed the vapours hanging nearer the earth. Sometimes the moon was totally eclipsed; at others, it shed a wan and ghastly glimmer over the masses rolling in the firmament. Not a star could be discerned, but, in their stead, streaks of lurid radiance, whence proceeding it was impossible to determine, shot ever and anon athwart the dusky vault, and added to the ominous and threatening appearance of the night.

Alarmed by these prognostications of a storm, and feeling too much exhausted from his late severe treatment to proceed further on foot, Wood endeavoured to find a tavern where he might warm and otherwise refresh himself. With this view he struck off into a narrow street on the left, and soon entered a small alehouse, over the door of which hung the sign of the "Welsh Trumpeter."

"Let me have a glass of brandy," said he, addressing the host.

"Too late, master," replied the landlord of the Trumpeter, in a surly tone, for he did not much like the appearance of his customer; "just shut up shop."

"Zounds! David Pugh, don't you know your old friend and countryman?" exclaimed the carpenter.

"Ah! Owen Wood, is it you?" cried David in astonishment. "What the devil makes you out so late? And what has happened to you, man, eh?--you seem in a queer plight."

"Give me the brandy, and I'll tell you," replied Wood.

"Here, wife--hostess--fetch me that bottle from the second shelf in the corner cupboard.--There, Mr. Wood," cried David, pouring out a glass of the spirit, and offering it to the carpenter, "that'll warm the cockles of your heart. Don't be afraid, man,--off with it. It's right Nantz. I keep it for my own drinking," he added in a lower tone.

Mr. Wood having disposed of the brandy, and pronounced himself much better, hurried close to the fire-side, and informed his friend in a few words of the inhospitable treatment he had experienced from the gentlemen of the Mint; whereupon Mr. Pugh, who, as well as the carpenter, was a descendant of Cadwallader, waxed extremely wrath; gave utterance to a number of fierce-sounding imprecations in the Welsh tongue; and was just beginning to express the greatest anxiety to catch some of the rascals at the Trumpeter, when Mr. Wood cut him short by stating his intention of crossing the river as soon as possible in order to avoid the storm.

"A storm!" exclaimed the landlord. "Gadzooks! I thought something was coming on; for when I looked at the weather-glass an hour ago, it had sunk lower than I ever remember it."

"We shall have a durty night on it, to a sartinty, landlord," observed an old one-eyed sailor, who sat smoking his pipe by the fire-side. "The glass never sinks in that way, d'ye see, without a hurricane follerin', I've knowed it often do so in the West

Injees. Moreover, a souple o' porpusses came up with the tide this mornin', and ha' bin flounderin' about i' the Thames abuv Lunnun Bridge all day long; and them say-monsters, you know, always proves sure fore runners of a gale."

"Then the sooner I'm off the better," cried Wood; "what's to pay, David?"

"Don't affront me, Owen, by asking such a question," returned the landlord; "hadn't you better stop and finish the bottle?"

"Not a drop more," replied Wood. "Enough's as good as a feast. Good night!"

"Well, if you won't be persuaded, and must have a boat, Owen," observed the landlord, "there's a waterman asleep on that bench will help you to as tidy a craft as any on the Thames. Halloa, Ben!" cried he, shaking a broad-backed fellow, equipped in a short-skirted doublet, and having a badge upon his arm,--"scullers wanted."

"Holloa! my hearty!" cried Ben, starting to his feet.

"This gentleman wants a pair of oars," said the landlord.

"Where to, master?" asked Ben, touching his woollen cap.

"Arundel Stairs," replied Wood, "the nearest point to Wych Street."

"Come along, master," said the waterman.

"Hark 'ee, Ben," said the old sailor, knocking the ashes from his pipe upon the hob; "you may try, but dash my timbers if you'll ever cross the Thames to-night."

"And why not, old saltwater?" inquired Ben, turning a quid in his mouth.

"'Cos there's a gale a-getting up as'll perwent you, young freshwater," replied the tar.

"It must look sharp then, or I shall give it the slip," laughed Ben: "the gale never yet blowed as could perwent my crossing the Thames. The weather's been foul enough for the last fortnight, but I've never turned my back upon it."

"May be not," replied the old sailor, drily; "but you'll find it too stiff for you to-night, anyhow. Howsomdever, if you *should* reach t'other side, take an old feller's advice, and don't be foolhardy enough to venter back again."

"I tell 'ee what, saltwater," said Ben, "I'll lay you my fare--and that'll be two shillin'--I'm back in an hour."

"Done!" cried the old sailor. "But vere'll be the use o' vinnin'? you von't live to pay me."

"Never fear," replied Ben, gravely; "dead or alive I'll pay you, if I lose. There's my thumb upon it. Come along, master."

"I tell 'ee what, landlord," observed the old sailor, quietly replenishing his pipe from a huge pewter tobacco-box, as the waterman and Wood quitted the house, "you've said good-b'ye to your friend."

"Odd's me! do you think so?" cried the host of the Trumpeter. "I'll run and bring him back. He's a Welshman, and I wouldn't for a trifle that any accident befel him."

"Never mind," said the old sailor, taking up a piece of blazing coal with the tongs, and applying it to his pipe; "let 'em try. They'll be back soon enough--or not at all."

Mr. Wood and the waterman, meanwhile, proceeded in the direction of St. Saviour's Stairs. Casting a hasty glance at the old and ruinous prison belonging to the liberty of the Bishop of Winchester (whose palace formerly adjoined the river), called the Clink, which gave its name to the street, along which he walked: and noticing, with some uneasiness, the melancholy manner in which the wind whistled through its barred casements, the carpenter followed his companion down an opening to the right, and presently arrived at the water-side.

Moored to the steps, several wherries were dancing in the rushing current, as if impatient of restraint. Into one of these the waterman jumped, and, having assisted Mr. Wood to a seat within it, immediately pushed from land. Ben had scarcely adjusted his oars, when the gleam of a lantern was seen moving towards the bank. A shout was heard at a little distance, and, the next moment, a person rushed with breathless haste to the stair-head.

"Boat there!" cried a voice, which Mr. Wood fancied he recognised.

"You'll find a waterman asleep under his tilt in one of them ere craft, if you look about, Sir," replied Ben, backing water as he spoke.

"Can't you take me with you?" urged the voice; "I'll make it well worth your while. I've a child here whom I wish to convey across the water without loss of time."

"A child!" thought Wood; it must be the fugitive Darrell. "Hold hard," cried he, addressing the waterman; "I'll give the gentleman a lift."

"Unpossible, master," rejoined Ben; "the tide's running down like a mill-sluice, and the wind's right in our teeth. Old saltwater was right. We shall have a reg'lar squall afore we gets across. D'ye hear how the wanes creaks on old Winchester

House? We shall have a touch on it ourselves presently. But I shall lose my wager if I stay a moment longer--so here goes." Upon which, he plunged his oars deeply into the stream, and the bark shot from the strand.

Mr. Wood's anxiety respecting the fugitive was speedily relieved by hearing another waterman busy himself in preparation for starting; and, shortly after, the dip of a second pair of oars sounded upon the river.

"Curse me, if I don't think all the world means to cross the Thames this fine night," observed Ben. "One'd think it rained fares, as well as blowed great guns. Why, there's another party on the stair-head inquiring arter scullers; and, by the mass! they appear in a greater hurry than any on us."

His attention being thus drawn to the bank, the carpenter beheld three figures, one of whom bore a torch, leap into a wherry of a larger size than the others, which immediately put off from shore. Manned by a couple of watermen, who rowed with great swiftness, this wherry dashed through the current in the track of the fugitive, of whom it was evidently in pursuit, and upon whom it perceptibly gained. Mr. Wood strained his eyes to catch a glimpse of the flying skiff. But he could only discern a black and shapeless mass, floating upon the water at a little distance, which, to his bewildered fancy, appeared absolutely standing still. To the practised eye of the waterman matters wore a very different air. He perceived clearly enough, that the chase was moving quickly; and he was also aware, from the increased rapidity with which the oars were urged, that every exertion was made on board to get out of the reach of her pursuers. At one moment, it seemed as if the flying bark was about to put to shore. But this plan (probably from its danger) was instantly aban doned; not, however, before her momentary hesitation had been taken advantage of by her pursuers, who, redoubling their efforts at this juncture, materially lessened the distance between them.

Ben watched these manoeuvres with great interest, and strained every sinew in his frame to keep ahead of the other boats.

"Them's catchpoles, I s'pose, Sir, arter the gemman with a writ?" he observed.

"Something worse, I fear," Wood replied.

"Why, you don't think as how they're crimps, do you?" Ben inquired.

"I don't know what I think," Wood answered sulkily; and he bent his eyes upon the water, as if he wished to avert his attention forcibly from the scene.

There is something that inspires a feeling of inexpressible melancholy in sailing on a dark night upon the Thames. The sounds that reach the ear, and the objects that meet the eye, are all calculated to awaken a train of sad and serious contemplation. The ripple of the water against the boat, as its keel cleaves through the stream--the darkling current hurrying by--the indistinctly-seen craft, of all forms and all sizes, hovering around, and making their way in ghost-like silence, or warning each other of their approach by cries, that, heard from afar, have something doleful in their note--the solemn shadows cast by the bridges--the deeper gloom of the echoing arches--the lights glimmering from the banks--the red reflection thrown upon the waves by a fire kindled on some stationary barge--the tall and fantastic shapes of the houses, as discerned through the obscurity;--these, and other sights and sounds of the same character, give a sombre colour to the thoughts of one who may choose to indulge in meditation at such a time and in such a place.

But it was otherwise with the carpenter. This was no night for the indulgence of dreamy musing. It was a night of storm and terror, which promised each moment to become more stormy and more terrible. Not a bark could be discerned on the river, except those already mentioned. The darkness was almost palpable; and the wind which, hitherto, had been blowing in gusts, was suddenly lulled. It was a dead calm. But this calm was more awful than the previous roaring of the blast.

Amid this portentous hush, the report of a pistol reached the carpenter's ears; and, raising his head at the sound, he beheld a sight which filled him with fresh apprehensions.

By the light of a torch borne at the stern of the hostile wherry, he saw that the pursuers had approached within a short distance of the object of their quest. The shot had taken effect upon the waterman who rowed the chase. He had abandoned his oars, and the boat was drifting with the stream towards the enemy. Escape was now impossible. Darrell stood erect in the bark, with his drawn sword in hand, prepared to repel the attack of his assailants, who, in their turn, seemed to await with impatience the moment which should deliver him into their power.

They had not to tarry long. In another instant, the collision took place. The watermen, who manned the larger wherry, immediately shipped their oars, grappled with the drifting skiff, and held it fast. Wood, then, beheld two persons, one of whom he recognised as Rowland, spring on board the chase. A fierce struggle ensued. There was a shrill cry, instantly succeeded by a deep splash.

"Put about, waterman, for God's sake!" cried Wood, whose humanity got the better of every personal consideration; "some one is overboard. Give way, and let us render what assistance we can to the poor wretch."

"It's all over with him by this time, master," replied Ben, turning the head of his boat, and rowing swiftly towards the scene of strife; "but d--n him, he was the chap as hit poor Bill Thomson just now, and I don't much care if he should be food for fishes."

As Ben spoke, they drew near the opposing parties. The contest was now carried on between Rowland and Darrell. The latter had delivered himself from one of his assailants, the attendant, Davies. Hurled over the sides of the skiff, the ruffian speedily found a watery grave. It was a spring-tide at half ebb; and the current, which was running fast and furiously, bore him instantly away. While the strife raged between the principals, the watermen in the larger wherry were occupied in stemming the force of the torrent, and endeavouring to keep the boats, they had lashed together, stationary. Owing to this circumstance, Mr. Wood's boat, impelled alike by oar and tide, shot past the mark at which it aimed; and before it could be again brought about, the struggle had terminated. For a few minutes, Darrell seemed to have the advantage in the conflict. Neither combatant could use his sword; and in strength the fugitive was evidently superior to his antagonist. The boat rocked violently with the struggle. Had it not been lashed to the adjoining wherry, it must have been upset, and have precipitated the opponents into the water. Rowland felt himself sinking beneath the powerful grasp of his enemy. He called to the other attendant, who held the torch. Understanding the appeal, the man snatched his master's sword from his grasp, and passed it through Darrell's body. The next moment, a heavy plunge told that the fugitive had been consigned to the waves.

Darrell, however, rose again instantly; and though mortally wounded, made a desperate effort to regain the boat.

"My child!" he groaned faintly.

"Well reminded," answered Rowland, who had witnessed his struggles with a smile of gratified vengeance; "I had forgotten the accursed imp in this confusion. Take it," he cried, lifting the babe from the bottom of the boat, and flinging it towards its unfortunate father.

The child fell within a short distance of Darrell, who, hearing the splash, struck out in that direction, and caught it before it sank. At this juncture, the sound of oars reached his ears, and he perceived Mr. Wood's boat bearing up towards him.

"Here he is, waterman," exclaimed the benevolent carpenter. "I see him!--row for your life!"

"That's the way to miss him, master," replied Ben coolly. "We must keep still. The tide'll bring him to us fast enough."

Ben judged correctly. Borne along by the current, Darrell was instantly at the boat's side.

"Seize this oar," vociferated the waterman.

"First take the child," cried Darrell, holding up the infant, and clinging to the oar with a dying effort.

"Give it me," returned the carpenter; "all's safe. Now lend me your own hand."

"My strength fails me," gasped the fugitive. "I cannot climb the boat. Take my child to--it is--oh God!--I am sinking--take it--take it!"

"Where?" shouted Wood.

Darrell attempted to reply. But he could only utter an inarticulate exclamation. The next moment his grasp relaxed, and he sank to rise no more.

Rowland, meantime, alarmed by the voices, snatched a torch from his attendant, and holding it over the side of the wherry, witnessed the incident just described.

"Confusion!" cried he; "there is another boat in our wake. They have rescued the child. Loose the wherry, and stand to your oars--quick--quick!"

These commands were promptly obeyed. The boat was set free, and the men resumed their seats. Rowland's purposes were, however, defeated in a manner as unexpected as appalling.

During the foregoing occurrences a dead calm prevailed. But as Rowland sprang to the helm, and gave the signal for pursuit, a roar like a volley of ordnance was heard aloft, and the wind again burst its bondage. A moment before, the surface of the stream was black as ink. It was now whitening, hissing, and seething like an enormous cauldron. The blast once more swept over the agitated river: whirled off the sheets of foam, scattered them far and wide in rain-drops, and left the raging torrent blacker than before. The gale had become a hurricane: that hurricane was the most terrible that ever laid waste our city. Destruction everywhere marked its course. Steeples toppled, and towers reeled beneath its fury. Trees were torn up by the roots; many houses were levelled to the ground; others were unroofed; the leads on the churches were ripped off, and "shrivelled up like scrolls of parchment." Nothing on land or water was spared by the remorseless gale. Most of the vessels lying in the river were driven from their moorings, dashed tumultuously against each other, or blown ashore. All was darkness, horror, confusion, ruin. Men fled from their tottering habitations, and returned to them scared by greater dangers. The end of the world seemed at hand.

At this time of universal havoc and despair,--when all London quaked at the voice of the storm,--the carpenter, who was exposed to its utmost fury, fared better than might have been anticipated. The boat in which he rode was not overset. Fortunately, her course had been shifted immediately after the rescue of the child; and, in consequence of this movement, she received the first shock of the hurricane, which blew from the southwest, upon her stern. Her head dipped deeply into the current, and she narrowly escaped being swamped. Righting, however, instantly afterwards, she scudded with the greatest rapidity over the boiling waves, to whose mercy she was now entirely abandoned. On this fresh outburst of the storm, Wood threw himself instinctively into the bottom of the boat, and clasping the little orphan to his breast, endeavoured to prepare himself to meet his fate.

While he was thus occupied, he felt a rough grasp upon his arm, and presently afterwards Ben's lips approached close to his ear. The waterman sheltered his mouth with his hand while he spoke, or his voice would have been carried away by the violence of the blast.

"It's all up, master," groaned Ben, "nothin' short of a merracle can save us. The boat's sure to run foul o' the bridge; and if she 'scapes stavin' above, she'll be swamped to a sartainty below. There'll be a fall of above twelve foot o' water, and think o' that on a night as 'ud blow a whole fleet to the devil."

Mr. Wood *did* think of it, and groaned aloud.

"Heaven help us!" he exclaimed; "we were mad to neglect the old sailor's advice."

"That's what troubles me," rejoined Ben. "I tell 'ee what, master, if you're more

fortinate nor I am, and get ashore, give old saltwater your fare. I pledged my thumb
that, dead or alive, I'd pay the wager if I lost; and I should like to be as good as my
word."

"I will--I will," replied Wood hastily. "Was that thunder?" he faltered, as a terrible clap was heard overhead.

"No; it's only a fresh gale," Ben returned: "hark! now it comes."

"Lord have mercy upon us, miserable sinners!" ejaculated Wood, as a fearful
gust dashed the water over the side of the boat, deluging him with spray.

The hurricane had now reached its climax. The blast shrieked, as if exulting in
its wrathful mission. Stunning and continuous, the din seemed almost to take away
the power of hearing. He, who had faced the gale, would have been instantly stifled.
Piercing through every crevice in the clothes, it, in some cases, tore them from
the wearer's limbs, or from his grasp. It penetrated the skin; benumbed the flesh;
paralysed the faculties. The intense darkness added to the terror of the storm. The
destroying angel hurried by, shrouded in his gloomiest apparel. None saw, though
all felt, his presence, and heard the thunder of his voice. Imagination, coloured by
the obscurity, peopled the air with phantoms. Ten thousand steeds appeared to be
trampling aloft, charged with the work of devastation. Awful shapes seemed to flit
by, borne on the wings of the tempest, animating and directing its fury. The actual
danger was lost sight of in these wild apprehensions; and many timorous beings
were scared beyond reason's verge by the excess of their fears.

This had well nigh been the case with the carpenter. He was roused from the
stupor of despair into which he had sunk by the voice of Ben, who roared in his ear,
"The bridge!--the bridge!"

CHAPTER VII.
Old London Bridge.

L ONDON, at the period of this history, boasted only a single bridge. But that bridge was more remarkable than any the metropolis now possesses. Covered with houses, from one end to the other, this reverend and pictur-esque structure presented the appearance of a street across the Thames. It was as if Grace-church Street, with all its shops, its magazines, and ceaseless throng of passengers, were stretched from the Middlesex to the Surrey shore. The houses were older, the shops gloomier, and the thoroughfare narrower, it is true; but the bustle, the crowd, the street-like air was the same. Then the bridge had arched gateways, bristling with spikes, and garnished (as all ancient gateways ought to be) with the heads of traitors. In olden days it boasted a chapel, dedicated to Saint Thomas; beneath which there was a crypt curiously constructed amid the arches, where "was sepultured Peter the Chaplain of Colechurch, who began the Stone Bridge at London;" and it still boasted an edifice (though now in rather a tumble-down condition) which had once vied with a palace,--we mean Nonesuch House. The other buildings stood close together in rows; and so valuable was every inch of room accounted, that, in many cases, cellars, and even habitable apartments, were constructed in the solid masonry of the piers.

Old London Bridge (the grandsire of the present erection) was supported on nineteen arches, each of which

Would a Rialto make for depth and height!

The arches stood upon enormous piers; the piers on starlings, or jetties, built far out into the river to break the force of the tide.

Roused by Ben's warning, the carpenter looked up and could just perceive the dusky outline of the bridge looming through the darkness, and rendered indistinctly visible by the many lights that twinkled from the windows of the lofty houses. As he gazed at these lights, they suddenly seemed to disappear, and a tremendous shock was felt throughout the frame of the boat. Wood started to his feet. He found that the skiff had been dashed against one of the buttresses of the bridge.

"Jump!" cried Ben, in a voice of thunder.

Wood obeyed. His fears supplied him with unwonted vigour. Though the starling was more than two feet above the level of the water, he alighted with his little charge--which he had never for an instant quitted--in safety upon it. Poor Ben was not so fortunate. Just as he was preparing to follow, the wherry containing Rowland and his men, which had drifted in their wake, was dashed against his boat. The violence of the collision nearly threw him backwards, and caused him to swerve as he sprang. His foot touched the rounded edge of the starling, and glanced off, precipitating him into the water. As he fell, he caught at the projecting masonry. But the stone was slippery; and the tide, which here began to feel the influence of the fall, was running with frightful velocity. He could not make good his hold. But, uttering a loud cry, he was swept away by the headlong torrent.

Mr. Wood heard the cry. But his own situation was too perilous to admit of his rendering any assistance to the ill-fated waterman. He fancied, indeed, that he beheld a figure spring upon the starling at the moment when the boats came in contact; but, as he could perceive no one near him, he concluded he must have been mistaken.

In order to make Mr. Wood's present position, and subsequent proceedings fully intelligible, it may be necessary to give some notion of the shape and structure of the platform on which he had taken refuge. It has been said, that the pier of each arch, or lock of Old London Bridge, was defended from the force of the tide by a huge projecting spur called a starling. These starlings varied in width, according to the bulk of the pier they surrounded. But they were all pretty nearly of the same length, and built somewhat after the model of a boat, having extremities as sharp and pointed as the keel of a canoe. Cased and ribbed with stone, and braced with horizontal beams of timber, the piles, which formed the foundation of these jetties, had resisted the strong encroachments of the current for centuries. Some of them are now buried at the bottom of the Thames. The starling, on which the carpenter stood, was the fourth from the Surrey shore. It might be three yards in width, and a few more in length; but it was covered with ooze and slime, and the waves continually broke over it. The transverse spars before mentioned were as slippery as ice; and the hollows between them were filled ankle-deep with water.

The carpenter threw himself flat upon the starling to avoid the fury of the wind. But in this posture he fared worse than ever. If he ran less risk of being blown over, he stood a much greater chance of being washed off, or stifled. As he lay on his back, he fancied himself gradually slipping off the platform. Springing to his feet in an ecstasy of terror, he stumbled, and had well nigh realized his worst apprehensions. He, next, tried to clamber up the flying buttresses and soffits of the pier, in the hope of reaching some of the windows and other apertures with which, as a man-of-war is studded with port-holes, the sides of the bridge were pierced. But this wild scheme was speedily abandoned; and, nerved by despair, the carpenter resolved to hazard an attempt, from the execution, almost from the contemplation, of which he had hitherto shrunk. This was to pass under the arch, along the narrow ledge of the starling, and, if possible, attain the eastern platform, where, protected by the bridge, he would suffer less from the excessive violence of the gale.

Assured, if he remained much longer where he was, he would inevitably perish, Wood recommended himself to the protection of Heaven, and began his perilous course. Carefully sustaining the child which, even in that terrible extremity, he had not the heart to abandon, he fell upon his knees, and, guiding himself with his right hand, crept slowly on. He had scarcely entered the arch, when the indraught was so violent, and the noise of the wind so dreadful and astounding, that he almost determined to relinquish the undertaking. But the love of life prevailed over his fears. He went on.

The ledge, along which he crawled, was about a foot wide. In length the arch exceeded seventy feet. To the poor carpenter it seemed an endless distance. When, by slow and toilsome efforts, he had arrived midway, something obstructed his further progress. It was a huge stone placed there by some workmen occupied in repairing the structure. Cold drops stood upon Wood's brow, as he encountered this obstacle. To return was impossible,--to raise himself certain destruction. He glanced downwards at the impetuous torrent, which he could perceive shooting past him with lightning swiftness in the gloom. He listened to the thunder of the fall now mingling with the roar of the blast; and, driven almost frantic by what he heard and saw, he pushed with all his force against the stone. To his astonishment and delight it yielded to the pressure, toppled over the ledge, and sank. Such was the hubbub and tumult around him, that the carpenter could not hear its plunge into the flood. His course, however, was no longer interrupted, and he crept on.

After encountering other dangers, and being twice, compelled to fling himself flat upon his face to avoid slipping from the wet and slimy pathway, he was at length about to emerge from the lock, when, to his inexpressible horror, he found he had lost the child!

All the blood in his veins rushed to his heart, and he shook in every limb as he made this discovery. A species of vertigo seized him. His brain reeled. He fancied that the whole fabric of the bridge was cracking over head,--that the arch was tumbling upon him,--that the torrent was swelling around him, whirling him off, and about to bury him in the deafening abyss. He shrieked with agony, and clung with desperate tenacity to the roughened stones. But calmer thoughts quickly succeeded. On taxing his recollection, the whole circumstance rushed to mind with painful distinctness. He remembered that, before he attempted to dislodge the stone, he had placed the child in a cavity of the pier, which the granite mass had been intended to fill. This obstacle being removed, in his eagerness to proceed, he had forgotten to take his little charge with him. It was still possible the child might be in safety. And so bitterly did the carpenter reproach himself with his neglect, that he resolved, at all risks, to go back in search of it. Acting upon this humane determination, he impelled himself slowly backwards,--for he did not dare to face the blast,--and with incredible labour and fatigue reached the crevice. His perseverance was amply rewarded. The child was still safe. It lay undisturbed in the remotest corner of the recess.

So overjoyed was the carpenter with the successful issue of his undertaking, that he scarcely paused a moment to recruit himself; but, securing the child, set out upon his return. Retracing his steps, he arrived, without further accident, at the eastern platform of the starling. As he anticipated, he was here comparatively screened from the fury of the wind; and when he gazed upon the roaring fall beneath him, visible through the darkness in a glistening sheet of foam, his heart overflowed with gratitude for his providential deliverance.

As he moved about upon the starling, Mr. Wood became sensible that he was not alone. Some one was standing beside him. This, then, must be the person whom he had seen spring upon the western platform at the time of the collision between the boats. The carpenter well knew from the obstacle which had interfered with his own progress, that the unknown could not have passed through the same lock as himself. But he might have crept along the left side of the pier, and beneath the further arch; whereas, Wood, as we have seen, took his course upon the right. The darkness prevented the carpenter from discerning the features or figure of the stranger; and the ceaseless din precluded the possibility of holding any communication by words with him. Wood, however, made known his presence to the individual by laying his hand upon his shoulder. The stranger started at the touch, and spoke. But his words were borne away by the driving wind.

Finding all attempts at conversation with his companion in misfortune in vain, Wood, in order to distract his thoughts, looked up at the gigantic structure standing, like a wall of solid darkness, before him. What was his transport on perceiving that a few yards above him a light was burning. The carpenter did not hesitate a moment. He took a handful of the gravelly mud, with which the platform was covered, and threw the small pebbles, one by one, towards the gleam. A pane of glass was shivered by each stone. The signal of distress was evidently understood. The light disappeared. The window was shortly after opened, and a rope ladder, with a lighted horn lantern attached to it, let down.

Wood grasped his companion's arm to attract his attention to this unexpected means of escape. The ladder was now within reach. Both advanced towards it, when, by the light of the lantern, Wood beheld, in the countenance of the stranger, the well-remembered and stern features of Rowland.

The carpenter trembled; for he perceived Rowland's gaze fixed first upon the infant, and then on himself.

"It *is* her child!" shrieked Rowland, in a voice heard above the howling of the tempest, "risen from this roaring abyss to torment me. Its parents have perished. And shall their wretched offspring live to blight my hopes, and blast my fame? Never!" And, with these words, he grasped Wood by the throat, and, despite his resistance, dragged him to the very verge of the platform.

All this juncture, a thundering crash was heard against the side of the bridge. A stack of chimneys, on the house above them, had yielded to the storm, and descended in a shower of bricks and stones.

When the carpenter a moment afterwards stretched out his hand, scarcely knowing whether he was alive or dead, he found himself alone. The fatal shower, from which he and his little charge escaped uninjured, had stricken his assailant and precipitated him into the boiling gulf.

"It's an ill wind that blows nobody good," thought the carpenter, turning his attention to the child, whose feeble struggles and cries proclaimed that, as yet, life had not been extinguished by the hardships it had undergone. "Poor little creature!" he muttered, pressing it tenderly to his breast, as he grasped the rope and clambered up to the window: "if thou hast, indeed, lost both thy parents, as that terrible man said just now, thou art not wholly friendless and deserted, for I myself will be a father to thee! And in memory of this dreadful night, and the death from which I have, been the means of preserving thee, thou shalt bear the name of THAMES DARRELL."

No sooner had Wood crept through the window, than nature gave way, and he fainted. On coming to himself, he found he had been wrapped in a blanket and put to bed with a couple of hot bricks to his feet. His first inquiries were concerning the child, and he was delighted to find that it still lived and was doing well. Every care had been taken of it, as well as of himself, by the humane inmates of the house in which he had sought shelter.

About noon, next day, he was able to move; and the gale having abated, he set out homewards with his little charge.

The city presented a terrible picture of devastation. London Bridge had suffered a degree less than most places. But it was almost choked up with fallen stacks of chimneys, broken beams of timber, and shattered tiles. The houses overhung in a frightful manner, and looked as if the next gust would precipitate them into the river. With great difficulty, Wood forced a path through the ruins. It was a work of no slight danger, for every instant a wall, or fragment of a building, came crashing to the ground. Thames Street was wholly impassable. Men were going hither and thither with barrows, and ladders and ropes, removing the rubbish, and trying to support the tottering habitations. Grace-church Street was entirely deserted, except by a few stragglers, whose curiosity got the better of their fears; or who, like the carpenter, were compelled to proceed along it. The tiles lay a foot thick in the road.

In some cases they were ground almost to powder; in others, driven deeply into the earth, as if discharged from a piece of ordnance. The roofs and gables of many of the houses had been torn off. The signs of the shops were carried to incredible distances. Here and there, a building might be seen with the doors and windows driven in, and all access to it prevented by the heaps of bricks and tilesherds.

Through this confusion the carpenter struggled on;--now ascending, now descending the different mountains of rubbish that beset his path, at the imminent peril of his life and limbs, until he arrived in Fleet Street. The hurricane appeared to have raged in this quarter with tenfold fury. Mr. Wood scarcely knew where he was. The old aspect of the place was gone. In lieu of the substantial habitations which he had gazed on overnight, he beheld a row of falling scaffoldings, for such they seemed.

It was a dismal and depressing sight to see a great city thus suddenly overthrown; and the carpenter was deeply moved by the spectacle. As usual, however, on the occasion of any great calamity, a crowd was scouring the streets, whose sole object was plunder. While involved in this crowd, near Temple Bar,--where the thoroughfare was most dangerous from the masses of ruin that impeded it,--an individual, whose swarthy features recalled to the carpenter one of his tormentors of the previous night, collared him, and, with bitter imprecations accused him of stealing his child. In vain Wood protested his innocence. The ruffian's companions took his part. And the infant, in all probability, would have been snatched from its preserver, if a posse of the watch (sent out to maintain order and protect property) had not opportunely arrived, and by a vigorous application of their halberts dispersed his persecutors, and set him at liberty.

Mr. Wood then took to his heels, and never once looked behind him till he reached his own dwelling in Wych Street. His wife met him at the door, and into her hands he delivered his little charge.

END OF THE FIRST EPOCH.

EPOCH THE SECOND. 1715.
THAMES DARRELL.

CHAPTER I.
The Idle Apprentice.

TWELVE years! How many events have occurred during that long interval! how many changes have taken place! The whole aspect of things is altered. The child has sprung into a youth; the youth has become a man; the man has already begun to feel the advances of age. Beauty has bloomed and faded. Fresh flowers of loveliness have budded, expanded, died. The fashions of the day have become antiquated. New customs have prevailed over the old. Parties, politics, and popular opinions have changed. The crown has passed from the brow of one monarch to that of another. Habits and tastes are no longer the same. We, ourselves, are scarcely the same we were twelve years ago.

Twelve years ago! It is an awful retrospect. Dare we look back upon the darkened vista, and, in imagination retrace the path we have trod? With how many vain hopes is it shaded! with how many good resolutions, never fulfilled, is it paved! Where are the dreams of ambition in which, twelve years ago, we indulged? Where are the aspirations that fired us--the passions that consumed us then? Has our success in life been commensurate with our own desires--with the anticipations formed of us by others? Or, are we not blighted in heart, as in ambition? Has not the loved one been estranged by doubt, or snatched from us by the cold hand of death? Is not the goal, towards which we pressed, further off than ever--the prospect before us cheerless as the blank behind?--Enough of this. Let us proceed with our tale.

Twelve years, then, have elapsed since the date of the occurrences detailed in the preceding division of this history. At that time, we were beneath the sway of Anne: we are now at the commencement of the reign of George the First. Passing at a glance over the whole of the intervening period; leaving in the words of the poet,

>   --The growth untried
> Of that wide gap--

we shall resume our narrative at the beginning of June, 1715.

One Friday afternoon, in this pleasant month, it chanced that Mr. Wood, who had been absent on business during the greater part of the day, returned (perhaps not altogether undesignedly) at an earlier hour than was expected, to his dwelling in Wych Street, Drury Lane; and was about to enter his workshop, when, not hearing any sound of labour issue from within, he began to suspect that an apprentice, of whose habits of industry he entertained some doubt, was neglecting his employment. Impressed with this idea, he paused for a moment to listen. But finding all continue silent, he cautiously lifted the latch, and crept into the room, resolved to punish the offender in case his suspicions should prove correct.

The chamber, into which he stole, like all carpenters' workshops, was crowded with the implements and materials of that ancient and honourable art. Saws, hammers, planes, axes, augers, adzes, chisels, gimblets, and an endless variety of tools were ranged, like a stand of martial weapons at an armoury, in racks against the walls. Over these hung levels, bevels, squares, and other instruments of measurement. Amid a litter of nails without heads, screws without worms, and locks without wards, lay a glue-pot and an oilstone, two articles which their owner was wont to term "his right hand and his left." On a shelf was placed a row of paint-jars; the contents of which had been daubed in rainbow streaks upon the adjacent closet and window sill. Divers plans and figures were chalked upon the walls; and the spaces between them were filled up with an almanack for the year; a godly ballad, adorned with a rude wood-cut, purporting to be " *The History of Chaste Susannah*;" an old print of the Seven Golden Candlesticks; an abstract of the various Acts of

Parliament against drinking, swearing, and all manner of profaneness; and a view of the interior of Doctor Daniel Burgess's Presbyterian meeting-house in Russell Court, with portraits of the reverend gentleman and the principal members of his flock. The floor was thickly strewn with sawdust and shavings; and across the room ran a long and wide bench, furnished at one end with a powerful vice; next to which three nails driven into the boards served, it would appear from the lump of unconsumed tallow left in their custody, as a substitute for a candlestick. On the bench was set a quartern measure of gin, a crust of bread, and a slice of cheese. Attracted by the odour of the latter dainty, a hungry cat had contrived to scratch open the paper in which it was wrapped, displaying the following words in large characters:--"THE HISTORY OF THE FOUR KINGS, OR CHILD'S BEST GUIDE TO THE GALLOWS." And, as if to make the moral more obvious, a dirty pack of cards was scattered, underneath, upon the sawdust. Near the door stood a pile of deal planks, behind which the carpenter ensconced himself in order to reconnoitre, unobserved, the proceedings of his idle apprentice.

Standing on tiptoe, on a joint-stool, placed upon the bench, with his back to the door, and a clasp-knife in his hand, this youngster, instead of executing his appointed task, was occupied in carving his name upon a beam, overhead. Boys, at the time of which we write, were attired like men of their own day, or certain charity-children of ours; and the stripling in question was dressed in black plush breeches, and a gray drugget waistcoat, with immoderately long pockets, both of which were evidently the cast-off clothes of some one considerably his senior. Coat, on the present occasion, he had none, it being more convenient, as well as agreeable to him, to pursue his avocations in his shirtsleeves; but, when fully equipped, he wore a large-cuffed, long-skirted garment, which had once been the property of his master.

In concealing himself behind the timber, Mr. Wood could not avoid making a slight shuffling sound. The noise startled the apprentice, who instantly suspended his labour, and gazed anxiously in the direction whence he supposed it proceeded. His face was that of a quick, intelligent-looking boy, with fine hazel eyes, and a clear olive complexion. His figure was uncommonly slim even for his age, which could not be more than thirteen; and the looseness of his garb made him appear thinner than he was in reality. But if his frame was immature, his looks were not so. He seemed to possess a penetration and cunning beyond his years--to hide a man's judgment under a boy's mask. The glance, which he threw at the door, was singularly expressive of his character: it was a mixture of alarm, effrontery, and resolution. In the end, resolution triumphed, as it was sure to do, over the weaker emotions, and he laughed at his fears. The only part of his otherwise-interesting countenance, to which one could decidedly object, was the mouth; a feature that, more than any other, is conceived to betray the animal propensities of the possessor. If this is true, it must be owned that the boy's mouth showed a strong tendency on his part to coarse indulgence. The eyes, too, though large and bright, and shaded by long lashes, seemed to betoken, as hazel eyes generally do in men, a faithless and uncertain disposition. The cheek-bones were prominent: the nose slightly depressed, with rather wide nostrils; the chin narrow, but well-formed; the forehead broad and lofty; and he possessed such an extraordinary flexibility of muscle in this region, that he could elevate his eye-brows at pleasure up to the very verge of his sleek and shining black hair, which, being closely cropped, to admit of his occasionally wearing a wig, gave a singular bullet-shape to his head. Taken altogether, his physiognomy resembled one of those vagabond heads which Murillo delighted to paint, and for which Guzman d'Alfarache, Lazarillo de Tormes, or Estevanillo Gonzalez might have sat:--faces that almost make one in love with roguery, they seem so full of vivacity and enjoyment. There was all the knavery, and more than all the drollery of a Spanish picaroon in the laughing eyes of the English apprentice; and, with a little more warmth and sunniness of skin on the side of the latter, the resemblance between them would have been complete.

Satisfied, as he thought, that he had nothing to apprehend, the boy resumed his task, chanting, as he plied his knife with redoubled assiduity, the following--not inappropriate strains:--

THE NEWGATE STONE.

When Claude Du Val was in Newgate thrown,
He carved his name on the dungeon stone;
Quoth a dubsman, who gazed on the shattered wall,
"You have carved your epitaph, Claude Du Val,
    With your chisel so fine, tra la!"

"This S wants a little deepening," mused the apprentice, retouching the letter in question; "ay, that's better."

> Du Val was hang'd, and the next who came
> On the selfsame stone inscribed his name:
> "Aha!" quoth the dubsman, with devilish glee,
> "Tom Waters your doom is the triple tree!
>   With your chisel so fine, tra la!"

"Tut, tut, tut," he cried, "what a fool I am to be sure! I ought to have cut John, not Jack. However, it don't signify. Nobody ever called me John, that I recollect. So I dare say I was christened Jack. Deuce take it! I was very near spelling my name with one P.

> Within that dungeon lay Captain Bew,
> Rumbold and Whitney--a jolly crew!
> All carved their names on the stone, and all
> Share the fate of the brave Du Val!
>   With their chisels so fine, tra la!

"Save us!" continued the apprentice, "I hope this beam doesn't resemble the Newgate stone; or I may chance, like the great men the song speaks of, to swing on the Tyburn tree for my pains. No fear o' that.--Though if my name should become as famous as theirs, it wouldn't much matter. The prospect of the gallows would never deter me from taking to the road, if I were so inclined.

> Full twenty highwaymen blithe and bold,
> Rattled their chains in that dungeon old;
> Of all that number there 'scaped not one
> Who carved his name on the Newgate Stone.
>   With his chisel so fine, tra la!

"There!" cried the boy, leaping from the stool, and drawing back a few paces on the bench to examine his performance,--"that'll do. Claude du Val himself couldn't have carved it better--ha! ha!"

The name inscribed upon the beam (of which, as it has been carefully preserved by the subsequent owners of Mr. Wood's habitation in Wych Street, we are luckily enabled to furnish a facsimile) was

"I've half a mind to give old Wood the slip, and turn highwayman," cried Jack, as he closed the knife, and put it in his pocket.

"The devil you have!" thundered a voice from behind, that filled the apprentice with dismay. "Come down, sirrah, and I'll teach you how to deface my walls in future. Come down, I say, instantly, or I'll make you." Upon which, Mr. Wood caught hold of Jack's leg, and dragged him off the bench.

"And so you'll turn highwayman, will you, you young dog?" continued the carpenter, cuffing him soundly,--"rob the mails, like Jack Hall, I suppose."

"Yes, I will," replied Jack sullenly, "if you beat me in that way."

Amazed at the boy's assurance, Wood left off boxing his ears for a moment, and, looking at him steadfastly, said in a grave tone, "Jack, Jack, you'll come to be hanged!"

"Better be hanged than hen-pecked," retorted the lad with a malicious grin.

"What do you mean by that, sirrah?" cried Wood, reddening with anger. "Do you dare to insinuate that Mrs. Wood governs me?"

"It's plain you can't govern yourself, at all events," replied Jack coolly; "but, be that as it may, I won't be struck for nothing."

"Nothing," echoed Wood furiously. "Do you call neglecting your work, and singing flash songs nothing? Zounds! you incorrigible rascal, many a master would have taken you before a magistrate, and prayed for your solitary confinement in Bridewell for the least of these offences. But I'll be more lenient, and content myself with merely chastising you, on condition--"

"You may do as you please, master," interrupted Jack, thrusting his hand into his pocket, as if in search of the knife; "but I wouldn't advise you to lay hands on me again."

Mr. Wood glanced at the hardy offender, and not liking the expression of his countenance, thought it advisable to postpone the execution of his threats to a more favourable opportunity. So, by way of gaining time, he resolved to question him further.

"Where did you learn the song I heard just now?" he demanded, in an authoritative tone.

"At the Black Lion in our street," replied Jack, without hesitation.

"The worst house in the neighbourhood--the constant haunt of reprobates and thieves," groaned Wood. "And who taught it you--the landlord, Joe Hind?"

"No; one Blueskin, a fellow who frequents the Lion," answered Jack, with a degree of candour that astonished his master nearly as much as his confidence. "It was that song that put it into my head to cut my name on the beam."

"A white wall is a fool's paper, Jack,--remember that," rejoined Wood. "Pretty company for an apprentice to keep!--pretty houses for an apprentice to frequent! Why, the rascal you mention is a notorious house-breaker. He was tried at the last Old Bailey sessions; and only escaped the gallows by impeaching his accomplices. Jonathan Wild brought him off."

"Do you happen to know Jonathan Wild, master?" inquired Jack, altering his tone, and assuming a more respectful demeanour.

"I've seen him some years ago, I believe," answered Wood; "and, though he must be much changed by this time, I dare say I should know him again."

"A short man, isn't he, about your height, Sir,--with a yellow beard, and a face as sly as a fox's?"

"Hem!" replied Wood, coughing slightly to conceal a smile; "the description's not amiss. But why do you ask?"

"Because--" stammered the boy.

"Speak out--don't be alarmed," said Wood, in a kind and encouraging tone. "If you've done wrong, confess it, and I'll forgive you!"

"I don't deserve to be forgiven!" returned Jack, bursting into tears; "for I'm afraid I've done very wrong. Do you know this, Sir?" he added, taking a key from his pocket.

"Where did you find it!" asked Wood.

"It was given me by a man who was drinking t'other night with Blueskin at the Lion! and who, though he slouched his hat over his eyes, and muffled his chin in a handkerchief, must have been Jonathan Wild."

"Where did *he* get it?" inquired Wood, in surprise.

"That I can't say. But he promised to give me a couple of guineas if I'd ascertain whether it fitted your locks."

"Zounds!" exclaimed Wood; "it's my old master-key. This key," he added, taking it from the boy, "was purloined from me by your father, Jack. What he intended to do with it is of little consequence now. But before he suffered at Tyburn, he charged your mother to restore it. She lost it in the Mint. Jonathan Wild must have stolen it from her."

"He must," exclaimed Jack, hastily; "but only let me have it till to-morrow, and if I don't entrap him in a snare from which, with all his cunning, he shall find it difficult to escape, my name's not Jack Sheppard."

"I see through your design, Jack," returned the carpenter, gravely; "but I don't like under-hand work. Even when you've a knave to deal with, let your actions be plain, and above-board. That's my maxim; and it's the maxim of every honest man. It would be a great matter, I must own, to bring Jonathan Wild to justice. But I can't consent to the course you would pursue--at least, not till I've given it due consideration. In regard to yourself, you've had a very narrow escape. Wild's intention, doubtless, was to use you as far as he found necessary, and then to sell you. Let this be a caution to you in future--with whom, and about what you deal. We're told, that 'Whoso is partner with a thief hateth his own soul.' Avoid taverns and bad company, and you may yet do well. You promise to become a first-rate workman. But you want one quality, without which all others are valueless. You want industry--you want steadiness. Idleness is the key of beggary, Jack. If you don't conquer this disgraceful propensity in time, you'll soon come to want; and then nothing can save you. Be warned by your father's fate. As you brew so must you drink. I've engaged to watch over you as a son, and I *will* do so as far as I'm able; but if you neglect my advice, what chance have I of benefitting you? On one point I've made up my mind--you shall either obey me, or leave me. Please yourself. Here are your indentures, if you choose to seek another master."

"I *will* obey you, master,--indeed I will!" implored Jack, seriously alarmed at the carpenter's calm displeasure.

"We shall see. Good words, without deeds, are rushes and reeds. And now take away those cards, and never let me see them again. Drive away the cat; throw that measure of gin through the window; and tell me why you've not so much as touched the packing-case for Lady Trafford, which I particularly desired you to complete against my return. It must be sent home this evening. She leaves town to-morrow."

"It shall be ready in two hours," answered Jack, seizing a piece of wood and a plane; "it isn't more than four o'clock. I'll engage to get the job done by six. I didn't expect you home before that hour, Sir."

"Ah, Jack," said Wood, shaking his head, "where there's a will there's a way. You can do anything you please. I wish I could get you to imitate Thames Darrell."

"I'm sure I understand the business of a carpenter much better than he does," replied Jack, adroitly adjusting the board, and using the plane with the greatest rapidity.

"Perhaps," replied Wood, doubtfully.

"Thames was always your favourite," observed Jack, as he fastened another piece of wood on the teeth of the iron stopper.

"I've made no distinction between you, hitherto," answered Wood; "nor shall I do so, unless I'm compelled."

"I've had the hard work to do, at all events," rejoined Jack, "But I won't complain. I'd do anything for Thames Darrell."

"And Thames Darrell would do anything for you, Jack," replied a blithe voice. "What's the matter, father!" continued the new-comer, addressing Wood. "Has Jack displeased you? If so, overlook his fault this once. I'm sure he'll do his best to content you. Won't you, Jack?"

"That I will," answered Sheppard, eagerly.

"When it thunders, the thief becomes honest," muttered Wood.

"Can I help you, Jack?" asked Thames, taking up a plane.

"No, no, let him alone," interposed Wood. "He has undertaken to finish this job by six o'clock, and I wish to see whether he'll be as good as his word."

"He'll have hard work to do it by that time, father," remonstrated Thames; "you'd better let me help him."

"On no account," rejoined Wood peremptorily. "A little extra exertion will teach him the advantage of diligence at the proper season. Lost ground must be regained. I need scarcely ask whether you've executed your appointed task, my dear? You're never behindhand."

Thames turned away at the question, which he felt might be construed into a reproach. But Sheppard answered for him.

"Darrell's job was done early this morning," he said; "and if I'd attended to his advice, the packing-case would have been finished at the same time."

"You trusted too much to your own skill, Jack," rejoined Thames. "If I could work as fast as you, I might afford to be as idle. See how he gets on, father," he added, appealing to Wood: "the box seems to grow under his hands."

"You're a noble-hearted little fellow, Thames," rejoined Wood, casting a look of pride and affection at his adopted son, whose head he gently patted; "and give promise of a glorious manhood."

Thames Darrell was, indeed, a youth of whom a person of far greater worldly consequence than the worthy carpenter might have been justly proud. Though a few months younger than his companion Jack Sheppard, he was half a head taller, and much more robustly formed. The two friends contrasted strikingly with each other. In Darrell's open features, frankness and honour were written in legible characters; while, in Jack's physiognomy, cunning and knavery were as strongly imprinted. In all other respects they differed as materially. Jack could hardly be accounted good-looking: Thames, on the contrary, was one of the handsomest boys possible. Jack's complexion was that of a gipsy; Darrell's as fresh and bright as a rose. Jack's mouth was coarse and large; Darrell's small and exquisitely carved, with the short, proud upper lip, which belongs to the highest order of beauty. Jack's nose was broad and flat; Darrell's straight and fine as that of Antinous. The expression pervading the countenance of the one was vulgarity; of the other, that which is rarely found, except in persons of high birth. Darrell's eyes were of that clear gray which it is difficult to distinguish from blue by day and black at night; and his rich brown hair, which he could not consent to part with, even on the promise of a new and modish peruke from his adoptive father, fell in thick glossy ringlets upon his shoulders; whereas Jack's close black crop imparted the peculiar bullet-shape we have noticed, to his head.

While Thames modestly expressed a hope that he might not belie the carpenter's favourable prediction, Jack Sheppard thought fit to mount a small ladder placed against the wall, and, springing with the agility of an ape upon a sort of frame, contrived to sustain short spars and blocks of timber, began to search about for a piece of wood required in the work on which he was engaged. Being in a great hurry, he took little heed where he set his feet; and a board giving way, he must have fallen, if he had not grasped a large plank laid upon the transverse beam immediately over his head.

"Take care, Jack," shouted Thames, who witnessed the occurrence; "that plank isn't properly balanced. You'll have it down."

But the caution came too late. Sheppard's weight had destroyed the equilibrium of the plank: it swerved, and slowly descended. Losing his presence of mind, Jack quitted his hold, and dropped upon the frame. The plank hung over his head. A moment more and he would have been crushed beneath the ponderous board, when a slight but strong arm arrested its descent.

"Get from under it, Jack!" vociferated Thames. "I can't hold it much longer-- it'll break my wrist. Down we come!" he exclaimed, letting go the plank, which fell with a crash, and leaping after Sheppard, who had rolled off the frame.

All this was the work of a minute.

"No bones broken, I hope," said Thames, laughing at Jack, who limped towards the bench, rubbing his shins as he went.

"All right," replied Sheppard, with affected indifference.

"It's a mercy you both escaped!" ejaculated Wood, only just finding his tongue. "I declare I'm all in a cold sweat. How came you, Sir," he continued, addressing Sheppard, "to venture upon that frame. I always told you some accident would happen."

"Don't scold him, father," interposed Thames; "he's been frightened enough already."

"Well, well, since you desire it, I'll say no more," returned Wood. "You hay'n't hurt your arm, I trust, my dear?" he added, anxiously.

"Only sprained it a little, that's all," answered Thames; "the pain will go off presently."

"Then you *are* hurt," cried the carpenter in alarm. "Come down stairs directly, and let your mother look at your wrist. She has an excellent remedy for a sprain. And do you, Jack, attend to your work, and mind you don't get into further mischief."

"Hadn't Jack better go with us?" said Thames. "His shin may need rubbing."

"By no means," rejoined Wood, hastily. "A little suffering will do him good. I meant to give him a drubbing. That bruise will answer the same purpose."

"Thames," said Sheppard in a low voice, as he threw a vindictive glance at the carpenter, "I shan't forget this. You've saved my life."

"Pshaw! you'd do as much for me any day, and think no more about it. It'll be your turn to save mine next."

"True, and I shan't be easy till my turn arrives."

"I tell you what, Jack," whispered Thames, who had noticed Sheppard's menacing glance, and dreaded some further indiscretion on his part, "if you really wish to oblige me, you'll get that packing-case finished by six o'clock. You *can* do it, if you will."

"And I *will*, if I can, depend upon it," answered Sheppard, with a laugh.

So saying, he manfully resumed his work; while Wood and Thames quitted the room, and went down stairs.

CHAPTER II.
Thames Darrell.

THAMES Darrell's arm having been submitted to the scrutiny of Mrs. Wood, was pronounced by that lady to be very much sprained; and she, forthwith, proceeded to bathe it with a reddish-coloured lotion. During this operation, the carpenter underwent a severe catechism as to the cause of the accident; and, on learning that the mischance originated with Jack Sheppard, the indignation of his helpmate knew no bounds; and she was with difficulty prevented from flying to the workshop to inflict summary punishment on the offender.

"I knew how it would be," she cried, in the shrill voice peculiar to a shrew, "when you brought that worthless hussy's worthless brat into the house. I told you no good would come of it. And every day's experience proves that I was right. But, like all your overbearing sex, you must have your own way. You'll never be guided by me--never!"

"Indeed, my love, you're entirely mistaken," returned the carpenter, endeavouring to deprecate his wife's rising resentment by the softest looks, and the meekest deportment.

So far, however, was this submission from producing the desired effect, that it seemed only to lend additional fuel to her displeasure. Forgetting her occupation in her anger, she left off bathing Darrell's wrist; and, squeezing his arm so tightly that the boy winced with pain, she clapped her right hand upon her hip, and turned, with flashing eyes and an inflamed countenance, towards her crest-fallen spouse.

"What!" she exclaimed, almost choked with passion,--"I advised you to burthen yourself with that idle and good-for-nothing pauper, who'm you ought rather to send to the workhouse than maintain at your own expense, did I! I advised you to take him as an apprentice; and, so far from getting the regular fee with him, to give him a salary? I advised you to feed him, and clothe him, and treat him like his betters; to put up with his insolence, and wink at his faults? I counselled all this, I suppose. You'll tell me next, I dare say, that I recommended you to go and visit his mother so frequently under the plea of charity; to give her wine, and provisions, and money; to remove her from the only fit quarters for such people--the Mint; and to place her in a cottage at Willesden, of which you must needs pay the rent? Marry, come up! charity should begin at home. A discreet husband would leave the dispensation of his bounty, where women are concerned, to his wife. And for my part, if I were inclined to exercise my benevolence at all, it should be in favour of some more deserving object than that whining, hypocritical Magdalene."

"It was the knowledge of this feeling on your part, my love, that made me act without your express sanction. I did all for the best, I'm sure. Mrs. Sheppard is--"

"I know what Mrs. Sheppard is, without your information, Sir. I haven't forgotten her previous history. You've your own reasons, no doubt, for bringing up her son--perhaps, I ought rather to say *your* son, Mr. Wood."

"Really, my love, these accusations are most groundless--this violence is most unnecessary."

"I can't endure the odious baggage. I hope I may never come near her."

"I hope you never may, my love," humbly acquiesced the carpenter.

"Is my house to be made a receptacle for all your natural children, Sir? Answer me that."

"Winny," said Thames, whose glowing cheek attested the effect produced upon him by the insinuation; "Winny," said he, addressing a pretty little damsel of some twelve years of age, who stood by his side holding the bottle of embrocation, "help me on with my coat, please. This is no place for me."

"Sit down, my dear, sit down," interposed Mrs. Wood, softening her asperity. "What I said about natural children doesn't apply to *you*. Don't suppose," she added, with a scornful glance at her helpmate, "that I would pay him the compliment of thinking he could possibly be the father of such a boy as you."

Mr. Wood lifted up his hands in mute despair.

"Owen, Owen," pursued Mrs. Wood, sinking into a chair, and fanning herself violently,--"what a fluster you have put me into with your violence, to be sure! And at the very time, too, when you know I'm expecting a visit from Mr. Kneebone, on his return from Manchester. I wouldn't have him see me in this state for the world. He'd never forgive you."

"Poh, poh, my dear! Mr. Kneebone invariably takes part with me, when any trifling misunderstanding arises between us. I only wish he was not a Papist and a Jacobite."

"Jacobite!" echoed Mrs. Wood. "Marry, come up! Mightn't he just as reasonably complain of your being a Hanoverian and a Presbyterian? It's all matter of opinion. And now, my love," she added, with a relenting look, "I'm content to make up our quarrel. But you must promise me not to go near that abandoned hussy at Willesden. One can't help being jealous, you know, even of an unworthy object."

Glad to make peace on any terms, Mr. Wood gave the required promise, though he could not help thinking that if either of them had cause to be jealous he was the party.

And here, we may be permitted to offer an observation upon the peculiar and unaccountable influence which ladies of a shrewish turn so frequently exercise over--we can scarcely, in this case, say--their lords and masters; an influence which seems not merely to extend to the will of the husband, but even to his inclinations. We do not remember to have met with a single individual, reported to be under petticoat government, who was not content with his lot,--nay, who so far from re-pining, did not exult in his servitude; and we see no way of accounting for this ap-parently inexplicable conduct--for which, among other phenomena of married life, various reasons have been assigned, though none entirely satisfactory to us--except upon the ground that these domineering dames possess some charm sufficiently strong to counteract the irritating effect of their tempers; some secret and attractive quality of which the world at large is in ignorance, and with which their husbands alone can be supposed to be acquainted. An influence of this description appeared to be exerted on the present occasion. The worthy carpenter was restored to instant good humour by a glance from his helpmate; and, notwithstanding the infliction he had just endured, he would have quarrelled with any one who had endeavoured to persuade him that he was not the happiest of men, and Mrs. Wood the best of wives.

"Women must have their wills while they live, since they can make none when they die," observed Wood, as he imprinted a kiss of reconciliation on the plump hand of his consort;--a sentiment to the correctness of which the party chiefly interested graciously vouchsafed her assent.

Lest the carpenter should be taxed with too much uxoriousness, it behoves us to ascertain whether the personal attractions of his helpmate would, in any degree, justify the devotion he displayed. In the first place, Mrs. Wood had the advantage of her husband in point of years, being on the sunny side of forty,--a period pronounced by competent judges to be the most fascinating, and, at the same time, most critical epoch of woman's existence,--whereas, he was on the shady side of fifty,--a term of life not generally conceived to have any special recommendation in female eyes. In the next place, she really had some pretensions to beauty. Accounted extremely pretty in her youth, her features and person expanded as she grew older, without much detriment to their original comeliness. Hers was beauty on a large scale no doubt; but it was beauty, nevertheless: and the carpenter thought her eyes as bright, her complexion as blooming, and her figure (if a little more buxom) quite as captivating as when he led her to the altar some twenty years ago.

On the present occasion, in anticipation of Mr. Kneebone's visit, Mrs. Wood was dressed with more than ordinary care, and in more than ordinary finery. A dove-coloured kincob gown, embroidered with large trees, and made very low in front, displayed to the greatest possible advantage, the rounded proportions of her figure; while a high-heeled, red-leather shoe did not detract from the symmetry of a very neat ankle, and a very small foot. A stomacher, fastened by imitation-diamond buckles, girded that part of her person, which should have been a waist; a coral necklace encircled her throat, and a few black patches, or mouches, as they were termed, served as a foil to the bloom of her cheek and chin. Upon a table, where they had been hastily deposited, on the intelligence of Darrell's accident, lay a pair of pink kid gloves, bordered with lace, and an enormous fan; the latter, when opened, represented the metamorphosis and death of Actaeon. From her stomacher, to which it was attached by a multitude of glittering steel chains, depended an immense turnip-shaped watch, in a pinchbeck case. Her hair was gathered up behind, in a sort of pad, according to the then prevailing mode; and she wore a muslin cap, and pinners with crow-foot edging. A black silk fur-belowed scarf covered her shoulders; and over the kincob gown hung a yellow satin apron, trimmed with white Persian.

But, in spite of her attractions, we shall address ourselves to the younger, and more interesting couple.

"I could almost find in my heart to quarrel with Jack Sheppard for occasioning you so much pain," observed little Winifred Wood, as, having completed her ministration to the best of her ability, she helped Thames on with his coat.

"I don't think you could find in your heart to quarrel with any one, Winny; much less with a person whom I like so much as Jack Sheppard. My arm's nearly well again. And I've already told you the accident was not Jack's fault. So, let's think no more about it."

"It's strange you should like Jack so much dear Thames. He doesn't resemble you at all."

"The very reason why I like him, Winny. If he *did* resemble me, I shouldn't care about him. And, whatever you may think, I assure you, Jack's a downright good-natured fellow."

Good-natured fellows are always especial favourites with boys. And, in applying the term to his friend, Thames meant to pay him a high compliment. And so Winifred understood him.

"Well," she said, in reply, "I may have done Jack an injustice. I'll try to think better of him in future."

"And, if you want an additional inducement to do so, I can tell you there's no one--not even his mother--whom he loves so well as you."

"Loves!" echoed Winifred, slightly colouring.

"Yes, loves, Winny. Poor fellow! he sometimes indulges the hope of marrying you, when he grows old enough."

"Thames!"

"Have I said anything to offend you?"

"Oh! no. But if you wouldn't have me positively dislike Jack Sheppard, you'll never mention such a subject again. Besides," she added, blushing yet more deeply, "it isn't a proper one to talk upon."

"Well then, to change it," replied Thames, gravely, "suppose I should be obliged to leave you."

Winifred looked as if she could not indulge such a supposition for a single moment.

"Surely," she said, after a pause, "you don't attach any importance to what my mother has just said. *She* has already forgotten it."

"But I never can forget it, Winny. I will no longer be a burthen to those upon whom I have no claim, but compassion."

As he said this, in a low and mournful, but firm voice, the tears gathered thickly in Winifred's dark eyelashes.

"If you are in earnest, Thames," she replied, with a look of gentle reproach, "you are very foolish; and, if in jest, very cruel. My mother, I'm sure, didn't intend to hurt your feelings. She loves you too well for that. And I'll answer for it, she'll never say a syllable to annoy you again."

Thames tried to answer her, but his voice failed him.

"Come! I see the storm has blown over," cried Winifred, brightening up.

"You're mistaken, Winny. Nothing can alter my determination. I shall quit this roof to-morrow."

The little girl's countenance fell.

"Do nothing without consulting my father--*your* father, Thames," she implored. "Promise me that."

"Willingly. And what's more, I promise to abide by his decision."

"Then, I'm quite easy," cried Winifred, joyfully.

"I'm sure he won't attempt to prevent me," rejoined Thames.

The slight smile that played upon Winifred's lips seemed to say that *she* was not quite so sure. But she made no answer.

"In case he should consent--"

"He never will," interrupted Winifred.

"In case he *should*, I say," continued Thames, "will *you* promise to let Jack Sheppard take my place in your affections, Winny?"

"Never!" replied the little damsel, "I can never love any one so much as you."

"Excepting your father."

Winifred was going to say "No," but she checked herself; and, with cheeks mantling with blushes, murmured, "I wish you wouldn't tease me about Jack Sheppard."

The foregoing conversation, having been conducted throughout in a low tone, and apart, had not reached the ears of Mr. and Mrs. Wood, who were, furthermore, engaged in a little conjugal tete-a-tete of their own. The last observation, however, caught the attention of the carpenter's wife.

"What's that you're saying about Jack Sheppard?" she cried.

"Thames was just observing--"

"Thames!" echoed Mrs. Wood, glancing angrily at her husband. "There's another instance of your wilfulness and want of taste. Who but *you* would have dreamed of giving the boy such a name? Why, it's the name of a river, not a Christian. No gentleman was ever called Thames, and Darrell *is* a gentleman, unless the whole story of his being found in the river is a fabrication!"

"My dear, you forget--"

"No, Mr. Wood, I forget nothing. I've an excellent memory, thank God! And I perfectly remember that everybody was drowned upon that occasion--except yourself and the child!"

"My love you're beside yourself--"

"I was beside myself to take charge of your--"

"Mother?" interposed Winifred.

"It's of no use," observed Thames quietly, but with a look that chilled the little damsel's heart;--"my resolution is taken."

"You at least appear to forget that Mr. Kneebone is coming, my dear," ventured Mr. Wood.

"Good gracious! so I do," exclaimed his amiable consort. "But you *do* agitate me so much. Come into the parlour, Winifred, and dry your eyes directly, or I'll send you to bed. Mr. Wood, I desire you'll put on your best things, and join us as soon as possible. Thames, you needn't tidy yourself, as you've hurt your arm. Mr. Kneebone will excuse you. Dear me! if there isn't his knock. Oh! I'm in such a fluster!"

Upon which, she snatched up her fan, cast a look into the glass, smoothed down her scarf, threw a soft expression into her features, and led the way into the next room, whither she was followed by her daughter and Thames Darrell.

CHAPTER III.
The Jacobite.

MR. William Kneebone was a woollen-draper of "credit and renown," whose place of business was held at the sign of the Angel (for, in those days, every shop had its sign), opposite Saint Clement's church in the Strand. A native of Manchester, he was the son of Kenelm Kneebone, a staunch Catholic, and a sergeant of dragoons, who lost his legs and his life while fighting for James the Second at the battle of the Boyne, and who had little to bequeath his son except his laurels and his loyalty to the house of Stuart.

The gallant woollen-draper was now in his thirty-sixth year. He had a handsome, jolly-looking face; stood six feet two in his stockings; and measured more than a cloth-yard shaft across the shoulders--athletic proportions derived from his father the dragoon. And, if it had not been for a taste for plotting, which was continually getting him into scrapes, he might have been accounted a respectable member of society.

Of late, however, his plotting had assumed a more dark and dangerous complexion. The times were such that, with the opinions he entertained, he could not remain idle. The spirit of disaffection was busy throughout the kingdom. It was on the eve of that memorable rebellion which broke forth, two months later, in Scotland. Since the accession of George the First to the throne in the preceding year, every effort had been made by the partisans of the Stuarts to shake the credit of the existing government, and to gain supporters to their cause. Disappointed in their hopes of the restoration of the fallen dynasty after the death of Anne, the adherents of the Chevalier de Saint George endeavoured, by sowing the seeds of dissension far and wide, to produce a general insurrection in his favour. No means were neglected to accomplish this end. Agents were dispersed in all directions--offers the most tempting held out to induce the wavering to join the Chevalier's standard. Plots were hatched in the provinces, where many of the old and wealthy Catholic families resided, whose zeal for the martyr of their religion (as the Chevalier was esteemed), sharpened by the persecutions they themselves endured, rendered them hearty and efficient allies. Arms, horses, and accoutrements were secretly purchased and distributed; and it is not improbable that, if the unfortunate prince, in whose behalf these exertions were made, and who was not deficient in courage, as he proved at the battle of Malplaquet, had boldly placed himself at the head of his party at an earlier period, he might have regained the crown of his ancestors. But the indecision, which had been fatal to his race, was fatal to him. He delayed the blow till the fortunate conjuncture was past. And when, at length, it *was* struck, he wanted energy to pursue his advantages.

But we must not anticipate the course of events. At the precise period of this history, the Jacobite party was full of hope and confidence. Louis the Fourteenth yet lived, and expectations were, therefore, indulged of assistance from France. The disgrace of the leaders of the late Tory administration had strengthened, rather than injured, their cause. Mobs were gathered together on the slightest possible pretext; and these tumultuous assemblages, while committing the most outrageous excesses, loudly proclaimed their hatred to the house of Hanover, and their determination to cut off the Protestant succession. The proceedings of this faction were narrowly watched by a vigilant and sagacious administration. The government was not deceived (indeed, every opportunity was sought by the Jacobites of parading their numbers,) as to the force of its enemies; and precautionary measures were taken to defeat their designs. On the very day of which we write, namely, the 10th of June 1715, Bolingbroke and Oxford were impeached of high treason. The Committee of Secrecy--that English Council of Ten--were sitting, with Walpole at their head; and the most extraordinary discoveries were reported to be made. On the same day, moreover, which, by a curious coincidence, was the birthday of the Chevalier de Saint George, mobs were collected together in the streets, and the health of that prince was publicly drunk under the title of James the Third; while, in many country towns, the bells were rung, and rejoicings held, as if for a reigning monarch:-- the cry of the populace almost universally being, "No King George, but a Stuart!"

The adherents of the Chevalier de Saint George, we have said, were lavish in promises to their proselytes. Posts were offered to all who chose to accept them. Blank commissions, signed by the prince, to be filled up by the name of the person, who could raise a troop for his service, were liberally bestowed. Amongst others, Mr. Kneebone, whose interest was not inconsiderable with the leaders of his faction, obtained an appointment as captain in a regiment of infantry, on the conditions above specified. With a view to raise recruits for his corps, the warlike woollen-draper started for Lancashire, under the colour of a journey on business. He was pretty successful in Manchester,--a town which may be said to have been the head-quarters of the disaffected. On his return to London, he found that applications had been made from a somewhat doubtful quarter by two individuals, for the posts of subordinate officers in his troop. Mr. Kneebone, or, as he would have preferred being styled, Captain Kneebone, was not perfectly satisfied with the recommendations forwarded by the applicants. But this was not a season in which to be needlessly scrupulous. He resolved to judge for himself. Accordingly, he was introduced to the two military aspirants at the Cross Shovels in the Mint, by our old acquaintance, Baptist Kettleby. The Master of the Mint, with whom the Jacobite captain had often had transactions before, vouched for their being men of honour and loyalty; and Kneebone was so well satisfied with his representations, that he at once closed the matter by administering to the applicants the oath of allegiance and fidelity to King James the Third, and several other oaths besides, all of which those gentlemen took with as little hesitation as the sum of money, afterwards tendered, to make the compact binding. The party, then, sat down to a bowl of punch; and, at its conclusion, Captain Kneebone regretted that an engagement to spend the evening with Mrs. Wood, would preclude the possibility of his remaining with his new friends as long as his inclinations prompted. At this piece of information, the two subordinate officers were observed to exchange glances; and, after a little agreeable raillery on their captain's gallantry, they begged permission to accompany him in his visit. Kneebone, who had drained his glass to the restoration of the house of Stuart, and the downfall of the house of Hanover, more frequently than was consistent with prudence, consented; and the trio set out for Wych Street, where they arrived in the jolliest humour possible.

CHAPTER IV.
Mr. Kneebone and his Friends.

MRS. Wood was scarcely seated before Mr. Kneebone made his appearance. To her great surprise and mortification he was not alone; but brought with him a couple of friends, whom he begged to introduce as Mr. Jeremiah Jackson, and Mr. Solomon Smith, chapmen, (or what in modern vulgar parlance would be termed bagmen) travelling to procure orders for the house of an eminent cloth manufacturer in Manchester. Neither the manners, the looks, nor the attire of these gentlemen prepossessed Mrs. Wood in their favour. Accordingly, on their presentation, Mr. Jeremiah Jackson and Mr. Solomon Smith received something very like a rebuff. Luckily, they were not easily discomposed. Two persons possessing a more comfortable stock of assurance could not be readily found. Imitating the example of Mr. Kneebone, who did not appear in the slightest degree disconcerted by his cool reception, each sank carelessly into a chair, and made himself at home in a moment. Both had very singular faces; very odd wigs, very much pulled over their brows; and very large cravats, very much raised above their chins. Besides this, each had a large black patch over his right eye, and a very queer twist at the left side of his mouth, so that if their object had been disguise, they could not have adopted better precautions. Mrs. Wood thought them both remarkably plain, but Mr. Smith decidedly the plainest of the two. His complexion was as blue as a sailor's jacket, and though Mr. Jackson had one of the ugliest countenances imaginable, he had a very fine set of teeth. That was something in his favour. One peculiarity she did not fail to notice. They were both dressed in every respect alike. In fact, Mr. Solomon Smith seemed to be Mr. Jeremiah Jackson's double. He talked in the same style, and pretty nearly in the same language; laughed in the same manner, and coughed, or sneezed at the same time. If Mr. Jackson took an accurate survey of the room with his one eye, Mr. Smith's solitary orb followed in the same direction. When Jeremiah admired the Compasses in the arms of the Carpenter's Company over the chimney-piece, or the portraits of the two eminent masters of the rule and plane, William Portington, and John Scott, Esquires, on either side of it, Solomon was lost in wonder. When Mr. Jackson noticed a fine service of old blue china in an open japan closet, Mr. Smith had never seen anything like it. And finally, when Jeremiah, having bestowed upon Mrs. Wood a very free-and-easy sort of stare, winked at Mr. Kneebone, his impertinence was copied to the letter by Solomon. All three, then, burst into an immoderate fit of laughter. Mrs. Wood's astonishment and displeasure momentarily increased. Such freedoms from such people were not to be endured. Her patience was waning fast. Still, in spite of her glances and gestures, Mr. Kneebone made no effort to check the unreasonable merriment of his companions, but rather seemed to encourage it. So Mrs. Wood went on fuming, and the trio went on laughing for some minutes, nobody knew why or wherefore, until the party was increased by Mr. Wood, in his Sunday habiliments and Sunday buckle. Without stopping to inquire into the cause of their mirth, or even to ask the names of his guests, the worthy carpenter shook hands with the one-eyed chapmen, slapped Mr. Kneebone cordially on the shoulder, and began to laugh as heartily as any of them.

Mrs. Wood could stand it no longer.

"I think you're all bewitched," she cried.

"So we are, Ma'am, by your charms," returned Mr. Jackson, gallantly.

"Quite captivated, Ma'am," added Mr. Smith, placing his hand on his breast.

Mr. Kneebone and Mr. Wood laughed louder than ever.

"Mr. Wood," said the lady bridling up, "my request may, perhaps, have some weight with *you*. I desire, Sir, you'll recollect yourself. Mr. Kneebone," she added, with a glance at that gentleman, which was meant to speak daggers, "will do as he pleases."

Here the chapmen set up another boisterous peal.

"No offence, I hope, my dear Mrs. W," said Mr. Kneebone in a conciliatory tone. "My friends, Mr. Jackson and Mr. Smith, may have rather odd ways with them; but--"

"They *have* very odd ways," interrupted Mrs. Wood, disdainfully.

"Our worthy friend was going to observe, Ma'am, that we never fail in our devotion to the fair sex," said Mr. Jackson.

"Never, Ma'am!" echoed Mr. Smith, "upon my conscience."

"My dear," said the hospitable carpenter, "I dare say Mr. Kneebone and his friends would be glad of a little refreshment."

"They shall have it, then," replied his better half, rising. "You base ingrate," she added, in a whisper, as she flounced past Mr. Kneebone on her way to the door, "how could you bring such creatures with you, especially on an occasion like this, when we haven't met for a fortnight!"

"Couldn't help it, my life," returned the gentleman addressed, in the same tone; "but you little know who those individuals are."

"Lord bless us! you alarm me. Who are they?"

Mr. Kneebone assumed a mysterious air; and bringing his lips close to Mrs. Wood's ear, whispered, "secret agents from France--you understand--friends to the cause--hem!"

"I see,--persons of rank!"

Mr. Kneebone nodded.

"Noblemen."

Mr. Kneebone smiled assent.

"Mercy on us! Well, I thought their manners quite out o' the common. And so, the invasion really is to take place after all; and the Chevalier de Saint George is to land at the Tower with fifty thousand Frenchmen; and the Hanoverian usurper's to be beheaded; and Doctor Sacheverel's to be made a bishop, and we're all to be--eh?"

"All in good time," returned Kneebone, putting his finger to his lips; "don't let your imagination run away with you, my charmer. That boy," he added, looking at Thames, "has his eye upon us."

Mrs. Wood, however, was too much excited to attend to the caution.

"O, lud!" she cried; "French noblemen in disguise! and so rude as I was! I shall never recover it!"

"A good supper will set all to rights," insinuated Kneebone. "But be prudent, my angel."

"Never fear," replied the lady. "I'm prudence personified. You might trust me with the Chevalier himself,--I'd never betray him. But why didn't you let me know they were coming. I'd have got something nice. As it is, we've only a couple of ducks--and they were intended for you. Winny, my love, come with me. I shall want you.--Sorry to quit your lord--worships, I mean,--I don't know what I mean," she added, a little confused, and dropping a profound curtsey to the disguised noblemen, each of whom replied by a bow, worthy, in her opinion, of a prince of the blood at the least,--"but I've a few necessary orders to give below."

"Don't mind us, Ma'am," said Mr. Jackson: "ha! ha!"

"Not in the least, Ma'am," echoed Mr. Smith: "ho! ho!"

"How condescending!" thought Mrs. Wood. "Not proud in the least, I declare. Well, I'd no idea," she continued, pursuing her ruminations as she left the room, "that people of quality laughed so. But it's French manners, I suppose."

CHAPTER V.
Hawk and Buzzard.

MRS. Wood's anxiety to please her distinguished guests speedily displayed itself in a very plentiful, if not very dainty repast. To the duckling, peas, and other delicacies, intended for Mr. Kneebone's special consumption, she added a few impromptu dishes, tossed off in her best style; such as lamb chops, broiled kidneys, fried ham and eggs, and toasted cheese. Side by side with the cheese (its never-failing accompaniment, in all seasons, at the carpenter's board) came a tankard of swig, and a toast. Besides these there was a warm gooseberry-tart, and a cold pigeon pie--the latter capacious enough, even allowing for its due complement of steak, to contain the whole produce of a dove-cot; a couple of lobsters and the best part of a salmon swimming in a sea of vinegar, and shaded by a forest of fennel. While the cloth was laid, the host and Thames descended to the cellar, whence they returned, laden with a number of flasks of the same form, and apparently destined to the same use as those depicted in Hogarth's delectable print--the Modern Midnight Conversation.

Mrs. Wood now re-appeared with a very red face; and, followed by Winifred, took her seat at the table. Operations then commenced. Mr. Wood carved the ducks; Mr. Kneebone helped to the pigeon-pie; while Thames unwired and uncorked a bottle of stout Carnarvonshire ale. The woollen-draper was no despicable trencherman in a general way; but his feats with the knife and fork were child's sport compared with those of Mr. Smith. The leg and wing of a duck were disposed of by this gentleman in a twinkling; a brace of pigeons and a pound of steak followed with equal celerity; and he had just begun to make a fierce assault upon the eggs and ham. His appetite was perfectly Gargantuan. Nor must it be imagined, that while he thus exercised his teeth, he neglected the flagon. On the contrary, his glass was never idle, and finding it not filled quite so frequently as he desired, he applied himself, notwithstanding the expressive looks and muttered remonstrances of Mr. Jackson, to the swig. The latter gentleman did full justice to the good things before him; but he drank sparingly, and was visibly annoyed by his companion's intemperance. As to Mr. Kneebone, what with flirting with Mrs. Wood, carving for his friends, and pledging the carpenter, he had his hands full. At this juncture, and just as a cuckoo-clock in the corner struck sis, Jack Sheppard walked into the room, with the packing-case under his arm.

"I was in the right, you see, father," observed Thames, smiling; "Jack *has* done his task."

"So I perceive," replied Wood.

"Where am I to take it to?" asked Sheppard.

"I told you that before," rejoined Wood, testily. "You must take it to Sir Rowland Trenchard's in Southampton Fields. And, mind, it's for his sister, Lady Trafford."

"Very well, Sir," replied Sheppard.

"Wet your whistle before you start, Jack," said Kneebone, pouring out a glass of ale. "What's that you're taking to Sir Rowland Trenchard's?"

"Only a box, Sir," answered Sheppard, emptying the glass.

"It's an odd-shaped one," rejoined Kneebone, examining it attentively. "But I can guess what it's for. Sir Rowland is one of *us*," he added, winking at his companions, "and so was his brother-in-law, Sir Cecil Trafford. Old Lancashire families both. Strict Catholics, and loyal to the backbone. Fine woman, Lady Trafford--a little on the wane though."

"Ah! you're so very particular," sighed Mrs. Wood.

"Not in the least," returned Kneebone, slyly, "not in the least. Another glass, Jack."

"Thank'ee, Sir," grinned Sheppard.

"Off with it to the health of King James the Third, and confusion to his enemies!"

"Hold!" interposed Wood; "that is treason. I'll have no such toast drunk at my table!"

"It's the king's birthday," urged the woollen draper.

"Not *my* king's," returned Wood. "I quarrel with no man's political opinions, but I will have my own respected!"

"Eh day!" exclaimed Mrs. Wood; "here's a pretty to-do about nothing. Marry, come up! I'll see who's to be obeyed. Drink the toast, Jack."

"At your peril, sirrah!" cried Wood.

"He was hanged that left his drink behind, you know, master," rejoined Sheppard. "Here's King James the Third, and confusion to his enemies!"

"Very well," said the carpenter, sitting down amid the laughter of the company.

"Jack!" cried Thames, in a loud voice, "you deserve to be hanged for a rebel as you are to your lawful king and your lawful master. But since we must have toasts," he added, snatching up a glass, "listen to mine: Here's King George the First! a long reign to him! and confusion to the Popish Pretender and his adherents!"

"Bravely done!" said Wood, with tears in his eyes.

"That's the kinchin as was to try the dub for us, ain't it?" muttered Smith to his companion as he stole a glance at Jack Sheppard.

"Silence!" returned Jackson, in a deep whisper; "and don't muddle your brains with any more of that Pharaoh. You'll need all your strength to grab him."

"What's the matter?" remarked Kneebone, addressing Sheppard, who, as he caught the single but piercing eye of Jackson fixed upon him, started and trembled.

"What's the matter?" repeated Mrs. Wood in a sharp tone.

"Ay, what's the matter, boy!" reiterated Jackson sternly. "Did you never see two gentlemen with only a couple of peepers between them before!"

"Never, I'll be sworn!" said Smith, taking the opportunity of filling his glass while his comrade's back was turned; "we're a nat'ral cur'osity."

"Can I have a word with you, master?" said Sheppard, approaching Wood.

"Not a syllable!" answered the carpenter, angrily. "Get about your business!"

"Thames!" cried Jack, beckoning to his friend.

But Darrell averted his head.

"Mistress!" said the apprentice, making a final appeal to Mrs. Wood.

"Leave the room instantly, sirrah!" rejoined the lady, bouncing up, and giving him a slap on the cheek that made his eyes flash fire.

"May I be cursed," muttered Sheppard, as he slunk away with (as the woollen-draper pleasantly observed) 'a couple of boxes in charge,' "if ever I try to be honest again!"

"Take a little toasted cheese with the swig, Mr. Smith," observed Wood. "That's an incorrigible rascal," he added, as Sheppard closed the door; "it's only to-day that I discovered--"

"What?" asked Jackson, pricking up his ears.

"Don't speak ill of him behind his back, father," interposed Thames.

"If I were your father, young gentleman," returned Jackson, enraged at the interruption, "I'd teach *you* not to speak till you were spoken to."

Thames was about to reply, but a glance from Wood checked him.

"The rebuke is just," said the carpenter; "at the same time, I'm not sorry to find you're a friend to fair play, which, as you seem to know, is a jewel. Open that bottle with a blue seal, my dear. Gentlemen! a glass of brandy will be no bad finish to our meal."

This proposal giving general satisfaction, the bottle circulated swiftly; and Smith found the liquor so much to his taste, that he made it pay double toll on its passage.

"Your son is a lad of spirit, Mr. Wood," observed Jackson, in a slightly-sarcastic tone.

"He's not my son," rejoined the carpenter.

"How, Sir?"

"Except by adoption. Thames Darrell is--"

"My husband nicknames him Thames," interrupted Mrs. Wood, "because he found him in the river!--ha! ha!"

"Ha! ha!" echoed Smith, taking another bumper of brandy; "he'll set the Thames on fire one of these days, I'll warrant him!"

"That's more than you'll ever do, you drunken fool!" growled Jackson, in an under tone: "be cautious, or you'll spoil all!"

"Suppose we send for a bowl of punch," said Kneebone.

"With all my heart!" replied Wood. And, turning to his daughter, he gave the necessary directions in a low tone.

Winifred, accordingly, left the room, and a servant being despatched to the nearest tavern, soon afterwards returned with a crown bowl of the ambrosian fluid. The tables were then cleared. Bottles and glasses usurped the place of dishes and plates. Pipes were lighted; and Mr. Kneebone began to dispense the fragrant fluid; begging Mrs. Wood, in a whisper, as he filled a rummer to the brim, not to forget the health of the Chevalier de Saint George--a proposition to which the lady immediately responded by drinking the toast aloud.

"The Chevalier shall hear of this," whispered the woollen-draper.

"You don't say so!" replied Mrs. Wood, delighted at the idea.

Mr. Kneebone assured her that he *did* say so; and, as a further proof of his sincerity, squeezed her hand very warmly under the table.

Mr. Smith, now, being more than half-seas over, became very uproarious, and, claiming the attention of the table, volunteered the following

DRINKING SONG.

I.

Jolly nose! the bright rubies that garnish thy tip
  Are dug from the mines of canary;
And to keep up their lustre I moisten my lip
  With hogsheads of claret and sherry.

II.

Jolly nose! he who sees thee across a broad glass
  Beholds thee in all thy perfection;
And to the pale snout of a temperate ass
  Entertains the profoundest objection.

III.

For a big-bellied glass is the palette I use,
  And the choicest of wine is my colour;

And I find that my nose takes the mellowest hues
  The fuller I fill it--the fuller!

IV.

Jolly nose! there are fools who say drink hurts the sight;
  Such dullards know nothing about it.
'T is better, with wine, to extinguish the light,
  Than live always, in darkness, without it!

"How long may it be since that boy was found in the way Mrs. Wood men-
tions?" inquired Jackson, as soon as the clatter that succeeded Mr. Smith's melody
had subsided.

"Let me see," replied Wood; "exactly twelve years ago last November."

"Why, that must be about the time of the Great Storm," rejoined Jackson.

"Egad!" exclaimed Wood, "you've hit the right nail on the head, anyhow. It *was*
on the night of the Great Storm that I found him."

"I should like to hear all particulars of the affair," said Jackson, "if it wouldn't
be troubling you too much."

Mr. Wood required little pressing. He took a sip of punch and commenced his
relation. Though meant to produce a totally different effect, the narrative seemed
to excite the risible propensities rather than the commiseration of his auditor; and
when Mr. Wood wound it up by a description of the drenching he had undergone
at the Mint pump, the other could hold out no longer, but, leaning back in his chair,
gave free scope to his merriment.

"I beg your pardon," he cried; "but really--ha! ha!--you must excuse me!--that
is so uncommonly diverting--ha! ha! Do let me hear it again?--ha! ha! ha!"

"Upon my word," rejoined Wood, "you seem vastly entertained by my misfor-
tunes."

"To be sure! Nothing entertains me so much. People always rejoice at the mis-
fortunes of others--never at their own! The droll dogs! how *they* must have enjoyed
it!--ha! ha!"

"I dare say they did. But I found it no laughing matter, I can assure you. And, though it's a long time ago, I feel as sore on the subject as ever."

"Quite natural! Never forgive an injury!--I never do!--ha! ha!"

"Really, Mr. Jackson, I could almost fancy we had met before. Your laugh reminds me of--of----"

"Whose, Sir?" demanded Jackson, becoming suddenly grave.

"You'll not be offended, I hope," returned Wood, drily, "if I say that your voice, your manner, and, above all, your very extraordinary way of laughing, put me strangely in mind of one of the 'droll dogs,' (as you term them,) who helped to perpetrate the outrage I've just described."

"Whom do you mean?" demanded Jackson.

"I allude to an individual, who has since acquired an infamous notoriety as a thief-taker; but who, in those days, was himself the associate of thieves."

"Well, Sir, his name?"

"Jonathan Wild."

"'Sblood!" cried Jackson, rising, "I can't sit still and hear Mr. Wild, whom I believe to be as honest a gentleman as any in the kingdom, calumniated!"

"Fire and fury!" exclaimed Smith, getting up with the brandy-bottle in his grasp; "no man shall abuse Mr. Wild in my presence! He's the right-hand of the community! We could do nothing without him!"

"We!" repeated Wood, significantly.

"Every honest man, Sir! He helps us to our own again."

"Humph!" ejaculated the carpenter.

"Surely," observed Thames, laughing, "to one who entertains so high an opinion of Jonathan Wild, as Mr. Jackson appears to do, it can't be very offensive to be told, that he's like him."

"I don't object to the likeness, if any such exists, young Sir," returned Jackson, darting an angry glance at Thames; "indeed I'm rather flattered by being thought to resemble a gentleman of Mr. Wild's figure. But I can't submit to hear the well-earned reputation of my friend termed an 'infamous notoriety.'"

"No, we can't stand that," hiccupped Smith, scarcely able to keep his legs.

"Well, gentlemen," rejoined Wood, mildly; "since Mr. Wild is a friend of yours, I'm sorry for what I said. I've no doubt he's as honest as either of you."

"Enough," returned Jackson, extending his hand; "and if I've expressed myself warmly, I'm sorry for it likewise. But you must allow me to observe, my good Sir, that you're wholly in the wrong respecting my friend. Mr. Wild never was the associate of thieves."

"Never," echoed Smith, emphatically, "upon my honour."

"I'm satisfied with your assurance," replied the carpenter, drily.

"It's more than I am," muttered Thames.

"I was not aware that Jonathan Wild was an acquaintance of yours, Mr. Jackson," said Kneebone, whose assiduity to Mrs. Wood had prevented him from paying much attention to the previous scene.

"I've known him all my life," replied the other.

"The devil you have! Then, perhaps, you can tell me when he intends to put his threat into execution?"

"What threat?" asked Jackson.

"Why, of hanging the fellow who acts as his jackal; one Blake, or Blueskin, I think he's called."

"You've been misinformed, Sir," interposed Smith. "Mr. Wild is incapable of such baseness."

"Bah!" returned the woollen-draper. "I see you don't know him as well as you pretend. Jonathan is capable of anything. He has hanged twelve of his associates already. The moment they cease to be serviceable, or become dangerous he lodges an information, and the matter's settled. He has always plenty of evidence in reserve. Blueskin is booked. As sure as you're sitting there, Mr. Smith, he'll swing after next Old Bailey sessions. I wouldn't be in his skin for a trifle!"

"But he may peach," said Smith casting an oblique glance at Jackson.

"It would avail him little if he did," replied Kneebone. "Jonathan does what he pleases in the courts."

"Very true," chuckled Jackson; "very true."

"Blueskin's only chance would be to carry *his* threat into effect," pursued the woollen-draper.

"Aha!" exclaimed Jackson. "*He* threatens, does he?"

"More than that," replied Kneebone; "I understand he drew a knife upon Jonathan, in a quarrel between them lately. And since then, he has openly avowed his determination of cutting his master's throat on the slightest inkling of treachery.

But, perhaps Mr. Smith will tell you I'm misinformed, also, on that point."

"On the contrary," rejoined Smith, looking askance at his companion, "I happen to *know* you're in the right."

"Well, Sir, I'm obliged to you," said Jackson; "I shall take care to put Mr. Wild on his guard against an assassin."

"And I shall put Blueskin on the alert against the designs of a traitor," rejoined Smith, in a tone that sounded like a menace.

"In my opinion," remarked Kneebone, "it doesn't matter how soon society is rid of two such scoundrels; and if Blueskin dies by the rope, and Jonathan by the hand of violence, they'll meet the fate they merit. Wild was formerly an agent to the Jacobite party, but, on the offer of a bribe from the opposite faction, he unhesitatingly deserted and betrayed his old employers. Of late, he has become the instrument of Walpole, and does all the dirty work for the Secret Committee. Several arrests of importance have been intrusted to him; but, forewarned, forearmed, we have constantly baffled his schemes;--ha! ha! Jonathan's a devilish clever fellow. But he can't have his eyes always about him, or he'd have been with us this morning at the Mint, eh, Mr. Jackson!"

"So he would," replied the latter: "so he would."

"With all his cunning, he may meet with his match," continued Kneebone, laughing. "I've set a trap for him."

"Take care you don't fall into it yourself," returned Jackson, with a slight sneer.

"Were I in your place," said Smith, "I should be apprehensive of Wild, because he's a declared enemy."

"And were I in *yours*," rejoined the woollen-draper, "I should be doubly apprehensive, because he's a professed friend. But we're neglecting the punch all this time. A bumper round, gentlemen. Success to our enterprise!"

"Success to our enterprise!" echoed the others, significantly.

"May I ask whether you made any further inquiries into the mysterious affair about which we were speaking just now?" observed Jackson, turning to the carpenter.

"I can't say I did," replied Wood, somewhat reluctantly; "what with the confusion incident to the storm, and the subsequent press of business, I put it off till it was too late. I've often regretted that I didn't investigate the matter. However, it doesn't much signify. All concerned in the dark transaction must have perished."

"Are you sure of that," inquired Jackson.

"As sure as one reasonably can be. I saw their boat swept away, and heard the roar of the fall beneath the bridge; and no one, who was present, could doubt the result. If the principal instigator of the crime, whom I afterwards encountered on the platform, and who was dashed into the raging flood by the shower of bricks, escaped, his preservation must have been indeed miraculous."

"Your own was equally so," said Jackson ironically. "What if he *did* escape?"

"My utmost efforts should be used to bring him to justice."

"Hum!"

"Have you any reason to suppose he survived the accident?" inquired Thames eagerly.

Jackson smiled and put on the air of a man who knows more than he cares to tell.

"I merely asked the question," he said, after he had enjoyed the boy's suspense for a moment.

The hope that had been suddenly kindled in the youth's bosom was as suddenly extinguished.

"If I thought he lived----" observed Wood.

"*If*," interrupted Jackson, changing his tone: "he *does* live. And it has been well for you that he imagines the child was drowned."

"Who is he?" asked Thames impatiently.

"You're inquisitive, young gentleman," replied Jackson, coldly. "When you're older, you'll know that secrets of importance are not disclosed gratuitously. Your adoptive father understands mankind better."

"I'd give half I'm worth to hang the villain, and restore this boy to his rights," said Mr. Wood.

"How do you know he *has* any rights to be restored to?" returned Jackson, with a grin. "Judging from what you tell me, I've no doubt he's the illegitimate offspring of some handsome, but lowborn profligate; in which case, he'll neither have name, nor wealth for his inheritance. The assassination, as you call it, was, obviously, the vengeance of a kinsman of the injured lady, who no doubt was of good family, upon her seducer. The less said, therefore, on this point the better; because, as nothing is to be gained by it, it would only be trouble thrown away. But, if you have any particular fancy for hanging the gentleman, who chose to take the law into his own hands--and I think your motive extremely disinterested and praiseworthy--why, it's just possible, if you make it worth my while, that your desires may be gratified."

"I don't see how this is to be effected, unless you yourself were present at the time," said Wood, glancing suspiciously at the speaker.

"I had no hand in the affair," replied Jackson, bluntly; "but I know those who had; and could bring forward evidence, if you require it."

"The best evidence would be afforded by an accomplice of the assassin," rejoined Thames, who was greatly offended by the insinuation as to his parentage.

"Perhaps you could point out such a party, Mr. Jackson?" said Wood, significantly.

"I could," replied Thames.

"Then you need no further information from me," rejoined Jackson, sternly.

"Stay!" cried Wood, "this is a most perplexing business--if you really are privy to the affair----"

"We'll talk of it to-morrow, Sir," returned Jackson, cutting him short. "In the mean time, with your permission, I'll just make a few minutes of our conversation."

"As many as you please," replied Wood, walking towards the chimney-piece, and taking down a constable's, staff, which hung upon a nail.

Jackson, mean time, produced a pocket-book; and, after deliberately sharpening the point of a pencil, began to write on a blank leaf. While he was thus occupied, Thames, prompted by an unaccountable feeling of curiosity, took up the pen-knife which the other had just used, and examined the haft. What he there noticed occasioned a marked change in his demeanour. He laid down the knife, and fixed a searching and distrustful gaze upon the writer, who continued his task, unconscious of anything having happened.

"There," cried Jackson, closing the book and rising, "that'll do. To-morrow at twelve I'll be with you, Mr. Wood. Make up your mind as to the terms, and I'll engage to find the man."

"Hold!" exclaimed the carpenter, in an authoritative voice: "we can't part thus. Thames, look the door." (An order which was promptly obeyed.) "Now, Sir, I must insist upon a full explanation of your mysterious hints, or, as I am headborough of the district, I shall at once take you into custody."

Jackson treated this menace with a loud laugh of derision.

"What ho!" he cried slapping Smith, who had fallen asleep with the brandy-bottle in his grasp, upon the shoulder. "It is time!"

"For what?" grumbled the latter, rubbing his eyes.

"For the caption!" replied Jackson, coolly drawing a brace of pistols from his pockets.

"Ready!" answered Smith, shaking himself, and producing a similar pair of weapons.

"In Heaven's name! what's all this?" cried Wood.

"Be still, and you'll receive no injury," returned Jackson. "We're merely about to discharge our duty by apprehending a rebel. Captain Kneebone! we must trouble you to accompany us."

"I've no intention of stirring," replied the woollen-draper, who was thus un-ceremoniously disturbed: "and I beg you'll sit down, Mr. Jackson."

"Come, Sir!" thundered the latter, "no trifling! Perhaps," he added, opening a warrant, "you'll obey this mandate?"

"A warrant!" ejaculated Kneebone, starting to his feet.

"Ay, Sir, from the Secretary of State, for *your* arrest! You're charged with high-treason."

"By those who've conspired with me?"

"No! by those who've entrapped you! You've long eluded our vigilance; but we've caught you at last!"

"Damnation!" exclaimed the woollen-draper; "that I should be the dupe of such a miserable artifice!"

"It's no use lamenting now, Captain! You ought rather to be obliged to us for allowing you to pay this visit. We could have secured you when you left the Mint. But we wished to ascertain whether Mrs. Wood's charms equalled your descrip-tion."

"Wretches!" screamed the lady; "don't dare to breathe your vile insinuations against me! Oh! Mr. Kneebone, are these your French noblemen?"

"Don't upbraid me!" rejoined the woollen-draper.

"Bring him along, Joe!" said Jackson, in a whisper to his comrade.

Smith obeyed. But he had scarcely advanced a step, when he was felled to the ground by a blow from the powerful arm of Kneebone, who, instantly possessing himself of a pistol, levelled it at Jackson's head.

"Begone! or I fire!" he cried.

"Mr. Wood," returned Jackson, with the utmost composure; "you're a headborough, and a loyal subject of King George. I call upon you to assist me in the apprehension of this person. You'll be answerable for his escape."

"Mr. Wood, I command you not to stir," vociferated the carpenter's better-half; "recollect you'll be answerable to me."

"I declare I don't know what to do," said Wood, burned by conflicting emotions. "Mr. Kneebone! you would greatly oblige me by surrendering yourself."

"Never!" replied the woollen-draper; "and if that treacherous rascal, by your side, doesn't make himself scarce quickly, I'll send a bullet through his brain."

"My death will lie at your door," remarked Jackson to the carpenter.

"Show me your warrant!" said Wood, almost driven to his wit's-end; "perhaps it isn't regular?"

"Ask him who he is?" suggested Thames.

"A good idea!" exclaimed the carpenter. "May I beg to know whom I've the pleasure of adressing? Jackson, I conclude, is merely an assumed name."

"What does it signify?" returned the latter, angrily.

"A great deal!" replied Thames. "If you won't disclose your name, I will for you! You are Jonathan Wild!"

"Further concealment is needless," answered the other, pulling off his wig and black patch, and resuming his natural tone of voice; "I *am* Jonathan Wild!"

"Say you so!" rejoined Kneebone; "then be this your passport to eternity."

Upon which he drew the trigger of the pistol, which, luckily for the individual against whom it was aimed, flashed in the pan.

"I might now send you on a similar journey!" replied Jonathan, with a bitter smile, and preserving the unmoved demeanour he had maintained throughout; "but I prefer conveying you, in the first instance, to Newgate. The Jacobite daws want a scarecrow."

So saying, he sprang, with a bound like that of a tiger-cat, against the throat of the woollen-draper. And so sudden and well-directed was the assault, that he completely overthrew his gigantic antagonist.

"Lend a hand with the ruffles, Blueskin!" he shouted, as that personage, who had just recovered from the stunning effects of the blow, contrived to pick himself up. "Look quick, d--n you, or we shall never master him!"

"Murder!" shrieked Mrs. Wood, at the top of her voice.

"Here's a pistol!" cried Thames, darting towards the undischarged weapon dropped by Blueskin in the scuffle, and pointing it at Jonathan. "Shall I shoot him?"

"Yes! yes! put it to his ear!" cried Mrs. Wood; "that's the surest way!"

"No! no! give it me!" vociferated Wood, snatching the pistol, and rushing to the door, against which he placed his back.

"I'll soon settle this business. Jonathan Wild!" he added, in a loud voice, "I command you to release your prisoner."

"So I will," replied Jonathan, who, with Blueskin's aid, had succeeded in slipping a pair of handcuffs over the woollen-draper's wrists, "when I've Mr. Walpole's order to that effect--but not before."

"You'll take the consequences, then?"

"Willingly."

"In that case I arrest you, and your confederate, Joseph Blake, alias Blueskin, on a charge of felony," returned Wood, brandishing his staff; "resist my authority, if you dare."

"A clever device," replied Jonathan; "but it won't serve your turn. Let us pass, Sir. Strike the gag, Blueskin."

"You shall not stir a footstep. Open the window, Thames, and call for assistance."

"Stop!" cried Jonathan, who did not care to push matters too far, "let me have a word with you, Mr. Wood."

"I'll have no explanations whatever," replied the carpenter, disdainfully, "except before a magistrate."

"At least state your charge. It is a serious accusation."

"It *is*," answered Wood. "Do you recollect this key? Do you recollect to whom you gave it, and for what purpose? or shall I refresh your memory?"

Wild appeared confounded.

"Release your prisoner," continued Wood, "or the window is opened."

"Mr. Wood," said Jonathan, advancing towards him, and speaking in a low tone, "the secret of your adopted son's birth is known to me. The name of his father's murderer is also known to me. I can help you to both,--nay, I *will* help you to both, if you do not interfere with my plans. The arrest of this person is of consequence to me. Do not oppose it, and I will serve you. Thwart me, and I become your mortal enemy. I have but to give a hint of that boy's existence in the proper quarter, and his life will not be worth a day's purchase."

"Don't listen to him, father," cried Thames, unconscious of what was passing; "there are plenty of people outside."

"Make your choice," said Jonathan.

"If you don't decide quickly, I'll scream," cried Mrs. Wood, popping her head through the window.

"Set your prisoner free!" returned Wood.

"Take off the ruffles, Blueskin," rejoined Wild. "You know my fixed determination," he added in a low tone, as he passed the carpenter. "Before to-morrow night that boy shall join his father."

So saying, he unlocked the door and strode out of the room.

"Here are some letters, which will let you see what a snake you've cherished in your bosom, you uxorious old dotard," said Blueskin, tossing a packet of papers to Wood, as he followed his leader.

"'Odd's-my-life! what's this?" exclaimed the carpenter, looking at the superscription of one of them. "Why, this is your writing Dolly, and addressed to Mr. Kneebone."

"My writing! no such thing!" ejaculated the lady, casting a look of alarm at the woollen-draper.

"Confusion! the rascal must have picked my pocket of your letters," whispered Kneebone, "What's to be done?"

"What's to be done! Why, I'm undone! How imprudent in you not to burn them. But men *are* so careless, there's no trusting anything to them! However, I must try to brazen it out.--Give me the letters, my love," she added aloud, and in her most winning accents; "they're some wicked forgeries."

"Excuse me, Madam," replied the carpenter, turning his back upon her, and sinking into a chair: "Thames, my love, bring me my spectacles. My heart misgives me. Fool that I was to marry for beauty! I ought to have remembered that a fair woman and a slashed gown always find some nail in the way."

CHAPTER VI.
The first Step towards the Ladder.

IF there is one thing on earth, more lovely than another, it is a fair girl of the tender age of Winifred Wood! Her beauty awakens no feeling beyond that of admiration. The charm of innocence breathes around her, as fragrance is diffused by the flower, sanctifying her lightest thought and action, and shielding her, like a spell, from the approach of evil. Beautiful is the girl of twelve,--who is neither child nor woman, but something between both, something more exquisite than either!

Such was the fairy creature presented to Thames Darrell, under the following circumstances.

Glad to escape from the scene of recrimination that ensued between his adopted parents, Thames seized the earliest opportunity of retiring, and took his way to a small chamber in the upper part of the house, where he and Jack were accustomed to spend most of their leisure in the amusements, or pursuits, proper to their years. He found the door ajar, and, to his surprise, perceived little Winifred seated at a table, busily engaged in tracing some design upon a sheet of paper. She did not hear his approach, but continued her occupation without raising her head.

It was a charming sight to watch the motions of her tiny fingers as she pursued her task; and though the posture she adopted was not the most favourable that might have been chosen for the display of her sylphlike figure, there was something in her attitude, and the glow of her countenance, lighted up by the mellow radiance of the setting sun falling upon her through the panes of the little dormer-window, that seemed to the youth inexpressibly beautiful. Winifred's features would have been pretty, for they were regular and delicately formed, if they had not been slightly marked by the small-pox;--a disorder, that sometimes spares more than it destroys, and imparts an expression to be sought for in vain in the smoothest complexion. We have seen pitted cheeks, which we would not exchange for dimples and a satin skin. Winifred's face had a thoroughly amiable look. Her mouth was worthy of her face; with small, pearly-white teeth; lips glossy, rosy, and pouting; and the sweetest smile imaginable, playing constantly about them. Her eyes were soft and blue, arched over by dark brows, and fringed by long silken lashes. Her hair was of the darkest brown, and finest texture; and, when unloosed, hung down to her heels. She was dressed in a little white frock, with a very long body, and very short sleeves, which looked (from a certain fullness about the hips,) as if it was intended to be worn with a hoop. Her slender throat was encircled by a black riband, with a small locket attached to it; and upon the top of her head rested a diminutive lace cap.

The room in which she sat was a portion of the garret, assigned, as we have just stated, by Mr. Wood as a play-room to the two boys; and, like most boy's play-rooms, it exhibited a total absence of order, or neatness. Things were thrown here and there, to be taken up, or again cast aside, as the whim arose; while the broken-backed chairs and crazy table bore the marks of many a conflict. The characters of the youthful occupants of the room might be detected in every article it contained. Darell's peculiar bent of mind was exemplified in a rusty broadsword, a tall grenadier's cap, a musket without lock or ramrod, a belt and cartouch-box, with other matters evincing a decided military taste. Among his books, Plutarch's Lives, and the Histories of Great Commanders, appeared to have been frequently consulted; but the dust had gathered thickly upon the Carpenter's Manual, and a Treatise on Trigonometry and Geometry. Beneath the shelf, containing these books, hung the fine old ballad of 'St. George for England' and a loyal ditty, then much in vogue, called 'True Protestant Gratitude, or, Britain's Thanksgiving for the First of August, Being the Day of His Majesty's Happy Accession to the Throne.' Jack Sheppard's library consisted of a few ragged and well-thumbed volumes abstracted from the tremendous chronicles bequeathed to the world by those Froissarts and Holinsheds of crime--the Ordinaries of Newgate. His vocal collection comprised a couple of flash songs pasted against the wall, entitled 'The Thief-Catcher's Prophecy,' and the 'Life and Death of the Darkman's Budge;' while his extraordinary mechanical skill was displayed in what he termed (Jack had a supreme contempt for orthography,) a 'Moddle of his Ma^{s}. Jale off Newgate;' another model of the pillory at

Fleet Bridge; and a third of the permanent gibbet at Tyburn. The latter specimen, of his workmanship was adorned with a little scarecrow figure, intended to represent a housebreaking chimney-sweeper of the time, described in Sheppard's own hand-writing, as 'Jack Hall a-hanging.' We must not omit to mention that a family group from the pencil of little Winifred, representing Mr. and Mrs. Wood in very characteristic attitudes, occupied a prominent place on the walls.

For a few moments, Thames regarded the little girl through the half-opened door in silence. On a sudden, a change came over her countenance, which, up to this moment, had worn a smiling and satisfied expression. Throwing down the pencil, she snatched up a piece of India-rubber, and exclaiming,--"It isn't at all like him! it isn't half handsome enough!" was about to efface the sketch, when Thames darted into the room.

"Who isn't it like?" he asked, endeavouring to gain possession of the drawing, which, af the sound of his footstep, she crushed between her fingers.

"I can't tell you!" she replied, blushing deeply, and clinching her little hand as tightly as possible; "it's a secret!"

"I'll soon find it out, then," he returned, playfully forcing the paper from her grasp.

"Don't look at it, I entreat," she cried.

But her request was unheeded. Thames unfolded the drawing, smoothed out its creases, and beheld a portrait of himself.

"I've a good mind not to speak to you again, Sir!" cried Winifred, with difficulty repressing a tear of vexation; "you've acted unfairly."

"I feel I have, dear Winny!" replied Thames, abashed at his own rudeness; "my conduct is inexcusable."

"I'll excuse it nevertheless," returned the little damsel, affectionately extending her hand to him.

"Why were you afraid to show me this picture, Winny?" asked the youth.

"Because it's not like you," was her answer.

"Well, like or not, I'm greatly pleased with it, and must beg it from you as a memorial----"

"Of what?" she interrupted, startled by his change of manner.

"Of yourself," he replied, in a mournful tone. "I shall value it highly, and will promise never to part with it. Winny, this is the last night I shall pass beneath your father's roof."

"Have you told him so?" she inquired, reproachfully. "No; but I shall, before he retires to rest."

"Then you *will* stay!" she cried, clapping her hands joyfully, "for I'm sure he won't part with you. Oh! thank you--thank you! I'm so happy!"

"Stop, Winny!" he answered, gravely; "I haven't promised yet."

"But you will,--won't you?" she rejoined, looking him coaxingly in the face.

Unable to withstand this appeal, Thames gave the required promise, adding,--
"Oh! Winny, I wish Mr. Wood had been my father, as well as yours."

"So do I!" she cried; "for then you would have been *really* my brother. No, I don't, either; because----"

"Well, Winny?"

"I don't know what I was going to say," she added, in some confusion; "only I'm sorry you were born a gentleman."

"Perhaps, I wasn't," returned Thames, gloomily, as the remembrance of Jonathan Wild's foul insinuation crossed him. "But never mind who, or what I am. Give me this picture. I'll keep it for your sake."

"I'll give you something better worth keeping," she answered, detaching the ornament from her neck, and presenting it to him; "this contains a lock of my hair, and may remind you sometimes of your little sister. As to the picture, I'll keep it myself, though, if you *do go I shall need no memorial of you*. I'd a good many things to say to you, besides--but you've put them all out of my head."

With this, she burst into tears, and sank with her face upon his shoulder. Thames did not try to cheer her. His own heart was too full of melancholy foreboding. He felt that he might soon be separated--perhaps, for ever--from the fond little creature he held in his arms, whom he had always regarded with the warmest fraternal affection, and the thought of how much she would suffer from the separation so sensibly affected him, that he could not help joining in her grief.

From this sorrowful state he was aroused by a loud derisive whistle, followed by a still louder laugh; and, looking up, he beheld the impudent countenance of Jack Sheppard immediately before him.

"Aha!" exclaimed Jack, with a roguish wink, "I've caught you,--have I?"

The carpenter's daughter was fair and free--
  Fair, and fickle, and false, was she!
  She slighted the journeyman, (meaning me!)
  And smiled on a gallant of high degree.
            Degree! degree!
  She smiled on a gallant of high degree.
  Ha! ha! ha!"

"Jack!" exclaimed Thames, angrily.

But Sheppard was not to be silenced. He went on with his song, accompanying it with the most ridiculous grimaces:

"When years were gone by, she began to rue
  Her love for the gentleman, (meaning you!)
  'I slighted the journeyman fond,' quoth she,
  'But where is my gallant of high degree?
            Where! where!
  Oh! where is my gallant of high degree?'
  Ho! ho! ho!"

"What are you doing here!" demanded Thames.

"Oh! nothing at all," answered Jack, sneeringly, "though this room's as much mine as yours, for that matter. 'But I don't desire to spoil sport,--not I. And, if you'll give me such a smack of your sweet lips, Miss, as you've just given Thames, I'll take myself off in less than no time."

The answer to this request was a "smack" of a very different description, bestowed upon Sheppard's outstretched face by the little damsel, as she ran out of the room.

"'Odd's! bodikins!" cried Jack, rubbing his cheek, "I'm in luck to-day. However, I'd rather have a blow from the daughter than the mother. I know who hits hardest. I tell you what, Thames," he added, flinging himself carelessly into a chair, "I'd give my right hand,--and that's no light offer for a carpenter's 'prentice,--if that little minx were half as fond of me as she is of you."

"That's not likely to be the case, if you go on in this way," replied Thames, sharply.

"Why, what the devil would you have had me do!--make myself scarce, eh? You should have tipped me the wink."

"No more of this," rejoined Thames, "or we shall quarrel."

"Who cares if we do?" retorted Sheppard, with a look of defiance.

"Jack," said the other, sternly; "don't provoke me further, or I'll give you a thrashing."

"Two can play at that game, my blood," replied Sheppard, rising, and putting himself into a posture of defence.

"Take care of yourself, then," rejoined Thames, doubling his fists, and advancing towards him: "though my right arm's stiff, I can use it, as you'll find."

Sheppard was no match for his opponent, for, though he possessed more science, he was deficient in weight and strength; and, after a short round, in which he had decidedly the worst of it, a well-directed hit on the *nob* stretched him at full length on the floor.

"That'll teach you to keep a civil tongue in your head for the future," observed Thames, as he helped Jack to his feet.

"I didn't mean to give offence," replied Sheppard, sulkily. "But, let me tell you, it's not a pleasant sight to see the girl one likes in the arms of another."

"You want another drubbing, I perceive," said Thames, frowning.

"No, I don't. Enough's as good as a feast of the dainties you provide. I'll think no more about her. Save us!" he cried, as his glance accidentally alighted on the drawing, which Winifred had dropped in her agitation. "Is this *her* work?"

"It is," answered Thames. "Do you see any likeness?"

"Don't I," returned Jack, bitterly. "Strange!" he continued, as if talking to himself. "How very like it is!"

"Not so strange, surely," laughed Thames, "that a picture should resemble the person for whom it's intended."

"Ay, but it *is* strange how much it resembles somebody for whom it's *not* intended. It's exactly like a miniature I have in my pocket."

"A miniature! Of whom?"

"That I can't say," replied Jack, mysteriously. "But, I half suspect, of your father."

"My father!" exclaimed Thames, in the utmost astonishment; "let me see it!"

"Here it is," returned Jack, producing a small picture in a case set with brilliants.

Thames took it, and beheld the portrait of a young man, apparently--judging from his attire--of high rank, whose proud and patrician features certainly presented a very striking resemblance to his own.

"You're right Jack," he said, after a pause, during which he contemplated the picture with the most fixed attention: "this must have been my father!"

"No doubt of it," answered Sheppard; "only compare it with Winny's drawing, and you'll find they're as like as two peas in a pod."

"Where did you get it?" inquired Thames.

"From Lady Trafford's, where I took the box."

"Surely, you haven't stolen it?"

"Stolen's an awkward word. But, as you perceive, I brought it away with me."

"It must be restored instantly,--be the consequences what they may."

"You're not going to betray me!" cried Jack, in alarm.

"I am not," replied Thames; "but I insist upon your taking it back at once."

"Take it back yourself," retorted Jack, sullenly. "I shall do no such thing."

"Very well," replied Thames, about to depart.

"Stop!" exclaimed Jack, planting himself before the door; "do you want to get me sent across the water?"

"I want to save you from disgrace and ruin," returned Thames.

"Bah!" cried Jack, contemptuously; "nobody's disgraced and ruined unless he's found out. I'm safe enough if you hold your tongue. Give me that picture, or I'll make you!"

"Hear me," said Thames, calmly; "you well know you're no match for me."

"Not at fisticuffs, perhaps," interrupted Jack, fiercely; "but I've my knife."

"You daren't use it."

"Try to leave the room, and see whether I daren't," returned Jack, opening the blade.

"I didn't expect this from you," rejoined Thames, resolutely. "But your threats won't prevent my leaving the room when I please, and as I please. Now, will you stand aside?"

"I won't," answered Jack, obstinately.

Thames said not another word, but marched boldly towards him, and seized him by the collar.

"Leave go!" cried Jack, struggling violently, and raising his hand, "or I'll maul you for life."

But Thames was not to be deterred from his purpose; and the strife might have terminated seriously, if a peace-maker had not appeared in the shape of little Winifred, who, alarmed by the noise, rushed suddenly into the room.

"Ah!" she screamed, seeing the uplifted weapon in Sheppard's hand, "don't hurt Thames--don't, dear Jack! If you want to kill somebody, kill me, not him."

And she flung herself between them.

Jack dropped the knife, and walked sullenly aside.

"What has caused this quarrel, Thames?" asked the little girl, anxiously.

"You," answered Jack, abruptly.

"No such thing," rejoined Thames. "I'll tell you all about it presently. But you must leave us now, dear Winny, Jack and I have something to settle between ourselves. Don't be afraid. Our quarrel's quite over."

"Are you sure of that?" returned Winifred, looking uneasily at Jack.

"Ay, ay," rejoined Sheppard; "he may do what he pleases,--hang me, if he thinks proper,--if *you* wish it."

With this assurance, and at the reiterated request of Thames, the little girl reluctantly withdrew.

"Come, come, Jack," said Thames, walking up to Sheppard, and taking his hand, "have done with this. I tell you once more, I'll say and do nothing to get you into trouble. Best assured of that. But I'm resolved to see Lady Trafford. Perhaps, she may tell me whose picture this is."

"So she may," returned Jack, brightening up; "it's a good idea. I'll go with you. But you must see her alone; and that'll be no easy matter to manage, for she's a great invalid, and has generally somebody with her. Above all, beware of Sir Rowland Trenchard. He's as savage and suspicious as the devil himself. I should never have noticed the miniature at all, if it hadn't been for him. He was standing by, rating her ladyship,--who can scarcely stir from the sofa,--while I was packing up her jewels in the case, and I observed that she tried to hide a small casket from him. His back was no sooner turned, than she slipped this casket into the box. The next minute, I contrived, without either of 'em perceiving me, to convey it into my own pocket. I was sorry for what I did afterwards; for, I don't know why, but, poor, lady! with her pale face, and black eyes, she reminded me of my mother."

"That, alone, ought to have prevented you from acting as you did, Jack," returned Thames, gravely.

"I should never have acted as I did," rejoined Sheppard, bitterly; "if Mrs. Wood hadn't struck me. That blow made me a thief. And, if ever I'm brought to the gallows, I shall lay my death at her door."

"Well, think no more about it," returned Thames. "Do better in future."

"I will, when I've had my revenge," muttered Jack. "But, take my advice, and keep out of Sir Rowland's way, or you'll get the poor lady into trouble as well as me."

"Never fear," replied Thames, taking up his hat. "Come, let's be off."

The two boys, then, emerged upon the landing, and were about to descend the stairs, when the voices of Mr. and Mrs. Wood resounded from below. The storm appeared to have blown over, for they were conversing in a very amicable manner with Mr. Kneebone, who was on the point of departing.

"Quite sorry, my good friend, there should have been any misunderstanding between us," observed the woollen-draper.

"Don't mention it," returned Wood, in the conciliatory tone of one who admits he has been in the wrong; "your explanation is perfectly satisfactory."

"We shall expect you to-morrow," insinuated Mrs. Wood; "and pray, don't bring anybody with you,--especially Jonathan Wild."

"No fear of that," laughed Kneebone.--"Oh! about that boy, Thames Darrell. His safety must be looked to. Jonathan's threats are not to be sneezed at. The rascal will be at work before the morning. Keep your eye upon the lad. And mind he doesn't stir out of your sight, on any pretence whatever, till I call."

"You hear that," whispered Jack.

"I do," replied Thames, in the same tone; "we haven't a moment to lose."

"Take care of yourself," said Mr. Wood, "and I'll take care of Thames. It's never a bad day that has a good ending. Good night! God bless you!"

Upon this, there was a great shaking of hands, with renewed apologies and protestations of friendship on both sides; after which Mr. Kneebone took his leave.

"And so, you really suspected me?" murmured Mrs. Wood, reproachfully, as they returned to the parlour. "Oh! you men! you men! Once get a thing into your head, and nothing will beat it out."

"Why, my love," rejoined her husband, "appearances, you must allow, were a little against you. But since you assure me *you* didn't write the letters, and Mr. Kneebone assures me *he* didn't receive them, I can't do otherwise than believe you. And I've made up my mind that a husband ought to believe only half that he hears, and nothing that he sees."

"An excellent maxim!" replied his wife, approvingly; "the best I ever heard you utter."

"I must now go and look after Thames," observed the carpenter.

"Oh! never mind him: he'll take no harm! Come with me into the parlour. I can't spare you at present. Heigho!"

"Now for it!" cried Jack, as the couple entered the room: "the coast's clear."

Thames was about to follow, when he felt a gentle grasp upon his arm. He turned, and beheld Winifred.

"Where are you going?" she asked.

"I shall be back presently," replied Thames, evasively.

"Don't go, I beg of you!" she implored. "You're in danger. I overheard what Mr. Kneebone said, just now."

"Death and the devil! what a cursed interruption!" cried Jack, impatiently. "If you loiter in this way, old Wood will catch us."

"If you stir, I'll call him!" rejoined Winifred. "It's you, Jack, who are persuading my brother to do wrong. Thames," she urged, "the errand, on which you're going, can't be for any good, or you wouldn't be afraid of mentioning it to my father."

"He's coming!" cried Jack, stamping his foot, with vexation. "Another moment, and it'll be too late."

"Winny, I *must* go!" said Thames, breaking from her.

"Stay, dear Thames!--stay!" cried the little girl. "He hears me not! he's gone!"

she added, as the door was opened and shut with violence; "something tells me I shall never see him again!"

When her father, a moment afterwards, issued from the parlour to ascertain the cause of the noise, he found her seated on the stairs, in an agony of grief.

"Where's Thames?" he hastily inquired.

Winifred pointed to the door. She could not speak.

"And Jack?"

"Gone too," sobbed his daughter.

Mr. Wood uttered something like an imprecation.

"God forgive me for using such a word!" he cried, in a troubled tone; "if I hadn't yielded to my wife's silly request, this wouldn't have happened!"

CHAPTER VII.
Brother and Sister.

ON the same evening, in a stately chamber of a noble old mansion of Elizabeth's time, situated in Southampton Fields, two persons were seated. One of these, a lady, evidently a confirmed invalid, and attired in deep mourning, reclined upon a sort of couch, or easy chair, set on wheels, with her head supported by cushions, and her feet resting upon a velvet footstool. A crutch, with a silver handle, stood by her side, proving the state of extreme debility to which she was reduced. It was no easy matter to determine her age, for, though she still retained a certain youthfulness of appearance, she had many marks in her countenance, usually indicating the decline of life, but which in her case were, no doubt, the result of constant and severe indisposition. Her complexion was wan and faded, except where it was tinged by a slight hectic flush, that made the want of colour more palpable; her eyes were large and black, but heavy and lustreless; her cheeks sunken; her frame emaciated; her dark hair thickly scattered with gray. When younger, and in better health, she must have been eminently lovely; and there were still the remains of great beauty about her. The expression, however, which would chiefly have interested a beholder, was that of settled and profound melancholy.

Her companion was a person of no inferior condition. Indeed it was apparent, from the likeness between them, that they were nearly related. He had the same dark eyes, though lighted by a fierce flame; the same sallow complexion; the same tall, thin figure, and majestic demeanour; the same proud cast of features. But here the resemblance stopped. The expression was wholly different. He looked melancholy enough, it is true. But his gloom appeared to be occasioned by remorse, rather than sorrow. No sterner head was ever beheld beneath the cowl of a monk, or the bonnet of an inquisitor. He seemed inexorable, and inscrutable as fate itself.

"Well, Lady Trafford," he said, fixing a severe look upon her. "You depart for Lancashire to-morrow. Have I your final answer?"

"You have, Sir Rowland," she answered, in a feeble tone, but firmly. "You shall have the sum you require, but----"

"But what, Madam!"

"Do not misunderstand me," she proceeded. "I give it to King James--not so you: for the furtherance of a great and holy cause, not for the prosecution of wild and unprofitable schemes."

Sir Rowland bit his lips to repress the answer that rose to them.

"And the will?" he said, with forced calmness. "Do you still refuse to make one!"

"I *have* made one," replied Lady Trafford.

"How?" cried her brother, starting.

"Rowland," she rejoined, "you strive in vain to terrify me into compliance with your wishes. Nothing shall induce me to act contrary to the dictates of my conscience. My will is executed, and placed in safe custody."

"In whose favour is it made?" he inquired, sternly.

"In favour of my son."

"You have no son," rejoined Sir Rowland, moodily.

"I *had* one," answered his sister, in a mournful voice; "and, perhaps, I have one still."

"If I thought so--" cried the knight fiercely; "but this is idle," he added, suddenly checking himself. "Aliva, your child perished with its father."

"And by whom were they both destroyed?" demanded his sister, raising herself by a painful effort, and regarding him with a searching glance.

"By the avenger of his family's dishonour--by your brother," he replied, coolly.

"Brother," cried Lady Trafford, her eye blazing with unnatural light, and her cheek suffused with a crimson stain: "Brother," she cried, lifting her thin fingers towards Heaven, "as God shall judge me, I was wedded to that murdered man!"

"A lie!" ejaculated Sir Rowland, furiously; "a black, and damning lie!"

"It is the truth," replied his sister, falling backwards upon the couch. "I will swear it upon the cross!"

"His name, then?" demanded the knight. "Tell me that, and I will believe you."

"Not now--not now!" she returned, with a shudder. "When I am dead you will learn it. Do not disquiet yourself. You will not have to wait long for the information. Rowland," she added, in an altered tone, "I am certain I shall not live many days. And if you treat me in this way, you will have my death to answer for, as well as the deaths of my husband and child. Let us part in peace. We shall take an eternal farewell of each other."

"Be it so!" rejoined Sir Rowland, with concentrated fury; "but before we *do* part, I am resolved to know the name of your pretended husband!"

"Torture shall not wrest it from me," answered his sister, firmly.

"What motive have you for concealment?" he demanded.

"A vow," she answered,--"a vow to my dead husband."

Sir Rowland looked at her for a moment, as if he meditated some terrible reply. He then arose, and, taking a few turns in the chamber, stopped suddenly before her.

"What has put it into your head that your son yet lives?" he asked.

"I have dreamed that I shall see him before I die," she rejoined.

"Dreamed!" echoed the knight, with a ghastly smile. "Is that all? Then learn from me that your hopes are visionary as their foundation. Unless he can arise from the bottom of the Thames, where he and his abhorred father lie buried, you will never behold him again in this world."

"Heaven have compassion on you, Rowland!" murmured his sister, crossing her hands and looking upwards; "you have none on me."

"I *will* have none till I have forced the villain's name from you!" he cried, stamping the floor with rage.

"Rowland, your violence is killing me," she returned, in a plaintive tone.

"His name, I say!--his name!" thundered the knight.

And he unsheathed his sword.

Lady Trafford uttered a prolonged scream, and fainted. When she came to herself, she found that her brother had quitted the room, leaving her to the care of a female attendant. Her first orders were to summon the rest of her servants to make immediate preparations for her departure for Lancashire.

"To-night, your ladyship?" ventured an elderly domestic.

"Instantly, Hobson," returned Lady Trafford; "as soon as the carriage can be brought round."

"It shall be at the door in ten minutes. Has your ladyship any further commands?"

"None whatever. Yet, stay! There is one thing I wish you to do. Take that box, and put it into the carriage yourself. Where is Sir Rowland?"

"In the library, your ladyship. He has given orders that no one is to disturb him. But there's a person in the hall--a very odd sort of man--waiting to see him, who won't be sent away."

"Very well. Lose not a moment, Hobson."

The elderly domestic bowed, took up the case, and retired.

"Your ladyship is far too unwell to travel," remarked the female attendant, assisting her to rise; "you'll never be able to reach Manchester."

"It matters not, Norris," replied Lady Trafford: "I would rather die on the road, than be exposed to another such scene as I have just encountered."

"Dear me!" sympathised Mrs. Norris. "I was afraid from the scream I heard, that something dreadful had happened, Sir Rowland has a terrible temper indeed--a shocking temper! I declare he frightens me out of my senses."

"Sir Rowland is my brother," resumed Lady Trafford coldly.

"Well that's no reason why he should treat your ladyship so shamefully, I'm sure. Ah! how I wish, poor dear Sir Cecil were alive! he'd keep him in order."

Lady Trafford sighed deeply.

"Your ladyship has never been well since you married Sir Cecil," rejoined Mrs. Norris. "For my part, I don't think you ever quite got over the accident you met with on the night of the Great Storm."

"Norris!" gasped Lady Trafford, trembling violently.

"Mercy on us! what have I said!" cried the attendant, greatly alarmed by the agitation of her mistress; "do sit down, your ladyship, while I run for the ratifia and rosa solis."

"It is past," rejoined Lady Trafford, recovering herself by a powerful effort; "but never allude to the circumstance again. Go and prepare for our departure."

In less time than Hobson had mentioned, the carriage was announced. And Lady Trafford having been carried down stairs, and placed within it, the postboy drove off, at a rapid pace for Barnet.

CHAPTER VIII.
Miching Mallecho.

SIR Rowland, meantime, paced his chamber with a quick and agitated step. He was ill at ease, though he would not have confessed his disquietude even to himself. Not conceiving that his sister--feeble as she was, and yielding as she had ever shown herself to his wishes, whether expressed or implied--would depart without consulting him, he was equally surprised and enraged to hear the servants busied in transporting her to the carriage. His pride, however, would not suffer him to interfere with their proceedings; much less could he bring himself to acknowledge that he had been in the wrong, and entreat Lady Trafford to remain, though he was well aware that her life might be endangered if she travelled by night. But, when the sound of the carriage-wheels died away, and he felt that she was actually gone, his resolution failed him, and he rang the bell violently.

"My horses, Charcam," he said, as a servant appeared.

The man lingered.

"'Sdeath! why am I not obeyed?" exclaimed the knight, angrily. "I wish to over-take Lady Trafford. Use despatch!"

"Her ladyship will not travel beyond Saint Alban's to-night, Sir Rowland, so Mrs. Norris informed me," returned Charcam, respectfully; "and there's a person without, anxious for an audience, whom, with submission, I think your honour would desire to see."

"Ah!" exclaimed Sir Rowland, glancing significantly at Charcam, who was a confidant in his Jacobite schemes; "is it the messenger from Orchard-Windham, from Sir William?"

"No, Sir Rowland."

"From Mr. Corbet Kynaston, then? Sir John Packington's courier was here yesterday."

"No, Sir Rowland."

"Perhaps he is from Lord Derwentwater, or Mr. Forster? News *is* expected from Northumberland."

"I can't exactly say, Sir Rowland. The gentleman didn't communicate his business to me. But I'm sure it's important."

Charcam said this, not because he knew anything about the matter; but, having received a couple of guineas to deliver the message, he, naturally enough, estimated its importance by the amount of the gratuity.

"Well, I will see him," replied the knight, after a moment's pause; "he may be from the Earl of Mar. But let the horses be in readiness. I shall ride to St. Alban's to-night."

So saying, he threw himself into a chair. And Charcam, fearful of another charge in his master's present uncertain mood, disappeared.

The person, shortly afterwards ushered into the room, seemed by the imperfect light,--for the evening was advancing, and the chamber darkened by heavy drapery,--to be a middle-sized middle-aged man, of rather vulgar appearance, but with a very shrewd aspect. He was plainly attired in a riding-dress and boots of the period, and wore a hanger by his side.

"Your servant, Sir Rowland," said the stranger, ducking his head, as he advanced.

"Your business, Sir?" returned the other, stiffly.

The new-comer looked at Charcam. Sir Rowland waved his hand, and the attendant withdrew.

"You don't recollect me, I presume?" premised the stranger, taking a seat.

The knight, who could ill brook this familiarity, instantly arose.

"Don't disturb yourself," continued the other, nowise disconcerted by the rebuke. "I never stand upon ceremony where I know I shall be welcome. We *have* met before."

"Indeed!" rejoined Sir Rowland, haughtily; "perhaps, you will refresh my memory as to the time, and place."

"Let me see. The time was the 26th of November, 1703: the place, the Mint in Southwark. I have a good memory, you perceive, Sir Rowland."

The knight staggered as if struck by a mortal wound. Speedily recovering himself, however, he rejoined, with forced calmness, "You are mistaken, Sir. I was in Lancashire, at our family seat, at the time you mention."

The stranger smiled incredulously.

"Well, Sir Rowland," he said, after a brief pause, during which the knight regarded him with a searching glance, as if endeavouring to recall his features, "I will not gainsay your words. You are in the right to be cautious, till you know with whom you have to deal; and, even then, you can't be too wary. 'Avow nothing, believe nothing, give nothing for nothing,' is my own motto. And it's a maxim of universal application: or, at least, of universal practice. I am not come here to play the part of your father-confessor. I am come to serve you."

"In what way, Sir?" demanded Trenchard, in astonishment.

"You will learn anon. You refuse me your confidence. I applaud your prudence: it is, however, needless. Your history, your actions, nay, your very thoughts are better known to me than to your spiritual adviser."

"Make good your assertions," cried Trenchard, furiously, "or----"

"To the proof," interrupted the stranger, calmly. "You are the son of Sir Montacute Trenchard, of Ashton-Hall, near Manchester. Sir Montacute had three children--two daughters and yourself. The eldest, Constance, was lost, by the carelessness of a servant, during her infancy, and has never since been heard of: the youngest, Aliva, is the present Lady Trafford. I merely mention these circumstances to show the accuracy of my information."

"If this is the extent of it, Sir," returned the knight, ironically, "you may spare yourself further trouble. These particulars are familiar to all, who have any title to the knowledge."

"Perhaps so," rejoined the stranger; "but I have others in reserve, not so generally known. With your permission, I will go on in my own way. Where I am in error, you can set me right.--Your father, Sir Montacute Trenchard, who had been a loyal subject of King James the Second, and borne arms in his service, on the abdication of that monarch, turned his back upon the Stuarts, and would never afterwards recognise their claims to the crown. It was said, that he received an affront from James, in the shape of a public reprimand, which his pride could not forgive. Be this as it may, though a Catholic, he died a friend to the Protestant succession."

"So far you are correct," observed Trenchard; "still, this is no secret."

"Suffer me to proceed," replied the stranger. "The opinions, entertained by the old knight, naturally induced him to view with displeasure the conduct of his son, who warmly espoused the cause he had deserted. Finding remonstrances of no avail, he had recourse to threats; and when threats failed, he adopted more decided measures."

"Ha!" ejaculated Trenchard.

"As yet," pursued the stranger, "Sir Montacute had placed no limit to his son's expenditure. He did not quarrel with Rowland's profusion, for his own revenues were ample; but he *did* object to the large sums lavished by him in the service of a faction he was resolved not to support. Accordingly, the old knight reduced his son's allowance to a third of its previous amount; and, upon further provocation, he even went so far as to alter his will in favour of his daughter, Aliva, who was then betrothed to her cousin, Sir Cecil Trafford."

"Proceed, Sir," said Trenchard, breathing hard.

"Under these circumstances, Rowland did what any other sensible person would do. Aware of his father's inflexibility of purpose, he set his wits to work to defeat the design. He contrived to break off his sister's match; and this he accomplished so cleverly, that he maintained the strictest friendship with Sir Cecil. For two years he thought himself secure; and, secretly engaged in the Jacobite schemes of the time, in which, also, Sir Cecil was deeply involved, he began to relax in his watchfulness over Aliva. About this time,--namely, in November, 1703--while young Trenchard was in Lancashire, and his sister in London, on a visit, he received a certain communication from his confidential servant, Davies, which, at once, destroyed his hopes. He learnt that his sister was privately married--the name or rank of her husband could not be ascertained--and living in retirement in an obscure dwelling in the Borough, where she had given birth to a son. Rowland's plans were quickly formed, and as quickly executed. Accompanied by Sir Cecil, who still continued passionately enamoured of his sister, and to whom he represented that she had fallen a victim to the arts of a seducer, he set off, at fiery speed, for the metropolis. Arrived there, their first object was to seek out Davies, by whom they were conducted to the lady's retreat,--a lone habitation, situated on the outskirts of Saint George's Fields in Southwark. Refused admittance, they broke open the door. Aliva's husband, who passed by the name of Darrell, confronted them sword in hand. For a few minutes he kept them at bay. But, urged by his wife's cries, who was more anxious for the preservation of her child's life than her own, he snatched up the infant, and made his escape from the back of the premises. Rowland and his companions instantly started in pursuit, leaving the lady to recover as she might. They tracked the fugitive to the Mint; but, like hounds at fault, they here lost all scent of their prey. Meantime, the lady had overtaken them; but, terrified by the menaces of her vindictive kinsmen, she did not dare to reveal herself to her husband, of whose concealment on the roof of the very house the party were searching she was aware. Aided by an individual, who was acquainted with a secret outlet from the tenement, Darrell escaped. Before his departure, he gave his assistant a glove. That glove is still preserved. In her endeavour to follow him, Aliva met with a severe fall, and was conveyed away, in a state of insensibility, by Sir Cecil. She was supposed to be lifeless; but she survived the accident, though she never regained her strength. Directed by the same individual, who had helped Darrell to steal a march upon him, Rowland, with Davies, and another attendant, continued the pursuit. Both the fugitive and his chasers embarked on the Thames. The elements were wrathful as their passions. The storm burst upon them in its fury. Unmindful of the terrors of the night, unscared by the danger that threatened him, Rowland consigned his sister's husband and his sister's child to the waves."

"Bring your story to an end, Sir," said Trenchard who had listened to the recital with mingled emotions of rage and fear.

"I have nearly done," replied the stranger.--"As Rowland's whole crew perished in the tempest, and he only escaped by miracle, he fancied himself free from detection. And for twelve years he has been so; until his long security, well-nigh obliterating remembrance of the deed, has bred almost a sense of innocence within his breast. During this period Sir Montacute has been gathered to his fathers. His title has descended to Rowland: his estates to Aliva. The latter has, since, been induced to unite herself to Sir Cecil, on terms originating with her brother, and which, however strange and unprecedented, were acquiesced in by the suitor."

Sir Rowland looked bewildered with surprise.

"The marriage was never consummated," continued the imperturbable stranger. "Sir Cecil is no more. Lady Trafford, supposed to be childless, broken in health and spirits, frail both in mind and body, is not likely to make another marriage. The estates must, ere long, revert to Sir Rowland."

"Are you man, or fiend?" exclaimed Trenchard, staring at the stranger, as he concluded his narration.

"You are complimentary, Sir Rowland," returned the other, with a grim smile.

"If you *are* human," rejoined Trenchard, with stern emphasis, "I insist upon knowing whence you derived your information?"

"I might refuse to answer the question, Sir Rowland. But I am not indisposed to gratify you. Partly, from your confessor; partly, from other sources."

"My confessor!" ejaculated the knight, in the extremity of surprise; "has *he* betrayed his sacred trust?"

"He has," replied the other, grinning; "and this will be a caution to you in future, how you confide a secret of consequence to a priest. I should as soon think of trusting a woman. Tickle the ears of their reverences with any idle nonsense you please: but tell them nothing you care to have repeated. I was once a disciple of Saint Peter myself, and speak from experience."

"Who are you?" ejaculated Trenchard, scarcely able to credit his senses.

"I'm surprised you've not asked that question before, Sir Rowland. It would have saved me much circumlocution, and you some suspense. My name is Wild-- Jonathan Wild."

And the great thief-taker indulged himself in a chuckle at the effect produced by this announcement. He was accustomed to such surprises, and enjoyed them.

Sir Rowland laid his hand upon his sword.

"Mr. Wild," he said, in a sarcastic tone, but with great firmness; "a person of your well-known sagacity must be aware that some secrets are dangerous to the possessor."

"I am fully aware of it, Sir Rowland," replied Jonathan, coolly; "but I have nothing to fear; because, in the first place, it will be to your advantage not to molest me; and, in the second, I am provided against all contingencies. I never hunt the human tiger without being armed. My janizaries are without. One of them is furnished with a packet containing the heads of the statement I have just related, which, if I don't return at a certain time, will be laid before the proper authorities. I have calculated my chances, you perceive."

"You have forgotten that you are in my power," returned the knight, sternly; "and that all your allies cannot save you from my resentment."

"I can at least, protect myself," replied Wild, with, provoking calmness. "I am accounted a fair shot, as well as a tolerable swordsman, and I will give proof of my skill in both lines, should occasion require it. I have had a good many desperate engagements in my time, and have generally come off victorious. I bear the marks of some of them about me still," he continued, taking off his wig, and laying bare a bald skull, covered with cicatrices and plates of silver. "This gash," he added, pointing to one of the larger scars, "was a wipe from the hanger of Tom Thurland, whom I apprehended for the murder of Mrs. Knap. This wedge of silver," pointing to another, "which would mend a coffee-pot, serves to stop up a breach made by Will Colthurst, who robbed Mr. Hearl on Hounslow-Heath. I secured the dog after he had wounded me. This fracture was the handiwork of Jack Parrot (otherwise called Jack the Grinder), who broke into the palace of the Bishop of Norwich. Jack was a comical scoundrel, and made a little too free with his grace's best burgundy, as well as his grace's favourite housekeeper. The Bishop, however, to show him the danger of meddling with the church, gave him a dance at Tyburn for his pains. Not a scar but has its history. The only inconvenience I feel from my shattered noddle is an incapacity to drink. But that's an infirmity shared by a great many sounder heads than mine. The hardest bout I ever had was with a woman--Sally Wells, who was afterwards lagged for shoplifting. She attacked me with a carving-knife, and, when I had disarmed her, the jade bit off a couple of fingers from my left hand. Thus, you see, I've never hesitated and never *shall* hesitate to expose my life where anything is to be gained. My profession has hardened me."

And, with this, he coolly re-adjusted his peruke.

"What do you expect to gain from this interview, Mr. Wild!" demanded Trenchard, as if he had formed a sudden resolution.

"Ah! now we come to business," returned Jonathan, rubbing his hands, gleefully. "These are my terms, Sir Rowland," he added, taking a sheet of paper from his pocket, and pushing it towards the knight.

Trenchard glanced at the document.

"A thousand pounds," he observed, gloomily, "is a heavy price to pay for doubtful secrecy, when *certain silence* might be so cheaply procured."

"You would purchase it at the price of your head," replied Jonathan, knitting his brows. "Sir Rowland," he added, savagely, and with somewhat of the look of a bull-dog before he flies at his foe, "if it were my pleasure to do so, I could crush you with a breath. You are wholly in my power. Your name, with the fatal epithet of 'dangerous' attached to it, stands foremost on the list of Disaffected now before the Secret Committee. I hold a warrant from Mr. Walpole for your apprehension."

"Arrested!" exclaimed Trenchard, drawing his sword.

"Put up your blade, Sir Rowland," rejoined Jonathan, resuming his former calm demeanour, "King James the Third will need it. I have no intention of arresting you. I have a different game to play; and it'll be your own fault, if you don't come off the winner. I offer you my assistance on certain terms. The proposal is so far from being exorbitant, that it should be trebled if I had not a fellow-feeling in the cause. To be frank with you, I have an affront to requite, which can be settled at the same time, and in the same way with your affair. That's worth something to me; for I don't mind paying for revenge. After all a thousand pounds is a trifle to rid you of an upstart, who may chance to deprive you of tens of thousands."

"Did I hear you aright?" asked Trenchard, with startling eagerness.

"Certainly," replied Jonathan, with the most perfect *sangfroid*, "I'll undertake to free you from the boy. That's part of the bargain."

"Is he alive!" vociferated Trenchard.

"To be sure," returned Wild; "he's not only alive, but likely for life, if we don't clip the thread."

Sir Rowland caught at a chair for support, and passed his hand across his brow, on which the damp had gathered thickly.

"The intelligence seems new to you. I thought I'd been sufficiently explicit," continued Jonathan. "Most persons would have guessed my meaning."

"Then it was *not* a dream!" ejaculated Sir Rowland in a hollow voice, and as if speaking to himself. "I *did* see them on the platform of the bridge--the child and his preserver! They were *not* struck by the fallen ruin, nor whelmed in the roaring flood,--or, if they *were*, they escaped as I escaped. God! I have cheated myself into a belief that the boy perished! And now my worst fears are realized--he lives!"

"As yet," returned Jonathan, with fearful emphasis.

"I cannot--dare not injure him," rejoined Trenchard, with a haggard look, and sinking, as if paralysed, into a chair.

Jonathan laughed scornfully.

"Leave him to me," he said. "He shan't trouble you further."

"No," replied Sir Rowland, who appeared completely prostrated. "I will struggle no longer with destiny. Too much blood has been shed already."

"This comes of fine feelings!" muttered Jonathan, contemptuously. "Give me your thorough-paced villain. But I shan't let him off thus. I'll try a strong dose.-- Am I to understand that you intend to plead guilty, Sir Rowland?" he added. "If so, I may as well execute my warrant."

"Stand off, Sir!" exclaimed Trenchard, starting suddenly backwards.

"I knew that would bring him to," thought Wild.

"Where is the boy?" demanded Sir Rowland.

"At present under the care of his preserver--one Owen Wood, a carpenter, by whom he was brought up."

"Wood!" exclaimed Trenchard,--"of Wych Street?"

"The same."

"A boy from his shop was here a short time ago. Could it be him you mean?"

"No. That boy was the carpenter's apprentice, Jack Sheppard. I've just left your nephew."

At this moment Charcam entered the room.

"Beg pardon, Sir Rowland," said the attendant, "but there's a boy from Mr. Wood, with a message for Lady Trafford."

"From whom?" vociferated Trenchard.

"From Mr. Wood the carpenter."

"The same who was here just now?"

"No, Sir Rowland, a much finer boy."

"'Tis he, by Heaven!" cried Jonathan; "this is lucky. Sir Rowland," he added, in a deep whisper, "do you agree to my terms?"

"I do," answered Trenchard, in the same tone.

"Enough!" rejoined Wild; "he shall not return."

"Have you acquainted him with Lady Trafford's departure?" said the knight, addressing Charcam, with as much composure as he could assume.

"No, Sir Rowland," replied the attendant, "as you proposed to ride to Saint

Albans to-night, I thought you might choose to see him yourself. Besides, there's something odd about the boy; for, though I questioned him pretty closely concerning his business, he declined answering my questions, and said he could only deliver his message to her ladyship. I thought it better not to send him away till I'd mentioned the circumstance to you."

"You did right," returned Trenchard.

"Where is he?" asked Jonathan.

"In the hall," replied Charcam.

"Alone?"

"Not exactly, Sir. There's another lad at the gate waiting for him--the same who was here just now, that Sir Rowland was speaking of, who fastened up the jewel-case for her ladyship."

"A jewel-case!" exclaimed Jonathan. "Ah, I see it all!" he cried, with a quick glance. "Jack Sheppard's fingers are lime-twigs. Was anything missed after the lad's departure, Sir Rowland?"

"Not that I'm aware of," said the knight.--"Stay! something occurs to me." And he conferred apart with Jonathan.

"That's it!" cried Wild when Trenchard concluded. "This young fool is come to restore the article--whatever it may be--which Lady Trafford was anxious to conceal, and which his companion purloined. It's precisely what such a simpleton would do. We have him as safe as a linnet in a cage; and could wring his neck round as easily. Oblige me by acting under my guidance in the matter, Sir Rowland. I'm an old hand at such things. Harkee," he added, "Mr. What's-your-name!"

"Charcam," replied the attendant, bowing.

"Very well, Mr. Charcoal, you may bring in the boy. But not a word to him of Lady Trafford's absence--mind that. A robbery has been committed, and your master suspects this lad as an accessory to the offence. He, therefore, desires to interrogate him. It will be necessary to secure his companion; and as you say he is not in the house, some caution must be used in approaching him, or he may chance to take to his heels, for he's a slippery little rascal. When you've seized him, cough thrice thus,--and two rough-looking gentlemen will make their appearance. Don't be alarmed by their manners, Mr. Charcoal. They're apt to be surly to strangers, but it soon wears off. The gentleman with the red beard will relieve you of your prisoner. The other must call a coach as quickly as he can."

"For whom, Sir?" inquired Charcam. "For me--his master, Mr. Jonathan Wild."

"Are you Mr. Jonathan Wild?" asked the attendant, in great trepidation.

"I *am*, Charcoal. But don't let my name frighten you. Though," said the thief-taker, with a complacent smile, "all the world seems to tremble at it. Obey my orders, and you've nothing to fear. About them quickly. Lead the lad to suppose that he'll be introduced to Lady Trafford. You understand me, Charcoal."

The attendant did *not* understand him. He was confounded by the presence in which he found himself. But, not daring to confess his want of comprehension, he made a profound reverence, and retired.

CHAPTER IX.
Consequences of the Theft.

How do you mean to act, Sir?" inquired Trenchard, as soon as they were left alone. "As circumstances shall dictate, Sir Rowland," returned Jonathan. "Something is sure to arise in the course of the investigation, of which I can take advantage. If not, I'll convey him to St. Giles's round-house on my own responsibility."

"Is this your notable scheme!" asked the knight, scornfully.

"Once there," proceeded Wild, without noticing the interruption, "he's as good as in his grave. The constable, Sharples, is in my pay. I can remove the prisoner at any hour of the night I think fit: and I *will* remove him. You must, know, Sir Rowland--for I've no secrets from you--that, in the course of my business I've found it convenient to become the owner of a small Dutch sloop; by means of which I can transmit any light ware,--such as gold watches, rings, and plate, as well as occasionally a bank or goldsmith's note, which has been *spoken with* by way of the mail,-- you understand me?--to Holland or Flanders, and obtain a secure and ready market for them. This vessel is now in the river, off Wapping. Her cargo is nearly shipped. She will sail, at early dawn to-morrow, for Rotterdam. Her commander, Rykhart Van Galgebrok, is devoted to my interests. As soon as he gets into blue water, he'll think no more of pitching the boy overboard than of lighting his pipe. This will be safer than cutting his throat on shore. I've tried the plan, and found it answer. The Northern Ocean keeps a secret better than the Thames, Sir Rowland. Before midnight, your nephew shall be safe beneath the hatches of the Zeeslang."

"Poor child!" muttered Trenchard, abstractedly; "the whole scene upon the river is passing before me. I hear the splash in the water--I see the white object floating like a sea-bird on the tide--it will not sink!"

"'Sblood!" exclaimed Jonathan, in a tone of ill-disguised contempt; "it won't do to indulge those fancies now. Be seated, and calm yourself."

"I have often conjured up some frightful vision of the dead," murmured the knight, "but I never dreamed of an interview with the living."

"It'll be over in a few minutes," rejoined Jonathan, impatiently; "in fact, it'll be over too soon for me. I like such interviews. But we waste time. Have the goodness to affix your name to that memorandum, Sir Rowland. I require nothing, you see, till my share of the contract is fulfilled."

Trenchard took up a pen.

"It's the boy's death-warrant," observed Jonathan, with a sinister smile.

"I cannot sign it," returned Trenchard.

"Damnation!" exclaimed Wild with a snarl, that displayed his glistening fangs to the farthest extremity of his mouth, "I'm not to be trifled with thus. That paper *must* be signed, or I take my departure."

"Go, Sir," rejoined the knight, haughtily.

"Ay, ay, I'll go, fast enough!" returned Jonathan, putting his hands into his pockets, "but not alone, Sir Rowland."

At this juncture, the door was flung open, and Charcam entered, dragging in Thames, whom he held by the collar, and who struggled in vain to free himself from the grasp imposed upon him.

"Here's one of the thieves, Sir Rowland!" cried the attendant. "I was only just in time. The young rascal had learnt from some of the women-servants that Lady Trafford was from home, and was in the very act of making off when I got down stairs. Come along, my Newgate bird!" he continued, shaking him with great violence.

Jonathan gave utterance to a low whistle.

"If things had gone smoothly," he thought, "I should have cursed the fellow's stupidity. As it is, I'm not sorry for the blunder."

Trenchard, meanwhile, whose gaze was fixed upon the boy, became livid as death, but he moved not a muscle.

"'T is he!" he mentally ejaculated.

"What do you think of your nephew, Sir Rowland?" whispered Jonathan, who sat with his back towards Thames, so that his features were concealed from the youth's view. "It would be a thousand pities, wouldn't it, to put so promising a lad out of the way?"

"Devil!" exclaimed the knight fiercely, "Give me the paper."

Jonathan hastily picked up the pen, and presented it to Trenchard, who attached his signature to the document.

"If I *am* the devil," observed Wild, "as some folks assert, and I myself am not unwilling to believe, you'll find that I differ from the generally-received notions of the arch-fiend, and faithfully execute the commands of those who confide their souls to my custody."

"Take hence this boy, then," rejoined Trenchard; "his looks unman me."

"Of what am I accused?" asked Thames, who though a good deal alarmed at first, had now regained his courage.

"Of robbery!" replied Jonathan in a thundering voice, and suddenly confronting him. "You've charged with assisting your comrade, Jack Sheppard, to purloin certain articles of value from a jewel-case belonging to Lady Trafford. Aha!" he continued, producing a short silver staff, which he carried constantly about with him, and uttering a terrible imprecation, "I see you're confounded. Down on your marrow-bones, sirrah! Confess your guilt, and Sir Rowland may yet save you from the gallows."

"I've nothing to confess," replied Thames, boldly; "I've done no wrong. Are *you* my accuser?"

"I am," replied Wild; "have you anything to allege to the contrary?"

"Only this," returned Thames: "that the charge is false, and malicious, and that *you* know it to be so."

"Is that all!" retorted Jonathan. "Come, I must search you my youngster!"

"You shan't touch me," rejoined Thames; and, suddenly bursting from Charcam, he threw himself at the feet of Trenchard. "Hear me, Sir Rowland!" he cried. "I am innocent, f have stolen nothing. This person--this Jonathan Wild, whom I beheld for the first time, scarcely an hour ago, in Wych Street, is--I know not why--my enemy. He has sworn that he'll take away my life!"

"Bah!" interrupted Jonathan. "You won't listen to this nonsense, Sir Rowland!"

"If you *are* innocent, boy," said the knight, controlling his emotion; "you have nothing to apprehend. But, what brought you here?"

"Excuse me, Sir Rowland. I cannot answer that question. My business is with Lady Trafford."

"Are you aware that I am her ladyship's brother?" returned the knight. "She has no secrets from me."

"Possibly not," replied Thames, in some confusion; "but I am not at liberty to speak."

"Your hesitation is not in your favour," observed Trenchard, sternly.

"Will he consent, to be searched?" inquired Jonathan.

"No," rejoined Thames, "I won't be treated like a common felon, if I can help it."

"You shall be treated according to your deserts, then," said Jonathan, maliciously. And, in spite of the boy's resistance, he plunged his hands into his pockets, and drew forth the miniature.

"Where did you get this from?" asked Wild, greatly surprised at the result of his investigation.

Thames returned no answer.

"I thought as much," continued Jonathan. "But we'll find a way to make you open your lips presently. Bring in his comrade," he added, in a whisper to Charcam; "I'll take care of him. And don't neglect my instructions this time." Upon which, with an assurance that he would not do so, the attendant departed.

"You can, of course, identify this picture as Lady Trafford's property?" pursued Jonathan, with a meaning glance, as he handed it to the knight.

"I can," replied Trenchard. "Ha!" he exclaimed, with a sudden start, as his glance fell upon the portrait; "how came this into your possession, boy?"

"Why don't you answer, sirrah?" cried Wild, in a savage tone, and striking him with the silver staff. "Can't you speak?"

"I don't choose," replied Thames, sturdily; "and your brutality shan't make me."

"We'll see that," replied Jonathan, dealing him another and more violent blow.

"Let him alone," said Trenchard authoritatively, "I have another question to propose. Do you know whoso portrait this is?"

"I do not," replied Thames, repressing his tears, "but I believe it to be the portrait of my father."

"Indeed!" exclaimed the knight, in astonishment. "Is your father alive?"

"No," returned Thames; "he was assassinated while I was an infant."

"Who told you this is his portrait?" demanded Trenchard.

"My heart," rejoined Thames, firmly; "which now tells me I am in the presence of his murderer."

"That's me," interposed Jonathan; "a thief-taker is always a murderer in the eyes of a thief. I'm almost sorry your suspicions are unfounded, if your father in any way resembled you, my youngster. But I can tell you who'll have the pleasure of hanging your father's son; and that's a person not a hundred miles distant from you at this moment--ha! ha!"

As he said this, the door was opened, and Charcam entered, accompanied by a dwarfish, shabby-looking man, in a brown serge frock, with coarse Jewish features, and a long red beard. Between the Jew and the attendant came Jack Sheppard; while a crowd of servants, attracted by the news, that the investigation of a robbery was going forward, lingered at the doorway in hopes of catching something of the proceedings.

When Jack was brought in, he cast a rapid glance around him, and perceiving Thames in the custody of Jonathan, instantly divined how matters stood. As he looked in this direction, Wild gave him a significant wink, the meaning of which he was not slow to comprehend.

"Get it over quickly," said Trenchard, in a whisper to the thief-taker.

Jonathan nodded assent.

"What's your name?" he said, addressing the audacious lad, who was looking about him as coolly as if nothing material was going on.

"Jack Sheppard," returned the boy, fixing his eyes upon a portrait of the Earl of Mar. "Who's that queer cove in the full-bottomed wig?"

"Attend to me, sirrah," rejoined Wild, sternly. "Do you know this picture?" he added, with another significant look, and pointing to the miniature.

"I do," replied Jack, carelessly.

"That's well. Can you inform us whence it came?"

"I should think so."

"State the facts, then."

"It came from Lady Trafford's jewel-box."

Here a murmur of amazement arose from the assemblage outside.

"Close the door!" commanded Trenchard, impatiently.

"In my opinion, Sir Rowland," suggested Jonathan; "you'd better allow the court to remain open."

"Be it so," replied the knight, who saw the force of this reasoning. "Continue the proceedings."

"You say that the miniature was abstracted from Lady Trafford's jewel-box," said Jonathan, in a loud voice. "Who took it thence?"

"Thames Darrell; the boy at your side."

"Jack!" cried Thames, in indignant surprise.

But Sheppard took no notice of the exclamation.

A loud buzz of curiosity circulated among the domestics; some of whom--especially the females--leaned forward to obtain a peep at the culprit.

"Si--lence!" vociferated Charcam, laying great emphasis on the last syllable.

"Were you present at the time of the robbery?" pursued Jonathan.

"I was," answered Sheppard.

"And will swear to it?"

"I will."

"Liar!" ejaculated Thames.

"Enough!" exclaimed Wild, triumphantly.

"Close the court, Mr. Charcoal. They've heard quite enough for my purpose," he muttered, as his orders were obeyed, and the domestics excluded. "It's too late to carry 'em before a magistrate now, Sir Rowland; so, with your permission, I'll give 'em a night's lodging in Saint Giles's round-house. You, Jack Sheppard, have nothing to fear, as you've become evidence against your accomplice. To-morrow, I shall carry you before Justice Walters, who'll take your information; and I've no doubt but Thames Darrell will be fully committed. Now, for the cage, my pretty canary-bird. Before we start, I'll accommodate you with a pair of ruffles." And he proceeded to handcuff his captive.

"Hear me!" cried Thames, bursting into tears. "I am innocent. I could not have committed this robbery. I have only just left Wych Street. Send for Mr. Wood, and you'll find that I've spoken the truth."

"You'd better hold your peace, my lad," observed Jonathan, in a menacing tone.

"Lady Trafford would not have thus condemned me!" cried Thames.

"Away with him!" exclaimed Sir Rowland, impatiently.

"Take the prisoners below, Nab," said Jonathan, addressing the dwarfish Jew; "I'll join you in an instant."

The bearded miscreant seized Jack by the waist, and Thames by the nape of the neck, and marched off, like the ogre in the fairy tale, with a boy under each arm, while Charcam brought upt the rear.

CHAPTER X.
Mother and Son.

THEY had scarcely been gone a moment, when a confused noise was heard without, and Charcam re-entered the room, with a countenance of the utmost bewilderment and alarm.

"What's the matter with the man?" demanded Wild.

"Her ladyship--" faltered the attendant.

"What of her?" cried the knight. "Is she returned!"

"Y--e--s, Sir Rowland," stammered Charcam.

"The devil!" ejaculated Jonathan. "Here's a cross-bite."

"But that's not all, your honour," continued Charcam; "Mrs. Norris says she's dying."

"Dying!" echoed the knight.

"Dying, Sir Rowland. She was taken dreadfully ill on the road, with spasms and short breath, and swoonings,--worse than ever she was before. And Mrs. Norris was so frightened that she ordered the postboys to drive back as fast as they could. She never expected to get her ladyship home alive."

"My God!" cried Trenchard, stunned by the intelligence, "I have killed her."

"No doubt," rejoined Wild, with a sneer; "but don't let all the world know it."

"They're lifting her out of the carriage," interposed Charcam; "will it please your honour to send for some advice and the chaplain?"

"Fly for both," returned Sir Rowland, in a tone of bitter anguish.

"Stay!" interposed Jonathan. "Where are the boys?"

"In the hall."

"Her ladyship will pass through it?"

"Of course; there's no other way."

"Then, bring them into this room, the first thing--quick! They must not meet, Sir Rowland," he added, as Charcam hastened to obey his instructions.

"Heaven has decreed it otherwise," replied the knight, dejectedly. "I yield to fate."

"Yield to nothing," returned Wild, trying to re-assure him; "above all, when your designs prosper. Man's fate is in his own hands. You are your nephew's executioner, or he is yours. Cast off this weakness. The next hour makes, or mars you for ever. Go to your sister, and do not quit her till all is over. Leave the rest to me."

Sir Rowland moved irresolutely towards the door, but recoiled before a sad spectacle. This was his sister, evidently in the last extremity. Borne in the arms of a couple of assistants, and preceded by Mrs. Norris, wringing her hands and wepping, the unfortunate lady was placed upon a couch. At the same time, Charcam, who seemed perfectly distracted by the recent occurrences, dragged in Thames, leaving Jack Sheppard outside in the custody of the dwarfish Jew.

"Hell's curses!" muttered Jonathan between his teeth; "that fool will ruin all. Take him away," he added, striding up to Charcam.

"Let him remain," interposed Trenchard.

"As you please, Sir Rowland," returned Jonathan, with affected indifference; "but I'm not going to hunt the deer for another to eat the ven'son, depend on 't."

But seeing that no notice was taken of the retort, he drew a little aside, and folded his arms, muttering, "This whim will soon be over. She can't last long. I can pull the strings of this stiff-necked puppet as I please."

Sir Rowland, meantime, throw himself on his knees beside his sister, and, clasping her chilly fingers within his own, besought her forgiveness in the most passionate terms. For a few minutes, she appeared scarcely sensible of his presence. But, after some restoratives had been administered by Mrs. Norris, she revived a little.

"Rowland," she said, in a faint voice, "I have not many minutes to live. Where is Father Spencer? I must have absolution. I have something that weighs heavily upon my mind."

Sir Rowland's brow darkened.

"I have sent for him," Aliva, he answered; "he will be here directly, with your medical advisers."

"They are useless," she returned. "Medicine cannot save mo now."

"Dear sister----"

"I should die happy, if I could behold my child."

"Comfort yourself, then, Aliva. You *shall* behold him."

"You are mocking me, Rowland. Jests are not for seasons like this."

"I am not, by Heaven," returned the knight, solemnly. "Leave us, Mrs. Norris, and do not return till Father Spencer arrives."

"Your ladyship----" hesitated Norris.

"Go!" said Lady Trafford; "it is my last request."

And her faithful attendant, drowned in tears, withdrew, followed by the two assistants.

Jonathan stepped behind a curtain.

"Rowland," said Lady Trafford, regarding him with a look of indescribable anxiety, "you have assured me that I shall behold my son. Where is he?"

"Within this room," replied the knight.

"Here!" shrieked Lady Trafford.

"Here," repeated her brother. "But calm yourself, dear sister, or the interview will be too much for you."

"I *am* calm--quite calm, Rowland," she answered, with lips whose agitation belied her words. "Then, the story of his death was false. I knew it. I was sure you could not have the heart to slay a child--an innocent child. God forgive you!"

"May He, indeed, forgive me!" returned Trenchard, crossing himself devoutly; "but my guilt is not the less heavy, because your child escaped. This hand consigned him to destruction, but another was stretched forth to save him. The infant was rescued from a watery-grave by an honest mechanic, who has since brought him up as his own son."

"Blessings upon him!" cried Lady Trafford, fervently. "But trifle with mo no longer. Moments are ages now. Let me see my child, if he is really here?"

"Behold him!" returned Trenchard, taking Thames (who had been a mute, but deeply-interested, witness of the scene) by the hand, and leading him towards her.

"Ah!" exclaimed Lady Trafford, exerting all her strength. "My sight is failing me. Let me have more light, that I may behold him. Yes!" she screamed, "these are his father's features! It is--it is my son!"

"Mother!" cried Thames; "are you, indeed, my mother?"

"I am, indeed--my own sweet boy!" she sobbed, pressing him tenderly to her breast.

"Oh!--to see you thus!" cried Thames, in an agony of affliction.

"Don't weep, my love," replied the lady, straining him still more closely to her. "I am happy--quite happy now."

During this touching interview, a change had come over Sir Rowland, and he half repented of what he had done.

"You can no longer refuse to tell me the name of this youth's father, Aliva," he said.

"I dare not, Rowland," she answered. "I cannot break my vow. I will confide it to Father Spencer, who will acquaint you with it when I am no more. Undraw the curtain, love," she added to Thames, "that I may look at you."

"Ha!" exclaimed her son, starting back, as he obeyed her, and disclosed Jonathan Wild.

"Be silent," said Jonathan, in a menacing whisper.

"What have you seen?" inquired Lady Trafford.

"My enemy," replied her son.

"Your enemy!" she returned imperfectly comprehending him. "Sir Rowland is your uncle--he will be your guardian--he will protect you. Will you not, brother?"

"Promise," said a deep voice in Trenchard's ear.

"He will kill me," cried Thames. "There is a man in this room who seeks my life."

"Impossible!" rejoined his mother.

"Look at these fetters," returned Thames, holding up his manacled wrists; "they were put on by my uncle's command."

"Ah!" shrieked Lady Trafford.

"Not a moment is to be lost," whispered Jonathan to Trenchard. "His life--or yours?"

"No one shall harm you more, my dear," cried Lady Trafford. "Your uncle *must* protect you. It will be his interest to do so. He will be dependent on you."

"Do what you please with him," muttered Trenchard to Wild.

"Take off these chains, Rowland," said Lady Trafford, "instantly, I command you."

"I will," replied Jonathan, advancing, and rudely seizing Thames.

"Mother!" cried the son, "help!"

"What is this?" shrieked Lady Trafford, raising herself on the couch, and extending her hands towards him. "Oh, God! would you take him from me?--would you murder him?"

"His father's name?--and he is free," rejoined Rowland, holding her arms.

"Release him first--and I will disclose it!" cried Lady Trafford; "on my soul, I will!"

"Speak then!" returned Rowland.

"Too late!" shrieked the lady, falling heavily backwards,--"too late!--oh!"

Heedless of her cries, Jonathan passed a handkerchief tightly over her son's mouth, and forced him out of the room.

When he returned, a moment or so afterwards, he found Sir Rowland standing by the lifeless body of his sister. His countenance was almost as white and rigid as that of the corpse by his side.

"This is your work," said the knight, sternly.

"Not entirely," replied Jonathan, calmly; "though I shouldn't be ashamed of it if it were. After all, you failed in obtaining the secret from her, Sir Rowland. Women are hypocrites to the last--true only to themselves."

"Peace!" cried the knight, fiercely.

"No offence," returned Jonathan. "I was merely about to observe that I am in possession of her secret."

"You!"

"Didn't I tell you that the fugitive Darrell gave me a glove! But we'll speak of this hereafter. You can *purchase* the information from me whenever you're so disposed. I shan't drive a hard bargain. To the point however. I came back to say, that I've placed your nephew in a coach; and, if you'll be at my lock in the Old Bailey an hour after midnight, you shall hear the last tidings of him."

"I will be there," answered Trenchard, gloomily.

"You'll not forget the thousand, Sir Rowland--short accounts, you know."

"Fear nothing. You shall have your reward."

"Thank'ee,--thank'ee. My house is the next door to the Cooper's Arms, in the Old Bailey, opposite Newgate. You'll find me at supper."

So saying, he bowed and departed.

"That man should have been an Italian bravo," murmured the knight, sinking into a chair: "he has neither fear nor compunction. Would I could purchase his apathy as easily as I can procure his assistance."

Soon after this Mrs. Norris entered the room, followed by Father Spencer. On approaching the couch, they found Sir Rowland senseless, and extended over the dead body of his unfortunate sister.

CHAPTER XI.
The Mohocks.

JONATHAN Wild, meanwhile, had quitted the house. He found a coach at the door, with the blinds carefully drawn up, and ascertained from a tall, ill-looking, though tawdrily-dressed fellow, who held his horse by the bridle, and whom he addressed as Quilt Arnold, that the two boys were safe inside, in the custody of Abraham Mendez, the dwarfish Jew. As soon as he had delivered his instructions to Quilt, who, with Abraham, constituted his body-guard, or janizaries, as he termed them, Jonathan mounted his steed, and rode off at a gallop. Quilt was not long in following his example. Springing upon the box, he told the coachman to make the best of his way to Saint Giles's. Stimulated by the promise of something handsome to drink, the man acquitted himself to admiration in the management of his lazy cattle. Crack went the whip, and away floundered the heavy vehicle through the deep ruts of the ill-kept road, or rather lane, (for it was little better,) which, then, led across Southampton Fields. Skirting the noble gardens of Montague House, (now, we need scarcely say, the British Museum,) the party speedily reached Great Russell Street,--a quarter described by Strype, in his edition of old Stow's famous *Survey*, "as being graced with the best buildings in all Bloomsbury, and the best inhabited by the nobility and gentry, especially the north side, as having gardens behind the houses, and the prospect of the pleasant fields up to Hampstead and Highgate; insomuch that this place, by physicians, is esteemed the most healthful of any in London." Neither of the parties outside bestowed much attention upon these stately and salubriously-situated mansions; indeed, as it was now not far from ten o'clock, and quite dark, they could scarcely discern them. But, in spite of his general insensibility to such matters, Quilt could not help commenting upon the delicious perfume wafted from the numerous flower-beds past which they were driving. The coachman answered by a surly grunt, and, plying his whip with redoubled zeal, shaped his course down Dyot Street; traversed that part of Holborn, which is now called Broad Street, and where two ancient alms-houses were, then, standing in the middle of that great thoroughfare, exactly opposite the opening of Compston Street; and, diving under a wide gateway on the left, soon reached a more open space, surrounded by mean habitations, coach-houses and stables, called Kendrick Yard, at the further end of which Saint Giles's round-house was situated.

No sooner did the vehicle turn the corner of this yard, than Quilt became aware, from the tumultuous sounds that reached his ears, as well as from the flashing of various lanterns at the door of the round-house, that some disturbance was going on; and, apprehensive of a rescue, if he drew up in the midst of the mob, he thought it prudent to come to a halt. Accordingly, he stopped the coach, dismounted, and hastened towards the assemblage, which, he was glad to find, consisted chiefly of a posse of watchmen and other guardians of the night. Quilt, who was an ardent lover of mischief, could not help laughing most heartily at the rueful appearance of these personages. Not one of them but bore the marks of having been engaged in a recent and severe conflict. Quarter-staves, bludgeons, brown-bills, lanterns, swords, and sconces were alike shivered; and, to judge from the sullied state of their habiliments, the claret must have been tapped pretty freely. Never was heard such a bawling as these unfortunate wights kept up. Oaths exploded like shells from a battery in full fire, accompanied by threats of direst vengeance against the individuals who had maltreated them. Here, might be seen a poor fellow whose teeth were knocked down his throat, spluttering out the most tremendous menaces, and gesticulating like a madman: there, another, whose nose was partially slit, vented imprecations and lamentations in the same breath. On the right, stood a bulky figure, with a broken rattle hanging out of his great-coat pocket, who held up a lantern to his battered countenance to prove to the spectators that both his orbs of vision were darkened: on the left, a meagre constable had divested himself of his shirt, to bind up with greater convenience a gaping cut in the arm.

"So, the Mohocks have been at work, I perceive," remarked Quilt, as he drew near the group.

"'Faith, an' you may say that," returned a watchman, who was wiping a ruddy stream from his brow; "they've broken the paice, and our pates into the bargain.

But shurely I'd know that vice," he added, turning his lantern towards the janizary. "Ah! Quilt Arnold, my man, is it you? By the powers! I'm glad to see you. The sight o' your 'andsome phiz allys does me good."

"I wish I could return the compliment, Terry. But your cracked skull is by no means a pleasing spectacle. How came you by the hurt, eh?"

"How did I come by it?--that's a nate question. Why, honestly enouch. It was lent me by a countryman o' mine; but I paid him back in his own coin--ha! ha!"

"A countryman of yours, Terry?"

"Ay, and a noble one, too, Quilt--more's the pity! You've heard of the Marquis of Slaughterford, belike?"

"Of course; who has not? He's the leader of the Mohocks, the general of the Scourers, the prince of rakes, the friend of the surgeons and glaziers, the terror of your tribe, and the idol of the girls!"

"That's him to a hair?" cried Terence, rapturously. "Och! he's a broth of a boy!"

"Why, I thought he'd broken your head, Terry?"

"Phooh! that's nothing? A piece o' plaster'll set all to rights; and Terry O'Flaherty's not the boy to care for the stroke of a supple-jack. Besides, didn't I tell you that I giv' him as good as he brought--and better! I jist touched him with my 'Evenin' Star,' as I call this shillelah," said the watchman, flourishing an immense bludgeon, the knob of which appeared to be loaded with lead, "and, by Saint Patrick! down he cum'd like a bullock."

"Zounds!" exclaimed Quilt, "did you kill him?"

"Not quite," replied Terence, laughing; "but I brought him to his senses."

"By depriving him of 'em, eh! But I'm sorry you hurt his lordship, Terry. Young noblemen ought to be indulged in their frolics. If they *do*, now and then, run away with a knocker, paint a sign, beat the watch, or huff a magistrate, they *pay* for their pastime, and that's sufficient. What more could any reasonable man--especially a watchman--desire? Besides, the Marquis, is a devilish fine fellow, and a particular friend of mine. There's not his peer among the peerage."

"Och! if he's a friend o' yours, my dear joy, there's no more to be said; and right sorry am I, I struck him. But, bloodan'-'ouns! man, if ould Nick himself were to hit me a blow, I'd be after givin' him another."

"Well, well--wait awhile," returned Quilt; "his lordship won't forget you. He's as generous as he's frolicsome."

As he spoke, the door of the round-house was opened, and a stout man, with a lantern in his hand, presented himself at the threshold.

"There's Sharples," cried Quilt.

"Whist!" exclaimed Terence; "he elevates his glim. By Jasus! he's about to spake to us."

"Gem'men o' the votch!" cried Sharples, as loudly as a wheezy cough would permit him, "my noble pris'ner--ough! ough;--the Markis o' Slaughterford----"

Further speech was cut short by a volley of execrations from the angry guardians of the night.

"No Mohocks! No Scourers!" cried the mob.

"Hear! hear!" vociferated Quilt.

"His lordship desires me to say--ough! ough!"

Fresh groans and hisses.

"Von't you hear me?--ough! ough!" demanded Sharples, after a pause.

"By all means," rejoined Quilt.

"Raise your vice, and lave off coughin'," added Terence.

"The long and the short o' the matter's this then," returned Sharples with dignity, "the Markis begs your acceptance o' ten guineas to drink his health."

The hooting was instantaneously changed to cheers.

"And his lordship, furthermore, requests me to state," proceeded Sharples, in a hoarse tone, "that he'll be responsible for the doctors' bill of all such gem'men as have received broken pates, or been otherwise damaged in the fray--ough! ough!"

"Hurrah!" shouted the mob.

"We're all damaged--we've all got broken pates," cried a dozen voices.

"Ay, good luck to him! so we have," rejoined Terence; "but we've no objection to take out the dochter's bill in drink."

"None whatever," replied the mob.

"Your answer, gem'men?" demanded Sharples.

"Long life to the Markis, and we accept his honourable proposal," responded the mob.

"Long life to the Marquis!" reiterated Terence; "he's an honour to ould Ireland!"

"Didn't I tell you how it would be?" remarked Quilt.

"Troth, and so did you," returned the watchman; "but I couldn't belave it. In futur', I'll keep the 'Evenin' Star' for his lordship's enemies."

"You'd better," replied Quilt. "But bring your glim this way. I've a couple of kinchens in yonder rattler, whom I wish to place under old Sharples's care."

"Be handy, then," rejoined Terence, "or, I'll lose my share of the smart money."

With the assistance of Terence, and a linkboy who volunteered his services, Quilt soon removed the prisoners from the coach, and leaving Sheppard to the custody of Abraham, proceeded to drag Thames towards the round-house. Not a word had been exchanged between the two boys on the road. Whenever Jack attempted to speak, he was checked by an angry growl from Abraham; and Thames, though his heart was full almost to bursting, felt no inclination to break the silence. His thoughts, indeed, were too painful for utterance, and so acute were his feelings, that, for some time, they quite overcame him. But his grief was of short duration. The elastic spirits of youth resumed their sway; and, before the coach stopped, his tears had ceased to flow. As to Jack Sheppard, he appeared utterly reckless and insensible, and did nothing but whistle and sing the whole way.

While he was dragged along in the manner just described, Thames looked around to ascertain, if possible, where he was; for he did not put entire faith in Jonathan's threat of sending him to the round-house, and apprehensive of something even worse than imprisonment. The aspect of the place, so far as he could discern through the gloom, was strange to him; but chancing to raise his eyes above the level of the surrounding habitations, he beheld, relieved against the sombre sky, the tall steeple of Saint Giles's church, the precursor of the present structure, which was not erected till some fifteen years later. He recognised this object at once. Jonathan had not deceived him.

"What's this here kinchen *in* for?" asked Terence, as he and Quilt strode along, with Thames between them.

"What for?" rejoined Quilt, evasively.

"Oh! nothin' partickler--mere curossity," replied Terence. "By the powers!" he added, turning his lantern full upon the face of the captive, "he's a nice genn-teel-lookin' kiddy, I must say. Pity he's ta'en to bad ways so airly."

"You may spare me your compassion, friend," observed Thames; "I am falsely detained."

"Of course," rejoined Quilt, maliciously; "every thief is so. If we were to wait till a prig was rightfully nabbed, we might tarry till doomsday. We never supposed you helped yourself to a picture set with diamonds--not we!"

"Is the guv'ner consarned in this job?" asked Terence, in a whisper.

"He is," returned Quilt, significantly. "Zounds! what's that!" he cried, as the noise of a scuffle was heard behind them. "The other kid's given my partner the slip. Here, take this youngster, Terry; my legs are lighter than old Nab's." And, committing Thames to the care of the watchman, he darted after the fugitive.

"Do you wish to earn a rich reward, my good friend?" said Thames to the watchman, as soon as they were left alone.

"Is it by lettin' you go, my darlin', that I'm to airn it?" inquired Terence. "If so, it won't pay. You're Mister Wild's pris'ner, and worse luck to it!"

"I don't ask you to liberate me," urged Thames; "but will you convey a message for me?"

"Where to, honey?"

"To Mr. Wood's, the carpenter in Wych Street. He lives near the Black Lion."

"The Black Lion!" echoed Terence. "I know the house well; by the same token that it's a flash crib. Och! many a mug o' bubb have I drained wi' the landlord, Joe Hind. And so Misther Wudd lives near the Black Lion, eh?"

"He does," replied Thames. "Tell him that I--his adopted son, Thames Darrell--am detained here by Jonathan Wild."

"Thames Ditton--is that your name?"

"No," replied the boy, impatiently; "Darrell--Thames Darrell."

"I'll not forget it. It's a mighty quare 'un, though. I never yet heard of a Christians as was named after the Shannon or the Liffy; and the Thames is no better than a dhurty puddle, compared wi' them two noble strames. But then you're an adopted son, and that makes all the difference. People do call their unlawful children strange names. Are you quite shure you haven't another alyas, Masther Thames Ditton?"

"Darrell, I tell you. Will you go? You'll be paid handsomely for your trouble."

"I don't mind the throuble," hesitated Terence, who was really a good-hearted fellow at the bottom; "and I'd like to sarve you if I could, for you look like a gentleman's son, and that goes a great way wi' me. But if Misther Wild were to find out that I thwarted his schames----"

"I'd not be in your skin for a trifle," interrupted Quilt, who having secured Sheppard, and delivered him to Abraham, now approached them unawares; "and it shan't be my fault if he don't hear of it."

"'Ouns!" ejaculated Terence, in alarm, "would you turn snitch on your old pal, Quilt?"

"Ay, if he plays a-cross," returned Quilt. "Come along, my sly shaver. With all your cunning, we're more than a match for you."

"But not for me," growled Terence, in an under tone.

"Remember!" cried Quilt, as he forced the captive along.

"Remember the devil!" retorted Terence, who had recovered his natural audacity. "Do you think I'm afeard of a beggarly thief-taker and his myrmidons? Not I. Master Thames Ditton, I'll do your biddin'; and you, Misther Quilt Arnold, may do your worst, I defy you."

"Dog!" exclaimed Quilt, turning fiercely upon him, "do you threaten?"

But the watchman eluded his grasp, and, mingling with the crowd, disappeared.

CHAPTER XII.
Saint Giles's Round-house.

SAINT Giles's Round-house was an old detached fabric, standing in an angle of Kendrick Yard. Originally built, as its name imports, in a cylindrical form, like a modern Martello tower, it had undergone, from time to time, so many alterations, that its symmetry was, in a great measure, destroyed. Bulging out more in the middle than at the two extremities, it resembled an enormous cask set on its end,--a sort of Heidelberg tun on a large scale,--and this resemblance was increased by the small circular aperture--it hardly deserved to be called a door--pierced, like the bung-hole of a barrell, through the side of the structure, at some distance from the ground, and approached by a flight of wooden steps. The prison was two stories high, with a flat roof surmounted by a gilt vane fashioned like a key; and, possessing considerable internal accommodation, it had, in its day, lodged some thousands of disorderly personages. The windows were small, and strongly grated, looking, in front, on Kendrick Yard, and, at the back, upon the spacious burial-ground of Saint Giles's Church. Lights gleamed from the lower rooms, and, on a nearer approach to the building, the sound of revelry might be heard from within.

Warned of the approach of the prisoners by the increased clamour, Sharples, who was busied in distributing the Marquis's donation, affected to throw the remainder of the money among the crowd, though, in reality, he kept back a couple of guineas, which he slipped into his sleeve, and running hastily up the steps, unlocked the door. He was followed, more leisurely, by the prisoners; and, during their ascent, Jack Sheppard made a second attempt to escape by ducking suddenly down, and endeavouring to pass under his conductor's legs. The dress of the dwarfish Jew was not, however, favourable to this expedient. Jack was caught, as in a trap, by the pendant tails of Abraham's long frock; and, instead of obtaining his release by his ingenuity, he only got a sound thrashing.

Sharples received them at the threshold, and holding his lantern towards the prisoners to acquaint himself with their features, nodded to Quilt, between whom and himself some secret understanding seemed to subsist, and then closed and barred the door.

"Vell," he growled, addressing Quilt, "you know who's here, I suppose?"

"To be sure I do," replied Quilt; "my noble friend, the Marquis of Slaughterford. What of that?"

"Vot 'o that!" echoed Sharples, peevishly: "Everythin'. Vot am I to do vith these young imps, eh?"

"What you generally do with your prisoners, Mr. Sharples," replied Quilt; "lock 'em up."

"That's easily said. But, suppose I've no place to lock 'em up in, how then?"

Quilt looked a little perplexed. He passed his arm under that of the constable, and drew him aside.

"Vell, vell," growled Sharples, after he had listened to the other's remonstrances, "it shall be done. But it's confounded inconvenient. One don't often get sich a vindfal as the Markis----"

"Or such a customer as Mr. Wild," edged in Quilt.

"Now, then, Saint Giles!" interposed Sheppard, "are we to be kept here all night?"

"Eh day!" exclaimed Sharples: "wot new-fledged bantam's this?"

"One that wants to go to roost," replied Sheppard. "So, stir your stumps, Saint Giles; and, if you mean to lock us up, use despatch."

"Comin'! comin'!" returned the constable, shuffling towards him.

"Coming!--so is midnight--so is Jonathan Wild," retorted Jack, with a significant look at Thames.

"Have you never an out-o-the-vay corner, into vich you could shtow these troublesome warmint?" observed Abraham. "The guv'ner'll be here afore midnight."

Darrell's attention was drawn to the latter part of this speech by a slight pressure on his foot. And, turning at the touch, he perceived Sheppard's glance fixed meaningly upon him.

"Stow it, Nab!" exclaimed Quilt, angrily; "the kinchen's awake."

"Awake!--to be sure I am, my flash cove," replied Sheppard; "I'm down as a hammer."

"I've just bethought me of a crib as'll serve their turn," interposed Sharples, "at any rate, they'll be out o' the vay, and as safe as two chicks in a coop."

"Lead the way to it then, Saint Giles," said Jack, in a tone of mock authority.

The place, in which they stood, was a small entrance-chamber, cut off, like the segment of a circle, from the main apartment, (of which it is needless to say it originally constituted a portion,) by a stout wooden partition. A door led to the inner room; and it was evident from the peals of merriment, and other noises, that, ever and anon, resounded from within, that this chamber was occupied by the Marquis and his friends. Against the walls hung an assortment of staves, brown-bills, (weapons then borne by the watch,) muskets, handcuffs, great-coats, and lanterns. In one angle of the room stood a disused fire-place, with a rusty grate and broken chimney-piece; in the other there was a sort of box, contrived between the wall and the boards, that looked like an apology for a cupboard. Towards this box Sharples directed his steps, and, unlocking a hatch in the door, disclosed a recess scarcely as large, and certainly not as clean, as a dog-kennel.

"Vill this do?" demanded the constable, taking the candle from the lantern, the better to display the narrow limits of the hole. "I call this ere crib the Little-Ease, artcr the runaway prentices' cells in Guildhall. I *have* squeezed three kids into it afore now. To be sure," he added, lowering his tone, "they wos little 'uns, and one on 'em was smothered--ough! ough!--how this cough chokes me!"

Sheppard, meanwhile, whose hands were at liberty, managed to possess himself, unperceived, of the spike of a halbert, which was lying, apart from the pole, upon a bench near him. Having secured this implement, he burst from his conductor, and, leaping into the hatch, as clowns generally spring into the clock-faces, when in pursuit of harlequin in the pantomime,--that is, back foremost,--broke into a fit of loud and derisive laughter, kicking his heels merrily all the time against the boards. His mirth, however, received an unpleasant check; for Abraham, greatly incensed by his previous conduct, caught him by the legs, and pushed him with such violence into the hole that the point of the spike, which he had placed in his pocket, found its way through his clothes to the flesh, inflicting a slight, but painful wound. Jack, who had something of the Spartan in his composition, endured his martyrdom without flinching; and carried his stoical indifference so far, as even to make a mocking grimace in Sharples's face, while that amiable functionary thrust Thames into the recess beside him.

"How go you like your quarters, sauce-box?" asked Sharples, in a jeering tone.

"Better than your company, Saint Giles," replied Sheppard; "so, shut the door, and make yourself scarce."

"That boy'll never rest till he finds his vay to Bridewell," observed Sharples.

"Or the street," returned Jack: "mind my words, the prison's not built that can keep me."

"We'll see that, young hempseed," replied Sharples, shutting the hatch furiously in his face, and locking it. "If you get out o' that cage, I'll forgive you. Now, come along, gem'men, and I'll show you some precious sport."

The two janizaries followed him as far as the entrance to the inner room, when Abraham, raising his finger to his lips, and glancing significantly in the direction of the boys, to explain his intention to his companions, closed the door after them, and stole softly back again, planting himself near the recess.

For a few minutes all was silent. At length Jack Sheppard observed:--"The coast's clear. They're gone into the next room."

Darrell returned no answer.

"Don't be angry with me, Thames," continued Sheppard, in a tone calculated, as he thought, to appease his companion's indignation. "I did all for the best, as I'll explain."

"I won't reproach you, Jack," said the other, sternly. "I've done with you."

"Not quite, I hope," rejoined Sheppard. "At all events, I've not done with you. If you owe your confinement to me, you shall owe your liberation to me, also."

"I'd rather lie here for ever, than be indebted to *you* for my freedom," returned Thames.

"I've done nothing to offend you," persisted Jack. "Nothing!" echoed the other, scornfully. "You've perjured yourself."

"That's my own concern," rejoined Sheppard. "An oath weighs little with me, compared with your safety."

"No more of this," interrupted Thames, "you make the matter worse by these excuses."

"Quarrel with me as much as you please, Thames, but hear me," returned Sheppard. "I took the course I pursued to serve you."

"Tush!" cried Thames; "you accused me to skreen yourself."

"On my soul, Thames, you wrong me!" replied Jack, passionately. "I'd lay down my life for yours."

"And you expect me to believe you after what has passed?"

"I do; and, more than that, I expect you to thank me."

"For procuring my imprisonment?"

"For saving your life."

"How?"

"Listen to me, Thames. You're in a more serious scrape than you imagine. I overheard Jonathan Wild's instructions to Quilt Arnold, and though he spoke in slang, and in an under tone, my quick ears, and acquaintance with the thieves' lingo, enabled me to make out every word he uttered. Jonathan is in league with Sir Rowland to make away with you. You are brought here that their designs may be carried into effect with greater security. Before morning, unless, we can effect an escape, you'll be kidnapped, or murdered, and your disappearance attributed to the negligence of the constable."

"Are you sure of this?" asked Thames, who, though as brave a lad as need be, could not repress a shudder at the intelligence.

"Certain. The moment I entered the room, and found you a prisoner in the hands of Jonathan Wild, I guessed how matters stood, and acted accordingly. Things haven't gone quite as smoothly as I anticipated; but they might have been worse. I *can* save you, and *will*. But, say we're friends."

"You're not deceiving me!" said Thames, doubtfully.

"I am not, by Heaven!" replied Sheppard, firmly.

"Don't swear, Jack, or I shall distrust you. I can't give you my hand; but you may take it."

"Thank you! thank you!" faltered Jack, in a voice full of emotion. "I'll soon free you from these bracelets."

"You needn't trouble yourself," replied Thames. "Mr. Wood will be here presently."

"Mr. Wood!" exclaimed Jack, in surprise. "How have you managed to communicate with him?"

Abraham, who had listened attentively to the foregoing conversation,--not a word of which escaped him,--now drew in his breath, and brought his ear closer to the boards.

"By means of the watchman who had the charge of me," replied Thames.

"Curse him!" muttered Abraham.

"Hist!" exclaimed Jack. "I thought I heard a noise. Speak lower. Somebody may be on the watch--perhaps, that old ginger-hackled Jew."

"I don't care if he is," rejoined Thames, boldly. "He'll learn that his plans will be defeated."

"He may learn how to defeat yours," replied Jack.

"So he may," rejoined Abraham, aloud, "so he may."

"Death and fiends!" exclaimed Jack; "the old thief *is* there. I knew it. You've betrayed yourself, Thames."

"Vot o' that?" chuckled Abraham. "*You* can shave him, you know."

"I *can*," rejoined Jack; "and you, too, old Aaron, if I'd a razor."

"How soon do you expect Mishter Vudd?" inquired the janizary, tauntingly.

"What's that to you?" retorted Jack, surlily.

"Because I shouldn't like to be out o' the vay ven he arrives," returned Abraham, in a jeering tone; "it vouldn't be vell bred."

"Vouldn't it!" replied Jack, mimicking his snuffling voice; "then shtay vere you are, and be cursed to you."

"It's all up," muttered Thames. "Mr. Wood will be intercepted. I've destroyed my only chance."

"Not your *only* chance, Thames," returned Jack, in the same undertone; "but your best. Never mind. We'll turn the tables upon 'em yet. Do you think we could manage that old clothesman between us, if we got out of this box?"

"I'd manage him myself, if my arms were free," replied Thames, boldly.

"Shpeak up, vill you?" cried Abraham, rapping his knuckles against the hatch. "I likes to hear vot you says. You *can* have no shecrets from me."

"Vy don't you talk to your partner, or Saint Giles, if you vant conversation,

Aaron?" asked Jack, slyly.

"Because they're in the next room, and the door's shut; that's vy, my jack-a-dandy!" replied Abraham, unsuspiciously.

"Oh! they are--are they?" muttered Jack, triumphantly; "that'll do. Now for it, Thames! Make as great a row as you can to divert his attention."

With this, he drew the spike from his pocket; and, drowning the sound of the operation by whistling, singing, shuffling, and other noises, contrived, in a few minutes, to liberate his companion from the handcuffs.

"Now, Jack," cried Thames, warmly grasping Sheppard's hand, "you are my friend again. I freely forgive you."

Sheppard cordially returned the pressure; and, cautioning Thames, "not to let the ruffles drop, or they might tell a tale," began to warble the following fragment of a robber melody:--

> "Oh! give me a chisel, a knife, or a file,
>   And the dubsmen shall find that I'll do it in style!
>   Tol-de-rol!"

"Vot the devil are you about, noisy?" inquired Abraham.

"Practising singing, Aaron," replied Jack. "Vot are you?"

"Practising patience," growled Abraham.

"Not before it's needed," returned Jack, aloud; adding in a whisper, "get upon my shoulders, Thames. Now you're up, take this spike. Feel for the lock, and prize it open,--you don't need to be told *how*. When it's done, I'll push you through. Take care of the old clothesman, and leave the rest to me.

> When the turnkey, next morning, stepp'd into his room,
>   The sight of the hole in the wall struck him dumb;
>   The sheriff's black bracelets lay strewn on the ground,
>   But the lad that had worn 'em could nowhere be found.
>   Tol-de-rol!"

As Jack concluded his ditty, the door flew open with a crash, and Thames sprang through the aperture.

This manoeuvre was so suddenly executed that it took Abraham completely by surprise. He was standing at the moment close to the hatch, with his ear at the keyhole, and received a severe blow in the face. He staggered back a few paces; and, before he could recover himself, Thames tripped up his heels, and, placing the point of the spike at his throat, threatened to stab him if he attempted to stir, or cry out. Nor had Jack been idle all this time. Clearing the recess the instant after his companion, he flew to the door of the inner room, and, locking it, took out the key. The policy of this step was immediately apparent. Alarmed by the noise of the scuffle, Quilt and Sharples rushed to the assistance of their comrade. But they were too late. The entrance was barred against them; and they had the additional mortification of hearing Sheppard's loud laughter at their discomfiture.

"I told you the prison wasn't built that could hold me," cried Jack.

"You're not out yet, you young hound," rejoined Quilt, striving ineffectually to burst open the door.

"But I soon shall be," returned Jack; "take these," he added, flinging the handcuffs against the wooden partition, "and wear 'em yourself."

"Halloo, Nab!" vociferated Quilt. "What the devil are you about! Will you allow yourself to be beaten by a couple of kids?"

"Not if I can help it," returned Abraham, making a desperate effort to regain his feet. "By my shalvation, boy," he added, fiercely, "if you don't take your hande off my peard, I'll sthrangle you."

"Help me, Jack!" shouted Thames, "or I shan't be able to keep the villain down."

"Stick the spike into him, then," returned Sheppard, coolly, "while I unbar the outlet."

But Thames had no intention of following his friend's advice. Contenting himself with brandishing the weapon in the Jew's eyes, he exerted all his force to prevent him from rising.

While this took place, while Quilt thundered at the inner door, and Jack drew back the bolts of the outer, a deep, manly voice was heard chanting--as if in contempt of the general uproar--the following strain:--

With pipe and punch upon the board,
    And smiling nymphs around us;
No tavern could more mirth afford
Than old Saint Giles's round-house!
        The round-house! the round-house!
    The jolly--jolly round-house!

"The jolly, jolly round-house!" chorussed Sheppard, as the last bar yielded to his efforts. "Hurrah! come along, Thames; we're free."

"Not sho fasht--not sho fasht!" cried Abraham, struggling with Thames, and detaining him; "if you go, you musht take me along vid you."

"Save yourself, Jack!" shouted Thames, sinking beneath the superior weight and strength of his opponent; "leave me to my fate!"

"Never," replied Jack, hurrying towards him. And, snatching the spike from Thames, he struck the janizary a severe blow on the head. "I'll make sure work this time," he added, about to repeat the blow.

"Hold!" interposed Thames, "he can do no more mischief. Let us be gone."

"As you please," returned Jack, leaping up; "but I feel devilishly inclined to finish him. However, it would only be robbing the hangman of his dues."

With this, he was preparing to follow his friend, when their egress was prevented by the sudden appearance of Jonathan Wild and Blueskin.

CHAPTER XIII.
The Magdalene.

THE household of the worthy carpenter, it may be conceived, was thrown into the utmost confusion and distress by the unaccountable disappearance of the two boys. As time wore on, and they did not return, Mr. Wood's anxiety grew so insupportable, that he seized his hat with the intention of sallying forth in search of them, though he did not know whither to bend his steps, when his departure was arrested by a gentle knock at the door.

"There he is!" cried Winifred, starting up, joyfully, and proving by the exclamation that her thoughts were dwelling upon one subject only. "There he is!"

"I fear not," said her father, with a doubtful shake of the head. "Thames would let himself in; and Jack generally finds an entrance through the backdoor or the shop-window, when he has been out at untimely hours. But, go and see who it is, love. Stay! I'll go myself."

His daughter, however, anticipated him. She flew to the door, but returned the next minute, looking deeply disappointed, and bringing the intelligence that it was "only Mrs. Sheppard."

"Who?" almost screamed Mrs. Wood.

"Jack Sheppard's mother," answered the little girl, dejectedly; "she has brought a basket of eggs from Willesden, and some flowers for you."

"For me!" vociferated Mrs. Wood, in indignant surprise. "Eggs for me! You mistake, child. They must be for your father."

"No; I'm quite sure she said they're for you," replied Winifred; "but she *does* want to see father."

"I thought as much," sneered Mrs. Wood.

"I'll go to her directly," said Wood, bustling towards the door. "I dare say she has called to inquire about Jack."

"I dare say no such thing," interposed his better half, authoritatively; "remain where you are, Sir."

"At all events, let me send her away, my dear," supplicated the carpenter, anxious to avert the impending storm.

"Do you hear me?" cried the lady, with increasing vehemence. "Stir a foot, at your peril."

"But, my love," still remonstrated Wood, "you know I'm going to look after the boys----"

"After Mrs. Sheppard, you mean, Sir," interrupted his wife, ironically. "Don't think to deceive me by your false pretences. Marry, come up! I'm not so easily deluded. Sit down, I command you. Winny, show the person into this room. I'll see her myself; and that's more than she bargained for, I'll be sworn."

Finding it useless to struggle further, Mr. Wood sank, submissively, into a chair, while his daughter hastened to execute her arbitrary parent's commission.

"At length, I have my wish," continued Mrs. Wood, regarding her husband with a glance of vindictive triumph. "I shall behold the shameless hussy, face to face; and, if I find her as good-looking as she's represented, I don't know what I'll do in the end; but I'll begin by scratching her eyes out."

In this temper, it will naturally be imagined, that Mrs. Wood's reception of the widow, who, at that moment, was ushered into the room by Winifred, was not particularly kind and encouraging. As she approached, the carpenter's wife eyed her from head to foot, in the hope of finding something in her person or apparel to quarrel with. But she was disappointed. Mrs. Sheppard's dress--extremely neat and clean, but simply fashioned, and of the plainest and most unpretending material,--offered nothing assailable; and her demeanour was so humble, and her looks so modest, that--if she had been ill-looking--she might, possibly, have escaped the shafts of malice preparing to be levelled against her. But, alas! she was beautiful--and beauty is a crime not to be forgiven by a jealous woman.

As the lapse of time and change of circumstances have wrought a remarkable alteration in the appearance of the poor widow, it may not be improper to notice it here. When first brought under consideration, she was a miserable and forlorn object; squalid in attire, haggard in looks, and emaciated in frame. Now, she was the very reverse of all this. Her dress, it has just been said, was neatness and simplicity itself. Her figure, though slight, had all the fulness of health; and her complexion--still pale, but without its former sickly cast,--contrasted agreeably, by its extreme fairness, with the dark brows and darker lashes that shaded eyes which, if they had lost some of their original brilliancy, had gained infinitely more in the soft and chastened lustre that replaced it. One marked difference between the poor outcast, who, oppressed by poverty, and stung by shame, had sought temporary relief in the stupifying draught,--that worst "medicine of a mind diseased,"--and those of the same being, freed from her vices, and restored to comfort and contentment, if not to happiness, by a more prosperous course of events, was exhibited in the mouth. For the fresh and feverish hue of lip which years ago characterised this feature, was now substituted a pure and wholesome bloom, evincing a total change of habits; and, though the coarse character of the mouth remained, in some degree, unaltered, it was so modified in expression, that it could no longer be accounted a blemish. In fact, the whole face had undergone a transformation. All its better points were improved, while the less attractive ones (and they were few in comparison) were subdued, or removed. What was yet more worthy of note was, that the widow's countenance had an air of refinement about it, of which it was utterly destitute before, and which seemed to intimate that her true position in society was far above that wherein accident had placed her.

"Well, Mrs. Sheppard," said the carpenter, advancing to meet her, and trying to look as cheerful and composed as he could; "what brings you to town, eh?--Nothing amiss, I trust?"

"Nothing whatever, Sir," answered the widow. "A neighbour offered me a drive to Paddington; and, as I haven't heard of my son for some time, I couldn't resist the temptation of stepping on to inquire after him, and to thank you for your great goodness to us both, I've brought a little garden-stuff and a few new-laid eggs for you, Ma'am," she added turning to Mrs. Wood, who appeared to be collecting her energies for a terrible explosion, "in the hope that they may prove acceptable. Here's a nosegay for you, my love," she continued, opening her basket, and presenting a fragrant bunch of flowers to Winifred, "if your mother will allow me to give it you."

"Don't touch it, Winny!" screamed Mrs. Wood, "it may be poisoned."

"I'm not afraid, mother," said the little girl, smelling at the bouquet. "How sweet these roses are! Shall I put them into water?"

"Put them where they came from," replied Mrs. Wood, severely, "and go to bed."

"But, mother, mayn't I sit up to see whether Thames returns?" implored Winifred.

"What can it matter to you whether he returns or not, child," rejoined Mrs. Wood, sharply. "I've spoken. And my word's law--with *you*, at least," she added, bestowing a cutting glance upon her husband.

The little girl uttered no remonstrance; but, replacing the flowers in the basket, burst into tears, and withdrew.

Mrs. Sheppard, who witnessed this occurrence with dismay, looked timorously at Wood, in expectation of some hint being given as to the course she had better pursue; but, receiving none, for the carpenter was too much agitated to attend to her, she ventured to express a fear that she was intruding.

"Intruding!" echoed Mrs. Wood; "to be sure you are! I wonder how you dare show your face in this house, hussy!"

"I thought you sent for me, Ma'am," replied the widow, humbly.

"So I did," retorted Mrs. Wood; "and I did so to see how far your effrontery would carry you."

"I'm sure I'm very sorry. I hope I haven't given any unintentional offence?" said the widow, again meekly appealing to Wood.

"Don't exchange glances with him under my very nose, woman!" shrieked Mrs. Wood; "I'll not bear it. Look at me, and answer me one question. And, mind! no prevaricating--nothing but the truth will satisfy me."

Mrs. Sheppard raised her eyes, and fixed them upon her interrogator.

"Are you not that man's mistress?" demanded Mrs. Wood, with a look meant to reduce her supposed rival to the dust.

"I am no man's mistress," answered the widow, crimsoning to her temples, but preserving her meek deportment, and humble tone.

"That's false!" cried Mrs. Wood. "I'm too well acquainted with your proceedings, Madam, to believe that. Profligate women are never reclaimed. *He* has told me sufficient of you--"

"My dear," interposed Wood, "for goodness' sake--"

"I *will* speak," screamed his wife, totally disregarding the interruption; "I *will* tell this worthless creature what I know about her,--and what I think of her."

"Not now, my love--not now," entreated Wood.

"Yes, *now*," rejoined the infuriated dame; "perhaps, I may never have another opportunity. She has contrived to keep out of my sight up to this time, and I've no doubt she'll keep out of it altogether for the future."

"That was my doing, dearest," urged the carpenter; "I was afraid if you saw her that some such scene as this might occur."

"Hear me, Madam, I beseech you," interposed Mrs. Sheppard, "and, if it please you to visit your indignation on any one let it be upon me, and not on your excellent husband, whose only fault is in having bestowed his charity upon so unworthy an object as myself."

"Unworthy, indeed!" sneered Mrs. Wood.

"To him I owe everything," continued the widow, "life itself--nay, more than life,--for without his assistance I should have perished, body and soul. He has been a father to me and my child."

"I never doubted the latter point, I assure you, Madam," observed Mrs. Wood.

"You have said," pursued the widow, "that she, who has once erred, is irreclaimable. Do not believe it, Madam. It is not so. The poor wretch, driven by desperation to the commission of a crime which her soul abhors, is no more beyond the hope of reformation than she is without the pale of mercy. I have suffered--I have sinned--I have repented. And, though neither peace nor innocence can be restored to my bosom; though tears cannot blot out my offences, nor sorrow drown my shame; yet, knowing that my penitence is sincere, I do not despair that my transgressions may be forgiven."

"Mighty fine!" ejaculated Mrs. Wood, contemptuously.

"You cannot understand me, Madam; and it is well you cannot. Blest with a fond husband, surrounded by every comfort, *you have never been assailed by the horrible temptations to which misery has exposed me*. You have never known what it is to want food, raiment, shelter. You have never seen the child within your arms perishing from hunger, and no relief to be obtained. You have never felt the hearts of all hardened against you; have never heard the jeer or curse from every lip; nor endured the insult and the blow from every hand. I *have* suffered all this. I could resist the tempter *now*, I am strong in health,--in mind. But *then*--Oh! Madam, there are moments--moments of darkness, which overshadow a whole existence--in the lives of the poor houseless wretches who traverse the streets, when reason is well-nigh benighted; when the horrible promptings of despair can, alone, be listened to; and when vice itself assumes the aspect of virtue. Pardon what I have said, Madam. I do not desire to extenuate my guilt--far less to defend it; but I would show you, and such as you--who, happily, are exempted from trials like mine--how much misery has to do with crime. And I affirm to you, on my own conviction, that she who falls, because she has not strength granted her to struggle with affliction, *may* be reclaimed,--may repent, and be forgiven,--even as she, whose sins, 'though many, were forgiven her'.

"It gladdens me to hear you talk thus, Joan," said Wood, in a voice of much emotion, while his eyes filled with tears, "and more than repays me for all I have done for you."

"If professions of repentance constitute a Magdalene, Mrs. Sheppard is one, no doubt," observed Mrs. Wood, ironically; "but I used to think it required something more than *mere words* to prove that a person's character was abused."

"Very right, my love," said Wood, "very sensibly remarked. So it does. Bu I can speak to that point. Mrs. Sheppard's conduct, from my own personal knowledge, has been unexceptionable for the last twelve years. During that period she has been a model of propriety."

"Oh! of course," rejoined Mrs. Wood; "I can't for an instant question such distinterested testimony. Mrs. Sheppard, I'm sure, will say as much for you. He's a model of conjugal attachment and fidelity, a pattern to his family, and an example to his neighbours. Ain't he, Madam?'"

"He is, indeed," replied the widow, fervently; "more--much more than that."

"He's no such thing!" cried Mrs. Wood, furiously. "He's a base, deceitful, tyrannical, hoary-headed libertine--that's what he is. But, I'll expose him. I'll proclaim his misdoings to the world; and, then, we shall see where he'll stand. Marry, come up! I'll show him what an injured wife can do. If all wives were of my mind and my spirit, husbands would soon be taught their own insignificance. But a time *will* come (and that before long,) when our sex will assert its superiority; and, when we have got the upper hand, let 'em try to subdue us if they can. But don't suppose, Madam, that anything I say has reference to you. I'm speaking of virtuous women-- of WIVES, Madam. Mistresses neither deserve consideration nor commiseration."

"I expect no commiseration," returned Mrs. Sheppard, gently, "nor do I need any. But, rather than be the cause of any further misunderstanding between you and my benefactor, I will leave London and its neighbourhood for ever."

"Pray do so, Madam," retorted Mrs. Wood, "and take your son with you."

"My son!" echoed the widow, trembling.

"Yes, your son, Madam. If you can do any good with him, it's more than we can. The house will be well rid of him, for a more idle, good-for-nothing reprobate never crossed its threshold."

"Is this true, Sir?" cried Mrs. Sheppard, with an agonized look at Wood. "I know you'll not deceive me. Is Jack what Mrs. Wood represents him?"

"He's not exactly what I could desire him to be, Joan," replied the carpenter, reluctantly, "But a ragged colt sometimes makes the best horse. He'll mend, I hope."

"Never," said Mrs. Wood,--"he'll never mend. He has taken more than one step towards the gallows already. Thieves and pickpockets are his constant companions."

"Thieves!" exclaimed Mrs. Sheppard, horror-stricken.

"Jonathan Wild and Blueskin have got him into their hands," continued Mrs. Wood.

"Impossible!" exclaimed the widow, wildly.

"If you doubt my word, woman," replied the carpenter's wife, coldly, "ask Mr. Wood."

"I know you'll contradict it, Sir," said the widow, looking at Wood as if she dreaded to have her fears confirmed,--"I know you will."

"I wish I could, Joan," returned the carpenter, sadly.

Mrs. Sheppard let fall her basket.

"My son," she murmured, wringing her hands piteously--, "my son the companion of thieves! My son in Jonathan Wild's power! It cannot be."

"Why not?" rejoined Mrs. Wood, in a taunting tone. "Your son's father was a thief; and Jonathan Wild (unless I'm misinformed,) was his friend,--so it's not unnatural he should show some partiality towards Jack."

"Jonathan Wild was my husband's bitterest enemy," said Mrs. Sheppard. "He first seduced him from the paths of honesty, and then betrayed him to a shameful death, and he has sworn to do the same thing by my son. Oh, Heavens; that I should have ever indulged a hope of happiness while that terrible man lives!"

"Compose yourself, Joan," said Wood; "all will yet be well."

"Oh, no,--no," replied Mrs. Sheppard, distractedly. "All cannot be well, if this is true. Tell me, Sir," she added, with forced calmness, and grasping Wood's arm; "what has Jack done? Tell me in a word, that I may know the worst. I can bear anything but suspense."

"You're agitating yourself unnecessarily, Joan," returned Wood, in a soothing voice. "Jack has been keeping bad company. That's the only fault I know of."

"Thank God for that!" ejaculated Mrs. Sheppard, fervently. "Then it is not too late to save him. Where is he, Sir? Can I see him?"

"No, that you can't," answered Mrs. Wood; "he has gone out without leave, and has taken Thames Darrell with him. If I were Mr. Wood, when he does return, I'd send him about his business. I wouldn't keep an apprentice to set my authority at defiance."

Mr. Wood's reply, if he intended any, was cut short by a loud knocking at the door.

"'Odd's-my-life!--what's that?" he cried, greatly alarmed.

"It's Jonathan Wild come back with a troop of constables at his heels, to search the house," rejoined Mrs. Wood, in equal trepidation. "We shall all be murdered. Oh! that Mr. Kneebone were here to protect me!"

"If it is Jonathan," rejoined Wood, "it is very well for Mr. Kneebone he's not here. He'd have enough to do to protect himself, without attending to you. I declare I'm almost afraid to go to the door. Something, I'm convinced, has happened to the boys."

"Has Jonathan Wild been here to-day?" asked Mrs. Sheppard, anxiously.

"To be sure he has!" returned Mrs. Wood; "and Blueskin, too. They're only just gone, mercy on us! what a clatter," she added, as the knocking was repeated more violently than before.

While the carpenter irresolutely quitted the room, with a strong presentiment of ill upon his mind, a light quick step was heard descending the stairs, and before he could call out to prevent it, a man was admitted into the passage.

"Is this Misther Wudd's, my pretty miss?" demanded the rough voice of the Irish watchman.

"It is", seplied Winifred; "have you brought any tidings of Thames Darrell!"

"Troth have I!" replied Terence: "but, bless your angilic face, how did you contrive to guess that?"

"Is he well?--is he safe?--is he coming back," cried the little girl, disregarding the question.

"He's in St. Giles's round-house," answered Terence; "but tell Mr. Wudd I'm here, and have brought him a message from his unlawful son, and don't be detainin' me, my darlin', for there's not a minute to lose if the poor lad's to be recused from the clutches of that thief and thief-taker o' the wurld, Jonathan Wild."

The carpenter, upon whom no part of this hurried dialogue had been lost, now made his appearance, and having obtained from Terence all the information which that personage could impart respecting the perilous situation of Thames, he declared himself ready to start to Saint Giles's at once, and ran back to the room for his hat and stick; expressing his firm determination, as he pocketed his constable's staff with which he thought it expedient to arm himself, of being direfully revenged upon the thief-taker: a determination in which he was strongly encouraged by his wife. Terence, meanwhile, who had followed him, did not remain silent, but recapitulated his story, for the benefit of Mrs. Sheppard. The poor widow was thrown into an agony of distress on learning that a robbery had been committed, in which her son (for she could not doubt that Jack was one of the boys,) was implicated; nor was her anxiety alleviated by Mrs. Wood, who maintained stoutly, that if Thames had been led to do wrong, it must be through the instrumentality of his worthless companion.

"And there you're right, you may dipind, marm," observed Terence. "Master Thames Ditt--what's his blessed name?--has honesty written in his handsome phiz; but as to his companion, Jack Sheppard, I think you call him, he's a born and bred thief. Lord bless you marm! we sees plenty on 'em in our purfession. Them young prigs is all alike. I seed he was one,--and a sharp un, too,--at a glance."

"Oh!" exclaimed the widow, covering her face with her hands.

"Take a drop of brandy before we start, watchman," said Wood, pouring out a glass of spirit, and presenting it to Terence, who smacked his lips as he disposed of it. "Won't you be persuaded, Joan?" he added, making a similar offer to Mrs. Sheppard, which she gratefully declined. "If you mean to accompany us, you may need it."

"You are very kind, Sir," returned the widow, "but I require no support. Nothing stronger than water has passed my lips for years."

"We may believe as much of that as we please, I suppose," observed the carpenter's wife, with a sneer. "Mr. Wood," she continued, in an authoritative tone, seeing her husband ready to depart, "one word before you set out. If Jack Sheppard or his mother ever enter this house again, I leave it--that's all. Now, do what you please. You know *my* fixed determination."

Mr. Wood made no reply; but, hastily kissing his weeping daughter, and bidding her be of good cheer, hurried off. He was followed with equal celerity by Terence and the widow. Traversing what remained of Wych Street at a rapid pace, and speeding along Drury Lane, the trio soon found themselves in Kendrick Yard. When they came to the round-house, Terry's courage failed him. Such was the terror inspired by Wild's vindictive character, that few durst face him who had given him cause for displeasure. Aware that he should incur the thief-taker's bitterest animosity by what he had done, the watchman, whose wrath against Quilt Arnold had evaporated during the walk, thought it more prudent not to hazard a meeting with his master, till the storm had, in some measure, blown over. Accordingly, having given Wood such directions as he thought necessary for his guidance, and received a handsome gratuity in return for his services, he departed.

It was not without considerable demur and delay on the part of Sharples that the carpenter and his companion could gain admittance to the round-house. Reconnoitring them through a small grated loophole, he refused to open the door till they had explained their business. This, Wood, acting upon Terry's caution, was most unwilling to do; but, finding he had no alternative, he reluctantly made known his errand and the bolts were undrawn. Once in, the constable's manner appeared totally changed. He was now as civil as he had just been insolent. Apologizing for their detention, he answered the questions put to him respecting the boys, by positively denying that any such prisoners had been entrusted to his charge, but offered to conduct him to every cell in the building to prove the truth of his assertion. He then barred and double-locked the door, took out the key, (a precautionary measure which, with a grim smile, he said he never omitted,) thrust it into his vest, and motioning the couple to follow him, led the way to the inner room. As Wood obeyed, his foot slipped; and, casting his eyes upon the floor, he perceived it splashed in several places with blood. From the freshness of the stains, which grew more frequent as they approached the adjoining chamber, it was evident some violence had been recently perpetrated, and the carpenter's own blood froze within his veins as he thought, with a thrill of horror, that, perhaps on this very spot, not many minutes before his arrival, his adopted son might have been inhumanly butchered. Nor was this impression removed as he stole a glance at Mrs. Sheppard, and saw from her terrified look that she had made the same alarming discovery as himself. But it was now too late to turn back, and, nerving himself for the shock he expected to encounter, he ventured after his conductor. No sooner had they entered the room than Sharples, who waited to usher them in, hastily retreated, closed the door, and turning the key, laughed loudly at the success of his stratagem. Vexation at his folly in suffering himself to be thus entrapped kept Wood for a short time silent. When he could find words, he tried by the most urgent solicitations to prevail upon the constable to let him out. But threats and entreaties--even promises were ineffectual; and the unlucky captive, after exhausting his powers of persuasion, was compelled to give up the point.

The room in which he was detained--that lately occupied by the Mohocks, who, it appeared, had been allowed to depart,--was calculated to inspire additional apprehension and disgust. Strongly impregnated with the mingled odours of tobacco, ale, brandy, and other liquors, the atmosphere was almost stifling. The benches running round the room, though fastened to the walls by iron clamps, had been forcibly wrenched off; while the table, which was similarly secured to the boards, was upset, and its contents--bottles, jugs, glasses, and bowls were broken and scattered about in all directions. Everything proclaimed the mischievous propensities of the recent occupants of the chamber.

Here lay a heap of knockers of all sizes, from the huge lion's head to the small brass rapper: there, a collection of sign-boards, with the names and calling of the owners utterly obliterated. On this side stood the instruments with which the latter piece of pleasantry had been effected,--namely, a bucket filled with paint and a brush: on that was erected a trophy, consisting of a watchman's rattle, a laced hat, with the crown knocked out, and its place supplied by a lantern, a campaign wig saturated with punch, a torn steen-kirk and ruffles, some half-dozen staves, and a broken sword.

As the carpenter's gaze wandered over this scene of devastation, his attention was drawn by Mrs. Sheppard towards an appalling object in one corner. This was the body of a man, apparently lifeless, and stretched upon a mattress, with his head bound up in a linen cloth, through which the blood had oosed. Near the body, which, it will be surmised, was that of Abraham Mendez, two ruffianly person-ages were seated, quietly smoking, and bestowing no sort of attention upon the new-comers. Their conversation was conducted in the flash language, and, though unintelligible to Wood, was easily comprehended by this companion, who learnt, to her dismay, that the wounded man had received his hurt from her son, whose courage and dexterity formed the present subject of their discourse. From other obscure hints dropped by the speakers, Mrs. Sheppard ascertained that Thames Darrell had been carried off--where she could not make out--by Jonathan Wild and Quilt Arnold; and that Jack had been induced to accompany Blueskin to the Mint. This intelligence, which she instantly communicated to the carpenter, drove him almost frantic. He renewed his supplications to Sharples, but with no better success than heretofore; and the greater part of the night was passed by him and the poor widow, whose anxiety, if possible, exceeded his own, in the most miserable state imaginable.

At length, about three o'clock, as the first glimmer of dawn became visible through the barred casements of the round-house, the rattling of bolts and chains at the outer door told that some one was admitted. Whoever this might be, the visit seemed to have some reference to the carpenter, for, shortly afterwards, Sharples made his appearance, and informed the captives they were free. Without waiting to have the information repeated, Wood rushed forth, determined as soon as he could procure assistance, to proceed to Jonathan Wild's house in the Old Bailey; while Mrs. Sheppard, whose maternal fears drew her in another direction, hurried off to the Mint.

CHAPTER XIV.
The Flash Ken.

IN an incredibly short space of time,--for her anxiety lent wings to her feet,--Mrs. Sheppard reached the debtor's garrison. From a scout stationed at the northern entrance, whom she addressed in the jargon of the place, with which long usage had formerly rendered her familiar, she ascertained that Blueskin, accompanied by a youth, whom she knew by the description must be her son, had arrived there about three hours before, and had proceeded to the Cross Shovels. This was enough for the poor widow. She felt she was now near her boy, and, nothing doubting her ability to rescue him from his perilous situation, she breathed a fervent prayer for his deliverance; and bending her steps towards the tavern in question, revolved within her mind as she walked along the best means of accomplishing her purpose. Aware of the cunning and desperate characters of the persons with whom she would have to deal,--aware, also, that she was in a quarter where no laws could be appealed to, nor assistance obtained, she felt the absolute necessity of caution. Accordingly, when she arrived at the Shovels, with which, as an old haunt in her bygone days of wretchedness she was well acquainted, instead of entering the principal apartment, which she saw at a glance was crowded with company of both sexes, she turned into a small room on the left of the bar, and, as an excuse for so doing, called for something to drink. The drawers at the moment were too busy to attend to her, and she would have seized the opportunity of examining, unperceived, the assemblage within, through a little curtained window that overlooked the adjoining chamber, if an impediment had not existed in the shape of Baptist Kettleby, whose portly person entirely obscured the view. The Master of the Mint, in the exercise of his two-fold office of governor and publican, was mounted upon a chair, and holding forth to his guests in a speech, to which Mrs. Sheppard was unwillingly compelled to listen.

"Gentlemen of the Mint," said the orator, "when I was first called, some fifty years ago, to the important office I hold, there existed across the water three places of refuge for the oppressed and persecuted debtor."

"We know it," cried several voices.

"It happened, gentlemen," pursued the Master, "on a particular occasion, about the time I've mentioned, that the Archduke of Alsatia, the Sovereign of the Savoy, and the Satrap of Salisbury Court, met by accident at the Cross Shovels. A jolly night we made of it, as you may suppose; for four such monarchs don't often come together. Well, while we were smoking our pipes, and quaffing our punch, Alsatia turns to me and says, 'Mint,' says he, 'you're well off here.'--'Pretty well,' says I; 'you're not badly off at the Friars, for that matter.'--'Oh! yes we are,' says he.--'How so?' says I.--'It's all up with us,' says he; 'they've taken away our charter.'--'They can't,' says I.--'They have,' says he.--'They can't, I tell you,' says I, in a bit of a passion; 'it's unconstitutional.'--'Unconstitutional or not,' says Salisbury Court and Savoy, speaking together, 'it's true. We shall become a prey to the Philistines, and must turn honest in self-defence.'--'No fear o' that,' thought I.--'I see how it'll be,' observed Alsatia, 'everybody'll pay his debts, and only think of such a state of things as that.'--'It's *not* to be thought of,' says I, thumping the table till every glass on it jingled; 'and I know a way as'll prevent it.'--'What is it, Mint?' asked all three.--'Why, hang every bailiff that sets a foot in your territories, and you're safe,' says I.--'We'll do it,' said they, filling their glasses, and looking as fierce as King George's grenadier guards; 'here's your health, Mint.' But, gentlemen, though they talked so largely, and looked so fiercely, they did *not* do it; they did *not* hang the bailiffs; and where are they?"

"Ay, where are they?" echoed the company with indignant derision.

"Gentlemen," returned the Master, solemnly, "it is a question easily answered--they are NOWHERE! Had they hanged the bailiffs, the bailiffs would not have hanged them. We ourselves have been similarly circumstanced. Attacked by an infamous and unconstitutional statute, passed in the reign of the late usurper, William of Orange, (for I may remark that, if the right king had been upon the throne, that illegal enactment would never have received the royal assent--the Stuarts-- Heaven preserve 'em!--always siding with the debtors); attacked in this outrageous

manner, I repeat, it has been all but '*up*' with US! But the vigorous resistance offered on that memorable occasion by the patriotic inhabitants of Bermuda to the
aggressions of arbitrary power, secured and established their privileges on a firm-
er basis than heretofore; and, while their pusillanimous allies were crushed and
annihilated, they became more prosperous than ever. Gentlemen, I am proud to
say that I originated--that I directed those measures. I hope to see the day, when
not Southwark alone, but London itself shall become one Mint,--when all men
shall be debtors, and none creditors,--when imprisonment for debt shall be utterly abolished,--when highway-robbery shall be accounted a pleasant pastime, and
forgery an accomplishment,--when Tyburn and its gibbets shall be overthrown,-
-capital punishments discontinued,--Newgate, Ludgate, the Gatehouse, and the
Compters razed to the ground,--Bridewell and Clerkenwell destroyed,--the Fleet,
the King's Bench, and the Marshalsea remembered only by name! But, in the mean
time, as that day may possibly be farther off than I anticipate, we are bound to make
the most of the present. Take care of yourselves, gentlemen, and your governor will
take care of you. Before I sit down, I have a toast to propose, which I am sure will be
received, as it deserves to be, with enthusiasm. It is the health of a stranger,--of Mr.
John Sheppard. His father was one of my old customers, and I am happy to find his
son treading in his steps. He couldn't be in better hands than those in which he has
placed himself. Gentlemen,--Mr. Sheppard's good health, and success to him!"

Baptist's toast was received with loud applause, and, as he sat down amid the
cheers of the company, and a universal clatter of mugs and glasses, the widow's
view was no longer obstructed. Her eye wandered quickly over that riotous and
disorderly assemblage, until it settled upon one group more riotous and disorderly
than the rest, of which her son formed the principal figure. The agonized mother
could scarcely repress a scream at the spectacle that met her gaze. There sat Jack,
evidently in the last stage of intoxication, with his collar opened, his dress disar-
ranged, a pipe in his mouth, a bowl of punch and a half-emptied rummer before
him,--there he sat, receiving and returning, or rather attempting to return,--for he
was almost past consciousness,--the blandishments of a couple of females, one of
whom had passed her arm round his neck, while the other leaned over the back of
his chair and appeared from her gestures to be whispering soft nonsense into his
ear.

Both these ladies possessed considerable personal attractions. The younger of the two, who was seated next to Jack, and seemed to monopolize his attention, could not be more than seventeen, though her person had all the maturity of twenty. She had delicate oval features, light, laughing blue eyes, a pretty *nez retrousse*, (why have we not the term, since we have the best specimens of the feature?) teeth of pearly whiteness, and a brilliant complexion, set off by rich auburn hair, a very white neck and shoulders,--the latter, perhaps, a trifle too much exposed. The name of this damsel was Edgeworth Bess; and, as her fascinations will not, perhaps, be found to be without some influence upon the future fortunes of her boyish admirer, we have thought it worth while to be thus particular in describing them. The other *bona roba*, known amongst her companions as Mistress Poll Maggot, was a beauty on a much larger scale,--in fact, a perfect Amazon. Nevertheless though nearly six feet high, and correspondingly proportioned, she was a model of symmetry, and boasted, with the frame of a Thalestris or a Trulla, the regular lineaments of the Medicean Venus. A man's laced hat,--whether adopted from the caprice of the moment, or habitually worn, we are unable to state,--cocked knowingly on her head, harmonized with her masculine appearance. Mrs. Maggot, as well as her companion Edgeworth Bess, was showily dressed; nor did either of them disdain the aid supposed to be lent to a fair skin by the contents of the patchbox. On an empty cask, which served him for a chair, and opposite Jack Sheppard, whose rapid progress in depravity afforded him the highest satisfaction, sat Blueskin, encouraging the two women in their odious task, and plying his victim with the glass as often as he deemed it expedient to do so. By this time, he had apparently accomplished all he desired; for moving the bottle out of Jack's reach, he appropriated it entirely to his own use, leaving the devoted lad to the care of the females. Some few of the individuals seated at the other tables seemed to take an interest in the proceedings of Blueskin and his party, just as a bystander watches any other game; but, generally speaking, the company were too much occupied with their own concerns to pay attention to anything else. The assemblage was for the most part, if not altogether, composed of persons to whom vice in all its aspects was too familiar to present much of novelty, in whatever form it was exhibited. Nor was Jack by any means the only stripling in the room. Not far from him was a knot of lads drinking, swearing, and playing at dice as eagerly and as skilfully as any of the older hands.

Near to these hopeful youths sat a fence, or receiver, bargaining with a clouter, or pickpocket, for a *suit*,--or, to speak in more intelligible language, a watch and seals, two *cloaks*, commonly called watch-cases, and a wedge-lobb, otherwise known as a silver snuff-box. Next to the receiver was a gang of housebreakers, laughing over their exploits, and planning fresh depredations; and next to the housebreakers came two gallant-looking gentlemen in long periwigs and riding-dresses, and equipped in all other respects for the road, with a roast fowl and a bottle of wine before them. Amid this varied throng,--varied in appearance, but alike in character,--one object alone, we have said, rivetted Mrs. Sheppard's attention; and no sooner did she in some degree recover from the shock occasioned by the sight of her son's debased condition, than, regardless of any other consideration except his instant removal from the contaminating society by which he was surrounded, and utterly forgetting the more cautious plan she meant to have adopted, she rushed into the room, and summoned him to follow her.

"Halloa!" cried Jack, looking round, and trying to fix his inebriate gaze upon the speaker,--"who's that?"

"Your mother," replied Mrs. Sheppard. "Come home directly, Sir."

"Mother be----!" returned Jack. "Who is it, Bess?"

"How should I know?" replied Edgeworth Bess. "But if it *is* your mother, send her about her business."

"That I will," replied Jack, "in the twinkling of a bedpost."

"Glad to see you once more in the Mint, Mrs. Sheppard," roared Blueskin, who anticipated some fun. "Come and sit down by me."

"Take a glass of gin, Ma'am," cried Poll Maggot, holding up a bottle of spirit; "it used to be your favourite liquor, I've heard."

"Jack, my love," cried Mrs. Sheppard, disregarding the taunt, "come away."

"Not I," replied Jack; "I'm too comfortable where I am. Be off!"

"Jack!" exclaimed his unhappy parent.

"Mr. Sheppard, if you please, Ma'am," interrupted the lad; "I allow nobody to call me Jack. Do I, Bess, eh?"

"Nobody whatever, love," replied Edgeworth Bess; "nobody but me, dear."

"And me," insinuated Mrs. Maggot. "My little fancy man's quite as fond of me as of you, Bess. Ain't you, Jacky darling?"

"Not quite, Poll," returned Mr. Sheppard; "but I love you next to her, and both of you better than *Her*," pointing with the pipe to his mother.

"Oh, Heavens!" cried Mrs. Sheppard.

"Bravo!" shouted Blueskin. "Tom Sheppard never said a better thing than that--ho! ho!"

"Jack," cried his mother, wringing her hands in distraction, "you'll break my heart!"

"Poh! poh!" returned her son; "women don't so easily break their hearts. Do they, Bess?"

"Certainly not," replied the young lady appealed to, "especially about their sons."

"Wretch!" cried Mrs. Sheppard, bitterly.

"I say," retorted Edgeworth Bess, with a very unfeminine imprecation, "I shan't stand any more of that nonsense. What do you mean by calling me wretch, Madam!" she added marching up to Mrs. Sheppard, and regarding her with an insolent and threatening glance.

"Yes--what do you mean, Ma'am?" added Jack, staggering after her.

"Come with me, my love, come--come," cried his mother, seizing his hand, and endeavouring to force him away.

"He shan't go," cried Edgeworth Bess, holding him by the other hand. "Here, Poll, help me!"

Thus exhorted, Mrs. Maggot lent her powerful aid, and, between the two, Jack was speedily relieved from all fears of being carried off against his will. Not content with this exhibition of her prowess, the Amazon lifted him up as easily as if he had been an infant, and placed him upon her shoulders, to the infinite delight of the company, and the increased distress of his mother.

"Now, let's see who'll dare to take him down," she cried.

"Nobody shall," cried Mr. Sheppard from his elevated position. "I'm my own master now, and I'll do as I please. I'll turn cracksman, like my father--rob old Wood--he has chests full of money, and I know where they're kept--I'll rob him, and give the swag to you, Poll--I'll--"

Jack would have said more; but, losing his balance, he fell to the ground, and, when taken up, he was perfectly insensible. In this state, he was laid upon a bench, to sleep off his drunken fit, while his wretched mother, in spite of her passionate supplications and resistance, was, by Blueskin's command, forcibly ejected from the house, and driven out of the Mint.

CHAPTER XV.
The Robbery in Willesden Church.

URING the whole of the next day and night, the poor widow hovered like a ghost about the precincts of the debtors' garrison,--for admission (by the Master's express orders,) was denied her. She could learn nothing of her son, and only obtained one solitary piece of information, which added to, rather than alleviated her misery,--namely, that Jonathan Wild had paid a secret visit to the Cross Shovels. At one time, she determined to go to Wych Street, and ask Mr. Wood's advice and assistance, but the thought of the reception she was likely to meet with from his wife deterred her from executing this resolution. Many other expedients occurred to her; but after making several ineffectual attempts to get into the Mint unobserved, they were all abandoned.

At length, about an hour before dawn on the second day--Sunday--having spent the early part of the night in watching at the gates of the robbers' sanctuary, and being almost exhausted from want of rest, she set out homewards. It was a long walk she had to undertake, even if she had endured no previous fatigue, but feeble as she was, it was almost more than she could accomplish. Daybreak found her winding her painful way along the Harrow Road; and, in order to shorten the distance as much as possible, she took the nearest cut, and struck into the meadows on the right. Crossing several fields, newly mown, or filled with lines of tedded hay, she arrived, not without great exertion, at the summit of a hill. Here her strength completely failed her, and she was compelled to seek some repose. Making her couch upon a heap of hay, she sank at once into a deep and refreshing slumber.

When she awoke, the sun was high in Heaven. It was a bright and beautiful day: *so* bright, so beautiful, that even her sad heart was cheered by it. The air, perfumed with the delicious fragrance of the new-mown grass, was vocal with the melodies of the birds; the thick foliage of the trees was glistening in the sunshine; all nature seemed happy and rejoicing; but, above all, the serene Sabbath stillness reigning around communicated a calm to her wounded spirit.

What a contrast did the lovely scene she now gazed upon present to the squalid neighbourhood she had recently quitted! On all sides, expanded prospects of country the most exquisite and most varied. Immediately beneath her lay Willesden,-- the most charming and secluded village in the neighbourhood of the metropolis-- with its scattered farm-houses, its noble granges, and its old grey church-tower just peeping above a grove of rook-haunted trees.

Towards this spot Mrs. Sheppard now directed her steps. She speedily reached her own abode,--a little cottage, standing in the outskirts of the village. The first circumstance that struck her on her arrival seemed ominous. Her clock had stopped-- stopped at the very hour on which she had quitted the Mint! She had not the heart to wind it up again.

After partaking of some little refreshment, and changing her attire, Mrs. Sheppard prepared for church. By this time, she had so far succeeded in calming herself, that she answered the greetings of the neighbours whom she encountered on her way to the sacred edifice--if sorrowfully, still composedly.

Every old country church is beautiful, but Willesden is the most beautiful country church we know; and in Mrs. Sheppard's time it was even more beautiful than at present, when the hand of improvement has proceeded a little too rashly with alterations and repairs. With one or two exceptions, there were no pews; and, as the intercourse with London was then but slight, the seats were occupied almost exclusively by the villagers. In one of these seats, at the end of the aisle farthest removed from the chancel, the widow took her place, and addressed herself fervently to her devotions.

The service had not proceeded far, when she was greatly disturbed by the entrance of a person who placed himself opposite her, and sought to attract her attention by a number of little arts, surveying her, as he did so, with a very impudent and offensive stare. With this person--who was no other than Mr. Kneebone--she was too well acquainted; having, more than once, been obliged to repel his advances; and, though his impertinence would have given her little concern at another season, it now added considerably to her distraction. But a far greater affliction was in store for her.

Just as the clergyman approached the altar, she perceived a boy steal quickly into the church, and ensconce himself behind the woollen-draper, who, in order to carry on his amatory pursuits with greater convenience, and at the same time display his figure (of which he was not a little vain) to the utmost advantage, preferred a standing to a sitting posture. Of this boy she had only caught a glimpse;--but that glimpse was sufficient to satisfy her it was her son,--and, if she could have questioned her own instinctive love, she could not question her antipathy, when she beheld, partly concealed by a pillar immediately in the rear of the woollen-draper, the dark figure and truculent features of Jonathan Wild. As she looked in this direction, the thief-taker raised his eyes--those gray, blood-thirsty eyes!--their glare froze the life-blood in her veins.

As she averted her gaze, a terrible idea crossed her. Why was he there? why did the tempter dare to invade that sacred spot! She could not answer her own questions, but vague fearful suspicions passed through her mind. Meanwhile, the service proceeded; and the awful command, "*Thou shalt not steal!*" was solemnly uttered by the preacher, when Mrs. Sheppard, who had again looked round towards her son, beheld a hand glance along the side of the woollen-draper. She could not see what occurred, though she guessed it; but she saw Jonathan's devilish triumphing glance, and read in it,--"Your son has committed a robbery--here--in these holy walls--he is mine--mine for ever!"

She uttered a loud scream, and fainted.

CHAPTER XVI.
Jonathan Wild's House in the Old Bailey.

JUST as St. Sepulchre's church struck one, on the eventful night of the 10th of June, (to which it will not be necessary to recur,) a horseman, mounted on a powerful charger, and followed at a respectful distance by an attendant, galloped into the open space fronting Newgate, and directed his course towards a house in the Old Bailey. Before he could draw in the rein, his steed--startled apparently by some object undistinguishable by the rider,--swerved with such suddenness as to unseat him, and precipitate him on the ground. The next moment, however, he was picked up, and set upon his feet by a person who, having witnessed the accident, flew across the road to his assistance.

"You're not hurt I hope, Sir Rowland?" inquired this individual.

"Not materially, Mr. Wild," replied the other, "a little shaken, that's all. Curses light on the horse!" he added, seizing the bridle of his steed, who continued snorting and shivering, as if still under the influence of some unaccountable alarm; "what can ail him?"

"I know what ails him, your honour," rejoined the groom, riding up as he spoke; "he's seen somethin' not o' this world."

"Most likely," observed Jonathan, with a slight sneer; "the ghost of some highwayman who has just breathed his last in Newgate, no doubt."

"May be," returned the man gravely.

"Take him home, Saunders," said Sir Rowland, resigning his faulty steed to the attendant's care, "I shall not require you further. Strange!" he added, as the groom departed; "Bay Stuart has carried me through a hundred dangers, but never played me such a trick before."

"And never should again, were he mine," rejoined Jonathan. "If the best nag ever foaled were to throw me in this unlucky spot, I'd blow his brains out."

"What do you mean, Sir?" asked Trenchard.

"A fall against Newgate is accounted a sign of death by the halter," replied Wild, with ill-disguised malignity.

"Tush!" exclaimed Sir Rowland, angrily.

"From that door," continued the thief-taker, pointing to the gloomy portal of the prison opposite which they were standing, "the condemned are taken to Tyburn. It's a bad omen to be thrown near that door."

"I didn't suspect you of so much superstition, Mr. Wild," observed the knight, contemptuously.

"Facts convince the most incredulous," answered Jonathan, drily. "I've known several cases where the ignominious doom I've mentioned has been foretold by such an accident as has just befallen you. There was Major Price--you must recollect him, Sir Rowland,--he stumbled as he was getting out of his chair at that very gate. Well, *he* was executed for murder. Then there was Tom Jarrot, the hackney-coachman, who was pitched off the box against yonder curbstone, and broke his leg. It was a pity he didn't break his neck, for he was hanged within the year. Another instance was that of Toby Tanner--"

"No more of this," interrupted Trenchard; "where is the boy?"

"Not far hence," replied Wild. "After all our pains we were near losing him, Sir Rowland."

"How so?" asked the other, distrustfully.

"You shall hear," returned Jonathan. "With the help of his comrade, Jack Sheppard, the young rascal made a bold push to get out of the round-house, where my janizaries had lodged him, and would have succeeded too, if, by good luck,--for the devil never deserts so useful an agent as I am, Sir Rowland,--I hadn't arrived in time to prevent him. As it was, my oldest and trustiest setter, Abraham Mendez, received a blow on the head from one of the lads that will deprive me of his services for a week to come,--if, indeed it does not disable him altogether. However, if I've lost one servant, I've gained another, that's one comfort. Jack Sheppard is now wholly in my hands."

"What is this to me, Sir?" said Trenchard, cutting him short.

"Nothing whatever," rejoined the thief-taker, coldly. "But it is much to me.

Jack Sheppard is to me what Thames Darrell is to you--an object of hatred. I owed his father a grudge: that I settled long ago. I owe his mother one, and will repay the debt, with interest, to her son. I could make away with him at once, as you are about to make away with your nephew, Sir Rowland,--but that wouldn't serve my turn. To be complete, my vengeance must be tardy. Certain of my prey, I can afford to wait for it. Besides, revenge is sweetened by delay; and I indulge too freely in the passion to rob it of any of its zest. I've watched this lad--this Sheppard--from infancy; and, though I have apparently concerned myself little about him, I have never lost sight of my purpose. I have suffered him to be brought up decently-- honestly; because I would make his fall the greater, and deepen the wound I meant to inflict upon his mother. From this night I shall pursue a different course; from this night his ruin may be dated. He is in the care of those who will not leave the task assigned to them--the utter perversion of his principles--half-finished. And when I have steeped him to the lips in vice and depravity; when I have led him to the commission of every crime; when there is neither retreat nor advance for him; when he has plundered his benefactor, and broken the heart of his mother--then-- but not till then, I will consign him to the fate to which I consigned his father. This I have sworn to do--this I will do."

"Not unless your skull's bullet-proof," cried a voice at his elbow; and, as the words were uttered, a pistol was snapped at his head, which,--fortunately or un- fortunately, as the reader pleases,--only burnt the priming. The blaze, however, was sufficient to reveal to the thief-taker the features of his intended assassin. They were those of the Irish watchman.

"Ah! Terry O'Flaherty!" vociferated Jonathan, in a tone that betrayed hot the slightest discomposure. "Ah! Terry O'Flaherty!" he cried, shouting after the Irish- man, who took to his heels as soon as he found his murderous attempt unsuccessful; "you may run, but you'll not get out of my reach. I'll put a brace of dogs on your track, who'll soon hunt you down. You shall swing for this after next sessions, or my name's not Jonathan Wild. I told you, Sir Rowland," he added, turning to the knight, and chuckling, "the devil never deserts me."

"Conduct me to your dwelling, Sir, without further delay," said Trenchard, sternly,--"to the boy."

"The boy's not at my house," replied Wild.

"Where is he, then?" demanded the other, hastily.

"At a place we call the Dark House at Queenhithe," answered Jonathan, "a sort of under-ground tavern or night-cellar, close to the river-side, and frequented by the crew of the Dutch skipper, to whose care he's to be committed. You need have no apprehensions about him, Sir Rowland. He's safe enough now. I left him in charge of Quilt Arnold and Rykhart Van Galgebrok--the skipper I spoke of--with strict orders to shoot him if he made any further attempt at escape; and they're not lads--the latter especially--to be trifled with. I deemed it more prudent to send him to the Dark House than to bring him here, in case of any search after him by his adoptive father--the carpenter Wood. If you choose, you can see him put on board the Zeeslang yourself, Sir Rowland. But, perhaps, you'll first accompany me to my dwelling for a moment, that we may arrange our accounts before we start. I've a few necessary directions to leave with my people, to put 'em on their guard against the chance of a surprise. Suffer me to precede you. This way, Sir Rowland."

The thief-taker's residence was a large dismal-looking, habitation, separated from the street by a flagged court-yard, and defended from general approach by an iron railing. Even in the daylight, it had a sombre and suspicious air, and seemed to slink back from the adjoining houses, as if afraid of their society. In the obscurity in which it was now seen, it looked like a prison, and, indeed, it was Jonathan's fancy to make it resemble one as much as possible. The windows were grated, the doors barred; each room had the name as well as the appearance of a cell; and the very porter who stood at the gate, habited like a jailer, with his huge bunch of keys at his girdle, his forbidding countenance and surly demeanour seemed to be borrowed from Newgate. The clanking of chains, the grating of locks, and the rumbling of bolts must have been music in Jonathan's ears, so much pains did he take to subject himself to such sounds. The scanty furniture of the rooms corresponded with their dungeon-like aspect. The walls were bare, and painted in stone-colour; the floors, devoid of carpet; the beds, of hangings; the windows, of blinds; and, excepting in the thief-taker's own audience-chamber, there was not a chair or a table about the premises; the place of these conveniences being elsewhere supplied by benches, and deal-boards laid across joint-stools. Great stone staircases leading no one knew whither, and long gloomy passages, impressed the occasional visitor with the idea that he was traversing a building of vast extent; and, though this was not the case in reality, the deception was so cleverly contrived that it seldom failed of producing the intended effect. Scarcely any one entered Mr. Wild's dwelling without apprehension, or quitted it without satisfaction. More strange stories were told of it than of any other house in London. The garrets were said to be tenanted by coiners, and artists employed in altering watches and jewelry; the cellars to be used as a magazine for stolen goods. By some it was affirmed that a subterranean communication existed between the thief-taker's abode and Newgate, by means of which he was enabled to maintain a secret correspondence with the imprisoned felons: by others, that an under-ground passage led to extensive vaults, where such malefactors as he chose to screen from justice might lie concealed till the danger was blown over. Nothing, in short, was too extravagant to be related of it; and Jonathan, who delighted in investing himself and his residence with mystery, encouraged, and perhaps originated, these marvellous tales. However this may be, such was the ill report of the place that few passed along the Old Bailey without bestowing a glance of fearful curiosity at its dingy walls, and wondering what was going on inside them; while fewer still, of those who paused at the door, read, without some internal trepidation, the formidable name--inscribed in large letters on its bright brass-plate--of JONATHAN WILD.

Arrived at his habitation, Jonathan knocked in a peculiar manner at the door, which was instantly opened by the grim-visaged porter just alluded to. No sooner had Trenchard crossed the threshold than a fierce barking was heard at the farther extremity of the passage, and, the next moment, a couple of mastiffs of the largest size rushed furiously towards him. The knight stood upon his defence; but he would unquestionably have been torn in pieces by the savage hounds, if a shower of oaths, seconded by a vigorous application of kicks and blows from their master, had not driven them growling off. Apologizing to Sir Rowland for this unpleasant reception, and swearing lustily at his servant for occasioning it by leaving the dogs at liberty, Jonathan ordered the man to light them to the audience-room. The command was sullenly obeyed, for the fellow did not appear to relish the rating. Ascending the stairs, and conducting them along a sombre gallery, in which Trenchard noticed that every door was painted black, and numbered, he stopped at the entrance of a chamber; and, selecting a key from the bunch at his girdle, unlocked it. Following his guide, Sir Rowland found himself in a large and lofty apartment, the extent of

which he could not entirely discern until lights were set upon the table. He then
looked around him with some curiosity; and, as the thief-taker was occupied in
giving directions to his attendant in an undertone, ample leisure was allowed him
for investigation. At the first glance, he imagined he must have stumbled upon a
museum of rarities, there were so many glass-cases, so many open cabinets, ranged
against the walls; but the next convinced him that if Jonathan was a virtuoso, his
tastes did not run in the ordinary channels. Trenchard was tempted to examine
the contents of some of these cases, but a closer inspection made him recoil from
them in disgust. In the one he approached was gathered together a vast assortment
of weapons, each of which, as appeared from the ticket attached to it, had been
used as an instrument of destruction. On this side was a razor with which a son
had murdered his father; the blade notched, the haft crusted with blood: on that,
a bar of iron, bent, and partly broken, with which a husband had beaten out his
wife's brains. As it is not, however, our intention to furnish a complete catalogue
of these curiosities, we shall merely mention that in front of them lay a large and
sharp knife, once the property of the public executioner, and used by him to dis-
sever the limbs of those condemned to death for high-treason; together with an immense two-pronged flesh-fork, likewise employed by the same terrible functionary
to plunge the quarters of his victims in the caldrons of boiling tar and oil. Every
gibbet at Tyburn and Hounslow appeared to have been plundered of its charnel
spoil to enrich the adjoining cabinet, so well was it stored with skulls and bones,
all purporting to be the relics of highwaymen famous in their day. Halters, each
of which had fulfilled its destiny, formed the attraction of the next compartment;
while a fourth was occupied by an array of implements of housebreaking almost
innumerable, and utterly indescribable. All these interesting objects were carefully
arranged, classed, and, as we have said, labelled by the thief-taker. From this singular collection Trenchard turned to regard its possessor, who was standing at a little
distance from him, still engaged in earnest discourse with his attendant, and, as he
contemplated his ruthless countenance, on which duplicity and malignity had set
their strongest seals, he could not help calling to mind all he had heard of Jonathan's
perfidiousness to his employers, and deeply regretting that he had placed himself in
the power of so unscrupulous a miscreant.

Jonathan Wild, at this time, was on the high-road to the greatness which he subsequently, and not long afterwards, obtained. He was fast rising to an eminence that no one of his nefarious profession ever reached before him, nor, it is to be hoped, will ever reach again. He was the Napoleon of knavery, and established an uncontrolled empire over all the practitioners of crime. This was no light conquest; nor was it a government easily maintained. Resolution, severity, subtlety, were required for it; and these were qualities which Jonathan possessed in an extraordinary degree. The danger or difficulty of an exploit never appalled him. What his head conceived his hand executed. Professing to stand between the robber and the robbed, he himself plundered both. He it was who formed the grand design of a robber corporation, of which he should be the sole head and director, with the right of delivering those who concealed their booty, or refused to share it with him, to the gallows. He divided London into districts; appointed a gang to each district; and a leader to each gang, whom he held responsible to himself. The country was partitioned in a similar manner. Those whom he retained about his person, or placed in offices of trust, were for the most part convicted felons, who, having returned from transportation before their term had expired, constituted, in his opinion, the safest agents, inasmuch as they could neither be legal evidences against him, nor withhold any portion of the spoil of which he chose to deprive them. But the crowning glory of Jonathan, that which raised him above all his predecessors in iniquity, and clothed this name with undying notoriety--was to come. When in the plenitude of his power, he commenced a terrible trade, till then unknown--namely, a traffic in human blood. This he carried on by procuring witnesses to swear away the lives of those persons who had incurred his displeasure, or whom it might be necessary to remove.

No wonder that Trenchard, as he gazed at this fearful being, should have some misgivings cross him.

Apparently, Jonathan perceived he was an object of scrutiny; for, hastily dismissing his attendant, he walked towards the knight.

"So, you're admiring my cabinet, Sir Rowland," he remarked, with a sinister smile; "it *is* generally admired; and, sometimes by parties who afterwards contribute to the collection themselves,--ha! ha! This skull," he added, pointing to a fragment of mortality in the case beside them, "once belonged to Tom Sheppard, the father of the lad I spoke of just now. In the next box hangs the rope by which he suffered. When I've placed another skull and another halter beside them, I shall be contented."

"To business, Sir!" said the knight, with a look of abhorrence.

"Ay, to business," returned Jonathan, grinning, "the sooner the better."

"Here is the sum you bargained for," rejoined Trenchard, flinging a pocket-book on the table; "count it."

Jonathan's eyes glistened as he told over the notes.

"You've given me more than the amount, Sir Rowland," he said, after he had twice counted them, "or I've missed my reckoning. There's a hundred pounds too much."

"Keep it," said Trenchard, haughtily.

"I'll place it to your account, Sir Rowland," answered the thief-taker, smiling significantly. "And now, shall we proceed to Queenhithe?"

"Stay!" cried the other, taking a chair, "a word with you, Mr. Wild."

"As many as you please, Sir Rowland," replied Jonathan, resuming his seat. "I'm quite at your disposal."

"I have a question to propose to you," said Trenchard, "relating to--" and he hesitated.

"Relating to the father of the boy--Thames Darrell," supplied Jonathan. "I guessed what was coming. You desire to know who he was, Sir Rowland. Well, you *shall* know."

"Without further fee?" inquired the knight.

"Not exactly," answered Jonathan, drily. "A secret is too valuable a commodity to be thrown away. But I said I wouldn't drive a hard bargain with you, and I won't. We are alone, Sir Rowland," he added, snuffing the candles, glancing cautiously around, and lowering his tone, "and what you confide to me shall never transpire,--at least to your disadvantage."

"I am at a loss to understand you Sir,", said Trenchard.

"I'll make myself intelligible before I've done," rejoined Wild. "I need not remind you, Sir Rowland, that I am aware you are deeply implicated in the Jacobite plot which is now known to be hatching."

"Ha!" ejaculated the other.

"Of course, therefore," pursued Jonathan, "you are acquainted with all the leaders of the proposed insurrection,--nay, must be in correspondence with them."

"What right have you to suppose this, Sir?" demanded Trenchard, sternly.

"Have a moment's patience, Sir Rowland," returned Wild; "and you shall hear. If you will furnish me with a list of these rebels, and with proofs of their treason, I will not only insure your safety, but will acquaint you with the real name and rank of your sister Aliva's husband, as well as with some particulars which will never otherwise reach your ears, concerning your lost sister, Constance."

"My sister Constance!" echoed the knight; "what of her?"

"You agree to my proposal, then?" said Jonathan.

"Do you take me for as great a villain as yourself, Sir?" said the knight, rising.

"I took you for one who wouldn't hesitate to avail himself of any advantage chance might throw in his way," returned the thief-taker, coldly. "I find I was in error. No matter. A time *may* come,--and that ere long,--when you will be glad to purchase my secrets, and your own safety, at a dearer price than the heads of your companions."

"Are you ready?" said Trenchard, striding towards the door.

"I am," replied Jonathan, following him, "and so," he added in an undertone, "are your captors."

A moment afterwards, they quitted the house.

CHAPTER XVII.
The Night-Cellar.

AFTER a few minutes' rapid walking, during which neither party uttered a word, Jonathan Wild and his companion had passed Saint Paul's, dived down a thoroughfare on the right, and reached Thames Street.

At the period of this history, the main streets of the metropolis were but imperfectly lighted, while the less-frequented avenues were left in total obscurity; but, even at the present time, the maze of courts and alleys into which Wild now plunged, would have perplexed any one, not familiar with their intricacies, to thread them on a dark night. Jonathan, however, was well acquainted with the road. Indeed, it was his boast that he could find his way through any part of London blindfolded; and by this time, it would seem, he had nearly arrived at his destination; for, grasping his companion's arm, he led him along a narrow entry which did not appear to have an outlet, and came to a halt. Cautioning the knight, if he valued his neck, to tread carefully, Jonathan then descended a steep flight of steps; and, having reached the bottom in safety, he pushed open a door, that swung back on its hinges as soon as it had admitted him; and, followed by Trenchard, entered the night-cellar.

The vault, in which Sir Rowland found himself, resembled in some measure the cabin of a ship. It was long and narrow, with a ceiling supported by huge uncovered rafters, and so low as scarcely to allow a tall man like himself to stand erect beneath it. Notwithstanding the heat of the season,--which was not, however, found particularly inconvenient in this subterranean region,--a large heaped-up fire blazed ruddily in one corner, and lighted up a circle of as villanous countenances as ever flame shone upon.

The guests congregated within the night-cellar were, in fact, little better than thieves; but thieves who confined their depredations almost exclusively to the vessels lying in the pool and docks of the river. They had as many designations as grades. There were game watermen and game lightermen, heavy horsemen and light horsemen, scuffle-hunters, and long-apron men, lumpers, journeymen coopers, mud-larks, badgers, and ratcatchers--a race of dangerous vermin recently, in a great measure, extirpated by the vigilance of the Thames Police, but at this period flourishing in vast numbers. Besides these plunderers, there were others with whom the disposal of their pillage necessarily brought them into contact, and who seldom failed to attend them during their hours of relaxation and festivity;--to wit, dealers in junk, old rags, and marine stores, purchasers of prize-money, crimps, and Jew receivers. The latter formed by far the most knavish-looking and unprepossessing portion of the assemblage. One or two of the tables were occupied by groups of fat frowzy women in flat caps, with rings on their thumbs, and baskets by their sides; and no one who had listened for a single moment to their coarse language and violent abuse of each other, would require to be told they were fish-wives from Billingsgate.

The present divinity of the cellar was a comely middle-aged dame, almost as stout, and quite as shrill-voiced, as the Billingsgate fish-wives above-mentioned, Mrs. Spurling, for so was she named, had a warm nut-brown complexion, almost as dark as a Creole; and a moustache on her upper lip, that would have done no discredit to the oldest dragoon in the King's service. This lady was singularly lucky in her matrimonial connections. She had been married four times: three of her husbands died of hempen fevers; and the fourth, having been twice condemned, was saved from the noose by Jonathan Wild, who not only managed to bring him off, but to obtain for him the situation of under-turnkey in Newgate.

On the appearance of the thief-taker, Mrs. Spurling was standing near the fire superintending some culinary preparation; but she no sooner perceived him, than hastily quitting her occupation, she elbowed a way for him and the knight through the crowd, and ushered them, with much ceremony, into an inner room, where they found the objects of their search, Quilt Arnold and Rykhart Van Galgebrok, seated at a small table, quietly smoking. This service rendered, without waiting for any farther order, she withdrew.

Both the janizary and the skipper arose as the others entered the room.

"This is the gentleman," observed Jonathan, introducing Trenchard to the Hollander, "who is about to intrust his young relation to your care."

"De gentleman may rely on my showing his relation all de attention in my power," replied Van Galgebrok, bowing profoundly to the knight; "but if any unforseen accident--such as a slip overboard--should befal de jonker on de voyage, he mushn't lay de fault entirely on my shoulders--haw! haw!"

"Where is he?" asked Sir Rowland, glancing uneasily around. "I do not see him."

"De jonker. He's here," returned the skipper, pointing significantly downwards. "Bring him out, Quilt."

So saying, he pushed aside the table, and the janizary stooping down, undrew a bolt and opened a trap-door.

"Come out!" roared Quilt, looking into the aperture. "You're wanted."

But as no answer was returned, he trust his arm up to the shoulder into the hole, and with some little difficulty and exertion of strength, drew forth Thames Darrell.

The poor boy, whose hands were pinioned behind him, looked very pale, but neither trembled, nor exhibited any other symptom of alarm.

"Why didn't you come out when I called you, you young dog?" cried Quilt in a savage tone.

"Because I knew what you wanted me for!" answered Thames firmly.

"Oh! you did, did you?" said the janizary. "And what do you suppose we mean to do with you, eh?"

"You mean to kill me," replied Thames, "by my cruel uncle's command. Ah! there he stands!" he exclaimed as his eye fell for the first time upon Sir Rowland. "Where is my mother?" he added, regarding the knight with a searching glance.

"Your mother is dead," interposed Wild, scowling.

"Dead!" echoed the boy. "Oh no--no! You say this to terrify me--to try me. But I will not believe you. Inhuman as he is, he would not kill her. Tell me, Sir," he added, advancing towards the knight, "tell me has this man spoken falsely?--Tell me my mother is alive, and do what you please with me."

"Tell him so, and have done with him, Sir Rowland," observed Jonathan coldly.

"Tell me the truth, I implore you," cried Thames. "Is she alive?"

"She is not," replied Trenchard, overcome by conflicting emotions, and unable to endure the boy's agonized look.

"Are you answered?" said Jonathan, with a grin worthy of a demon.

"My mother!--my poor mother!" ejaculated Thames, falling on his knees, and bursting into tears. "Shall I never see that sweet face again,--never feel the pressure of those kind hands more--nor listen to that gentle voice! Ah! yes, we shall meet again in Heaven, where I shall speedily join you. Now then," he added more calmly, "I am ready to die. The only mercy you can show me is to kill me."

"Then we won't even show you that mercy," retorted the thief-taker brutally. "So get up, and leave off whimpering. Your time isn't come yet."

"Mr. Wild," said Trenchard, "I shall proceed no further in this business. Set the boy free."

"If I disobey you, Sir Rowland," replied the thief-taker, "you'll thank me for it hereafter. Gag him," he added, pushing Thames rudely toward Quilt Arnold, "and convey him to the boat."

"A word," cried the boy, as the janizary was preparing to obey his master's orders. "What has become of Jack Sheppard?"

"Devil knows!" answered Quilt; "but I believe he's in the hands of Blueskin, so there's no doubt he'll soon be on the high-road to Tyburn."

"Poor Jack!" sighed Thames. "You needn't gag me," he added, "I'll not cry out."

"We won't trust you, my youngster," answered the janizary. And, thrusting a piece of iron into his mouth, he forced him out of the room.

Sir Rowland witnessed these proceedings like one stupified. He neither attempted to prevent his nephew's departure, nor to follow him.

Jonathan kept his keen eye fixed upon him, as he addressed himself for a moment to the Hollander.

"Is the case of watches on board?" he asked in an under tone.

"Ja," replied the skipper.

"And the rings?"

"Ja."

"That's well. You must dispose of the goldsmith's note I gave you yesterday, as soon as you arrive at Rotterdam. It'll be advertised to-morrow."

"De duivel!" exclaimed Van Galgebrok, "Very well. It shall be done as you direct. But about dat jonker," he continued, lowering his voice; "have you anything to add consarnin' him? It's almosht a pity to put him onder de water."

"Is the sloop ready to sail?" asked Wild, without noticing the skipper's remark.

"Ja," answered Van; "at a minut's nodish."

"Here are your despatches," said Jonathan with a significant look, and giving him a sealed packet. "Open them when you get on board--not before, and act as they direct you."

"I ondershtand," replied the skipper, putting his finger to his nose; "it shall be done."

"Sir Rowland," said Jonathan, turning to the knight, "will it please you to remain here till I return, or will you accompany us?"

"I will go with you," answered Trenchard, who, by this time, had regained his composure, and with it all his relentlessness of purpose.

"Come, then," said Wild, marching towards the door, "we've no time to lose."

Quitting the night-cellar, the trio soon arrived at the riverside. Quilt Arnold was stationed at the stair-head, near which the boat containing the captive boy was moored. A few words passed between him and the thief-taker as the latter came up; after which, all the party--with the exception of Quilt, who was left on shore--embarked within the wherry, which was pushed from the strand and rowed swiftly along the stream--for the tide was in its favour--by a couple of watermen. Though scarcely two hours past midnight, it was perfectly light. The moon had arisen, and everything could be as plainly distinguished as during the day. A thin mist lay on the river, giving the few craft moving about in it a ghostly look. As they approached London Bridge, the thief-taker whispered Van Galgebrok, who acted as steersman, to make for a particular arch--near the Surrey shore. The skipper obeyed, and in another moment, they swept through the narrow lock. While the watermen were contending with the eddies occasioned by the fall below the bridge, Jonathan observed a perceptible shudder run through Trenchard's frame.

"You remember that starling, Sir Rowland," he said maliciously, "and what occurred on it, twelve years ago?"

"Too well," answered the knight, frowning. "Ah! what is that?" he cried, pointing to a dark object floating near them amid the boiling waves, and which presented a frightful resemblance to a human face.

"We'll see," returned the thief-taker. And, stretching out his hand, he lifted the dark object from the flood.

It proved to be a human head, though with scarcely a vestige of the features remaining. Here and there, patches of flesh adhered to the bones, and the dank dripping hair hanging about what had once been the face, gave it a ghastly appearance.

"It's the skull of a *rebel*," said Jonathan, with marked emphasis on the word, "blown by the wind from a spike on the bridge above us. I don't know whose brainless head it may be, but it'll do for my collection." And he tossed it carelessly into the bottom of the boat.

After this occurence, not a word was exchanged between them until they came in sight of the sloop, which was lying at anchor off Wapping. Arrived at her side, it was soon evident, from the throng of seamen in Dutch dresses that displayed themselves, that her crew were on the alert, and a rope having been thrown down to the skipper, he speedily hoisted himself on deck. Preparations were next made for taking Thames on board. Raising him in his arms, Jonathan passed the rope round his body, and in this way the poor boy was drawn up without difficulty.

While he was swinging in mid air, Thames regarded his uncle with a stern look, and cried in a menacing voice, "We shall meet again."

"Not in this world," returned Jonathan. "Weigh anchor, Van!" he shouted to the skipper, "and consult your despatches."

"Ja--ja," returned the Hollander. And catching hold of Thames, he quitted the deck.

Shortly afterwards, he re-appeared with the information that the captive was safe below; and giving the necessary directions to his crew, before many minutes had elapsed, the Zeeslang spread her canvass to the first breeze of morning.

By the thief-taker's command, the boat was then rowed toward a muddy inlet, which has received in more recent times the name of Execution Dock. As soon as she reached this spot, Wild sprang ashore, and was joined by several persons,-- among whom was Quilt Arnold, leading a horse by the bridle,--he hastened down the stairs to meet him. A coach was also in attendance, at a little distance.

Sir Rowland, who had continued absorbed in thought, with his eyes fixed upon the sloop, as she made her way slowly down the river, disembarked more leisurely.

"At length I am my own master," murmured the knight, as his foot touched the strand.

"Not so, Sir Rowland," returned Jonathan; "you are my prisoner."

"How!" ejaculated Trenchard, starting back and drawing his sword.

"You are arrested for high treason," rejoined Wild, presenting a pistol at his head, while he drew forth a parchment,--"here is my warrant."

"Traitor!" cried Sir Rowland--"damned--double-dyed traitor!"

"Away with him," vociferated Jonathan to his myrmidons, who, having surrounded Trenchard, hurried him off to the coach before he could utter another word,--"first to Mr. Walpole, and then to Newgate. And now, Quilt," he continued, addressing the janizary, who approached him with the horse, "fly to St. Giles's roundhouse, and if, through the agency of that treacherous scoundrel, Terry O'Flaherty, whom I've put in my Black List, old Wood should have found his way there, and have been detained by Sharpies as I directed, you may release him. I don't care how soon he learns that he has lost his adopted son. When I've escorted you proud fool to his new quarters, I'll proceed to the Mint and look after Jack Sheppard."

With this, he mounted his steed and rode off.

CHAPTER XVIII.
How Jack Sheppard broke out of the
Cage at Willesden.

THE heart-piercing scream uttered by Mrs. Sheppard after the commission of the robbery in Willesden church was productive of unfortunate consequences to her son. Luckily, she was bereft of consciousness, and was thus spared the additional misery of witnessing what afterwards befell him. Startled by the cry, as may be supposed, the attention of the whole congregation was drawn towards the quarter whence it proceeded. Amongst others, a person near the door, roused by the shriek, observed a man make his exit with the utmost precipitation. A boy attempted to follow; but as the suspicions of the lookers-on were roused by the previous circumstances, the younger fugitive was seized and detained. Meanwhile, Mr. Kneebone, having been alarmed by something in the widow's look before her feelings found vent in the manner above described, thrust his hand instinctively into his coat in search of his pocket-book,--about the security of which, as it contained several letters and documents implicating himself and others in the Jacobite plot, he was, not unnaturally, solicitous,--and finding it gone, he felt certain he had been robbed. Turning quickly round, in the hope of discovering the thief, he was no less surprised than distressed--for in spite of his faults, the woollen-draper was a good-natured fellow--to perceive Jack Sheppard in custody. The truth at once flashed across his mind. This, then, was the cause of the widow's wild inexplicable look,--of her sudden shriek! Explaining his suspicious in a whisper to Jack's captor, who proved to be a church-warden and a constable, by name John Dump,--Mr. Kneebone begged him to take the prisoner into the churchyard. Dump instantly complied, and as soon as Jack was removed from the sacred edifice, his person was searched from head to foot--but without success. Jack submitted to this scrutiny with a very bad grace, and vehemently protested his innocence. In vain did the woollen-draper offer to set him free if he would restore the stolen article, or give up his associate, to whom it was supposed he might have handed it. He answered with the greatest assurance, that he knew nothing whatever of the matter--had seen no pocket-book, and no associate to give up. Nor did he content himself with declaring his guiltlessness of the crime imputed to him, but began in his turn to menace his captor and accuser, loading the latter with the bitterest upbraidings. By this time, the churchyard was crowded with spectators, some of whom dispersed in different directions in quest of the other robber. But all that could be ascertained in the village was, that a man had ridden off a short time before in the direction of London. Of this man Kneebone resolved to go in pursuit; and leaving Jack in charge of the constable, he proceeded to the small inn,--which bore then, as it bears now, the name of the Six Bells,--where, summoning the hostler, his steed was instantly brought him, and, springing on its back, he rode away at full speed.

Meanwhile, after a consultation between Mr. Dump and the village authorities, it was agreed to lock up the prisoner in the cage. As he was conveyed thither, an incident occurred that produced a considerable impression on the feelings of the youthful offender. Just as they reached the eastern outlet of the churchyard--where the tall elms cast a pleasant shade over the rustic graves--a momentary stoppage took place. At this gate two paths meet. Down that on the right the young culprit was dragged--along that on the left a fainting woman was borne in the arms of several females. It was his mother, and as he gazed on her pallid features and motionless frame, Jack's heart severely smote him. He urged his conductors to a quicker pace to get out of sight of the distressing spectacle, and even felt relieved when he was shut out from it and the execrations of the mob by the walls of the little prison.

The cage at Willesden was, and is--for it is still standing--a small round building about eight feet high, with a pointed tiled roof, to which a number of boards, inscribed with the names of the parish officers, and charged with a multitude of admonitory notices to vagrants and other disorderly persons, are attached. Over these boards the two arms of a guide-post serve to direct the way-farer--on the right hand to the neighbouring villages of Neasdon and Kingsbury, and on the left to the Edgeware Road and the healthy heights of Hampstead. The cage has a strong door, with an iron grating at the top, and further secured by a stout bolt and padlock. It is picturesquely situated beneath a tree on the high road, not far from the little hostel before mentioned, and at no great distance from the church.

For some time after he was locked up in this prison Jack continued in a very dejected state. Deserted by his older companion in iniquity, and instigator to crime, he did not know what might become of him; nor, as we have observed, was the sad spectacle he had just witnessed, without effect. Though within the last two days he had committed several heinous offences, and one of a darker dye than any with which the reader has been made acquainted, his breast was not yet so callous as to be wholly insensible to the stings of conscience. Wearied at length with thinking on the past, and terrified by the prospect of the future, he threw himself on the straw with which the cage was littered, and endeavoured to compose himself to slumber. When he awoke, it was late in the day; but though he heard voices outside, and now and then caught a glimpse of a face peeping at him through the iron grating over the door, no one entered the prison, or held any communication with him. Feeling rather exhausted, it occurred to him that possibly some provisions might have been left by the constable; and, looking about, he perceived a pitcher of water and a small brown loaf on the floor. He ate of the bread with great appetite, and having drunk as much as he chose of the water, poured the rest on the floor. His hunger satisfied, his spirits began to revive, and with this change of mood all his natural audacity returned. And here he was first visited by that genius which, in his subsequent career, prompted him to so many bold and successful attempts. Glancing around his prison, he began to think it possible he might effect an escape from it. The door was too strong, and too well secured, to break open,--the walls too thick: but the ceiling,--if he could reach it--there, he doubted not, he could make an outlet. While he was meditating flight in this way, and tossing about on the straw, he chanced upon an old broken and rusty fork. Here was an instrument which might be of the greatest service to him in accomplishing his design. He put it carefully aside, resolved to defer the attempt till night. Time wore on somewhat slowly with the prisoner, who had to control his impatience in the best way he could; but as the shades of evening were darkening, the door was unlocked, and Mr. Dump popped his head into the cage. He brought another small loaf, and a can with which he replenished the pitcher, recommending Jack to be careful, as he would get

nothing further till morning. To this Jack replied, that he should be perfectly contented, provided he might have a small allowance of gin. The latter request, though
treated with supreme contempt by Mr. Dump, made an impression on some one
outside; for not long after the constable departed, Jack heard a tap at the door, and
getting up at the summons, he perceived the tube of a pipe inserted between the
bars. At once divining the meaning of this ingenious device, he applied his mouth
to the tube, and sucked away, while the person outside poured spirit into the bowl.
Having drunk as much as he thought prudent, and thanked his unknown friend for
his attention, Jack again lay down on the straw, and indulged himself with another
nap, intending to get up as soon as it was perfectly dark. The strong potation he had
taken, combined with fatigue and anxiety he had previously undergone, made him
oversleep himself, and when he awoke it was just beginning to grow light. Cursing
himself for his inertness, Jack soon shook off this drowsiness, and set to work in earnest. Availing himself of certain inequalities in the door, he soon managed to climb
up to the roof; and securing his feet against a slight projection in the wall, began to
use the fork with great effect. Before many minutes elapsed, he had picked a large
hole in the plaster, which showered down in a cloud of dust; and breaking off several laths, caught hold of a beam, by which he held with one hand, until with the
other he succeeded, not without some difficulty, in forcing out one of the tiles. The
rest was easy. In a few minutes more he had made a breach in the roof wide enough
to allow him to pass through. Emerging from this aperture, he was about to descend,
when he was alarmed by hearing the tramp of horses' feet swiftly approaching, and
had only time to hide himself behind one of the largest sign-boards before alluded
to when two horsemen rode up. Instead of passing on, as Jack expected, these persons stopped opposite the cage, when one of them, as he judged from the sound, for
he did not dare to look out of his hiding place, dismounted. A noise was next heard,
as if some instrument were applied to the door with the intent to force it open, and
Jack's fears were at once dispelled, At first, he had imagined they were officers of
justice, come to convey him to a stronger prison: but the voice of one of the parties,
which he recognised, convinced him they were his friends.

"Look quick, Blueskin, and be cursed to you!" was growled in the deep tones of
Jonathan Wild. "We shall have the whole village upon us while you're striking the
jigger. Use the gilt, man!"

"There's no need of picklock or crow-bar, here, Mr. Wild," cried Jack, placing his hat on the right arm of the guide-post, and leaning over the board, "I've done the trick myself."

"Why, what the devil's this?" vociferated Jonathan, looking up. "Have you broken out of the cage, Jack?"

"Something like it," replied the lad carelessly.

"Bravo!" cried the thief-taker approvingly.

"Well, that beats all I ever heard of!" roared Blueskin.

"But are you really there?"

"No, I'm here," answered Jack, leaping down. "I tell you what, Mr. Wild," he added, laughing, "it must be a stronger prison than Willesden cage that can hold me."

"Ay, ay," observed Jonathan, "you'll give the keepers of his Majesty's jails some trouble before you're many years older, I'll warrant you. But get up behind, Blueskin. Some one may observe us."

"Come, jump up," cried Blueskin, mounting his steed, "and I'll soon wisk you to town. Edgeworth Bess and Poll Maggot are dying to see you. I thought Bess would have cried her pretty eyes out when she heard you was nabbed. You need give yourself no more concern about Kneebone. Mr. Wild has done his business."

"Ay--ay," laughed Jonathan. "The pocket-book you prigged contained the letters I wanted. He's now in spring-ankle warehouse with Sir Rowland Trenchard. So get up, and let's be off."

"Before I leave this place, I must see my mother."

"Nonsense," returned Jonathan gruffly. "Would you expose yourself to fresh risk? If it hadn't been for her you wouldn't have been placed in your late jeopardy."

"I don't care for that," replied Jack. "See her I *will*. Leave me behind: I'm not afraid. I'll be at the Cross Shovels in the course of the day."

"Nay, if you're bent upon this folly," observed Wild, who appeared to have his own reasons for humouring the lad, "I shan't hinder you. Blueskin will take care of the horses, and I'll go with you."

So saying, he dismounted; and flinging his bridle to his companion, and ordering him to ride off to a little distance, he followed Jack, who had quitted the main road, and struck into a narrow path opposite the cage. This path, bordered on each side by high privet hedges of the most beautiful green, soon brought them to a stile.

"There's the house," said Jack, pointing to a pretty cottage, the small wooden porch of which was covered with roses and creepers, with a little trim garden in front of it. "I'll be back in a minute."

"Don't hurry yourself," said Jonathan, "I'll wait for you here."

CHAPTER XIX.
Good and Evil.

A S Jack opened the gate, and crossed the little garden, which exhibited in every part the neatness and attention of its owner, he almost trembled at the idea of further disturbing her peace of mind. Pausing with the intention of turning back, he glanced in the direction of the village church, the tower of which could just be seen through the trees. The rooks were cawing amid the boughs, and all nature appeared awaking to happiness. From this peaceful scene Jack's eye fell upon Jonathan, who, seated upon the stile, under the shade of an elder tree, was evidently watching him. A sarcastic smile seemed to play upon the chief-taker's lips; and abashed at his own irresolution, the lad went on.

After knocking for some time at the door without effect, he tried the latch, and to his surprise found it open. He stepped in with a heavy foreboding of calamity. A cat came and rubbed herself against him as he entered the house, and seemed by her mewing to ask him for food. That was the only sound he heard.

Jack was almost afraid of speaking; but at length he summoned courage to call out "Mother!"

"Who's there?" asked a faint voice from the bed.

"Your son," answered the boy.

"Jack," exclaimed the widow, starting up and drawing back the curtain. "Is it indeed you, or am I dreaming?"

"You're not dreaming, mother," he answered. "I'm come to say good bye to you, and to assure you of my safety before I leave this place."

"Where are you going?" asked his mother.

"I hardly know," returned Jack; "but it's not safe for me to remain much longer here."

"True," replied the widow, upon whom all the terrible recollections of the day before crowded, "I know it isn't. I won't keep you long. But tell me how have you escaped from the confinement in which you were placed--come and sit by me-- here--upon the bed--give me your hand--and tell me all about it."

Her son complied, and sat down upon the patch-work coverlet beside her.

"Jack," said Mrs. Sheppard, clasping him with a hand that burnt with fever, "I have been ill--dreadfully ill--I believe delirious--I thought I should have died last night--I won't tell you what agony you have caused me--I won't reproach you. Only promise me to amend--to quit your vile companions--and I will forgive you- -will bless you. Oh! my dear, dear son, be warned in time. You are in the hands of a wicked, a terrible man, who will not stop till he has completed your destruction. Listen to your mother's prayers, and do not let her die broken-hearted."

"It is too late," returned Jack, sullenly; "I can't be honest if I would."

"Oh! do not say so," replied his wretched parent. "It is never too late. I know you are in Jonathan Wild's power, for I saw him near you in the church; and if ever the enemy of mankind was permitted to take human form, I beheld him then. Be- ware of him, my son! Beware of him! You know not what villany he is capable of. Be honest, and you will be happy. You are yet a child; and though you have strayed from the right path, a stronger hand than your own has led you thence. Return, I implore of you, to your master,--to Mr. Wood. Acknowledge your faults. He is all kindness, and will overlook them for your poor father's sake--for mine. Return to him, I say--"

"I can't," replied Jack, doggedly.

"Can't!" repeated his mother. "Why not?"

"I'll tell you," cried a deep voice from the back of the bed. And immediately afterwards the curtain was drawn aside, and disclosed the Satanic countenance of Jonathan Wild, who had crept into the house unperceived, "I'll tell you, why he can't go back to his master," cried the thief-taker, with a malignant grin. "He has robbed him."

"Robbed him!" screamed the widow. "Jack!"

Her son averted his gaze.

"Ay, robbed him," reiterated Jonathan. "The night before last, Mr. Wood's house was broken into and plundered. Your son was seen by the carpenter's wife in company with the robbers. Here," he added, throwing a handbill on the bed, "are the particulars of the burglary, with the reward for Jack's apprehension."

"Ah!" ejaculated the widow, hiding her face.

"Come," said Wild, turning authoritatively to Jack,--"you have overstayed your time."

"Do not go with him, Jack!" shrieked his mother. "Do not--do not!"

"He must!" thundered Jonathan, "or he goes to jail."

"If you must go to prison, I will go with you," cried Mrs. Sheppard: "but avoid that man as you would a serpent."

"Come along," thundered Jonathan.

"Hear me, Jack!" shrieked his mother. "You know not what you do. The wretch you confide in has sworn to hang you. As I hope for mercy, I speak the truth!--let him deny it if he can."

"Pshaw!" said Wild. "I could hang him now if I liked. But he may remain with you if he pleases: I sha'n't hinder him."

"You hear, my son," said the widow eagerly. "Choose between good and evil;--between him and me. And mind, your life,--more than your life--hangs upon your choice."

"It does so," said Wild. "Choose, Jack."

The lad made no answer, but left the room.

"He is gone!" cried Mrs. Sheppard despairingly.

"For ever!" said the thief-taker, preparing to follow.

"Devil!" cried the widow, catching his arm, and gazing with frantic eagerness in his face, "how many years will you give my son before you execute your terrible threat?"

"NINE!" answered Jonathan sternly.

END OF THE SECOND EPOCH.

EPOCH THE THIRD. 1724
THE PRISON-BREAKER.

CHAPTER I.
The Return.

NEARLY nine years after the events last recorded, and about the middle of May, 1724, a young man of remarkably prepossessing appearance took his way, one afternoon, along Wych Street; and, from the curiosity with which he regarded the houses on the left of the road, seemed to be in search of some particular habitation. The age of this individual could not be more than twenty-one; his figure was tall, robust, and gracefully proportioned; and his clear gray eye and open countenance bespoke a frank, generous, and resolute nature. His features were regular, and finely-formed; his complexion bright and blooming,--a little shaded, however, by travel and exposure to the sun; and, with a praiseworthy contempt for the universal and preposterous fashion then prevailing, of substituting a peruke for the natural covering of the head, he allowed his own dark-brown hair to fall over his shoulders in ringlets as luxuriant as those that distinguished the court gallant in Charles the Second's days--a fashion, which we do not despair of seeing revived in our own days. He wore a French military undress of the period, with high jack-boots, and a laced hat; and, though his attire indicated no particular rank, he had completely the air of a person of distinction. Such was the effect produced upon the passengers by his good looks and manly deportment, that few--especially of the gentler and more susceptible sex--failed to turn round and bestow a second glance upon the handsome stranger. Unconscious of the interest he excited, and entirely occupied by his own thoughts--which, if his bosom could have been examined, would have been found composed of mingled hopes and fears--the young man walked on till he came to an old house, with great projecting bay windows on the first floor, and situated as nearly as possible at the back of St. Clement's church. Here he halted; and, looking upwards, read, at the foot of an immense sign-board, displaying a gaudily-painted angel with expanded pinions and an olive-branch, not the name he expected to find, but that of WILLIAM KNEEBONE, WOOLLEN-DRAPER.

Tears started to the young man's eyes on beholding the change, and it was with difficulty he could command himself sufficiently to make the inquiries he desired to do respecting the former owner of the house. As he entered the shop, a tall portly personage advanced to meet him, whom he at once recognised as the present proprietor. Mr. Kneebone was attired in the extremity of the mode. A full-curled wig descended half-way down his back and shoulders; a neckcloth of "right Mechlin" was twisted round his throat so tightly as almost to deprive him of breath, and threaten him with apoplexy; he had lace, also, at his wrists and bosom; gold clocks to his hose, and red heels to his shoes. A stiff, formally-cut coat of cinnamon-coloured cloth, with rows of plate buttons, each of the size of a crown piece, on the sleeves, pockets, and skirts, reached the middle of his legs; and his costume was completed by the silver-hilted sword at his side, and the laced hat under his left arm.

Bowing to the stranger, the woollen-draper very politely requested to know his business.

"I'm almost afraid to state it," faltered the other; "but, may I ask whether Mr. Wood, the carpenter, who formerly resided here, is still living?"

"If you feel any anxiety on his account, Sir, I'm happy to be able to relieve it," answered Kneebone, readily. "My good friend, Owen Wood,--Heaven preserve him!--*is* still living. And, for a man who'll never see sixty again, he's in excellent preservation, I assure you."

"You delight me with the intelligence," said the stranger, entirely recovering his cheerfulness of look.

"I began to fear, from his having quitted the old place, that some misfortune must have befallen him."

"Quite the contrary," rejoined the woollen-draper, laughing good-humouredly. "Everything has prospered with him in an extraordinary manner. His business has thriven; legacies have unexpectedly dropped into his lap; and, to crown all, he has made a large fortune by a lucky speculation in South-Sea stock,--made it, too, where so many others have lost fortunes, your humble servant amongst the number--ha! ha! In a word, Sir, Mr. Wood is now in very affluent circumstances. He stuck to the shop as long as it was necessary, and longer, in my opinion. When he left these premises, three years ago, I took them from him; or rather--to deal frankly with you,--he placed me in them rent-free, for, I'm not ashamed to confess it, I've had losses, and heavy ones; and, if it hadn't been for him, I don't know where I should have been. Mr. Wood, Sir," he added, with much emotion, "is one of the best of men, and would be the happiest, were it not that--" and he hesitated.

"Well, Sir?" cried the other, eagerly.

"His wife is still living," returned Kneebone, drily.

"I understand," replied the stranger, unable to repress a smile. "But, it strikes me, I've heard that Mrs. Wood was once a favourite of yours."

"So she was," replied the woollen-draper, helping himself to an enormous pinch of snuff with the air of a man who does not dislike to be rallied about his gallantry,--"so she was. But those days are over--quite over. Since her husband has laid me under such a weight of obligation, I couldn't, in honour, continue--hem!" and he took another explanatory pinch. "Added to which, she is neither so young as she was, nor, is her temper by any means improved--hem!"

"Say no more on the subject, Sir," observed the stranger, gravely; "but let us turn to a more agreeable one--her daughter."

"That is a far more agreeable one, I must confess," returned Kneebone, with a self-sufficient smirk.

The stranger looked at him as if strongly disposed to chastise his impertinence.

"Is she married?" he asked, after a brief pause.

"Married!--no--no," replied the woollen-draper. "Winifred Wood will never marry, unless the grave can give up its dead. When a mere child she fixed her affections upon a youth named Thames Darrell, whom her father brought up, and who perished, it is supposed, about nine years ago; and she has determined to remain faithful to his memory."

"You astonish me," said the stranger, in a voice full of emotion.

"Why it *is* astonishing, certainly," remarked Kneebone, "to find any woman constant--especially to a girlish attachment; but such is the case. She has had offers innumerable; for where wealth and beauty are combined, as in her instance, suitors are seldom wanting. But she was not to be tempted."

"She is a matchless creature!" exclaimed the young man.

"So I think," replied Kneebone, again applying to the snuff-box, and by that means escaping the angry glance levelled at him by his companion.

"I have one inquiry more to make of you, Sir," said the stranger, as soon as he had conquered his displeasure, "and I will then trouble you no further. You spoke just now of a youth whom Mr. Wood brought up. As far as I recollect, there were two. What has become of the other?"

"Why, surely you don't mean Jack Sheppard?" cried the woollen-draper in surprise.

"That was the lad's name," returned the stranger.

"I guessed from your dress and manner, Sir, that you must have been long absent from your own country," said Kneebone; "and now I'm convinced of it, or you wouldn't have asked that question. Jack Sheppard is the talk and terror of the whole town. The ladies can't sleep in their beds for him; and as to the men, they daren't go to bed at all. He's the most daring and expert housebreaker that ever used a crow-bar. He laughs at locks and bolts; and the more carefully you guard your premises from him, the more likely are you to insure an attack. His exploits and escapes are in every body's mouth. He has been lodged in every round-house in the metropolis, and has broken out of them all, and boasts that no prison can hold him. We shall see. His skill has not been tried. At present, he is under the protection of Jonathan Wild."

"Does that villain still maintain his power?" asked the stranger sternly.

"He does," replied Kneebone, "and, what is more surprising, it seems to increase. Jonathan completely baffles and derides the ends of justice. It is useless to contend with him, even with right on your side. Some years ago, in 1715, just before the Rebellion, I was rash enough to league myself with the Jacobite party, and by Wild's machinations got clapped into Newgate, whence I was glad to escape with my head upon my shoulders. I charged the thief-taker, as was the fact, with having robbed me, by means of the lad Sheppard, whom he instigated to deed, of the very pocket-book he produced in evidence against me; but it was of no avail--I couldn't obtain a hearing. Mr. Wood fared still worse. Bribed by a certain Sir Rowland Trenchard, Jonathan kidnapped the carpenter's adopted son, Thames Darrell, and placed him in the hands of a Dutch Skipper, with orders to throw him overboard when he got out to sea; and though this was proved as clear as day, the rascal managed matters so adroitly, and gave such a different complexion to the whole affair, that he came off with flying colours. One reason, perhaps, of his success in this case might be, that having arrested his associate in the dark transaction, Sir Rowland Trenchard, on a charge of high treason, he was favoured by Walpole, who found his account in retaining such an agent. Be this as it may, Jonathan remained the victor; and shortly afterwards,--at the price of a third of his estate, it was whispered,--he procured Trenchard's liberation from confinement."

At the mention of the latter occurrence, a dark cloud gathered upon the stranger's brow.

"Do you know anything further of Sir Rowland?" he asked.

"Nothing more than this," answered Kneebone,--"that after the failure of his projects, and the downfall of his party, he retired to his seat, Ashton Hall, near Manchester, and has remained there ever since, entirely secluded from the world."

The stranger was for a moment lost in reflection.

"And now, Sir," he said, preparing to take his departure, "will you add to the obligation already conferred by informing me where I can meet with Mr. Wood?"

"With pleasure," replied the woollen-draper. "He lives at Dollis Hill, a beautiful spot near Willesden, about four or five miles from town, where he has taken a farm. If you ride out there, and the place is well worth a visit, for the magnificent view it commands of some of the finest country in the neighbourhood of London,--you are certain to meet with him. I saw him yesterday, and he told me he shouldn't stir from home for a week to come. He called here on his way back, after he had been to Bedlam to visit poor Mrs. Sheppard."

"Jack's mother?" exclaimed the young man. "Gracious Heaven!--is she the inmate of a mad-house?"

"She is, Sir," answered the woollen-draper, sadly, "driven there by her son's misconduct. Alas! that the punishment of his offences should fall on her head. Poor soul! she nearly died when she heard he had robbed his master; and it might have been well if she had done so, for she never afterwards recovered her reason. She rambles continually about Jack, and her husband, and that wretch Jonathan, to whom, as far as can be gathered from her wild ravings, she attributes all her misery. I pity her from the bottom of my heart. But, in the midst of all her affliction, she has found a steady friend in Mr. Wood, who looks after her comforts, and visits her constantly. Indeed, I've heard him say that, but for his wife, he would shelter her under his own roof. That, Sir, is what I call being a Good Samaritan."

The stranger said nothing, but hastily brushed away a tear. Perceiving he was about to take leave, Kneebone ventured to ask whom he had had the honour of addressing.

Before the question could be answered, a side-door was opened, and a very handsome woman of Amazonian proportions presented herself, and marched familiarly up to Mr. Kneebone. She was extremely showily dressed, and her large hooped petticoat gave additional effect to her lofty stature. As soon as she noticed the stranger, she honoured him with an extremely impudent stare, and scarcely endeavoured to disguise the admiration with which his good looks impressed her.

"Don't you perceive, my dear Mrs. Maggot, that I'm engaged," said Kneebone, a little disconcerted.

"Who've you got with you?" demanded the Amazon, boldly.

"The gentleman is a stranger to me, Poll," replied the woollen-draper, with increased embarrassment. "I don't know his name." And he looked at the moment as if he had lost all desire to know it.

"Well, he's a pretty fellow at all events," observed Mrs. Maggot, eyeing him from head to heel with evident satisfaction;--"a devilish pretty fellow!"

"Upon my word, Poll," said Kneebone, becoming very red, "you might have a little more delicacy than to tell him so before my face."

"What!" exclaimed Mrs. Maggot, drawing up her fine figure to its full height; "because I condescend to live with you, am I never to look at another man,--especially at one so much to my taste as this? Don't think it!"

"You had better retire, Madam," said the woollen-draper, sharply, "if you can't conduct yourself with more propriety."

"Order those who choose to obey you," rejoined the lady scornfully. "Though you lorded it over that fond fool, Mrs. Wood, you shan't lord it over me, I can promise you. That for you!" And she snapped her fingers in his face.

"Zounds!" cried Kneebone, furiously. "Go to your own room, woman, directly, or I'll make you!"

"Make me!" echoed Mrs. Maggot, bursting into a loud contemptuous laugh. "Try!"

Enraged at the assurance of his mistress, the woollen-draper endeavoured to carry his threat into execution, but all his efforts to remove her were unavailing. At length, after he had given up the point from sheer exhaustion, the Amazon seized him by the throat, and pushed him backwards with such force that he rolled over the counter.

"There!" she cried, laughing, "that'll teach you to lay hands upon me again. You should remember, before you try your strength against mine, that when I rescued you from the watch, and you induced me to come and live with you, I beat off four men, any of whom was a match for you--ha! ha!"

"My dear Poll!" said Kneebone, picking himself up, "I entreat you to moderate yourself."

"Entreat a fiddlestick!" retorted Mrs. Maggot: "I'm tired of you, and will go back to my old lover, Jack Sheppard. He's worth a dozen of you. Or, if this good-looking young fellow will only say the word, I'll go with him."

"You may go, and welcome, Madam!" rejoined Kneebone, spitefully. "But, I should think, after the specimen you've just given of your amiable disposition, no person would be likely to saddle himself with such an incumbrance."

"What say you, Sir?" said the Amazon, with an engaging leer at the stranger. "*You* will find me tractable enough; and, with *me* by, your side you need fear neither constable nor watchman. I've delivered Jack Sheppard from many an assault. I can wield a quarterstaff as well as a prize-fighter, and have beaten Figg himself at the broadsword. Will you take me?"

However tempting Mrs. Maggot's offer may appear, the young man thought fit to decline it, and, after a few words of well-merited compliment on her extraordinary prowess, and renewed thanks to Mr. Kneebone, he took his departure.

"Good bye!" cried Mrs. Maggot, kissing her hand to him. "I'll find you out. And now," she added, glancing contemptuously at the woollen-draper, "I'll go to Jack Sheppard."

"You shall first go to Bridewell, you jade!" rejoined Kneebone. "Here, Tom," he added, calling to a shop-boy, "run and fetch a constable."

"He had better bring half-a-dozen," said the Amazon, taking up a cloth-yard wand, and quietly seating herself; "one won't do."

On leaving Mr. Kneebone's house, the young man hastened to a hotel in the neighbourhood of Covent Garden, where, having procured a horse, he shaped his course towards the west end of the town. Urging his steed along Oxford Road,--as that great approach to the metropolis was then termed,--he soon passed Marylebone Lane, beyond which, with the exception of a few scattered houses, the country was completely open on the right, and laid out in pleasant fields and gardens; nor did he draw in the rein until he arrived at Tyburn-gate, where, before he turned off upon the Edgeware Road, he halted for a moment, to glance at the place of execution. This "fatal retreat for the unfortunate brave" was marked by a low wooden railing, within which stood the triple tree. Opposite the gallows was an open gallery, or scaffolding, like the stand at a racecourse, which, on state occasions, was crowded with spectators. Without the inclosure were reared several lofty gibbets, with their ghastly burthens. Altogether, it was a hideous and revolting sight. Influenced, probably, by what he had heard from Mr. Kneebone, respecting the lawless career of Jack Sheppard, and struck with the probable fate that awaited him, the young man, as he contemplated this scene, fell into a gloomy reverie. While he was thus musing, two horsemen rode past him; and, proceeding to a little distance, stopped likewise. One of them was a stout square-built man, with a singularly swarthy complexion, and harsh forbidding features. He was well mounted, as was his companion; and had pistols in his holsters, and a hanger at his girdle. The other individual, who was a little in advance, was concealed from the stranger's view. Presently, however, a sudden movement occurred, and disclosed his features, which were those of a young man of nearly his own age. The dress of this person was excessively showy, and consisted of a scarlet riding-habit, lined and faced with blue, and bedizened with broad gold lace, a green silk-knit waistcoat, embroidered with silver, and decorated with a deep fringe, together with a hat tricked out in the same gaudy style. His figure was slight, but well-built; and, in stature he did not exceed five feet four. His complexion was pale; and there was something sinister in the expression of his large black eyes. His head was small and bullet-shaped, and he did not wear a wig, but had his sleek black hair cut off closely round his temples. A mutual recognition took place at the same instant between the stranger and this individual. Both started. The latter seemed inclined to advance and address the former; but suddenly changing his mind, he shouted to his companion in tones familiar to the stranger's ear; and, striking spurs into his steed, dashed off at full speed along the Edgeware Road. Impelled by a feeling, into which we shall not pause to inquire, the stranger started after them; but they were better mounted, and soon distanced him. Remarking that they struck off at a turning on the left, he took the same road, and soon found himself on Paddington-Green. A row of magnificent, and even then venerable, elms threw their broad arms over this pleasant spot. From a man, who was standing beneath the shade of one these noble trees, information was obtained that the horsemen had ridden along the Harrow Road. With a faint view of overtaking them the pursuer urged his steed to a quicker pace. Arrived at Westbourne-Green--then nothing more than a common covered with gorse and furzebushes, and boasting only a couple of cottages and an alehouse--he perceived through the hedges the objects of his search slowly ascending the gentle hill that rises from Kensall-Green.

By the time he had reached the summit of this hill, he had lost all trace of them; and the ardour of the chase having in some measure subsided, he began to reproach himself for his folly, in having wandered--as he conceived--so far out of his course. Before retracing his steps, however, he allowed his gaze to range over the vast and beautiful prospect spread out beneath him, which is now hidden, from the traveller's view by the high walls of the General Cemetery, and can, consequently, only be commanded from the interior of that attractive place of burial,--and which, before it was intersected by canals and railroads, and portioned out into hippodromes, was exquisite indeed. After feasting his eye upon this superb panorama, he was about to return, when he ascertained from a farmer that his nearest road to Willesden would be down a lane a little further on, to the right. Following this direction, he opened a gate, and struck into one of the most beautiful green lanes imaginable; which, after various windings, conducted him into a more frequented road, and eventually brought him to the place he sought. Glancing at the finger-post over the cage, which has been described as situated at the outskirts of the village, and seeing no directions to Dollis Hill, he made fresh inquiries as to where it lay, from an elderly man, who was standing with another countryman near the little prison.

"Whose house do you want, master?" said the man, touching his hat.

"Mr. Wood's," was the reply.

"There is Dollis Hill," said the man, pointing to a well-wooded eminence about a mile distant, "and there," he added, indicating the roof of a house just visible above a grove of trees "is Mr. Wood's. If you ride past the church, and mount the hill, you'll come to Neasdon and then you'll not have above half a mile to go."

The young man thanked his informant, and was about to follow his instructions, when the other called after him----

"I say, master, did you ever hear tell of Mr. Wood's famous 'prentice?"

"What apprentice?" asked the stranger, in surprise.

"Why, Jack Sheppard, the notorious house-breaker,--him as has robbed half Lunnun, to be sure. You must know, Sir, when he was a lad, the day after he broke into his master's house in Wych Street, he picked a gentleman's pocket in our church, during sarvice time,--that he did, the heathen. The gentleman catched him i' th' fact, and we shut him up for safety i' that pris'n. But," said the fellow, with a laugh, "he soon contrived to make his way out on it, though. Ever since he's become so famous, the folks about here ha' christened it Jack Sheppard's cage. His mother used to live i' this village, just down yonder; but when her son took to bad ways, she went distracted,--and now she's i' Bedlam, I've heerd."

"I tell e'e what, John Dump," said the other fellow, who had hitherto preserved silence, "I don't know whether you talkin' o' Jack Sheppard has put him into my head or not; but I once had him pointed out to me, and if that *were* him as I seed then, he's just now ridden past us, and put up at the Six Bells."

"The deuce he has!" cried Dump. "If you were sure o' that we might seize him, and get the reward for his apprehension."

"That 'ud be no such easy matter," replied the countryman. "Jack's a desperate fellow, and is always well armed; besides, he has a comrade with him. But I'll tell e'e what we *might* do----"

The young man heard no more. Taking the direction pointed out, he rode off. As he passed the Six Bells, he noticed the steeds of the two horsemen at the door; and glancing into the house, perceived the younger of the two in the passage. The latter no sooner beheld him than he dashed hastily into an adjoining room. After debating with himself whether he should further seek an interview, which, though, now in his power, was so sedulously shunned by the other party, he decided in the negative; and contenting himself with writing upon a slip of paper the hasty words,--"You are known by the villagers,--be upon your guard,"--he gave it to the ostler, with instructions to deliver it instantly to the owner of the horse he pointed out, and pursued his course.

Passing the old rectory, and still older church, with its reverend screen of trees, and slowly ascending a hill side, from whence he obtained enchanting peeps of the spire and college of Harrow, he reached the cluster of well-built houses which constitute the village of Neasdon. From this spot a road, more resembling the drive through a park than a public thoroughfare, led him gradually to the brow of Dollis Hill. It was a serene and charming evening, and twilight was gently stealing over the face of the country. Bordered by fine timber, the road occasionally offered glimpses of a lovely valley, until a wider opening gave a full view of a delightful and varied prospect. On the left lay the heights of Hampstead, studded with villas, while farther off a hazy cloud marked the position of the metropolis. The stranger concluded he could not be far from his destination, and a turn in the road showed him the house.

Beneath two tall elms, whose boughs completely overshadowed the roof, stood Mr. Wood's dwelling,--a plain, substantial, commodious farm-house. On a bench at the foot of the trees, with a pipe in his mouth, and a tankard by his side, sat the worthy carpenter, looking the picture of good-heartedness and benevolence. The progress of time was marked in Mr. Wood by increased corpulence and decreased powers of vision,--by deeper wrinkles and higher shoulders, by scantier breath and a fuller habit. Still he looked hale and hearty, and the country life he led had imparted a ruddier glow to his cheek. Around him were all the evidences of plenty. A world of haystacks, bean-stacks, and straw-ricks flanked the granges adjoining his habitation; the yard was crowded with poultry, pigeons were feeding at his feet, cattle were being driven towards the stall, horses led to the stable, a large mastiff was rattling his chain, and stalking majestically in front of his kennel, while a number of farming-men were passing and repassing about their various occupations. At the back of the house, on a bank, rose an old-fashioned terrace-garden, full of apple-trees and other fruit-trees in blossom, and lively with the delicious verdure of early spring.

Hearing the approach of the rider, Mr. Wood turned to look at him. It was now getting dusk, and he could only imperfectly distinguish the features and figure of the stranger.

"I need not ask whether this is Mr. Wood's," said the latter, "since I find him at his own gate."

"You are right, Sir," said the worthy carpenter, rising. "I am Owen Wood, at your service."

"You do not remember me, I dare say," observed the stranger.

"I can't say I do," replied Wood. "Your voice seems familiar to me--and--but I'm getting a little deaf--and my eyes don't serve me quite so well as they used to do, especially by this light."

"Never mind," returned the stranger, dismounting; "you'll recollect me by and by, I've no doubt. I bring you tidings of an old friend."

"Then you're heartily welcome, Sir, whoever you are. Pray, walk in. Here, Jem, take the gentleman's horse to the stable--see him dressed and fed directly. Now, Sir, will you please to follow me?"

Mr. Wood then led the way up a rather high and, according to modern notions, incommodious flight of steps, and introduced his guest to a neat parlour, the windows of which were darkened by pots of flowers and creepers. There was no light in the room; but, notwithstanding this, the young man did not fail to detect the buxom figure of Mrs. Wood, now more buxom and more gorgeously arrayed than ever,--as well as a young and beautiful female, in whom he was at no loss to recognise the carpenter's daughter.

Winifred Wood was now in her twentieth year. Her features were still slightly marked by the disorder alluded to in the description of her as a child,--but that was the only drawback to her beauty. Their expression was so amiable, that it would have redeemed a countenance a thousand times plainer than hers. Her figure was perfect,--tall, graceful, rounded,--and, then, she had deep liquid blue eyes, that rivalled the stars in lustre. On the stranger's appearance, she was seated near the window busily occupied with her needle.

"My wife and daughter, Sir," said the carpenter, introducing them to his guest.

Mrs. Wood, whose admiration for masculine beauty was by no means abated, glanced at the well-proportioned figure of the young man, and made him a very civil salutation. Winifred's reception was kind, but more distant, and after the slight ceremonial she resumed her occupation.

"This gentleman brings us tidings of an old friend, my dear," said the carpenter.

"Ay, indeed! And who may that be?" inquired his wife.

"One whom you may perhaps have forgotten," replied the stranger, "but who can never forget the kindness he experienced at your hands, or at those of your excellent husband."

At the sound of his voice every vestige of colour fled from Winifred's cheeks, and the work upon which she was engaged fell from her hand.

"I have a token to deliver to you," continued the stranger, addressing her.

"To me?" gasped Winifred.

"This locket," he said, taking a little ornament attached to a black ribband from his breast, and giving it her,--"do you remember it?"

"I do--I do!" cried Winifred.

"What's all this?" exclaimed Wood in amazement.

"Do you not know me, father?" said the young man, advancing towards him, and warmly grasping his hand. "Have nine years so changed me, that there is no trace left of your adopted son?"

"God bless me!" ejaculated the carpenter, rubbing his eyes, "can--can it be?"

"Surely," screamed Mrs. Wood, joining the group, "it isn't Thames Darrell come to life again?"

"It is--it is!" cried Winifred, rushing towards him, and flinging her arms round his neck,--"it is my dear--dear brother!"

"Well, this is what I never expected to see," said the carpenter, wiping his eyes; "I hope I'm not dreaming! Thames, my dear boy, as soon as Winny has done with you, let me embrace you."

"My turn comes before yours, Sir," interposed his better half. "Come to my arms, Thames! Oh! dear! Oh! dear!"

To repeat the questions and congratulations which now ensued, or describe the extravagant joy of the carpenter, who, after he had hugged his adopted son to his breast with such warmth as almost to squeeze the breath from his body, capered around the room, threw his wig into the empty fire-grate, and committed various other fantastic actions, in order to get rid of his superfluous satisfaction--to describe the scarcely less extravagant raptures of his spouse, or the more subdued, but not less heartfelt delight of Winifred, would be a needless task, as it must occur to every one's imagination. Supper was quickly served; the oldest bottle of wine was brought from the cellar; the strongest barrel of ale was tapped; but not one of the party could eat or drink--their hearts were too full.

Thames sat with Winifred's hand clasped in his own, and commenced a recital of his adventures, which may be briefly told. Carried out to sea by Van Galgebrok, and thrown overboard, while struggling with the waves, he had been picked up by a French fishing-boat, and carried to Ostend. After encountering various hardships and privations for a long time, during which he had no means of communicating with England, he, at length, found his way to Paris, where he was taken notice of by Cardinal Dubois, who employed him as one of his secretaries, and subsequently advanced to the service of Philip of Orleans, from whom he received a commission. On the death of his royal patron, he resolved to return to his own country; and, after various delays, which had postponed it to the present time, he had succeeded in accomplishing his object.

Winifred listened to his narration with the profoundest attention; and, when it concluded, her tearful eye and throbbing bosom told how deeply her feelings had been interested.

The discourse, then, turned to Darrell's old playmate, Jack Sheppard; and Mr. Wood, in deploring his wild career, adverted to the melancholy condition to which it had reduced his mother.

"For my part, it's only what I expected of him," observed Mrs. Wood, "and I'm sorry and surprised he hasn't swung for his crimes before this. The gallows has groaned for him for years. As to his mother, I've no pity for her. She deserves what has befallen her."

"Dear mother, don't say so," returned Winifred. "One of the consequences of criminal conduct, is the shame and disgrace which--worse than any punishment the evil-doer can suffer--is brought by it upon the innocent relatives; and, if Jack had considered this, perhaps he would not have acted as he has done, and have entailed so much misery on his unhappy parent."

"I always detested Mrs. Sheppard," cried the carpenter's wife bitterly; "and, I repeat, Bedlam's too good for her."

"My dear," observed Wood, "you should be more charitable--"

"Charitable!" repeated his wife, "that's your constant cry. Marry, come up! I've been a great deal too charitable. Here's Winny always urging you to go and visit Mrs. Sheppard in the asylum, and take her this, and send her that;--and I've never prevented you, though such mistaken liberality's enough to provoke a saint. And, then, forsooth, she must needs prevent your hanging Jack Sheppard after the robbery in Wych Street, when you might have done so. Perhaps you'll call that charity: I call it defeating the ends of justice. See what a horrible rascal you've let loose upon the world!"

"I'm sure, mother," rejoined Winifred, "if any one was likely to feel resentment, I was; for no one could be more frightened. But I was sorry for poor Jack--as I am still, and hoped he would mend."

"Mend!" echoed Mrs. Wood, contemptuously, "he'll never mend till he comes to Tyburn."

"At least, I will hope so," returned Winifred. "But, as I was saying, I was most dreadfully frightened on the night of the robbery! Though so young at the time, I remember every circumstance distinctly. I was sitting up, lamenting your departure, dear Thames, when, hearing an odd noise, I went to the landing, and, by the light of a dark lantern, saw Jack Sheppard, stealing up stairs, followed by two men with crape on their faces. I'm ashamed to say that I was too much terrified to scream out--but ran and hid myself."

"Hold your tongue!" cried Mrs. Wood. "I declare you throw me into an ague. Do you think I forget it? Didn't they help themselves to all the plate and the money--to several of my best dresses, and amongst others, to my favourite kincob gown; and I've never been able to get another like it! Marry, come up! I'd hang 'em all, if I could. Were such a thing to happen again, I'd never let Mr. Wood rest till he brought the villains to justice."

"I hope such a thing never *will* happen again, my dear," observed Wood, mildly, "but, when it does, it will be time to consider what course we ought to pursue."

"Let them attempt it, if they dare!" cried Mrs. Wood, who had worked herself into a passion; "and, I'll warrant 'em, the boldest robber among 'em shall repent it, if he comes across me."

"No doubt, my dear," acquiesced the carpenter, "no doubt."

Thames, who had been more than once on the point of mentioning his accidental rencounter with Jack Sheppard, not being altogether without apprehension, from the fact of his being in the neighbourhood,--now judged it more prudent to say nothing on the subject, from a fear of increasing Mrs. Wood's displeasure; and he was the more readily induced to do this, as the conversation began to turn upon his own affairs. Mr. Wood could give him no further information respecting Sir Rowland Trenchard than what he had obtained from Kneebone; but begged him to defer the further consideration of the line of conduct he meant to pursue until the morrow, when he hoped to have a plan to lay before him, of which he would approve.

The night was now advancing, and the party began to think of separating. As Mrs. Wood, who had recovered her good humour, quitted the room she bestowed a hearty embrace on Thames, and she told him laughingly, that she would "defer all *she* had to propose to him until to-morrow."

To-morrow! She never beheld it.

After an affectionate parting with Winifred, Thames was conducted by the carpenter to his sleeping apartment--a comfortable cosy chamber; such a one, in short, as can only be met with in the country, with its dimity-curtained bed, its sheets fragrant of lavender, its clean white furniture, and an atmosphere breathing of freshness. Left to himself, he took a survey of the room, and his heart leaped as he beheld over the, chimney-piece, a portrait of himself. It was a copy of the pencil sketch taken of him nine years ago by Winifred, and awakened a thousand tender recollections.

When about to retire to rest, the rencounter with Jack Sheppard again recurred to him, and he half blamed himself for not acquainting Mr. Wood with the circumstances, and putting him upon his guard against the possibility of an attack. On weighing the matter over, he grew so uneasy that he resolved to descend, and inform him of his misgivings. But, when he got to the door with this intention, he became ashamed of his fears; and feeling convinced that Jack--bad as he might be--was not capable of such atrocious conduct as to plunder his benefactor twice, he contented himself with looking to the priming of his pistols, and placing them near him, to be ready in case of need, he threw himself on the bed and speedily fell asleep.

CHAPTER II.
The Burglary at Dollis Hill.

THAMES Darrell's fears were not, however, groundless. Danger, in the form he apprehended, was lurking outside: nor was he destined to enjoy long repose. On receiving the warning note from the ostler, Jack Sheppard and his companion left Willesden, and taking--as a blind--the direction of Harrow, returned at night-fall by a by-lane to Neasdon, and put up at a little public-house called the Spotted Dog. Here they remained till midnight when, calling for their reckoning and their steeds, they left the house.

It was a night well-fitted to their enterprise, calm, still, and profoundly dark. As they passed beneath the thick trees that shade the road to Dollis Hill, the gloom was almost impenetrable. The robbers proceeded singly, and kept on the grass skirting the road, so that no noise was made by their horses' feet.

As they neared the house, Jack Sheppard, who led the way, halted and addressed his companion in a low voice:--

"I don't half like this job, Blueskin," he said; "it always went against the grain. But, since I've seen the friend and companion of my childhood, Thames Darrell, I've no heart for it. Shall we turn back?"

"And disappoint Mr. Wild, Captain?" remonstrated the other, in a deferential tone. "You know this is a pet project. It might be dangerous to thwart him."

"Pish!" cried Jack: "I don't value his anger a straw. All our fraternity are afraid of him; but I laugh at his threats. He daren't quarrel with me: and if he does, let him look to himself. I've my own reasons for disliking this job."

"Well, you know I always act under your orders, Captain," returned Blueskin; "and if you give the word to retreat, I shall obey, of course: but I know what Edgeworth Bess will say when we go home empty-handed."

"Why what will she say?" inquired Sheppard.

"That we were afraid," replied the other; "but never mind her."

"Ay; but I do mind her," cried Jack upon whom his comrade's observation had produced the desired effect. "We'll do it."

"That's right, Captain," rejoined Blueskin. "You pledged yourself to Mr. Wild--"

"I did," interrupted Jack; "and I never yet broke an engagement. Though a thief, Jack Sheppard is a man of his word."

"To be sure he is," acquiesced Blueskin. "I should like to meet the man who would dare to gainsay it."

"One word before we begin, Blueskin," said Jack, authoritatively; "in case the family should be alarmed--mind, no violence. There's one person in the house whom I wouldn't frighten for the world."

"Wood's daughter, I suppose?" observed the other.

"You've hit it," answered Sheppard.

"What say you to carrying her off, Captain?" suggested Blueskin. "If you've a fancy for the girl, we might do it."

"No--no," laughed Jack. "Bess wouldn't bear a rival. But if you wish to do old Wood a friendly turn, you may bring his wife."

"I shouldn't mind ridding him of her," said Blueskin, gruffly; "and if she comes in my way, may the devil seize me if I don't make short work with her!"

"You forget," rejoined Jack, sternly, "I've just said I'll have no violence--mind that."

With this, they dismounted; and fastening their horses to a tree, proceeded towards the house. It was still so dark, that nothing could be distinguished except the heavy masses of timber by which the premises were surrounded; but as they advanced, lights were visible in some of the windows. Presently they came to a wall, on the other side of which the dog began to bark violently; but Blueskin tossed him a piece of prepared meat, and uttering a low growl, he became silent. They then clambered over a hedge, and scaling another wall, got into the garden at the back of the house. Treading with noiseless step over the soft mould, they soon reached the building. Arrived there, Jack felt about for a particular window; and having discovered the object of his search, and received the necessary implements from his companion, he instantly commenced operations. In a few seconds, the shutter flew open,--then the window,--and they were in the room. Jack now carefully closed the shutters, while Blueskin struck a light, with which he set fire to a candle. The room they were in was a sort of closet, with the door locked outside; but this was only a moment's obstacle to Jack, who with a chisel forced back the bolt. The operation was effected with so much rapidity and so little noise, that even if any one had been on the alert, he could scarcely have detected it. They then took off their boots, and crept stealthily up stairs, treading upon the point of their toes so cautiously, that not a board creaked beneath their weight. Pausing at each door on the landing, Jack placed his ear to the keyhole, and listened intently. Having ascertained by the breathing which room Thames occupied, he speedily contrived to fasten him in. He then tried the door of Mr. Wood's bed-chamber--it was locked, with the key left in it. This occasioned a little delay; but Jack, whose skill as a workman in the particular line he had chosen was unequalled, and who laughed at difficulties, speedily cut out a panel by means of a centre-bit and knife, took the key from the other side, and unlocked the door. Covering his face with a crape mask, and taking the candle from his associate, Jack entered the room; and, pistol in hand, stepped up to the bed, and approached the light to the eyes of the sleepers. The loud noise proceeding from the couch proved that their slumbers were deep and real; and unconscious of the danger in which she stood, Mrs. Wood turned over to obtain a more comfortable position. During this movement, Jack grasped the barrel of his pistol, held in his breath, and motioned to Blueskin, who bared a long knife, to keep still. The momentary alarm over, he threw a piece of-wash leather over a bureau, so as to deaden the sound, and instantly broke it open with a small crow-bar. While he was filling his pockets with golden coin from this store, Blueskin had pulled the plate-chest from under the bed, and having forced it open, began filling a canvass bag with its contents,--silver coffee-pots, chocolate-dishes, waiters trays, tankards, goblets, and candlesticks. It might be supposed that these articles, when thrust together into the bag, would have jingled; but these skilful practitioners managed matters so well that no noise was made. After rifling the room of everything portable, including some of Mrs. Wood's ornaments and wearing apparel, they prepared to depart. Jack then intimated his intention of visiting Winifred's chamber, in which several articles of value were known to be kept; but as, notwithstanding his reckless character, he still retained a feeling of respect for the object of his boyish affections, he would not suffer Blueskin to accompany him, so he commanded him to keep watch over the sleepers--strictly enjoining him, however, to do them no injury. Again having recourse to the centre-bit,--for Winifred's door was locked,--Jack had nearly cut out a panel, when a sudden outcry was raised in the carpenter's chamber. The next moment, a struggle was heard, and Blueskin appeared at the door, followed by Mrs. Wood.

Jack instandly extinguished the light, and called to his comrade to come after him.

But Blueskin found it impossible to make off,--at least with the spoil,--Mrs. Wood having laid hold of the canvass-bag.

"Give back the things!" cried the, lady. "Help!--help, Mr. Wood!"

"Leave go!" thundered Blueskin--"leave go--you'd better!"--and he held the sack as firmly as he could with one hand, while with the other he searched for his knife.

"No, I won't leave go!" screamed Mrs. Wood. "Fire!--murder--thieves!--I've got one of 'em!"

"Come along," cried Jack.

"I can't," answered Blueskin. "This she-devil has got hold of the sack. Leave go, I tell you!" and he forced open the knife with his teeth.

"Help!--murder!--thieves!" screamed Mrs. Wood;--"Owen--Owen!--Thames, help!"

"Coming!" cried Mr. Wood, leaping from the bed. "Where are you?"

"Here," replied Mrs. Wood. "Help--I'll hold him!"

"Leave her," cried Jack, darting down stairs, amid a furious ringing of bells,--"the house is alarmed,--follow me!"

"Curses light on you!" cried Blueskin, savagely; "since you won't be advised, take your fate."

And seizing her by the hair, he pulled back her head, and drew the knife with all his force across her throat. There was a dreadful stifled groan, and she fell heavily upon the landing.

The screams of the unfortunate woman had aroused Thames from his slumbers. Snatching-up his pistols, he rushed to the door, but to his horror found it fastened.

He heard the struggle on the landing, the fall of the heavy body, the groan,--and excited almost to frenzy by his fears, he succeeded in forcing open the door. By this time, several of the terrified domestics appeared with lights. A terrible spectacle was presented to the young man's gaze:--the floor deluged with blood--the mangled and lifeless body of Mrs. Wood,--Winifred fainted in the arms of a female attendant,--and Wood standing beside them almost in a state of distraction. Thus, in a few minutes, had this happy family been plunged into the depths of misery. At this juncture, a cry was raised by a servant from below, that the robbers were flying through the garden. Darting to a window looking in that direction, Thames threw it up, and discharged both his pistols, but without effect. In another minute, the tramp of horses' feet told that the perpetrators of the outrage had effected their escape.

CHAPTER III.
Jack Sheppard's Quarrel with Jonathan Wild.

SCARCELY an hour after the horrible occurrence just related, as Jonathan Wild was seated in the audience-chamber of his residence at the Old Bailey, occupied, like Peachum, (for whose portrait he sat,) with his account-books and registers, he was interrupted by the sudden entrance of Quilt Arnold, who announced Jack Sheppard and Blueskin.

"Ah!" cried Wild, laying down his pen and looking up with a smile of satisfaction. "I was just thinking of you Jack. What news. Have you done the trick at Dollis Hill?--brought off the swag--eh?"

"No," answered Jack, flinging himself sullenly into a chair, "I've not."

"Why how's this?" exclaimed Jonathan. "Jack Sheppard failed! I'd not believe it, if any one but himself told me so."

"I'v not failed," returned Jack, angrily; "but we've done too much."

"I'm no reader of riddles," said Jonathan. "Speak plainly."

"Let this speak for me," said Sheppard, tossing a heavy bag of money towards him. "You can generally understand that language. There's more than I undertook to bring. It has been purchased by blood!"

"What! have you cut old Wood's throat?" asked Wild, with great unconcern, as he took up the bag.

"If I *had*, you'd not have seen me here," replied Jack, sullenly. "The blood that has been spilt is that of his wife."

"It was her own fault," observed Blueskin, moodily. "She wouldn't let me go. I did it in self-defence."

"I care not why you did it," said Jack, sternly. "We work together no more."

"Come, come, Captain," remonstrated Blueskin. "I thought you'd have got rid of your ill-humour by this time. You know as well as I do that it was accident."

"Accident or not," rejoined Sheppard; "you're no longer pall of mine."

"And so this is my reward for having made you the tip-top cracksman you are," muttered Blueskin;--"to be turned off at a moment's notice, because I silenced a noisy woman. It's too hard. Think better of it."

"My mind's made up," rejoined Jack, coldly,--"we part to-night."

"I'll not go," answered the other. "I love you like a son, and will follow you like a dog. You'd not know what to do without me, and shan't drive me off."

"Well!" remarked Jonathan, who had paid little attention to the latter part of the conversation: "this is an awkward business certainly: but we must do the best we can in it. You must keep out of the way till it's blown over. I can accommodate you below."

"I don't require it," returned Sheppard. "I'm tired of the life I'm leading. I shall quit it and go abroad."

"I'll go with you," said Blueskin.

"Before either of you go, you will ask my permission," said Jonathan, coolly.

"How!" exclaimed Sheppard. "Do you mean to say you will interfere--"

"I mean to say this," interrupted Wild, with contemptuous calmness, "that I'll neither allow you to leave England nor the profession you've engaged in. I wouldn't allow you to be honest even if you could be so,--which I doubt. You are my slave-- and such you shall continue.'"

"Slave?" echoed Jack.

"Dare to disobey," continued Jonathan: "neglect my orders, and I will hang you."

Sheppard started to his feet.

"Hear me," he cried, restraining himself with difficulty. "It is time you should know whom you have to deal with. Henceforth, I utterly throw off the yoke you have laid upon me. I will neither stir hand nor foot for you more. Attempt to molest me, and I split. You are more in my power than I am in yours. Jack Sheppard is a match for Jonathan Wild, any day."

"That he is," added Blueskin, approvingly.

Jonathan smiled contemptuously.

"One motive alone shall induce me to go on with you," said Jack.

"What's that?" asked Wild.

"The youth whom you delivered to Van Galgebrok,--Thames Darrell, is returned."

"Impossible!" cried Jonathan. "He was thrown overboard, and perished at sea."

"He is alive," replied Jack, "I have seen him, and might have conversed with him if I had chosen. Now, I know you can restore him to his rights, if you choose. Do so; and I am yours as heretofore."

"Humph!" exclaimed Jonathan.

"Your answer!" cried Sheppard. "Yes, or no?"

"I will make no terms with you," rejoined Wild, sternly. "You have defied me, and shall feel my power. You have been useful to me, or I would not have spared you thus long. I swore to hang you two years ago, but I deferred my purpose."

"Deferred!" echoed Sheppard.

"Hear me out," said Jonathan. "You came hither under my protection, and you shall depart freely,--nay, more, you shall have an hour's grace. After that time, I shall place my setters on your heels."

"You cannot prevent my departure," replied Jack, dauntlessly, "and therefore your offer is no favour. But I tell you in return, I shall take no pains to hide myself. If you want me, you know where to find me."

"An hour," said Jonathan, looking at his watch,--"remember!"

"If you send for me to the Cross Shovels in the Mint, where I'm going with Blueskin, I will surrender myself without resistance," returned Jack.

"You will spare the officers a labour then," rejoined Jonathan.

"Can't I settle this business, Captain," muttered Blueskin, drawing a pistol.

"Don't harm him," said Jack, carelessly: "he dares not do it."

So saying, he left the room.

"Blueskin," said Jonathan, as that worthy was about to follow, "I advise you to remain with me."

"No," answered the ruffian, moodily. "If you arrest him, you must arrest me also."

"As you will," said Jonathan, seating himself.

Jack and his comrade went to the Mint, where he was joined by Edgeworth

Bess, with whom he sat down most unconcernedly to supper. His revelry, how-ever, was put an end at the expiration of the time mentioned by Jonathan, by the entrance of a posse of constables with Quilt Arnold and Abraham Mendez at their head. Jack, to the surprise of all his companions, at once surrendered himself: but Blueskin would have made a fierce resistance, and attempted a rescue if he had not been ordered by his leader to desist. He then made off. Edgeworth Bess, who passed for Sheppard's wife, was secured. They were hurried before a magistrate, and charged by Jonathan Wild with various robberies; but, as Jack Sheppard stated that he had most important disclosures to make, as well as charges to bring forward against his accuser, he was committed with his female companion to the New Prison in Clerkenwell for further examination.

CHAPTER IV.
Jack Sheppard's Escape from the New Prison.

IN consequence of Jack Sheppard's desperate character, it was judged expedient by the keeper of the New Prison to load him with fetters of unusual weight, and to place him in a cell which, from its strength and security, was called the Newgate Ward. The ward in which he was confined, was about six yards in length, and three in width, and in height, might be about twelve feet. The windows which were about nine feet from the floor, had no glass; but were secured by thick iron bars, and an oaken beam. Along the floor ran an iron bar to which Jack's chain was attached, so that he could move along it from one end of the chamber to the other. No prisoner except Edgeworth Bess was placed in the same cell with him. Jack was in excellent spirits; and by his wit, drollery and agreeable demeanour, speedily became a great favourite with the turnkey, who allowed him every indulgence consistent with his situation. The report of his detention caused an immense sensation. Numberless charges were preferred against him, amongst others, information was lodged of the robbery at Dollis Hill, and murder of Mrs. Wood, and a large reward offered for the apprehension of Blueskin; and as, in addition to this, Jack had threatened to impeach Wild, his next examination was looked forward to with the greatest interest.

The day before this examination was appointed to take place--the third of the prisoner's detention--an old man, respectably dressed, requested permission to see him. Jack's friends were allowed to visit him,; but as he had openly avowed his intention of attempting an escape, their proceedings were narrowly watched. The old man was conducted to Jack's cell by the turnkey, who remained near him during their interview. He appeared to be a stranger to the prisoner, and the sole motive of his visit, curiosity. After a brief conversation, which Sheppard sustained with his accustomed liveliness, the old man turned to Bess and addressed a few words of common-place gallantry to her. While this was going on, Jack suddenly made a movement which attracted the turnkey's attention; and during that interval the old man slipped some articles wrapped in a handkerchief into Bess's hands, who instantly secreted them in her bosom. The turnkey looked round the next moment, but the manoeuvre escaped his observation. After a little further discourse the old man took his departure.

Left alone with Edgeworth Bess, Jack burst into a loud laugh of exultation.

"Blueskin's a friend in need," he said. "His disguise was capital; but I detected it in a moment. Has he given you the tools?"

"He has," replied Bess, producing the handkerchief.

"Bravo," cried Sheppard, examining its contents, which proved to be a file, a chisel, two or three gimblets, and a piercer. "Jonathan Wild shall find it's not easy to detain me. As sure as he is now living, I'll pay him a visit in the Old Bailey before morning. And then I'll pay off old scores. It's almost worth while being sent to prison to have the pleasure of escaping. I shall now be able to test my skill." And running on in this way, he carefully concealed the tools.

Whether the turnkey entertained any suspicion of the old man, Jack could not tell, but that night he was more than usually rigorous in his search; and having carefully examined the prisoners and finding nothing to excite his suspicions, he departed tolerably satisfied.

As soon as he was certain he should be disturbed no more, Jack set to work, and with the aid of the file in less than an hour had freed himself from his fetters. With Bess's assistance he then climbed up to the window, which, as has just been stated, was secured by iron bars of great thickness crossed by a stout beam of oak. The very sight of these impediments, would have appalled a less courageous spirit than Sheppard's--but nothing could daunt him. To work then he went, and with wonderful industry filed off two of the iron bars. Just as he completed this operation, the file broke. The oaken beam, nine inches in thickness, was now the sole but most formidable obstacle to his flight. With his gimblet he contrived to bore a number of holes so close together that at last one end of the bar, being completely pierced through, yielded; and pursuing the same with the other extremity, it fell out altogether.

This last operation was so fatiguing, that for a short time he was obliged to pause to recover the use of his fingers. He then descended; and having induced Bess to take off some part of her clothing, he tore the gown and petticoat into shreds and twisted them into a sort of rope which he fastened to the lower bars of the window. With some difficulty he contrived to raise her to the window, and with still greater difficulty to squeeze her through it--her bulk being much greater than his own. He then made a sort of running noose, passed it over her body, and taking firmly hold of the bars, prepared to guide her descent. But Bess could scarcely summon resolution enough to hazard the experiment; and it was only on Jack's urgent intreaties, and even threats, that she could be prevailed on to trust herself to the frail tenure of the rope he had prepared. At length, however, she threw herself off; and Jack carefully guiding the rope she landed in safety.

The next moment he was by her side.

But the great point was still unaccomplished. They had escaped from the New Prison, it is true; but the wall of Clerkenwell Bridewell, by which that jail was formerly surrounded, and which was more than twenty feet high, and protected by formidable and bristling *chevaux de frise*, remained to be scaled. Jack, however, had an expedient for mastering this difficulty. He ventured to the great gates, and by inserting his gimblets into the wood at intervals, so as to form points upon which he could rest his foot, he contrived, to ascend them; and when at the top, having fastened a portion of his dress to the spikes, he managed, not without considerable risk, to draw up his female companion. Once over the iron spikes, Bess exhibited no reluctance to be let down on the other side of the wall. Having seen his mistress safe down, Jack instantly descended, leaving the best part of his clothes, as a memorial of his flight, to the jailor.

And thus he effected his escape from the New Prison.

CHAPTER V.
The Disguise.

IN a hollow in the meadows behind the prison whence Jack Sheppard had escaped,--for, at this time, the whole of the now thickly-peopled district north of Clerkenwell Bridewell was open country, stretching out in fertile fields in the direction of Islington--and about a quarter of a mile off, stood a solitary hovel, known as Black Mary's Hole. This spot, which still retains its name, acquired the appellation from an old crone who lived there, and who, in addition to a very equivocal character for honesty, enjoyed the reputation of being a witch. Without inquiring into the correctness of the latter part of the story, it may be sufficient to state, that Black Mary was a person in whom Jack Sheppard thought he could confide, and, as Edgeworth Bess was incapable of much further exertion, he determined to leave her in the old woman's care till the following night, while he shifted for himself and fulfilled his design--for, however rash or hazardous a project might be, if once conceived, Jack always executed it,--of visiting Jonathan Wild at his house in the Old Bailey.

It was precisely two o'clock on the morning of Whit-monday, the 25th of May 1724, when the remarkable escape before detailed was completed: and, though it wanted full two hours to daybreak, the glimmer of a waning moon prevented it from being totally dark. Casting a hasty glance, as he was about to turn an angle of the wall, at the great gates and upper windows of the prison, and perceiving no symptoms of pursuit, Jack proceeded towards the hovel at a very deliberate pace, carefully assisting his female companion over every obstacle in the road, and bearing her in his arms when, as was more than once the case, she sank from fright and exhaustion. In this way he crossed one or two public gardens and a bowling-green,--the neighbourhood of Clerkenwell then abounded in such places of amusement,--

passed the noted Ducking Pond, where Black Mary had been frequently immersed; and, striking off to the left across the fields, arrived in a few minutes at his destination.

Descending the hollow, or rather excavation,--for it was an old disused clay-pit, at the bottom of which the cottage was situated,--he speedily succeeded in arousing the ancient sibyl, and having committed Edgeworth Bess to her care, with a promise of an abundant reward in case she watched diligently over her safety, and attended to her comforts till his return,--to all which Black Mary readily agreed,--he departed with a heart lightened of half its load.

Jack's first object was to seek out Blueskin, whom he had no doubt he should find at the New Mint, at Wapping, for the Old Mint no longer afforded a secure retreat to the robber; and, with this view, he made the best of his way along a bye-lane leading towards Hockley-in-the-Hole. He had not proceeded far when he was alarmed by the tramp of a horse, which seemed to be rapidly approaching, and he had scarcely time to leap the hedge and conceal himself behind a tree, when a tall man, enveloped in an ample cloak, with his hat pulled over his brows, rode by at full speed. Another horseman followed quickly at the heels of the first; but just as he passed the spot where Jack stood, his steed missed its footing, and fell. Either ignorant of the accident, or heedless of it, the foremost horseman pursued his way without even turning his head.

Conceiving the opportunity too favourable to be lost, Jack sprang suddenly over the hedge, and before the man, who was floundering on the ground with one foot in the stirrup, could extricate himself from his embarrassing position, secured his pistols, which he drew from the holsters, and held them to his head. The fellow swore lustily, in a voice which Jack instantly recognised as that of Quilt Arnold, and vainly attempted to rise and draw his sword.

"Dog!" thundered Sheppard, putting the muzzle of the pistol so close to the janizary's ear, that the touch of the cold iron made him start, "don't you know me?"

"Blood and thunder!" exclaimed Quilt, opening his eyes with astonishment. "It can't be Captain Sheppard!"

"It *is*," replied Jack; "and you had better have met the devil on your road than me. Do you remember what I said when you took me at the Mint four days ago? I told you my turn would come. It *has* come,--and sooner than you expected."

"So I find, Captain," rejoined Quilt, submissively; "but you're too noble-hearted to take advantage of my situation. Besides, I acted for others, and not for myself."

"I know it," replied Sheppard, "and therefore I spare your life."

"I was sure you wouldn't injure me, Captain," remarked Quilt, in a wheedling tone, while he felt about for his sword; "you're far too brave to strike a fallen man."

"Ah! traitor!" cried Jack, who had noticed the movement; "make such another attempt, and it shall cost you your life." So saying, he unbuckled the belt to which the janizary's hanger was attached, and fastened it to his own girdle.

"And now," he continued, sternly, "was it your master who has just ridden by?"

"No," answered Quilt, sullenly.

"Who, then?" demanded Jack. "Speak, or I fire!"

"Well, if you *will* have it, it's Sir Rowland Trenchard."

"Sir Rowland Trenchard!" echoed Jack, in amazement. "What are you doing with him?"

"It's a long story, Captain, and I've no breath to tell it,--unless you choose to release me," rejoined Quilt.

"Get up, then," said Jack, freeing his foot from the stirrup. "Now--begin."

Quilt, however, seemed unwilling to speak.

"I should be sorry to proceed to extremities," continued Sheppard, again raising the pistol.

"Well, since you force me to betray my master's secrets," replied Quilt, sullenly, "I've ridden express to Manchester to deliver a message to Sir Rowland."

"Respecting Thames Darrell?" observed Jack.

"Why, how the devil did you happen to guess that?" cried the janizary.

"No matter," replied Sheppard. "I'm glad to find I'm right. You informed Sir Rowland that Thames Darrell was returned?"

"Exactly so," replied Quilt, "and he instantly decided upon returning to London with me. We've ridden post all the way, and I'm horribly tired, or you wouldn't have mastered me so easily."

"Perhaps not," replied Jack, to whom an idea had suddenly occurred. "Now, Sir, I'll trouble you for your coat. I've left mine on the spikes of the New Prison, and must borrow yours."

"Why, surely you can't be in earnest, Captain. You wouldn't rob Mr. Wild's chief janizary?"

"I'd rob Mr. Wild himself if I met him," retorted Jack. "Come, off with it, sirrah, or I'll blow out your brains, in the first place, and strip you afterwards."

"Well, rather than you should commit so great a crime, Captain, here it is," replied Quilt, handing him the garment in question. "Anything else?"

"Your waistcoat."

"'Zounds! Captain, I shall get my death of cold. I was in hopes you'd be content with my hat and wig."

"I shall require them as well," rejoined Sheppard; "and your boots."

"My boots! Fire and fury! They won't fit you; they are too large. Besides, how am I to ride home without them?"

"Don't distress yourself," returned Jack, "you shall walk. Now," he added, as his commands were reluctantly obeyed, "help me on with them."

Quilt knelt down, as if he meant to comply; but, watching his opportunity, he made a sudden grasp at Sheppard's leg, with the intention of overthrowing him.

But Jack was too nimble for him. Striking out his foot, he knocked half a dozen teeth down the janizary's throat; and, seconding the kick with a blow on the head from the butt-end of the pistol, stretched him, senseless and bleeding on the ground.

"Like master like man," observed Jack as he rolled the inanimate body to the side of the road. "From Jonathan Wild's confidential servant what could be expected but treachery?"

With this, he proceeded to dress himself in Quilt Arnold's clothes, pulled the wig over his face and eyes so as completely to conceal his features, slouched the hat over his brows, drew the huge boots above his knees, and muffled himself up in the best way he could. On searching the coat, he found, amongst other matters, a mask, a key, and a pocket-book. The latter appeared to contain several papers, which Jack carefully put by, in the hope that they might turn out of importance in a scheme of vengeance which he meditated against the thief-taker. He then mounted the jaded hack, which had long since regained its legs, and was quietly browsing the grass at the road-side, and, striking spurs into its side, rode off. He had not proceeded far when he encountered Sir Rowland, who, having missed his attendant, had returned to look after him.

"What has delayed you?" demanded the knight impatiently.

"My horse has had a fall," replied Jack, assuming to perfection--for he was a capital mimic,--the tones of Quilt Arnold. "It was some time before I could get him to move."

"I fancied I heard voices," rejoined Sir Rowland.

"So did I," answered Jack; "we had better move on. This is a noted place for highwaymen."

"I thought you told me that the rascal who has so long been the terror of the town--Jack Sheppard--was in custody."

"So he is," returned Jack; "but there's no saying how long he may remain so. Besides, there are greater rascals than Jack Sheppard at liberty, Sir Rowland."

Sir Rowland made no reply, but angrily quickened his pace. The pair then descended Saffron-hill, threaded Field-lane, and, entering Holborn, passed over the little bridge which then crossed the muddy waters of Fleet-ditch, mounted Snow-hill, and soon drew in the bridle before Jonathan Wild's door. Aware of Quilt Arnold's mode of proceeding, Jack instantly dismounted, and, instead of knocking, opened the door with the pass-key. The porter instantly made his appearance, and Sheppard ordered him to take care of the horses.

"Well, what sort of journey have you had, Quilt?" asked the man as he hastened to assist Sir Rowland to dismount.

"Oh! we've lost no time, as you perceive," replied Jack. "Is the governor within?"

"Yes; you'll find him in the audience-chamber. He has got Blueskin with him."

"Ah! indeed! what's he doing here?" inquired Jack.

"Come to buy off Jack Sheppard, I suppose," replied the fellow. "But it won't do. Mr. Wild has made up his mind, and, when that's the case, all the persuasion on earth won't turn him. Jack will be tried to-morrow; and, as sure as my name's Obadiah Lemon he'll take up his quarters at the King's-Head," pointing to Newgate, "over the way."

"Well, we shall see," replied Jack. "Look to the horses, Obadiah. This way, Sir

Rowland."

As familiar as Quilt Arnold himself with every part of Wild's mysterious abode, as well as with the ways of its inmates, Jack, without a moment's hesitation, took up a lamp which was burning in the hall, and led his companion up the great stone stairs. Arrived at the audience-chamber, he set down the light upon a stand, threw open the door, and announced in a loud voice, but with the perfect intonation of the person he represented,--"Sir Rowland Trenchard."

Jonathan, who was engaged in conversation with Blueskin, instantly arose, and bowed with cringing ceremoniousness to the knight. The latter haughtily returned his salutation, and flung himself, as if exhausted, into a chair.

"You've arrived sooner than I expected, Sir Rowland," observed the thief-taker. "Lost no time on the road--eh!--I didn't expect you till to-morrow at the earliest. Excuse me an instant while I dismiss this person.--You've your answer, Blueskin," he added, pushing that individual, who seemed unwilling to depart, towards the door; "it's useless to urge the matter further. Jack is registered in the Black Book."

"One word before I go," urged Blueskin.

"Not a syllable," replied Wild. "If you talk as long as an Old Bailey counsel, you'll not alter my determination."

"Won't my life do as well as his?" supplicated the other.

"Humph!" exclaimed Jonathan, doubtfully. "And you would surrender your-self--eh?"

"I'll surrender myself at once, if you'll engage to bring him off; and you'll get the reward from old Wood. It's two hundred pounds. Recollect that."

"Faithful fellow!" murmured Jack. "I forgive him his disobedience."

"Will you do it?" persisted Blueskin.

"No," replied Wild; "and I've only listened to your absurd proposal to see how far your insane attachment to this lad would carry you."

"I *do* love him," cried Blueskin, "and that's the long and short of it. I've taught him all he can do; and there isn't his fellow, and never will be again. I've seen many a clever cracksman, but never one like him. If you hang Jack Sheppard, you'll cut off the flower o' the purfession. But I'll not believe it of you. It's all very well to read him a lesson, and teach him obedience; but you've gone far enough for that."

"Not quite," rejoined the thief-taker, significantly.

"Well," growled Blueskin, "you've had my offer."

"And you my warning," retorted Wild. "Good night!"

"Blueskin," whispered Jack, in his natural tones, as the other passed him, "wait without."

"Power o' mercy!" cried Blueskin starting.

"What's the matter?" demanded Jonathan, harshly.

"Nothin'--nothin'," returned Blueskin; "only I thought--"

"You saw the hangman, no doubt," said Jack. "Take courage, man; it is only Quilt Arnold. Come, make yourself scarce. Don't you see Mr. Wild's busy." And then he added, in an under tone, "Conceal yourself outside, and be within call."

Blueskin nodded, and left the room. Jack affected to close the door, but left it slightly ajar.

"What did you say to him?" inquired Jonathan, suspiciously.

"I advised him not to trouble you farther about Jack Sheppard," answered the supposed janizary.

"He seems infatuated about the lad," observed Wild. "I shall be obliged to hang him to keep him company. And now, Sir Rowland," he continued, turning to the knight, "to our own concerns. It's a long time since we met, eight years and more. I hope you've enjoyed your health. 'Slife! you are wonderfully altered. I should scarcely have known you."

The knight was indeed greatly changed. Though not much passed the middle term of life, he seemed prematurely stricken with old age. His frame was wasted, and slightly bent; his eyes were hollow, his complexion haggard, and his beard, which had remained unshorn during his hasty journey, was perfectly white. His manner, however, was as stern and haughty as ever, and his glances retained their accustomed fire.

"I did not come hither to consult you as to the state of my health, Sir," he observed, displeased by Jonathan's allusion to the alteration in his appearance.

"True," replied Wild. "You were no doubt surprised by the unlooked-for intelligence I sent you of your nephew's return?"

"Was it unlooked-for on your part?" demanded the knight, distrustfully.

"On my soul, yes," rejoined Jonathan. "I should as soon have expected the bones of Tom Sheppard to reunite themselves and walk out of that case, as Thames Darrell to return. The skipper, Van Galgebrok, affirmed to me,--nay, gave me the additional testimony of two of his crew,--that he was thrown overboard. But it appears he was picked up by fishermen, and carried to France, where he has remained ever since, and where it would have been well for him if he had remained altogether."

"Have you seen him?" asked Trenchard.

"I have," replied Wild; "and nothing but the evidence of my senses would have made me believe he was living, after the positive assurance I received to the contrary. He is at present with Mr. Wood,--the person whom you may remember adopted him,--at Dollis Hill, near Willesden; and it's a singular but fortunate circumstance, so far as we are concerned, that Mrs. Wood chanced to be murdered by Blueskin, the fellow who just left the room, on the very night of his return, as it has thrown the house into such confusion, and so distracted them, that he has had no time as yet for hostile movements."

"And what course do you propose to pursue in reference to him?" asked Sir Rowland.

"My plan is a very simple one," rejoined the thief-taker smiling bitterly. "I would treat him as you treated his father, Sir Rowland."

"Murder him!" cried Trenchard shuddering.

"Ay, murder him, if you like the term," returned Wild. "I should call it putting him out of the way. But no matter how you phrase it, the end is the same."

"I cannot consent to it," replied Sir Rowland firmly. "Since the sea has spared him, I will spare him. It is in vain to struggle against the arm of fate. I will shed no more blood."

"And perish upon the gibbet," rejoined Jonathan contemptuously.

"Flight is still left me," replied Trenchard. "I can escape to France."

"And do you think I'll allow you to depart," cried Jonathan in a menacing tone, "and compromise *my* safety? No, no. We are linked together in this matter, and must go through with it. You cannot--shall not retreat."

"Death and hell!" cried Sir Rowland, rising and drawing his sword; "do you think you can shackle my free will, villain?"

"In this particular instance I do, Sir Rowland," replied Jonathan, calmly, "because you are wholly in my power. But be patient, I am your fast friend. Thames Darrell MUST die. Our mutual safety requires it. Leave the means to me."

"More blood! more blood!" cried Trenchard, passing his hand with agony across his brow. "Shall I never banish those horrible phantoms from my couch--the father with his bleeding breast and dripping hair!--the mother with her wringing hands and looks of vengeance and reproach!--And must another be added to their number--their son! Horror!--let me be spared this new crime! And yet the gibbet--my name tarnished--my escutcheon blotted by the hangman!--No, I cannot submit to that."

"I should think not," observed Jonathan, who had some practice in the knight's moods, and knew how to humour him. "It's a miserable weakness to be afraid of bloodshed.--The general who gives an order for wholesale carnage never sleeps a wink the less soundly for the midnight groans of his victims, and we should deride him as a coward if he did. And life is much the same, whether taken in battle, on the couch, or by the road-side. Besides those whom I've slain with my own hands, I've brought upwards of thirty persons to the gallows. Most of their relics are in yonder cases; but I don't remember that any of them have disturbed my rest. The mode of destruction makes no difference. It's precisely the same thing to me to bid my janizaries cut Thames Darrell's throat, as to order Jack Sheppard's execution."

As Jonathan said this, Jack's hand involuntarily sought a pistol.

"But to the point," continued Wild, unconscious of the peril in which the remark had placed him,--"to the point. On the terms that procured your liberation from Newgate, I will free you from this new danger."

"Those terms were a third of my estate," observed Trenchard bitterly.

"What of that," rejoined Jonathan. "Any price was better than your head. If Thames Darrell escapes, you will lose both life and property."

"True, true," replied the knight, with an agonized look; "there is no alternative."

"None whatever," rejoined Wild. "Is it a bargain?"

"Take half of my estate--take all--my life, if you will--I am weary of it!" cried Trenchard passionately.

"No," replied Jonathan, "I'll not take you at your word, as regards the latter proposition. We shall both, I hope, live to enjoy our shares--long after Thames Darrell is forgotten--ha! ha! A third of your estate I accept. And as these things should always be treated as matters of business, I'll just draw up a memorandum of our arrangement."

And, as he spoke, he took up a sheet of paper, and hastily traced a few lines upon it.

"Sign this," he said, pushing the document towards Sir Rowland.

The knight mechanically complied with his request.

"Enough!" cried Jonathan, eagerly pocketing the memorandum. "And now, in return for your liberality, I'll inform you of a secret with which it is important you should be acquainted."

"A secret!" exclaimed Trenchard. "Concerning whom?"

"Mrs. Sheppard," replied Jonathan, mysteriously.

"Mrs. Sheppard!" echoed Jack, surprised out of his caution.

"Ah!" exclaimed Wild, looking angrily towards his supposed attendant.

"I beg pardon, Sir," replied Jack, with the accent and manner of the janizary; "I was betrayed into the exclamation by my surprise that anything in which Sir Rowland Trenchard was interested could have reference to so humble a person as Mrs. Sheppard."

"Be pleased, then, in future not to let your surprise find vent in words," rejoined Jonathan, sternly. "My servants, like Eastern mutes, must have eyes, and ears,--and *hands*, if need be,--but no tongues. You understand me, sirrah?"

"Perfectly," replied Jack. "I'm dumb."

"Your secret?" demanded Trenchard, impatiently.

"I need not remind you, Sir Rowland," replied Wild, "that you had two sisters--Aliva and Constance."

"Both are dead," observed the knight, gloomily.

"Not so;" answered Wild. "Constance is yet living."

"Constance alive? Impossible!" ejaculated Trenchard.

"I've proofs to the contrary," replied Jonathan.

"If this is the case, where is she?"

"In Bedlam," replied the thief-taker, with a Satanic grin.

"Gracious Heaven!" exclaimed the knight, upon whom a light seemed suddenly to break. "You mentioned Mrs. Sheppard. What has she to with Constance Trenchard?"

"Mrs. Sheppard *is* Constance Trenchard," replied Jonathan, maliciously.

Here Jack Sheppard was unable to repress an exclamation of astonishment.

"Again," cried Jonathan, sternly: "beware!"

"What!" vociferated Trenchard. "My sister the wife of one condemned felon! the parent of another! It cannot be."

"It *is* so, nevertheless," replied Wild. "Stolen by a gipsy when scarcely five years old, Constance Trenchard, after various vicissitudes, was carried to London, where she lived in great poverty, with the dregs of society. It is useless to trace out her miserable career; though I can easily do so if you require it. To preserve herself, however, from destitution, or what she considered worse, she wedded a journeyman carpenter, named Sheppard."

"Alas! that one so highly born should submit to such a degradation?" groaned the knight.

"I see nothing surprising in it," rejoined Jonathan. "In the first place, she had no knowledge of her birth; and, consequently, no false pride to get rid of. In the second, she was wretchedly poor, and assailed by temptations of which you can form no idea. Distress like hers might palliate far greater offences than she ever committed. With the same inducements we should all do the same thing. Poor girl! she was beautiful once; so beautiful as to make *me*, who care little for the allurements of women, fancy myself enamoured of her."

Jack Sheppard again sought his pistol, and was only withheld from levelling it at the thief-taker's head, by the hope that he might gather some further information respecting his mother. And he had good reason before long to congratulate himself on his forbearance.

"What proof have you of the truth of this story?" inquired Trenchard.

"This," replied Jonathan, taking a paper from a portfolio, and handing it to the knight, "this written evidence, signed by Martha Cooper, the gipsy, by whom the girl was stolen, and who was afterwards executed for a similar crime. It is attested, you will observe, by the Reverend Mr. Purney, the present ordinary of Newgate."

"I am acquainted with Mr. Purney's hand-writing," said Jack, advancing, "and can at once decide whether this is a forgery or not."

"Look at it, then," said Wild, giving him the portfolio.

"It's the ordinary's signature, undoubtedly," replied Jack.

And as he gave back the portfolio to Sir Rowland he contrived, unobserved, to slip the precious document into his sleeve, and from thence into his pocket.

"And, does any of our bright blood flow in the veins of a ruffianly housebreaker?" cried Trenchard, with a look of bewilderment. "I'll not believe it."

"Others may, if you won't," muttered Jack, retiring. "Thank Heaven! I'm not basely born."

"Now, mark me," said Jonathan, "and you'll find I don't do things by halves. By your father, Sir Montacute Trenchard's will, you are aware,--and, therefore, I need not repeat it, except for the special purpose I have in view,--you are aware, I say, that, by this will, in case your sister Aliva, died without issue, or, on the death of such issue, the property reverts to Constance and *her* issue."

"I hear," said Sir Rowland, moodily.

"And I," muttered Jack.

"Thames Darrell once destroyed," pursued Jonathan. "Constance--or, rather, Mrs. Sheppard--becomes entitled to the estates; which eventually--provided he escaped the gallows--would descend to her son."

"Ha!" exclaimed Jack, drawing in his breath, and leaning forward with intense curiosity.

"Well, Sir?" gasped Sir Rowland.

"But this need give you no uneasiness," pursued Jonathan; "Mrs. Sheppard, as I told you, is in Bedlam, an incurable maniac; while her son is in the New Prison, whence he will only be removed to Newgate and Tyburn."

"So you think," muttered Jack, between his ground teeth.

"To make your mind perfectly easy on the score of Mrs. Sheppard," continued Jonathan; "after we've disposed of Thames Darrell, I'll visit her in Bedlam; and, as I understand I form one of her chief terrors, I'll give her such a fright that I'll engage she shan't long survive it."

"Devil!" muttered Jack, again grasping his pistol. But, feeling secure of vengeance, he determined to abide his time.

"And now, having got rid of the minor obstacles," said Jonathan, "I'll submit a plan for the removal of the main difficulty. Thames Darrell, I've said, is at Mr. Wood's at Dollis Hill, wholly unsuspicious of any designs against him, and, in fact, entirely ignorant of your being acquainted with his return, or even of his existence. In this state, it will be easy to draw him into a snare. To-morrow night--or rather to-night, for we are fast verging on another day--I propose to lure him out of the house by a stratagem which I am sure will prove infallible; and, then, what so easy as to knock him on the head. To make sure work of it, I'll superintend the job myself. Before midnight, I'll answer for it, it shall be done. My janizaries shall go with me. You hear what I say, Quilt?" he added, looking at Jack.

"I do," replied Sheppard.

"Abraham Mendez will like the task,--for he has entertained a hatred to the memory of Thames Darrell ever since he received the wound in the head, when the two lads attempted to break out of St. Giles's round-house. I've despatched him to the New Prison. But I expect him back every minute."

"The New Prison!" exclaimed Sheppard. "What is he gone there for?"

"With a message to the turnkey to look after his prisoner," replied Wild, with a cunning smile. "Jack Sheppard had a visitor, I understand, yesterday, and may make an attempt to escape. It's as well to be on the safe side."

"It is," replied Jack.

At this moment, his quick ears detected the sound of footsteps on the stairs. He drew both his pistols, and prepared for a desperate encounter.

"There is another mystery I would have solved," said Trenchard, addressing Wild; "you have told me much, but not enough."

"What do you require further?" asked Jonathan.

"The name and rank of Thames Darrell's father," said the knight.

"Another time," replied the thief-taker, evasively.

"I will have it now," rejoined Trenchard, "or our agreement is void."

"You cannot help yourself, Sir Rowland," replied Jonathan, contemptuously.

"Indeed!" replied the knight, drawing his sword, "the secret, villain, or I will force it from you."

Before Wild could make any reply, the door was thrown violently open, and Abraham Mendez rushed into the room, with a face of the utmost consternation.

"He hash eshcaped!" cried the Jew.

"Who? Jack!" exclaimed Jonathan.

"Yesh," replied Abraham. "I vent to de New Prish'n, and on wishitin' his shel vid de turnkey, vot should ve find but de shains on de ground, de vinder broken, and Jack and Agevorth Besh gone."

"Damnation!" cried Jonathan, stamping his foot with uncontrollable rage. "I'd rather have given a thousand pounds than this had happened. But he might have broken out of prison, and yet not got over the wall of Clerkenwell Bridewell. Did you search the yard, fool?"

"Ve did," replied Abraham; "and found his fine goat and ruffles torn to shtrips on de shpikes near de creat cate. It vosh plain he vent dat vay."

Jonathan gave utterance to a torrent of imprecations.

While he thus vented his rage, the door again opened, and Quilt Arnold rushed into the room, bleeding, and half-dressed.

"'Sblood! what's this!" cried Jonathan, in the utmost surprise. "Quilt Arnold, is that you?"

"It is, Sir," sputtered the janizary. "I've been robbed, maltreated, and nearly murdered by Jack Sheppard."

"By Jack Sheppard!" exclaimed the thief-taker.

"Yes; and I hope you'll take ample vengeance upon him," said Quilt.

"I will, when I catch him, rely on it," rejoined Wild.

"You needn't go far to do that," returned Quilt; "there he stands."

"Ay, here I am," said Jack, throwing off his hat and wig, and marching towards the group, amongst whom there was a general movement of surprise at his audacity. "Sir Rowland, I salute you as your nephew."

"Back, villain!" said the knight, haughtily. "I disown you. The whole story of your relationship is a fabrication."

"Time will show," replied Jack with equal haughtiness. "But, however, it may turn out, I disown *you*."

"Well, Jack," said Jonathan, who had looked at him with surprise not unmixed with admiration, "you are a bold and clever fellow, I must allow. Were I not Jonathan Wild, I'd be Jack Sheppard. I'm almost sorry I've sworn to hang you. But, it can't be helped. I'm a slave to my word. Were I to let you go, you'd say I feared you. Besides, you've secrets which must not be disclosed. Nab and Quilt to the door! Jack, you are my prisoner."

"And you flatter yourself you can detain me?" laughed Jack.

"At least I'll try," replied Jonathan, sarcastically. "You must be a cleverer lad than even I take you for, if you get out of this place."

"What ho! Blueskin!" shouted Jack.

"Here I am, Captain," cried a voice from without. And the door was suddenly thrown open, and the two janizaries felled to the ground by the strong arm of the stalwart robber.

"Your boast, you see, was a little premature, Mr. Wild," said Sheppard. "Adieu, my worthy uncle. Fortunately, I've secured the proof of my birth."

"Confusion!" thundered Wild. "Close the doors below! Loose the dogs! Curses! they don't hear me! I'll ring the alarm-bell." And he raised his arm with the intention of executing his purpose, when a ball from Jack's pistol passed through the back of his hand, shattering the limb. "Aha! my lad!" he cried without appearing to regard the pain of the wound; "now I'll show you no quarter." And, with the uninjured hand he drew a pistol, which he fired, but without effect, at Jack.

"Fly, Captain, fly!" vociferated Blueskin; "I shan't be able to keep these devils down. Fly! they shall knock me on the head--curse 'em!--before they shall touch you."

"Come along!" cried Jack, darting through the door. "The key's on the outside--quick! quick!"

Instantly alive to this chance, Blueskin broke away. Two shots were fired at him by Jonathan; one of which passed through his hat, and the other through the fleshy part of his arm; but he made good his retreat. The door was closed--locked,--and the pair were heard descending the stairs.

"Hell's curses!" roared Jonathan. "They'll escape. Not a moment is to be lost."

So saying, he took hold of a ring in the floor, and disclosed a flight of steps, down which he hurried, followed by the janizaries. This means of communication instantly brought them to the lobby. But Jack and his companion were already gone.

Jonathan threw open the street-door. Upon the pavement near the court lay the porter, who had been prostrated by a blow from the butt-end of a pistol. The man, who was just able to move, pointed towards Giltspur-street. Jonathan looked in that direction, and beheld the fugitives riding off in triumph.

"To-night it is *their* turn," said Jonathan, binding up his wounded fingers with a handkerchief. "To-morrow it will be *mine*."

CHAPTER VI.
Winifred receives two Proposals.

THE tragical affair at Dollis Hill, it need scarcely be said, was a dreadful blow to the family. Mr. Wood bore up with great fortitude against the shock, attended the inquest, delivered his evidence with composure, and gave directions afterwards for the funeral, which took place on the day but one following--Sunday. As soon, however, as the last solemn rites were over, and the remains of the unfortunate woman committed to their final resting-place in Willesden churchyard, his firmness completely deserted him, and he sank beneath the weight of his affliction. It was fortunate that by this time Winifred had so far recovered, as to be able to afford her father the best and only solace that, under the circumstances, he could have received,--her personal attentions.

The necessity which had previously existed of leaving the ghastly evidence of the murderous deed undisturbed,--the presence of the mangled corpse,--the bustle of the inquest, at which her attendance was required,--all these circumstances produced a harrowing effect upon the young girl's imagination. But when all was over, a sorrowful calm succeeded, and, if not free from grief, she was tranquil. As to Thames, though deeply and painfully affected by the horrible occurrence that had marked his return to his old friends, he was yet able to control his feelings, and devote himself to the alleviation of the distress of the more immediate sufferers by the calamity.

It was Sunday evening--a soft delicious evening, and, from the happy, *cheerful* look of the house, none would have dreamed of the dismal tragedy so lately acted within its walls. The birds were singing blithely amid the trees,--the lowing of the cows resounded from the yard,--a delicious perfume from the garden was wafted through the open window,--at a distance, the church-bells of Willesden were heard tolling for evening service. All these things spoke of peace;--but there are seasons when the pleasantest external influences have a depressing effect on the mind, by painfully recalling past happiness. So, at least, thought one of two persons who were seated together in a small back-parlour of the house at Dollis Hill. She was a lovely girl, attired in deep mourning, and having an expression of profound sorrow on her charming features. Her companion was a portly handsome man, also dressed in a full suit of the deepest mourning, with the finest of lace at his bosom and wrists, and a sword in a black sheath by his side. These persons were Mr. Kneebone and Winifred.

The funeral, it has just been said, took place on that day. Amongst others who attended the sad ceremony was Mr. Kneebone. Conceiving himself called upon, as the intimate friend of the deceased, to pay this last tribute of respect to her memory, he appeared as one of the chief mourners. Overcome by his affliction, Mr. Wood had retired to his own room, where he had just summoned Thames. Much to her annoyance, therefore, Winifred was left alone with the woollen-draper, who following up a maxim of his own, "that nothing was gained by too much bashfulness," determined to profit by the opportunity. He had only been prevented, indeed, by a fear of Mrs. Wood from pressing his suit long ago. This obstacle removed, he thought he might now make the attempt. Happen what might, he could not be in a worse position.

"We have had a sad loss, my dear Winifred," he began,--"for I must use the privilege of an old friend, and address you by that familiar name,--we have had a sad loss in the death of your lamented parent, whose memory I shall for ever revere."

Winifred's eyes filled with tears. This was not exactly what the woollen-draper desired. So he resolved to try another tack.

"What a very remarkable thing it is," he observed, applying to his snuff-box, "that Thames Darrell, whom we all supposed dead,"--Kneebone in his heart sincerely wished he *had* been so,--"should turn out to be alive after all. Strange, I shouldn't know him when he called on me."

"It *is* strange," replied Winifred, artlessly. "I knew him at once."

"Of course," rejoined Kneebone, a little maliciously, "but that's easily accounted for. May I be permitted, as a very old and very dear friend of your lamented parent, whose loss I shall ever deplore, to ask you one question?"

"Undoubtedly," replied Winifred.

"And you will answer it frankly?"

"Certainly."

"Now for it," thought the woollen-draper, "I shall, at least, ascertain how the land lies.--Well, then, my dear," he added aloud, "do you still entertain the strong attachment you did to Captain Darrell?"

Winifred's cheeks glowed with blushes, and fixing her eyes, which flashed with resentment, upon the questioner, she said:

"I have promised to answer your question, and I will do so. I love him as a brother."

"*Only* as a brother?" persisted Kneebone.

If Winifred remained silent, her looks would have disarmed a person of less assurance than the woollen-draper.

"If you knew how much importance I attach to your answer," he continued passionately, "you would not refuse me one. Were Captain Darrell to offer you his hand, would you accept it?"

"Your impertinence deserves very different treatment, Sir," said Winifred; "but, to put an end to this annoyance, I will tell you--I would not."

"And why not?" asked Kneebone, eagerly.

"I will not submit to be thus interrogated," said Winifred, angrily.

"In the name of your lamented parent, whose memory I shall for ever revere, I implore you to answer me," urged Kneebone, "why--why would you not accept him?"

"Because our positions are different," replied Winifred, who could not resist this appeal to her feelings.

"You are a paragon of prudence and discretion," rejoined the woollen-draper, drawing his chair closer to hers. "Disparity of rank is ever productive of unhappiness in the married state. When Captain Darrell's birth is ascertained, I've no doubt he'll turn out a nobleman's son. At least, I hope so for his sake as well as my own," he added, mentally. "He has quite the air of one. And now, my angel, that I am acquainted with your sentiments on this subject, I shall readily fulfil a promise which I made to your lamented parent, whose loss I shall ever deplore."

"A promise to my mother?" said Winifred, unsuspiciously.

"Yes, my angel, to *her*--rest her soul! She extorted it from me, and bound me by a solemn oath to fulfil it."

"Oh! name it."

"You are a party concerned. Promise me that you will not disobey the injunctions of her whose memory we must both of us ever revere. Promise me."

"If in my power--certainly. But, what is it! What *did* you promise?"

"To offer you my heart, my hand, my life," replied Kneebone, falling at her feet.

"Sir!" exclaimed Winifred, rising.

"Inequality of rank can be no bar to *our* union," continued Kneebone. "Heaven be praised, I am not the son of a nobleman."

In spite of her displeasure, Winifred could not help smiling at the absurdity of this address. Taking this for encouragement, her suitor proceeded still more extravagantly. Seizing her hand he covered it with kisses.

"Adorable girl!" he cried, in the most impassioned tone, and with the most impassioned look he could command. "Adorable girl, I have long loved you to desperation. Your lamented mother, whose loss I shall ever deplore, perceived my passion and encouraged it. Would she were alive to back my suit!"

"This is beyond all endurance," said Winifred, striving to withdraw her hand. "Leave me, Sir; I insist."

"Never!" rejoined Kneebone, with increased ardour,--"never, till I receive from your own lips the answer which is to make me the happiest or the most miserable of mankind. Hear me, adorable girl! You know not the extent of my devotion. No mercenary consideration influences me. Love--admiration for your matchless beauty alone sways me. Let your father--if he chooses, leave all his wealth to his adopted son. I care not. Possessed of *you*, I shall have a treasure such as kings could not boast."

"Pray cease this nonsense," said Winifred, "and quit the room, or I will call for assistance."

At this juncture, the door opened, and Thames entered the room. As the woollen-draper's back was towards him, he did not perceive him, but continued his passionate addresses.

"Call as you please, beloved girl," he cried, "I will not stir till I am answered. You say that you only love Captain Darrell as a brother--"

"Mr. Kneebone!"

"That you would not accept him were he to offer--"

"Be silent, Sir."

"He then," continued the woollen-draper, "is no longer considered--"

"How, Sir?" cried Thames, advancing, "what is the meaning of your reference to my name? Have you dared to insult this lady? If so--"

"Insult her!" replied Kneebone, rising, and endeavouring to hide his embarrassment under a look of defiance. "Far from, it, Sir. I have made her an honourable proposal of marriage, in compliance with the request of her lamented parent, whose memory--"

"Dare to utter that falsehood in my hearing again, scoundrel," interrupted Thames fiercely, "and I will put it out of your power to repeat the offence. Leave the room! leave the house, Sir! and enter it again at your peril."

"I shall do neither, Sir," replied Kneebone, "unless I am requested by this lady to withdraw,--in which case I shall comply with her request. And you have to thank her presence, hot-headed boy, that I do not chastise your insolence as it deserves."

"Go, Mr. Kneebone,--pray go!" implored Winifred. "Thames, I entreat--"

"Your wishes are my laws, beloved, girl," replied Kneebone, bowing profoundly. "Captain Darren," he added, sternly, "you shall hear from me."

"When you please, Sir," said Thames, coldly.

And the woollen-draper departed.

"What is all this, dear Winny?" inquired Thames, as soon as they were alone.

"Nothing--nothing," she answered, bursting into tears. "Don't ask me about it now."

"Winny," said Thames, tenderly, "something which that self-sufficient fool has said has so far done me a service in enabling me to speak upon a subject which I have long had upon my lips, but have not had courage to utter."

"Thames!"

"You seem to doubt my love," he continued,--"you seem to think that change of circumstances may produce some change in my affections. Hear me then, now, before I take one step to establish my origin, or secure my rights. Whatever those rights may be, whoever I am, my heart is yours. Do you accept it?"

"Dear Thames!"

"Forgive this ill-timed avowal of my love. But, answer me. Am I mistaken? Is your heart mine?"

"It is--it is; and has ever been," replied Winifred, falling upon his neck.

Lovers' confidences should be respected. We close the chapter.

CHAPTER VII.
Jack Sheppard warns Thames Darrell.

ON the following night--namely Monday,--the family assembled together, for the first time since the fatal event, in the chamber to which Thames had been introduced on his arrival at Dollis Hill. As this had been Mrs. Wood's favourite sitting-room, and her image was so intimately associated with it, neither the carpenter nor his daughter could muster courage to enter it before. Determined, however, to conquer the feeling as soon as possible, Wood had given orders to have the evening meal served there; but, notwithstanding all his good resolutions upon his first entrance, he had much ado to maintain his self-command. His wife's portrait had been removed from the walls, and the place it had occupied was only to be known by the cord by which it had been suspended. The very blank, however, affected him more deeply than if it had been left. Then a handkerchief was thrown over the cage, to prevent the bird from singing; it was *her* favourite canary. The flowers upon the mantel-shelf were withered and drooping--*she* had gathered them. All these circumstances,--slight in themselves, but powerful in their effect,--touched the heart of the widowed carpenter, and added to his depression.

Supper was over. It had been discussed in silence. The cloth was removed, and Wood, drawing the table as near the window as possible--for it was getting dusk--put on his spectacles, and opened that sacred volume from which the best consolation in affliction is derived, and left the lovers--for such they may now be fairly termed--to their own conversation. Having already expressed our determination not to betray any confidences of this sort, which, however interesting to the parties concerned, could not possibly be so to others, we shall omit also the "love passages," and proceeding to such topics as may have general interest, take up the discourse at the point when Thames Darrell expressed his determination of starting for Manchester, as soon as Jack Sheppard's examination had taken place.

"I am surprised we have received no summons for attendance to-day," he remarked; "perhaps the other robber may be secured."

"Or Jack have escaped," remarked Winny.

"I don't think that's likely. But, this sad affair disposed of, I will not rest till I have avenged my murdered parents."

"'*The avenger of blood himself shall slay the murderer*'," said Wood, who was culling for himself certain texts from the scriptures.

"It is the voice of inspiration," said Thames; "and I receive it as a solemn command. The villain has enjoyed his security too long."

"'*Bloody and deceitful men shall not live half their days*'," said Wood, reading aloud another passage.

"And yet, *he* has been spared thus long; perhaps with a wise purpose," rejoined Thames. "But, though the storm has spared him, I will not."

"'*No doubt*,'" said Wood, who had again turned over the leaves of the sacred volume--', "no doubt this man is a murderer, whom, though he escaped the seas, yet vengeance suffereth not to live'."

"No feelings of consanguinity shall stay my vengeance," said Thames, sternly. "I will have no satisfaction but his life."

"'Thou shalt take no satisfaction for the life of a murderer which is guilty of death, but he shall surely be put to death'," said Wood referring to another text.

"Do not steel your heart against him, dear Thames," interposed Winifred.

"'*And thine eye shall not pity*,'" said her father, in a tone of rebuke, "'but, life shall be for life, eye for eye, tooth for tooth, hand for hand, foot for foot.'"

As these words were delivered by the carpenter with stern emphasis, a female servant entered the room, and stated that a gentleman was at the door, who wished to speak with Captain Darell on business of urgent importance.

"With me?" said Thames. "Who is it?"

"He didn't give his name, Sir," replied the maid; "but he's a young gentleman."

"Don't go near him, dear Thames," said Winifred; "he may have some ill intention."

"Pshaw!" cried Thames. "What! refuse to see a person who desires to speak with me. Say I will come to him."

"Law! Miss," observed the maid, "there's nothing mischievous in the person's appearance, I'm sure. He's as nice and civil-spoken a gentleman as need be; by the same token," she added, in an under tone, "that he gave me a span new crown piece."

"'The thief cometh in the night, and the troop of robbers spoileth without,'" said Wood, who had a text for every emergency.

"Lor' ha' mussy, Sir!--how you *do* talk," said the woman; "this is no robber, I'm sure. I should have known at a glance if it was. He's more like a lord than--"

As she spoke, steps were heard approaching; the door was thrown open, and a young man marched boldly into the room.

The intruder was handsomely, even richly, attired in a scarlet riding-suit, embroidered with gold; a broad belt, to which a hanger was attached, crossed his shoulders; his boots rose above his knee, and he carried a laced hat in his hand. Advancing to the middle of the chamber, he halted, drew himself up, and fixed his dark, expressive eyes, on Thames Darrell. His appearance excited the greatest astonishment and consternation amid the group. Winifred screamed. Thames sprang to his feet, and half drew his sword, while Wood, removing his spectacles to assure himself that his eyes did not deceive him, exclaimed in a tone and with a look that betrayed the extremity of surprise--"Jack Sheppard!"

"Jack Sheppard!" echoed the maid. "Is this Jack Sheppard? Oh, la! I'm undone! We shall all have our throats cut! Oh! oh!" And she rushed, screaming, into the passage where she fell down in a fit.

The occasion of all this confusion and dismay, meanwhile, remained perfectly motionless; his figure erect, and with somewhat of dignity in his demeanour. He kept his keen eyes steadily fixed on Thames, as if awaiting to be addressed.

"Your audacity passes belief," cried the latter, as soon as his surprise would allow him utterance. "If you have contrived to break out of your confinement, villain, this is the last place where you ought to show yourself."

"And, therefore, the first I would visit," replied Jack, boldly. "But, pardon my intrusion. I was *resolved* to see you. And, fearing you might not come to me, I forced my way hither, even with certainty of discomposing your friends."

"Well, villain!" replied Thames, "I know not the motive of your visit. But, if you have come to surrender yourself to justice, it is well. You cannot depart hence."

"Cannot?" echoed Jack, a slight smile crossing his features. "But, let that pass. My motive in coming hither is to serve you, and save your life. If you choose to re-quite me by detaining me, you are at liberty to do so. I shall make no defence. That I am not ignorant of the reward offered for my capture this will show," he added, taking a large placard headed '*Murder*' from his pocket, and throwing it on the floor. "My demeanour ought to convince you that I came with no hostile intention. And, to show you that I have no intention of flying, I will myself close and lock the door. There is the key. Are you now satisfied?"

"No," interposed Wood, furiously, "I shall never be satisfied till I see you hanged on the highest gibbet at Tyburn."

"A time may come when you will be gratified, Mr. Wood," replied Jack, calm-ly.

"May come!--it *will* come!--it *shall* come!" cried the carpenter, shaking his hand menacingly at him. "I have some difficulty in preventing myself from becoming your executioner. Oh! that I should have nursed such a viper!"

"Hear me, Sir," said Jack.

"No, I won't hear you, murderer," rejoined Wood.

"I am no murderer," replied Sheppard. "I had no thought of injuring your wife, and would have died rather than commit so foul a crime."

"Think not to delude me, audacious wretch," cried the carpenter. "Even if you are not a principal, you are an accessory. If you had not brought your companion here, it would not have happened. But you shall swing, rascal,--you shall swing."

"My conscience acquits me of all share in the offence," replied Jack, humbly. "But the past is irremediable, and I did not come hither to exculpate myself, I came to save *your* life," he added, turning to Thames.

"I was not aware it was in danger," rejoined Darrell.

"Then you ought to be thankful to me for the warning. You *are* in danger."

"From some of your associates?"

"From your uncle, from *my* uncle,--Sir Rowland Trenchard."

"What means this idle boasting, villain?" said Thames. "*Your* uncle, Sir Row-land?"

"It is no idle boasting," replied the other. "You are cousin to the housebreaker, Jack Sheppard."

"If it were so, he would have great reason to be proud of the relationship, truly," observed Wood, shrugging his shoulders.

"It is easy to make an assertion like this," said Thames, contemptuously.

"And equally easy to prove it," replied Jack, giving him the paper he had abstracted from Wild. "Read that."

Thames hastily cast his eyes over it, and transferred it, with a look of incredulity, to Wood.

"Gracious Heavens! this is more wonderful than all the rest," cried the carpenter, rubbing his eyes. "Thames, this is no forgery."

"You believe it, father?"

"From the bottom of my heart. I always thought Mrs. Sheppard superior to her station."

"So did I," said Winifred. "Let me look at the paper."

"Poor soul!--poor soul!" groaned Wood, brushing the tears from his vision. "Well, I'm glad she's spared this. Oh! Jack, Jack, you've much to answer for!"

"I have, indeed," replied Sheppard, in a tone of contrition.

"If this document is correct," continued Wood, "and I am persuaded it is so,-- you are as unfortunate as wicked. See what your misconduct has deprived you of-- see what you might have been. This is retribution."

"I feel it," replied Jack, in a tone of agony, "and I feel it more on my poor mother's account than my own."

"She has suffered enough for you," said Wood.

"She has, she has," said Jack, in a broken voice.

"Weep on, reprobate," cried the carpenter, a little softened. "Those tears will do you good."

"Do not distress him, dear father," said Winifred; "he suffers deeply. Oh, Jack! repent, while it is yet time, of your evil conduct. I will pray for you."

"I cannot repent,--I cannot pray," replied Jack, recovering his hardened demeanour. "I should never have been what I am, but for you."

"How so?" inquired Winifred.

"I loved you," replied Jack,--"don't start--it is over now--I loved you, I say, as a boy. *hopelessly*, and it made me desperate. And now I find, when it is too late, that I *might* have deserved you--that I am as well born as Thames Darrell. But I mustn't think of these things, or I shall grow mad. I have said your life is in danger, Thames. Do not slight my warning. Sir Rowland Trenchard is aware of your return to England. I saw him last night at Jonathan Wild's, after my escape from the New Prison. He had just arrived from Manchester, whence he had been summoned by that treacherous thief-taker. I overheard them planning your assassination. It is to take place to-night."

"O Heavens!" screamed Winifred, while her father lifted up his hands in silent horror.

"And when I further tell you," continued Jack, "that, after yourself and my mother, I am the next heir to the estates of my grandfather, Sir Montacute Trenchard, you will perhaps own that my caution is sufficiently disinterested."

"Could I credit your wild story, I might do so," returned Thames, with a look of perplexity.

"Here are Jonathan Wild's written instructions to Quilt Arnold," rejoined Sheppard, producing the pocket-book he had found in the janizary's clothes. "This letter will vouch for me that a communication has taken place between your enemies."

Thames glanced at the despatch, and, after a moment's reflection, inquired, "In what way is the attempt upon my life to be made?"

"That I couldn't ascertain," replied Jack; "but I advise you to be upon your guard. For aught I know, they may be in the neighbourhood at this moment."

"Here!" ejaculated Wood, with a look of alarm. "Oh lord! I hope not."

"This I do know," continued Jack,--"Jonathan Wild superintends the attack."

"Jonathan Wild!" repeated the carpenter, trembling. "Then it's all over with us. Oh dear!--how sorry I am I ever left Wych Street. We may be all murdered in this unprotected place, and nobody be the wiser."

"There's some one in the garden at this moment," cried Jack; "I saw a face at the window."

"Where--where?" cried Thames.

"Don't stir," replied Jack. "I will at once convince you of the truth of my assertions, and ascertain whether the enemy really is at hand."

So saying, he advanced towards the window, threw open the sash, and called out in the voice of Thames Darrell, "Who's there?"

He was answered by a shot from a pistol. The ball passed over his head, and lodged in the ceiling.

"I was right," replied Jack, returning as coolly as if nothing had happened. "It is Jonathan. Your uncle--*our* uncle is with him. I saw them both."

"May I trust you?" cried Thames, eagerly.

"You may," replied Jack: "I'll fight for you to the last gasp."

"Follow me, then," cried Thames, drawing his sword, and springing through the window.

"To the world's end," answered Jack, darting after him.

"Thames!--Thames!" cried Winifred, rushing to the window. "He will be murdered!--Help!"

"My child!--my love!" cried Wood, dragging her forcibly back.

Two shots were fired, and presently the clashing of swords was heard below.

After some time, the scuffle grew more and more distant, until nothing could be heard.

Wood, meanwhile, had summoned his men-servants, and having armed them with such weapons as could be found, they proceeded to the garden, where the first object they encountered was Thames Darrell, extended on the ground, and weltering in his blood. Of Jack Sheppard or the assailants they could not discover a single trace.

As the body was borne to the house in the arms of the farming-men, Mr. Wood fancied he heard the exulting laugh of Jonathan Wild.

CHAPTER VIII.
Old Bedlam.

WHEN Thames Darrell and Jack Sheppard sprang through the window, they were instantly assailed by Wild, Trenchard, and their attendants. Jack attacked Jonathan with such fury, that he drove him into a shrubbery, and might perhaps have come off the victor, if his foot had not slipped as he made a desperate lunge. In this state it would have been all over with him, as, being stunned by the fall, it was some moments before he could recover himself, if another party had not unexpectedly come to his rescue. This was Blueskin, who burst through the trees, and sword in hand assaulted the thief-taker. As soon as Jack gained his legs, he perceived Blueskin lying, as he thought, dead in the plantation, with a severe cut across his temples, and while he was stooping to assist him, he heard groans at a little distance. Hastening in the direction of the sound, he discovered Thames Darrell, stretched upon the ground.

"Are you hurt, Thames?" asked Jack, anxiously.

"Not dangerously, I hope," returned Thames; "but fly--save yourself."

"Where are the assassins?" cried Sheppard.

"Gone," replied the wounded man. "They imagine their work is done. But I may yet live to thwart them."

"I will carry you to the house, or fetch Mr. Wood," urged Jack.

"No, no," rejoined Thames; "fly--or I will not answer for your safety. If you desire to please me, you will go."

"And leave you thus?" rejoined Jack. "I cannot do it."

"Go, I insist," cried Thames, "or take the consequences upon yourself. I cannot protect you."

Thus urged, Jack reluctantly departed. Hastening to the spot where he had tied his horse to a tree, he vaulted into the saddle, and rode off across the fields,--for he was fearful of encountering the hostile party,--till he reached the Edgeware Road. Arrived at Paddington, he struck across Marylebone Fields,--for as yet the New Road was undreamed of,--and never moderated his speed until he reached the city. His destination was the New Mint. At this place of refuge, situated in the heart of Wapping, near the river-side, he arrived in less than an hour, in a complete state of exhaustion.

In consequence of the infamous abuse of its liberties, an act for the entire suppression of the Old Mint was passed in the ninth year of the reign of George the First, not many months before the date of the present epoch of this history; and as, after the destruction of Whitefriars, which took place in the reign of Charles the Second, owing to the protection afforded by its inmates to the Levellers and Fifth-monarchy-men, when the inhabitants of Alsatia crossed the water, and settled themselves in the borough of Southwark,--so now, driven out of their fastnesses, they again migrated, and recrossing the Thames, settled in Wapping, in a miserable quarter between Artichoke Lane and Nightingale Lane, which they termed the New Mint. Ousted from his old retreat, the Cross Shovels, Baptist Kettleby opened another tavern, conducted upon the same plan as the former, which he denominated the Seven Cities of Refuge. His subjects, however, were no longer entirely under his control; and, though he managed to enforce some little attention to his commands, it was evident his authority was waning fast. Aware that they would not be allowed to remain long unmolested, the New Minters conducted themselves so outrageously, and with such extraordinary insolence, that measures were at this time being taken for their effectual suppression.

To the Seven Cities of Refuge Jack proceeded. Having disposed of his steed and swallowed a glass of brandy, without taking any other refreshment, he threw himself on a couch, where he sank at once into a heavy slumber. When he awoke it was late in the day, and he was surprised to find Blueskin seated by his bed-side, watching over him with a drawn sword on his knee, a pistol in each hand, and a blood-stained cloth bound across his brow.

"Don't disturb yourself," said his follower, motioning him to keep still; "it's all right."

"What time is it?" inquired Jack.

"Past noon," replied Blueskin. "I didn't awake you, because you seemed tired."

"How did you escape?" asked Sheppard, who, as he shook off his slumber, began to recall the events of the previous night.

"Oh, easily enough," rejoined the other. "I suppose I must have been senseless for some time; for, on coming to myself, I found this gash in my head, and the ground covered with blood. However, no one had discovered me, so I contrived to drag myself to my horse. I thought if you were living, and not captured, I should find you here,--and I was right. I kept watch over you, for fear of a surprise on the part of Jonathan. But what's to be done?"

"The first thing I do," replied Jack, "will be to visit my poor mother in Bedlam."

"You'd better take care of your mother's son instead," rejoined Blueskin. "It's runnin' a great risk."

"Risk, or no risk, I shall go," replied Jack. "Jonathan has threatened to do her some mischief. I am resolved to see her, without delay, and ascertain if it's possible to remove her."

"It's a hopeless job," grumbled Blueskin, "and harm will come of it. What are you to do with a mad mother at a time when you need all your wits to take care of yourself?"

"Don't concern yourself further about me," returned Jack. "Once for all, I shall go."

"Won't you take me?"

"No; you must await my return here."

"Then I must wait a long time," grumbled Blueskin. "You'll never return."

"We shall see," replied Jack. "But, if I should *not* return, take this purse to Edgeworth Bess. You'll find her at Black Mary's Hole."

And, having partaken of a hasty breakfast, he set out. Taking his way along East Smithfield, mounting Little Tower-hill, and threading the Minories and Hounsditch, he arrived without accident or molestation, at Moorfields.

Old Bethlehem, or Bedlam,--every trace of which has been swept away, and the hospital for lunatics removed to Saint George's Field,--was a vast and magnificent structure. Erected in Moorfields in 1675, upon the model of the Tuileries, it is said that Louis the Fourteenth was so incensed at the insult offered to his palace, that he had a counterpart of St. James's built for offices of the meanest description. The size and grandeur of the edifice, indeed, drew down the ridicule of several of the wits of the age: by one of whom--the facetious Tom Brown--it was said, "Bedlam is a pleasant place, and abounds with amusements;--the first of which is the building, so stately a fabric for persons wholly insensible of the beauty and use of it: the outside being a perfect mockery of the inside, and admitting of two amusing queries,--Whether the persons that ordered the building of it, or those that inhabit it, were the maddest? and, whether the name and thing be not as disagreeable as harp and harrow." By another--the no less facetious Ned Ward--it was termed, "A costly college for a crack-brained society, raised in a mad age, when the chiefs of the city were in a great danger of losing their senses, and so contrived it the more noble for their own reception; or they would never have flung away so much money to so foolish a purpose." The cost of the building exceeded seventeen thousand pounds. However the taste of the architecture may be questioned, which was the formal French style of the period, the general effect was imposing. Including the wings, it presented a frontage of five hundred and forty feet. Each wing had a small cupola; and, in the centre of the pile rose a larger dome, surmounted by a gilded ball and vane. The asylum was approached by a broad gravel walk, leading through a garden edged on either side by a stone balustrade, and shaded by tufted trees. A wide terrace then led to large iron gates,' over which were placed the two celebrated figures of Raving and Melancholy Madness, executed by the elder Cibber, and commemorated by Pope in the Dunciad, in the well-known lines:--

Close to those walls where Folly holds her throne,
And laughs to think Monroe would take her down,
Where, o'er the gates, by his famed father's hand,
Great Cibber's brazen, brainless brothers stand."

Internally, it was divided by two long galleries, one over the other. These galleries were separated in the middle by iron grates. The wards on the right were occupied by male patients, on the left by the female. In the centre of the upper gallery was a spacious saloon, appropriated to the governors of the asylum. But the besetting evil of the place, and that which drew down the severest censures of the writers above-mentioned, was that this spot,--which of all others should have been most free from such intrusion--was made a public exhibition. There all the loose characters thronged, assignations were openly made, and the spectators diverted themselves with the vagaries of its miserable inhabitants.

Entering the outer gate, and traversing the broad gravel walk before-mentioned, Jack ascended the steps, and was admitted, on feeing the porter, by another iron gate, into the hospital. Here he was almost stunned by the deafening clamour resounding on all sides. Some of the lunatics were rattling their chains; some shrieking; some singing; some beating with frantic violence against the doors. Altogether, it was the most dreadful noise he had ever heard. Amidst it all, however, there were several light-hearted and laughing groups walking from cell to cell to whom all this misery appeared matter of amusement. The doors of several of the wards were thrown open for these parties, and as Jack passed, he could not help glancing at the wretched inmates. Here was a poor half-naked creature, with a straw crown on his head, and a wooden sceptre in his hand, seated on the ground with all the dignity of a monarch on his throne. There was a mad musician, seemingly rapt in admiration of the notes he was extracting from a child's violin. Here was a terrific figure gnashing his teeth, and howling like a wild beast;--there a lover, with hands clasped together and eyes turned passionately upward. In this cell was a huntsman, who had fractured his skull while hunting, and was perpetually hallooing after the hounds;--in that, the most melancholy of all, the grinning gibbering lunatic, the realization of "moody madness, laughing wild."

Hastening from this heart-rending spectacle, Jack soon reached the grating that divided the men's compartment from that appropriated to the women. Inquiring for Mrs. Sheppard, a matron offered to conduct him to her cell.

"You'll find her quiet enough to-day, Sir," observed the woman, as they walked along; "but she has been very outrageous latterly. Her nurse says she may live some time; but she seems to me to be sinking fast."

"Heaven help her!" sighed Jack. "I hope not."

"Her release would be a mercy," pursued the matron. "Oh! Sir, if you'd seen her as I've seen her, you'd not wish her a continuance of misery."

As Jack made no reply, the woman proceeded.

"They say her son's taken at last, and is to be hanged. I'm glad of it, I'm sure; for it's all owing to him his poor mother's here. See what crime does, Sir. Those who act wickedly bring misery on all connected with them. And so gentle as the poor creature is, when she's not in her wild fits--it would melt a heart of stone to see her. She will cry for days and nights together. If Jack Sheppard could behold his mother in this state, he'd have a lesson he'd never forget--ay, and a severer one than even the hangman could read him. Hardened as he may be, that would touch him. But he has never been near her--never."

Rambling in this way, the matron at length came to a halt, and taking out a key, pointed to a door and said, "This is Mrs. Sheppard's ward, Sir."

"Leave us together, my good woman," said Jack, putting a guinea into her hand.

"As long as you please, Sir," answered the matron, dropping a curtsey. "There, Sir," she added, unlocking the door, "you can go in. Don't be frightened of her. She's not mischievous--and besides she's chained, and can't reach you."

So saying, she retired, and Jack entered the cell.

Prepared as he was for a dreadful shock, and with his nerves strung to endure it, Jack absolutely recoiled before the appalling object that met his gaze. Cowering in a corner upon a heap of straw sat his unfortunate mother, the complete wreck of what she had been. Her eyes glistened in the darkness--for light was only admitted through a small grated window--like flames, and, as she fixed them on him, their glances seemed to penetrate his very soul. A piece of old blanket was fastened across her shoulders, and she had no other clothing except a petticoat. Her arms and feet were uncovered, and of almost skeleton thinness. Her features were meagre, and ghastly white, and had the fixed and horrible stamp of insanity. Her head had been shaved, and around it was swathed a piece of rag, in which a few straws were stuck. Her thin fingers were armed with nails as long as the talons of a bird. A chain, riveted to an iron belt encircling her waist, bound her to the wall. The cell in which she was confined was about six feet long and four wide; the walls were scored all over with fantastic designs, snatches of poetry, short sentences and names,--the work of its former occupants, and of its present inmate.

When Jack entered the cell, she was talking to herself in the muttering unconnected way peculiar to her distracted condition; but, after her eye had rested on him some time, the fixed expression of her features relaxed, and a smile crossed them. This smile was more harrowing even than her former rigid look.

"You are an angel," she cried, with a look beaming with delight.

"Rather a devil," groaned her son, "to have done this."

"You are an angel, I say," continued the poor maniac; "and my Jack would have been like you, if he had lived. But he died when he was a child--long ago--long ago--long ago."

"Would he had done so!" cried Jack.

"Old Van told me if he grew up he would be hanged. He showed me a black mark under his ear, where the noose would be tied. And so I'll tell you what I did--"

And she burst into a laugh that froze Jack's blood in his veins.

"What did you do?" he asked, in a broken voice.

"I strangled him--ha! ha! ha!--strangled him while he was at my breast--ha! ha!"--And then with a sudden and fearful change of look, she added, "That's what has driven me mad, I killed my child to save him from the gallows--oh! oh! One man hanged in a family is enough. If I'd not gone mad, they would have hanged me."

"Poor soul!" ejaculated her son.

"I'll tell you a dream I had last night," continued the unfortunate being. "I was at Tyburn. There was a gallows erected, and a great mob round it--thousands of people, and all with white faces like corpses. In the midst of them there was a cart with a man in it--and that man was Jack--my son Jack--they were going to hang him. And opposite to him, with a book in his hand,--but it couldn't be a prayer-book,--sat Jonathan Wild, in a parson's cassock and band. I knew him in spite of his dress. And when they came to the gallows, Jack leaped out of the cart, and the hangman tied up Jonathan instead--ha! ha! How the mob shouted and huzzaed--and I shouted too--ha! ha! ha!"

"Mother!" cried Jack, unable to endure this agonizing scene longer. "Don't you know me, mother?"

"Ah!" shrieked Mrs. Sheppard. "What's that?--Jack's voice!"

"It is," replied her son.

"The ceiling is breaking! the floor is opening! he is coming to me!" cried the unhappy woman.

"He stands before you," rejoined her son.

"Where?" she cried. "I can't see him. Where is he?"

"Here," answered Jack.

"Are you his ghost, then?"

"No--no," answered Jack. "I am your most unhappy son."

"Let me touch you, then; let me feel if you are really flesh and blood," cried the poor maniac, creeping towards him on all fours.

Jack did not advance to meet her. He could not move; but stood like one stupified, with his hands clasped together, and eyes almost starting out of their sockets, fixed upon his unfortunate parent.

"Come to me!" cried the poor maniac, who had crawled as far as the chain would permit her,--"come to me!" she cried, extending her thin arm towards him.

Jack fell on his knees beside her.

"Who are you?" inquired Mrs. Sheppard, passing her hands over his face, and gazing at him with a look that made him shudder.

"Your son," replied Jack,--"your miserable, repentant son."

"It is false," cried Mrs. Sheppard. "You are not. Jack was not half your age when he died. They buried him in Willesden churchyard after the robbery."

"Oh, God!" cried Jack, "she does not know me. Mother--dear mother!" he added, clasping her in his arms, "Look at me again."

"Off!" she exclaimed, breaking from his embrace with a scream. "Don't touch me. I'll be quiet. I'll not speak of Jack or Jonathan. I won't dig their graves with my nails. Don't strip me quite. Leave me my blanket! I'm very cold at night. Or, if you must take off my clothes, don't dash cold water on my head. It throbs cruelly."

"Horror!" cried Jack.

"Don't scourge me," she cried, trying to hide herself in the farthest corner of the cell. "The lash cuts to the bone. I can't bear it. Spare me, and I'll be quiet--quiet--quiet!"

"Mother!" said Jack, advancing towards her.

"Off!" she cried with a prolonged and piercing shriek. And she buried herself beneath the straw, which she tossed above her head with the wildest gestures.

"I shall kill her if I stay longer," muttered her son, completely terrified.

While he was considering what would be best to do, the poor maniac, over whose bewildered brain another change had come, raised her head from under the straw, and peeping round the room, asked in a low voice, "If they were gone?"

"Who?" inquired Jack.

"The nurses," she answered.

"Do they treat you ill?" asked her son.

"Hush!" she said, putting her lean fingers to her lips. "Hush!--come hither, and I'll tell you."

Jack approached her.

"Sit beside me," continued Mrs. Sheppard. "And, now I'll tell you what they do. Stop! we must shut the door, or they'll catch us. See!" she added, tearing the rag from her head,--"I had beautiful black hair once. But they cut it all off."

"I shall go mad myself if I listen to her longer," said Jack, attempting to rise. "I must go."

"Don't stir, or they'll chain you to the wall," said his mother detaining him. "Now, tell me why they brought you here?"

"I came to see you, dear mother!" answered Jack.

"Mother!" she echoed,--"mother! why do you call me by that name?"

"Because you are my mother."

"What!" she exclaimed, staring eagerly in his face. "Are you my son? Are you Jack?"

"I am," replied Jack. "Heaven be praised she knows me at last."

"Oh, Jack!" cried his mother, falling upon his neck, and covering him with kisses.

"Mother--dear mother!" said Jack, bursting into tears.

"You will never leave me," sobbed the poor woman, straining him to her breast.

"Never--never!"

The words were scarcely pronounced, when the door was violently thrown open, and two men appeared at it. They were Jonathan Wild and Quilt Arnold.

"Ah!" exclaimed Jack, starting to his feet.

"Just in time," said the thief-taker. "You are my prisoner, Jack."

"You shall take my life first," rejoined Sheppard.

And, as he was about to put himself into a posture of defence, his mother clasped him in her arms.

"They shall not harm you, my love!" she exclaimed.

The movement was fatal to her son. Taking advantage of his embarrassed position, Jonathan and his assistant rushed upon him, and disarmed him.

"Thank you, Mrs. Sheppard," cried the thief-taker, as he slipped a pair of handcuffs over Jack's wrists, "for the help you have given us in capturing your son. Without you, we might have had some trouble."

Aware apparently in some degree, of the mistake she had committed, the poor maniac sprang towards him with frantic violence, and planted her long nails in his cheek.

"Keep off, you accursed jade!" roared Jonathan, "--off, I say, or--" And he struck her a violent blow with his clenched hand.

The miserable woman staggered, uttered a deep groan, and fell senseless on the straw.

"Devil!" cried Jack; "that blow shall cost you your life."

"It'll not need to be repeated, at all events," rejoined Jonathan, looking with a smile of malignant satisfaction at the body. "And, now,--to Newgate."

CHAPTER IX.
Old Newgate.

AT the beginning of the twelfth century,--whether in the reign of Henry the First, or Stephen is uncertain,--a fifth gate was added to the four principal entrances of the city of London; then, it is almost needless to say, surrounded by ramparts, moats, and other defences. This gate, called *Newgate*, "as being latelier builded than the rest," continued, for upwards of three hundred years, to be used as a place of imprisonment for felons and trespassers; at the end of which time, having grown old, ruinous, and "horribly loathsome," it was rebuilt and enlarged by the executors of the renowned Sir Richard Whittington, the Lord Mayor of London: whence it afterwards obtained amongst a certain class of students, whose examinations were conducted with some strictness at the Old Bailey, and their highest degrees taken at Hyde-park-corner, the appellation of Whittington's College, or, more briefly, the Whit. It may here be mentioned that this gate, destined to bequeath its name--a name, which has since acquired a terrible significance,--to every successive structure erected upon its site, was granted, in 1400, by charter by Henry the Sixth to the citizens of London, in return for their royal services, and thenceforth became the common jail to that city and the county of Middlesex. Nothing material occurred to Newgate, until the memorable year 1666, when it was utterly destroyed by the Great Fire. It is with the building raised after this direful calamity that our history has to deal.

Though by no means so extensive or commodious as the modern prison, Old Newgate was a large and strongly-built pile. The body of the edifice stood on the south side of Newgate Street, and projected at the western extremity far into the area opposite Saint Sepulchre's Church. One small wing lay at the north of the gate, where Giltspur Street Compter now stands; and the Press Yard, which was detached from the main building, was situated at the back of Phoenix Court. The south or principal front, looking, *down* the Old Bailey, and not *upon it*, as is the case of the present structure, with its massive walls of roughened freestone,--in some places darkened by the smoke, in others blanched, by exposure to the weather,--its heavy projecting cornice, its unglazed doubly-grated windows, its gloomy porch decorated with fetters, and defended by an enormous iron door, had a stern and striking effect. Over the Lodge, upon a dial was inscribed the appropriate motto, " *Venio sicut fur*." The Gate, which crossed Newgate Street, had a wide arch for carriages, and a postern, on the north side, for foot-passengers. Its architecture was richly ornamental, and resembled the style of a triumphal entrance to a capital, rather than a dungeon having battlements and hexagonal towers, and being adorned on the western side with a triple range of pilasters of the Tuscan order, amid the intercolumniations of which were niches embellished with statues. The chief of these was a figure of Liberty, with a cat at her feet, in allusion to the supposed origin of the fortunes of its former founder, Sir Richard Whittington. On the right of the postern against the wall was affixed a small grating, sustaining the debtor's box; and any pleasure which the passer-by might derive from contemplating the splendid structure above described was damped at beholding the pale faces and squalid figures of the captives across the bars of its strongly-grated windows. Some years after the date of this history, an immense ventilator was placed at the top of the Gate, with the view of purifying the prison, which, owing to its insufficient space and constantly-crowded state, was never free from that dreadful and contagious disorder, now happily unknown, the jail-fever. So frightful, indeed, were the ravages of this malady, to which debtors and felons were alike exposed, that its miserable victims were frequently carried out by cart-loads, and thrown into a pit in the burial-ground of Christ-church, without ceremony.

Old Newgate was divided into three separate prisons,--the Master's Side, the Common Side, and the Press Yard. The first of these, situated a the south of the building, with the exception of one ward over the gateway, was allotted to the better class of debtors, whose funds enabled them to defray their chamber-rent, fees, and garnish. The second, comprising the bulk of the jail, and by many degrees worse in point of accommodation, having several dismal and noisome wards under ground, was common both to debtors and malefactors,--an association little favourable to the morals or comforts of the former, who, if they were brought there with any notions of honesty, seldom left with untainted principles. The last,--in all respects the best and airiest of the three, standing, as has been before observed, in Phoenix Court, at the rear of the main fabric,--was reserved for state-offenders, and such persons as chose to submit to the extortionate demands of the keeper: from twenty to five hundred pounds premium, according to the rank and means of the applicant, in addition to a high weekly rent, being required for accommodation in this quarter. Some excuse for this rapacity may perhaps be found in the fact, that five thousand pounds was paid for the purchase of the Press Yard by Mr. Pitt, the then governor of Newgate. This gentleman, tried for high treason, in 1716, on suspicion of aiding Mr. Forster, the rebel general's escape, but acquitted, reaped a golden harvest during the occupation of his premises by the Preston rebels, when a larger sum was obtained for a single chamber than (in the words of a sufferer on the occasion) "would have paid the rent of the best house in Saint James's Square or Piccadilly for several years."

Nor was this all. Other, and more serious impositions, inasmuch as they affected a poorer class of persons, were practised by the underlings of the jail. On his first entrance, a prisoner, if unable or unwilling to comply with the exactions of the turnkeys, was thrust into the Condemned Hold with the worst description of criminals, and terrified by threats into submission. By the old regulations, the free use of strong liquors not being interdicted, a tap-house was kept in the Lodge, and also in a cellar on the Common Side,--under the superintendence of Mrs. Spurling, formerly, it may be remembered, the hostess of the Dark House at Queenhithe,-- whence wine, ale, and brandy of inferior quality were dispensed, in false measures, and at high prices, throughout the prison, which in noise and debauchery rivalled, if it did not surpass, the lowest tavern.

The chief scene of these disgusting orgies,--the cellar, just referred to,--was a large low-roofed vault, about four feet below the level of the street, perfectly dark, unless when illumined by a roaring fire, and candles stuck in pyramidal lumps of clay, with a range of butts and barrels at one end, and benches and tables at the other, where the prisoners, debtors, and malefactors male and female, assembled as long as their money lasted, and consumed the time in drinking, smoking, and gaming with cards and dice. Above was a spacious hall, connected with it by a flight of stone steps, at the further end of which stood an immense grated door, called in the slang of the place "The Jigger," through the bars of which the felons in the upper wards were allowed to converse with their friends, or if they wished to enter the room, or join the revellers below, they were at liberty to do so, on payment of a small fine. Thus, the same system of plunder was everywhere carried on. The jailers robbed the prisoners: the prisoners robbed one another.

Two large wards were situated in the Gate; one of which, the Stone Ward, appropriated to the master debtors, looked towards Holborn; the other called the Stone Hall, from a huge stone standing in the middle of it, upon which the irons of criminals under sentence of death were knocked off previously to their being taken to the place of execution, faced Newgate Street. Here the prisoners took exercise; and a quaint, but striking picture has been left of their appearance when so engaged, by the author of the English Rogue. "At my first being acquainted with the place," says this writer, in the 'Miseries of a Prison,' "the prisoners, methought, walking up and down the Stone Hall, looked like so many wrecks upon the sea. Here the ribs of a thousand pounds beating against the Needles--those dangerous rocks, credulity here floated, to and fro, silks, stuffs, camlets, and velvet, without giving place to each other, according to their dignity; here rolled so many pipes of canary, whose bungholes lying open, were so damaged that the merchant may go hoop for his money," A less picturesque, but more truthful, and, therefore, more melancholy description of the same scene, is furnished by the shrewd and satirical Ned Ward, who informs us, in the "Delectable History of Whittington's College," that "When the prisoners are disposed to recreate themselves with walking, they go up into a spacious room, called the Stone Hall; where, when you see them taking a turn together, it would puzzle one to know which is the gentleman, which the mechanic, and which the beggar, for they are all suited in the same garb of squalid poverty, making a spectacle of more pity than executions; only to be out at the elbows is in fashion here, and a great indecorum not to be threadbare."

In an angle of the Stone Hall was the Iron Hold, a chamber containing a vast assortment of fetters and handcuffs of all weights and sizes. Four prisoners, termed "The Partners," had charge of this hold. Their duty was to see who came in, or went out; to lock up, and open the different wards; to fetter such prisoners as were ordered to be placed in irons; to distribute the allowances of provision; and to maintain some show of decorum; for which latter purpose they were allowed to carry whips and truncheons. When any violent outrage was committed,--and such matters were of daily, sometimes hourly, occurrence,--a bell, the rope of which descended into the hall, brought the whole of the turnkeys to their assistance. A narrow passage at the north of the Stone Hall led to the Bluebeard's room of this enchanted castle, a place shunned even by the reckless crew who were compelled to pass it. It was a sort of cooking-room, with an immense fire-place flanked by a couple of cauldrons, and was called Jack Ketch's Kitchen, because the quarters of persons executed for treason were there boiled by the hangman in oil, pitch, and tar, before they were affixed on the city gates, or on London Bridge. Above this revolting spot was the female debtor's ward; below it a gloomy cell, called Tangier; and, lower still, the Stone Hold, a most terrible and noisome dungeon, situated underground, and un-visited by a single ray of daylight. Built and paved with stone, without beds, or any other sort of protection from the cold, this dreadful hole, accounted the most dark and dismal in the prison, was made the receptacle of such miserable wretches as could not pay the customary fees. Adjoining it was the Lower Ward,--"Though, in what degree of latitude it was situated," observes Ned Ward, "I cannot positively demonstrate, unless it lay ninety degrees beyond the North Pole; for, instead of being dark there but half a year, it is dark all the year round." It was only a shade better than the Stone Hold. Here were imprisoned the fines; and, "perhaps," adds the before-cited authority, "if he behaved himself, an outlawed person might creep in among them." Ascending the gate once more on the way back, we find over the Stone Hall another large room, called Debtors' Hall, facing Newgate Street, with "very good air and light." A little too much of the former, perhaps; as the windows being unglazed, the prisoners were subjected to severe annoyance from the weather and easterly winds.

Of the women felons' rooms nothing has yet been said. There were two. One called Waterman's Hall, a horrible place adjoining the postern under the gate, whence, through a small barred aperture, they solicited alms from the passengers: the other, a large chamber, denominated My Lady's Hold, was situated in the high-est part of the jail, at the northern extremity. Neither of these wards had beds, and the unfortunate inmates were obliged to take their rest on the oaken floor. The condition of the rooms was indescribably filthy and disgusting; nor were the habits of the occupants much more cleanly. In other respects, they were equally indecorous and offensive. "It is with no small concern," writes an anonymous historian of Newgate, "that I am obliged to observe that the women in every ward of this prison are exceedingly worse than the worst of the men not only in respect to their mode of living, but more especially as to their conversation, which, to their great shame, is as profane and wicked as hell itself can possibly be."

There were two Condemned Holds,--one for each sex. That for the men lay near the Lodge, with which it was connected by a dark passage. It was a large room, about twenty feet long and fifteen broad, and had an arched stone roof. In fact, it had been anciently the right hand postern under the gate leading towards the city. The floor was planked with oak, and covered with iron staples, hooks, and ringbolts, with heavy chains attached to them. There was only one small grated window in this hold, which admitted but little light.

Over the gateway towards Snow Hill, were two strong wards, called the Castle and the Red Room. They will claim particular attention hereafter.

Many other wards,--especially on the Master Debtor's side,--have been necessarily omitted in the foregoing hasty enumeration. But there were two places of punishment which merit some notice from their peculiarity. The first of these, the Press Room, a dark close chamber, near Waterman's Hall, obtained its name from an immense wooden machine kept in it, with which such prisoners as refused to plead to their indictments were pressed to death--a species of inquisitorial torture not discontinued until so lately as the early part of the reign of George the Third, when it was abolished by an express statute. Into the second, denominated the Bilbowes,--also a dismal place,--refractory prisoners were thrust, and placed in a kind of stocks, whence the name.

The Chapel was situated in the south-east angle of the jail; the ordinary at the time of this history being the Reverend Thomas Purney; the deputy chaplain, Mr. Wagstaff.

Much has been advanced by modern writers respecting the demoralising effect of prison society; and it has been asserted, that a youth once confined in Newgate, is certain to come out a confirmed thief. However this may be now, it was unquestionably true of old Newgate. It was the grand nursery of vice.--"A famous university," observes Ned Ward, in the London Spy, "where, if a man has a mind to educate a hopeful child in the daring science of padding; the light-fingered subtlety of shoplifting: the excellent use of jack and crow; for the silently drawing bolts, and forcing barricades; with the knack of sweetening; or the most ingenious dexterity of picking pockets; let him but enter in this college on the Common Side, and confine him close to his study but for three months; and if he does not come out qualified to take any degree of villainy, he must be the most honest dunce that ever had the advantage of such eminent tutors."

To bring down this imperfect sketch of Newgate to the present time, it may be mentioned, that, being found inadequate to the purpose required, the old jail was pulled down in 1770. Just at the completion of the new jail, in 1780, it was assailed by the mob during the Gordon riots, fired, and greatly damaged. The devastations, however, were speedily made good, and, in two years more, it was finished.

It is a cheering reflection, that in the present prison, with its clean, well-white-washed, and well-ventilated wards, its airy courts, its infirmary, its improved regulations, and its humane and intelligent officers, many of the miseries of the old jail are removed. For these beneficial changes society is mainly indebted to the unremitting exertions of the philanthropic HOWARD.

CHAPTER X.
How Jack Sheppard got out of the Condemned Hold.

ONDAY, the 31st of August 1724,--a day long afterwards remembered by the officers of Newgate,--was distinguished by an unusual influx of visitors to the Lodge. On that morning the death warrant had arrived from Windsor, ordering Sheppard for execution, (since his capture by Jonathan Wild in Bedlam, as related in a former chapter, Jack had been tried, convicted, and sentenced to death,) together with three other malefactors on the following Friday. Up to this moment, hopes had been entertained of a respite, strong representations in his favour having been made in the highest quarter; but now that his fate seemed sealed, the curiosity of the sight-seeing public to behold him was redoubled. The prison gates were besieged like the entrance of a booth at a fair; and the Condemned Hold where he was confined, and to which visitors were admitted at the moderate rate of a guinea a-head, had quite the appearance of a showroom. As the day wore on, the crowds diminished,--many who would not submit to the turnkey's demands were sent away ungratified,--and at five o'clock, only two strangers, Mr. Shotbolt, the head turnkey of Clerkenwell Prison, and Mr. Griffin, who held the same office in Westminster Gatehouse were left in the Lodge. Jack, who had formerly been in the custody of both these gentlemen, gave them a very cordial welcome; apologized for the sorry room he was compelled to receive them in; and when they took leave, insisted on treating them to a double bowl of punch, which they were now discussing with the upper jailer, Mr. Ireton, and his two satellites, Austin and Langley. At a little distance from the party, sat a tall, sinister-looking personage, with harsh inflexible features, a gaunt but muscular frame, and large bony hands. He was sipping a glass of cold gin and water, and smoking a short black pipe. His name was Marvel, and his avocation, which was as repulsive as his looks, was that of public executioner. By his side sat a remarkably stout dame, to whom he paid as much attention as it was in his iron nature to pay. She had a nut-brown skin, a swarthy upper lip, a merry black eye, a prominent bust, and a tun-like circumference of waist. A widow for the fourth time, Mrs. Spurling, (for she it was,) either by her attractions of purse or person, had succeeded in moving the stony heart of Mr. Marvel, who, as he had helped to deprive her of her former husbands, thought himself in duty bound to offer to supply their place. But the lady was not so easily won; and though she did not absolutely reject him, gave him very slight hopes. Mr. Marvel, therefore, remained on his probation. Behind Mrs. Spurling stood her negro attendant, Caliban; a hideous, misshapen, malicious monster, with broad hunched shoulders, a flat nose, and ears like those of a wild beast, a head too large for his body, and a body too long for his legs. This horrible piece of deformity, who acted as drawer and cellarman, and was a constant butt to the small wits of the jail, was nicknamed the Black Dog of Newgate.

In the general survey of the prison, taken in the preceding chapter, but little was said of the Lodge. It may be well, therefore, before proceeding farther, to describe it more minutely. It was approached from the street by a flight of broad stone steps, leading to a ponderous door, plated with iron, and secured on the inner side by huge bolts, and a lock, with wards of a prodigious size. A little within stood a second door, or rather wicket, lower than the first, but of equal strength, and surmounted by a row of sharp spikes. As no apprehension was entertained of an escape by this outlet,--nothing of the kind having been attempted by the boldest felon ever incarcerated in Newgate,--both doors were generally left open during the daytime. At six o'clock, the wicket was shut; and at nine, the jail was altogether locked up. Not far from the entrance, on the left, was a sort of screen, or partition-wall, reaching from the floor to the ceiling, formed of thick oaken planks riveted together by iron bolts, and studded with broad-headed nails. In this screen, which masked the entrance of a dark passage communicating with the Condemned Hold, about five feet from the ground, was a hatch, protected by long spikes set six inches apart, and each of the thickness of an elephant's tusk. The spikes almost touched the upper part of the hatch: scarcely space enough for the passage of a hand being left between their points and the beam. Here, as has already been observed, condemned malefactors were allowed to converse with such of their guests as had not interest or money enough to procure admission to them in the hold. Beyond the hatch, an angle, formed by a projection in the wall of some three or four feet, served to hide a door conducting to the interior of the prison. At the farther end of the Lodge, the floor was raised to the height of a couple of steps; whence the whole place, with the exception of the remotest corner of the angle before-mentioned, could be commanded at a single glance. On this elevation a table was now placed, around which sat the turnkeys and their guests, regaling themselves on the fragrant beverage provided by the prisoner. A brief description will suffice for them. They were all stout ill-favoured men, attired in the regular jail-livery of scratch wig and snuff-coloured suit; and had all a strong family likeness to each other. The only difference between the officers of Newgate and their brethren was, that they had enormous bunches of keys at their girdles, while the latter had left their keys at home.

"Well, I've seen many a gallant fellow in my time, Mr. Ireton," observed the chief turnkey of Westminster Gatehouse, as he helped himself to his third glass of punch; "but I never saw one like Jack Sheppard."

"Nor I," returned Ireton, following his example: "and I've had some experience too. Ever since he came here, three months ago, he has been the life and soul of the place; and now the death warrant has arrived, instead of being cast down, as most men would be, and as all others *are*, he's gayer than ever. Well, I shall be sorry to lose him, Mr. Griffin. We've made a pretty penny by him--sixty guineas this blessed day."

"No more!" cried Griffin, incredulously; "I should have thought you must have made double that sum at least."

"Not a farthing more, I assure you," rejoined Ireton, pettishly; "we're all on the square here. I took the money myself, and *ought* to know."

"Oh! certainly," answered Griffin; "certainly."

"I offered Jack five guineas as his share," continued Ireton; "but he wouldn't take it himself, and gave it to the poor debtors and felons, who are now drinking it out in the cellar on the Common Side."

"Jack's a noble fellow," exclaimed the head-jailer of Clerkenwell Prison, raising his glass; "and, though he played me a scurvy trick, I'll drink to his speedy deliverance."

"At Tyburn, eh, Mr. Shotbolt?" rejoined the executioner. "I'll pledge you in that toast with all my heart."

"Well, for my part," observed Mrs. Spurling, "I hope he may never see Tyburn. And, if I'd my own way with the Secretary of State, he never *should*. It's a thousand pities to hang so pretty a fellow. There haven't been so many ladies in the Lodge since the days of Claude Du Val, the gentleman highwayman; and they all declare it'll break their hearts if he's scragged."

"Bah!" ejaculated Marvel, gruffly.

"You think our sex has no feeling, I suppose, Sir," cried Mrs. Spurling, indignantly; "but I can tell you we have. And, what's more, I tell you, if Captain Sheppard *is* hanged, you need never hope to call *me* Mrs. Marvel."

"'Zounds!" cried the executioner, in astonishment. "Do you know what you are talking about, Mrs. Spurling? Why, if Captain Sheppard should get off, it 'ud be fifty guineas out of my way. There's the grand laced coat he wore at his trial, which I intend for my wedding-dress."

"Don't mention such a thing, Sir," interrupted the tapstress. "I couldn't bear to see you in it. Your speaking of the trial brings the whole scene to my mind. Ah! I shall never forget the figure Jack cut on that occasion. What a buzz of admiration ran round the court as he appeared! And, how handsome and composed he looked! Everybody wondered that such a stripling could commit such desperate robberies. His firmness never deserted him till his old master, Mr. Wood, was examined. Then he *did* give way a bit. And when Mr. Wood's daughter,--to whom, I've heard tell, he was attached years ago,--was brought up, his courage forsook him altogether, and he trembled, and could scarcely stand. Poor young lady! *She* trembled too, and was unable to give her evidence. When sentence was passed there wasn't a dry eye in the court."

"Yes, there was one," observed Ireton.

"I guess who you mean," rejoined Shotbolt. "Mr. Wild's."

"Right," answered Ireton. "It's strange the antipathy he bears to Sheppard. I was standing near Jack at that awful moment, and beheld the look Wild fixed on him. It was like the grin of a fiend, and made my flesh creep on my bones. When the prisoner was removed from the dock, we met Jonathan as we passed through the yard. He stopped us, and, addressing Jack in a taunting tone, said, 'Well, I've been as good as my word!'--'True,' replied Sheppard; 'and I'll be as good as mine!'

And so they parted."

"And I hope he will, if it's anything to Jonathan's disadvantage," muttered Mrs. Spurling, half aside.

"I'm surprised Mr. Wild hasn't been to inquire after him to-day," observed Langley; "it's the first time he's missed doing so since the trial."

"He's gone to Enfield after Blueskin, who has so long eluded his vigilance," rejoined Austin. "Quilt Arnold called this morning to say so. Certain information, it seems, has been received from a female, that Blueskin would be at a flash-ken near the Chase at five o'clock to-day, and they're all set out in the expectation of nabbing him."

"Mr. Wild had a narrow escape lately, in that affair of Captain Darrell," observed Shotbolt.

"I don't exactly know the rights of that affair," rejoined Griffin, with some curiosity.

"Nor any one else, I suspect," answered Ireton, winking significantly. "It's a mysterious transaction altogether. But, as much as is known is this: Captain Darrell, who resides with Mr. Wood at Dollis Hill, was assaulted and half-killed by a party of ruffians, headed, he swore, by Mr. Wild, and his uncle, Sir Rowland Trenchard. Mr. Wild, however, proved, on the evidence of his own servants, that he was at the Old Bailey at the time; and Sir Rowland proved that *he* was in Manchester. So the charge was dismissed. Another charge was then brought against them by the Captain, who accused them of kidnapping him when a boy, and placing him in the hands of a Dutch skipper, named Van Galgebrok, with instructions to throw him overboard, which was done, though he afterwards escaped. But this accusation, for want of sufficient evidence, met with the same fate as the first, and Jonathan came off victorious. It was thought, however, if the skipper *could* have been found, that the result of the case would have been materially different. This was rather too much to expect; for we all know, if Mr. Wild wishes to keep a man out of the way, he'll speedily find the means to do so."

"Ay, ay," cried the jailers, laughing.

"I could have given awkward evidence in that case, if I'd been so inclined," said Mrs. Spurling, "ay and found Van Galgebrok too. But I never betray an old customer."

"Mr. Wild is a great man," said the hangman, replenishing his pipe, "and we owe him much, and ought to support him. Were any thing to happen to him, Newgate wouldn't be what it is, nor Tyburn either."

"Mr. Wild has given you some employment, Mr. Marvel," remarked Shotbolt.

"A little, Sir," replied the executioner, with a grim smile.

"Out of the twelve hundred subjects I've tucked up, I may safely place half to his account. If ever he requires my services, he shall find I'm not ungrateful. And though I say it that shouldn't say it, no man can tie a better knot. Mr. Wild, gentlemen, and the nubbin' cheat."

"Fill your glasses, gentlemen," observed Ireton, "and I'll tell you a droll thing Jack said this morning. Amongst others who came to see him, was a Mr. Kneebone, a woollen-draper in Wych Street, with whose pockets, it appears, Jack, when a lad, made a little too free. As this gentleman was going away, he said to Jack in a jesting manner, 'that he should be glad to see him to-night at supper.' Upon which the other answered, 'that he accepted his invitation with pleasure, and would make a point of waiting upon him,' Ha! ha! ha!"

"*Did* he say so?" cried Shotbolt. "Then I advise you to look sharply after him, Mr. Ireton; for may I be hanged myself if I don't believe he'll be as good as his word."

At this juncture, two women, very smartly attired in silk hoods and cloaks, appeared at the door of the Lodge.

"Ah! who have we here?" exclaimed Griffin.

"Only Jack's two wives--Edgeworth Bess and Poll Maggot," replied Austin, laughing.

"They can't go into the Condemned Hold," said Ireton, consequentially; "it's against Mr. Wild's orders. They must see the prisoner at the hatch."

"Very well, Sir," replied Austin, rising and walking towards them. "Well, my pretty dears," he added, "--to see your husband, eh? You must make the most of your time. You won't have him long. You've heard the news, I suppose?"

"That the death warrant's arrived," returned Edgeworth Bess, bursting into a flood of tears; "oh, yes! we've heard it."

"How does Jack bear it?" inquired Mrs. Maggot.

"Like a hero," answered Austin.

"I knew he would," replied the Amazon. "Come Bess,--no whimpering. Don't unman him. Are we to see him here?"

"Yes, my love."

"Well, then, lose no time in bringing him to us," said Mrs. Maggot. "There's a guinea to drink our health," she added, slipping a piece of money into his hand.

"Here, Caliban," shouted the under-turnkey, "unlock Captain Sheppard's padlock, and tell him his wives are in the Lodge waiting to see him."

"Iss, Massa Austin," replied the black. And taking the keys, he departed on the errand.

As soon as he was gone, the two women divested themselves of their hoods and cloaks, and threw them, as if inadvertently, into the farthest part of the angle in the wall. Their beautifully proportioned figures and rather over-displayed shoulders attracted the notice of Austin, who inquired of the chief turnkey "whether he should stand by them during the interview?"

"Oh! never mind them," said Mrs. Spurling, who had been hastily compounding another bowl of punch. "Sit down, and enjoy yourself. I'll keep a look out that nothing happens."

By this time Caliban had returned, and Jack appeared at the hatch. He was wrapped in a loose dressing-gown of light material, and stood near the corner where the women's dresses had just been thrown down, quite out of sight of all the party, except Mrs. Spurling, who sat on the right of the table.

"Have you got Jonathan out of the way?" he asked, in an eager whisper.

"Yes, yes," replied Edgeworth Bess. "Patience Kite has lured him to Enfield on a false scent after Blueskin. You need fear no interruption from him, or any of his myrmidons."

"That's well!" cried Jack. "Now stand before me, Poll. I've got the watch-spring saw in my sleeve. Pretend to weep both of you as loudly as you can. This spike is more than half cut through. I was at work at it yesterday and the day before. Keep up the clamour for five minutes, and I'll finish it."

Thus urged, the damsels began to raise their voices in loud lamentation.

"What the devil are you howling about?" cried Langley. "Do you think we are to be disturbed in this way? Make less noise, hussies, or I'll turn you out of the Lodge."

"For shame, Mr. Langley," rejoined Mrs. Spurling: "I blush for you, Sir! To call yourself a man, and interfere with the natural course of affection! Have you no feeling for the situation of those poor disconsolate creatures, about to be bereaved of all they hold dear? Is it nothing to part with a husband to the gallows? I've lost four in the same way, and know what it is." Here she began to blubber loudly for sympathy.

"Comfort yourself, my charmer," said Mr. Marvel, in a tone intended to be consolatory. "I'll be their substitute."

"You!" cried the tapstress, with a look of horror: "Never!"

"Confusion!" muttered Jack, suddenly pausing in his task, "the saw has broken just as I am through the spike."

"Can't we break it off?" replied Mrs. Maggot.

"I fear not," replied Jack, despondingly.

"Let's try, at all events," returned the Amazon.

And grasping the thick iron rod, she pushed with all her force against it, while Jack seconded her efforts from within. After great exertions on both parts, the spike yielded to their combined strength, and snapped suddenly off.

"Holloa--what's that?" cried Austin, starting up.

"Only my darbies," returned Jack, clinking his chains.

"Oh! that was all, was it?" said the turnkey, quietly reseating himself.

"Now, give me the woollen cloth to tie round my fetters," whispered Sheppard. "Quick."

"Here it is," replied Edgeworth Bess.

"Give me your hand, Poll, to help me through," cried Jack, as he accomplished the operation. "Keep a sharp look out, Bess."

"Stop!" interposed Edgeworth Bess; "Mr. Langley is getting up, and coming this way. We're lost."

"Help me through at all hazards, Poll," cried Jack, straining towards the opening.

"The danger's past," whispered Bess. "Mrs. Spurling has induced him to sit down again. Ah! she looks this way, and puts her finger to her lips. She comprehends what we're about. We're all safe!"

"Don't lose a moment then," cried Jack, forcing himself into the aperture, while the Amazon, assisted by Bess, pulled him through it.

"There!" cried Mrs. Maggot, as she placed him without noise upon the ground; "you're safe so far."

"Come, my disconsolate darlings," cried Austin, "it only wants five minutes to six. I expect Mr. Wild here presently. Cut it as short as you can."

"Only two minutes more, Sir," intreated Edgeworth Bess, advancing towards him in such a manner as to screen Jack, who crept into the farthest part of the angle,--"only two minutes, and we've done."

"Well, well, I'm not within a minute," rejoined the turnkey.

"We shall never be able to get you out unseen, Jack," whispered Poll Maggot. "You must make a bold push."

"Impossible," replied Sheppard, in the same tone. "That would be certain destruction. I can't run in these heavy fetters. No: I must face it out. Tell Bess to slip out, and I'll put on her cloak and hood."

Meanwhile, the party at the table continued drinking and chatting as merrily as before.

"I can't help thinking of Jack Sheppard's speech to Mr. Kneebone," observed Shotbolt, as he emptied his tenth tumbler; "I'm sure he's meditating an escape, and hopes to accomplish it to-night."

"Poh! poh!" rejoined Ireton; "it was mere idle boasting. I examined the Condemned Hold myself carefully this morning, and didn't find a nail out of its place. Recollect, he's chained to the ground by a great horse-padlock, and is never unloosed except when he comes to that hatch. If he escapes at all, it must be before our faces."

"It wouldn't surprise me if he did," remarked Griffin. "He's audacity enough for anything. He got out in much the same way from the Gatehouse,--stole the keys, and passed through a room where I was sitting half-asleep in a chair."

"Caught you napping, eh?" rejoined Ireton, with a laugh. "Well, he won't do that here. I'll forgive him if he does."

"And so will I," said Austin. "We're too wide awake for that. Ain't we, partner?" he added, appealing to Langley, whom punch had made rather dozy.

"I should think so," responded the lethargic turnkey, with a yawn.

During this colloquy, Jack had contrived unobserved to put on the hood and cloak, and being about the size of the rightful owner, presented a very tolerable resemblance to her. This done, Edgeworth Bess, who watched her opportunity, slipped out of the Lodge.

"Halloa!" exclaimed Austin, who had caught a glimpse of her departing figure, "one of the women is gone!"

"No--no," hastily interposed Mrs. Spurling; "they're both here. Don't you see they're putting on their cloaks?"

"That's false!" rejoined Marvel, in a low tone; "I perceive what has taken place."

"Oh! goodness!" ejaculated the tapstress, in alarm. "You won't betray him."

"Say the word, and I'm mum," returned the executioner.

"Will you be mine!"

"It's a very unfair advantage to take--very," replied Mrs. Spurling; "however I consent."

"Then I'll lend a helping hand. I shall lose my fees and the laced coat. But it's better to have the bride without the weddin' dress, than the weddin' dress without the bride."

At this moment, Saint Sepulchre's clock struck six.

"Close the wicket, Austin," vociferated Ireton, in an authoritative tone.

"Good bye!" cried Jack, as if taking leave of his mistresses, "to-morrow, at the same time."

"We'll be punctual," replied Mrs. Maggot. "Good bye, Jack! Keep up your spirits."

"Now for it!--life or death!" exclaimed Jack, assuming the gait of a female, and stepping towards the door.

As Austin rose to execute his principal's commands, and usher the women to the gate, Mrs. Spurling and Marvel rose too. The latter walked carelessly towards the hatch, and leaning his back against the place whence the spike had been removed, so as completely to hide it, continued smoking his pipe as coolly as if nothing had happened.

Just as Jack gained the entrance, he heard a man's footstep behind him, and aware that the slightest indiscretion would betray him, he halted, uncertain what to do.

"Stop a minute, my dear," cried Austin. "You forget that you promised me a kiss the last time you were here."

"Won't one from me do as well?" interposed Mrs. Maggot.

"Much better," said Mrs. Spurling, hastening to the rescue. "I want to speak to Edgeworth Bess myself."

So saying, she planted herself between Jack and the turnkey. It was a moment of breathless interest to all engaged in the attempt.

"Come--the kiss!" cried Austin, endeavouring to pass his arm familiarly round the Amazon's waist.

"Hands off!" she exclaimed, "or you'll repent it."

"Why, what'll you do?" demanded the turnkey.

"Teach you to keep your distance!" retorted Mrs. Maggot, dealing him a buffet that sent him reeling several yards backwards.

"There! off with you!" whispered Mrs. Spurling, squeezing Jack's arm, and pushing him towards the door, "and, don't come here again."

Before Austin could recover himself, Jack and Mrs. Maggot had disappeared.

"Bolt the wicket!" shouted Ireton, who, with the others, had been not a little entertained by the gallant turnkey's discomfiture.

This was done, and Austin returned with a crest-fallen look to the table. Upon which Mrs. Spurling, and her now accepted suitor, resumed their seats.

"You'll be as good as your word, my charmer," whispered the executioner.

"Of course," responded the widow, heaving a deep sigh. "Oh! Jack! Jack!--you little know what a price I've paid for you!"

"Well, I'm glad those women are gone," remarked Shotbolt. "Coupling their presence with Jack's speech, I couldn't help fearing some mischief might ensue."

"That reminds me he's still at large," returned Ireton. "Here, Caliban, go and fasten his padlock."

"Iss, Massa Ireton," replied the black.

"Stop, Caliban," interposed Mrs. Spurling, who wished to protract the discovery of the escape as long as possible. "Before you go, bring me the bottle of pineapple rum I opened yesterday. I should like Mr. Ireton and his friends to taste it. It is in the lower cupboard. Oh! you haven't got the key--then I must have it, I suppose. How provoking!" she added, pretending to rummage her pockets; "one never *can* find a thing when one wants it."

"Never mind it, my dear Mrs. Spurling," rejoined Ireton; "we can taste the rum when he returns. We shall have Mr. Wild here presently, and I wouldn't for the world--Zounds!" he exclaimed, as the figure of the thief-taker appeared at the wicket, "here he is. Off with you, Caliban! Fly, you rascal!"

"Mr. Wild here!" exclaimed Mrs. Spurling in alarm. "Oh gracious! he's lost."

"Who's lost?" demanded Ireton.

"The key," replied the widow.

All the turnkeys rose to salute the thief-taker, whose habitually-sullen countenance looked gloomier than usual. Ireton rushed forward to open the wicket for him.

"No Blueskin, I perceive, Sir," he observed, in a deferential tone, as Wild entered the Lodge.

"No," replied Jonathan, moodily. "I've been deceived by false information. But the wench who tricked me shall bitterly repent it. I hope this is all. I begin to fear I might be purposely go out of the way. Nothing has gone wrong here?"

"Nothing whatever," replied Ireton. "Jack is just gone back to the Condemned Hold. His two wives have been here."

"Ha!" exclaimed Jonathan, with a sudden vehemence that electrified the chief turnkey; "what's this! a spike gone! 'Sdeath! the women, you say, have been here. He has escaped."

"Impossible, Sir," replied Ireton, greatly alarmed.

"Impossible!" echoed Wild, with a fearful imprecation. "No, Sir, it's quite possible--more than possible. It's certain. I'll lay my life he's gone. Come with me to the Condemned Hold directly, and, if I find my fears confirmed, I'll--"

He was here interrupted by the sudden entrance of the black, who rushed precipitately into the room, letting fall the heavy bunch of keys in his fright.

"O Massa Ireton! Massa Wild!" ejaculated Caliban, "Shack Sheppart gone!"

"Gone? you black devil!--Gone?" cried Ireton.

"Iss, Massa. Caliban sarch ebery hole in de place, but Shack no dere. Only him big hoss padlock--noting else."

"I knew it," rejoined Wild, with concentrated rage; "and he escaped you all, in broad day, before your faces. You may well say it's impossible! His Majesty's jail of

Newgate is admirably guarded, I must say. Ireton, you are in league with him."

"Sir," said the chief turnkey, indignantly.

"You *are*, Sir," thundered Jonathan; "and, unless you find him, you shan't hold your place a week. I don't threaten idly, as you know. And you, Austin; and you Langley, I say the same thing to you."

"But, Mr. Wild," implored the turnkeys.

"I've said it," rejoined Jonathan, peremptorily. "And you, Marvel, you must have been a party--"

"I, Sir!"

"If he's not found, I'll get a new hangman."

"Zounds!" cried Marvel, "I--"

"Hush!" whispered the tapstress, "or I retract my promise."

"Mrs. Spurling," said Jonathan, who overheard the whisper, "you owe your situation to me. If you have aided Jack Sheppard's escape, you shall owe your discharge to me also."

"As you please, Sir," replied the tapstress, coolly. "And the next time Captain Darrell wants a witness, I promise you he shan't look for one in vain."

"Ha! hussy, dare you threaten?" cried Wild; but, checking himself, he turned to Ireton and asked, "How long have the women been gone?"

"Scarcely five minutes," replied the latter.

"One of you fly to the market," returned Jonathan; "another to the river; a third to the New Mint. Disperse in every direction. We'll have him yet. A hundred pounds to the man who takes him."

So saying, he rushed out, followed by Ireton and Langley.

"A hundred pounds!" exclaimed Shotbolt. "That's a glorious reward. Do you think he'll pay it?"

"I'm sure of it," replied Austin.

"Then I'll have it before to-morrow morning," said the keeper of the New Prison, to himself. "If Jack Sheppard sups with Mr. Kneebone, I'll make one of the party."

CHAPTER XI.
Dollis Hill revisited.

ABOUT an hour after the occurrences at Newgate, the door of the small back-parlour already described at Dollis Hill was opened by Winifred, who, gliding noiselessly across the room, approached a couch, on which was extended a sleeping female, and, gazing anxiously at her pale careworn countenance, murmured,--"Heaven be praised! she still slumbers--slumbers peacefully. The opiate has done its duty. Poor thing! how beautiful she looks! but how like death!"

Deathlike, indeed, was the repose of the sleeper,--deathlike and deep. Its very calmness was frightful. Her lips were apart, but no breath seemed to issue from them; and, but for a slight--very slight palpitation of the bosom, the vital principle might be supposed to be extinct. This lifeless appearance was heightened by the extreme sharpness of her features--especially the nose and chin,--and by the emaciation of her limbs, which was painfully distinct through her drapery. Her attenuated arms were crossed upon her breast; and her black brows and eyelashes contrasted fearfully with the livid whiteness of her skin. A few short, dark locks, escaping from beneath her head-dress, showed that her hair had been removed, and had only been recently allowed to grow again.

"Poor Mrs. Sheppard!" sighed Winifred, as she contemplated the beautiful wreck before her,--"Poor Mrs. Sheppard! when I see her thus, and think of all she has endured, of all she may yet have to endure, I could almost pray for her release from trouble. I dare not reflect upon the effect that her son's fate,--if the efforts to save him are ineffectual,--may have upon her enfeebled frame, and still worse upon her mind. What a mercy that the blow aimed at her by the ruffian, Wild, though it brought her to the brink of the grave, should have restored her to reason! Ah! she stirs."

As she said this, she drew a little aside, while Mrs. Sheppard heaved a deep sigh, and opened her eyes, which now looked larger, blacker, and more melancholy than ever.

"Where am I?" she cried, passing her hand across her brow.

"With your friends, dear Mrs. Sheppard," replied Winifred, advancing.

"Ah! you are there, my dear young lady," said the widow, smiling faintly; "when I first waken, I'm always in dread of finding myself again in that horrible asylum."

"You need never be afraid of that," returned Winifred, affectionately; "my father will take care you never leave him more."

"Oh! how much I owe him!" said the widow, with fervour, "for bringing me here, and removing me from those dreadful sights and sounds, that would have driven me distracted, even if I had been in my right mind. And how much I owe *you*, too, dearest Winifred, for your kindness and attention. Without you I should never have recovered either health or reason. I can never be grateful enough. But, though I cannot reward you, Heaven will."

"Don't say anything about it, dear Mrs. Sheppard," rejoined Winifred, controlling her emotion, and speaking as cheerfully as she could; "I would do anything in the world for you, and so would my father, and so would Thames; but he *ought*, for he's your nephew, you know. We all love you dearly."

"Bless you! bless you!" cried Mrs. Sheppard, averting her face to hide her tears.

"I mustn't tell you what Thames means to do for you if ever he gains his rights," continued Winifred; "but I *may* tell you what my father means to do."

"He has done too much already," answered the widow. "I shall need little more."

"But, *do* hear what it is," rejoined Winifred; "you know I'm shortly to be united to your nephew,--that is," she added, blushing, "when he can be married by his right name, for my father won't consent to it before."

"Your father will never oppose your happiness, my dear, I'm sure," said Mrs. Sheppard; "but, what has this to do with me?"

"You shall hear," replied Winifred; "when this marriage takes place, you and I shall be closely allied, but my father wishes for a still closer alliance."

"I don't unterstand you," returned Mrs. Sheppard.

"To be plain, then," said Winifred, "he has asked me whether I have any objection to you as a mother."

"And what--what was your answer?" demanded the widow, eagerly.

"Can't you guess?" returned Winifred, throwing her arms about her neck. "That he couldn't choose any one so agreeable to me."

"Winifred," said Mrs. Sheppard, after a brief pause, during which she appeared overcome by her feelings,--she said, gently disengaging herself from the young girl's embrace, and speaking in a firm voice, "you must dissuade your father from this step."

"How?" exclaimed the other. "Can you not love him?"

"Love him!" echoed the widow. "The feeling is dead within my breast. My only love is for my poor lost son. I can esteem him, regard him; but, love him as he *ought* to be loved--that I cannot do."

"Your esteem is all he will require," urged Winifred.

"He has it, and will ever have it," replied Mrs. Sheppard, passionately,--"he has my boundless gratitude, and devotion. But I am not worthy to be any man's wife-- far less *his* wife. Winifred, you are deceived in me. You know not what a wretched guilty thing I am. You know not in what dark places my life has been cast; with what crimes it has been stained. But the offences I *have* committed are venial in comparison with what I should commit were I to wed your father. No--no, it must never be."

"You paint yourself worse than you are, dear Mrs. Sheppard," rejoined Winifred kindly. "Your faults were the faults of circumstances."

"Palliate them as you may," replied the widow, gravely, "they *were* faults; and as such, cannot be repaired by a greater wrong. If you love me, do not allude to this subject again."

"I'm sorry I mentioned it at all, since it distresses you," returned Winifred; "but, as I knew my father intended to propose to you, if poor Jack should be respited--"

"*If* he should be respited?" repeated Mrs. Sheppard, with startling eagerness. "Does your father doubt it? Speak! tell me!"

Winifred made no answer.

"Your hesitation convinces me he does," replied the widow. "Is Thames returned from London?"

"Not yet," replied the other; "but I expect him every minute. My father's chief fear, I must tell you, is from the baneful influence of Jonathan Wild."

"That fiend is ever in my path," exclaimed Mrs. Sheppard, with a look, the wildness of which greatly alarmed her companion. "I cannot scare him thence."

"Hark!" cried Winifred, "Thames is arrived. I hear the sound of his horse's feet in the yard. Now you will learn the result."

"Heaven support me!" cried Mrs. Sheppard, faintly.

"Breathe at this phial," said Winifred.

Shortly afterwards,--it seemed an age to the anxious mother,--Mr. Wood entered the room, followed by Thames. The latter looked very pale, either from the effect of his wound, which was not yet entirely healed, or from suppressed emotion,--partly, perhaps, from both causes,--and wore his left arm in a sling.

"Well!" cried Mrs. Sheppard, raising herself, and looking at him as if her life depended upon the answer. "He is respited?"

"Alas! no," replied Thames, sadly. "The warrant for his execution is arrived. There is no further hope."

"My poor son!" groaned the widow, sinking backwards.

"Heaven have mercy on his soul!" ejaculated Wood.

"Poor Jack!" cried Winifred, burying her face in her lover's bosom.

Not a word was uttered for some time, nor any sound heard except the stilled sobs of the unfortunate mother.

At length, she suddenly started to her feet; and before Winifred could prevent her, staggered up to Thames.

"When is he to suffer?" she demanded, fixing her large black eyes, which burnt with an insane gleam, upon him.

"On Friday," he replied.

"Friday!" echoed Mrs. Sheppard; "and to-day is Monday. He has three days to live. Only three days. Three short days. Horrible!"

"Poor soul! her senses are going again," said Mr. Wood, terrified by the wildness of her looks. "I was afraid it would be so."

"Only three days," reiterated the widow, "three short short days,--and then all is over. Jonathan's wicked threat is fulfilled at last. The gallows is in view--I see it with all its hideous apparatus!--ough!" and shuddering violently, she placed her hands before her, as if to exclude some frightful vision from her sight.

"Do not despair, my sweet soul," said Wood, in a soothing tone.

"Do not despair!" echoed Mrs. Sheppard, with a laugh that cut the ears of those who listened to it like a razor,--"Do not despair! And who or what shall give me comfort when my son is gone? I have wept till my eyes are dry,--suffered till my heart is broken,--prayed till the voice of prayer is dumb,--and all of no avail. He will be hanged--hanged--hanged. Ha! ha! What have I left but despair and madness? Promise me one thing, Mr. Wood," she continued, with a sudden change of tone, and convulsively clutching the carpenter's arm, "promise it me."

"Anything, my dear," replied Wood, "What is it?"

"Bury us together in one grave in Willesden churchyard. There is a small yew-tree west of the church. Beneath that tree let us lie. In one grave, mind. Do you promise to do this?"

"Solemnly," rejoined the carpenter.

"Enough," said the widow, gratefully. "I must see him to-night."

"Impossible, dear Mrs. Sheppard," said Thames. "To-morrow I will take you to him."

"To-morrow will be too late," replied the widow, in a hollow voice, "I feel it will. I must go to-night, or I shall never behold him again. I must bless him before I die. I have strength enough to drag myself there, and I do not want to return."

"Be pacified, sweet soul," said Wood, looking meaningly at Thames; "you *shall* go, and I will accompany you."

"A mother's blessing on you," replied Mrs. Sheppard, fervently. "And now," she added, with somewhat more composure, "leave me, dear friends, I entreat, for a few minutes to collect my scattered thoughts--to prepare myself for what I have to go through--to pray for my son."

"Shall we do so?" whispered Winifred to her father.

"By all means," returned Wood; "don't delay an instant." And, followed by the young couple, who gazed wistfully at the poor sufferer, he hastily quitted the room, and locked the door after him.

Mrs. Sheppard was no sooner alone than she fell upon her knees by the side of the couch, and poured forth her heart in prayer. So absorbed was she by her passionate supplications that she was insensible to anything passing around her, until she felt a touch upon her shoulder, and heard a well-known voice breathe in her ear--"Mother!"

She started at the sound as if an apparition had called her, screamed, and fell into her son's outstretched arms. "Mother! dear mother!" cried Jack, folding her to his breast.

"My son! my dear, dear son!" returned Mrs. Sheppard, returning his embrace with all a parent's tenderness.

Jack was completely overcome. His chest heaved violently, and big tears coursed rapidly down his cheeks.

"I don't deserve it," he said, at length; "but I would have risked a thousand deaths to enjoy this moment's happiness."

"And you must have risked much to obtain it, my love. I have scarcely recovered from the shock of hearing of your condemnation, when I behold you free!"

"Not two hours since," rejoined Jack, "I was chained down in the Condemned Hold in Newgate. With a small saw, conveyed to me a few days since by Thames Darrell, which I contrived to conceal upon my person, I removed a spike in the hatch, and, with the aid of some other friends, worked my way out. Having heard from Thames that you were better, and that your sole anxiety was about me, I came to give you the *first* intelligence of my escape."

"Bless you for it. But you will stay here?"

"I dare not. I must provide for my safety."

"Mr. Wood will protect you," urged Mrs. Sheppard.

"He has not the power--perhaps not the will to do so. And if he would, I would not subject him to the annoyance. The moment my escape is known, a large reward will be placed on my head. My dress, my person will be minutely described. Jonathan Wild and his bloodhounds, with a hundred others, incited by the reward, will be upon my track. Nay, for aught I know, some of them may even now have got scent of me."

"You terrify me," cried Mrs. Sheppard. "Oh! if this is the case, do not stay an instant. Fly! fly!"

"As soon as I can do so with safety, I will return, or send to you," said Jack.

"Do not endanger yourself on my account," rejoined his mother. "I am quite easy now; receive my blessing, my dear son; and if we never meet again, rest assured my last prayer shall be for you."

"Do not talk thus, dear mother," returned Jack, gazing anxiously at her pale countenance, "or I shall not be able to quit you. You must live for me."

"I will try to do so," replied the widow, forcing a smile. "One last embrace. I need not counsel you to avoid those fatal courses which have placed you in such fearful jeopardy."

"You need not," replied Jack, in a tone of the deepest compunction. "And, oh! forgive me, though I can never forgive myself, for the misery I have caused you."

"Forgive you!" echoed his mother, with a look radiant with delight. "I have nothing to forgive. Ah!" she screamed, with a sudden change of manner; and pointing to the window, which Jack had left open, and at which a dark figure was standing, "there is Jonathan Wild!"

"Betrayed!" exclaimed Jack, glancing in the same direction. "The door!--the door!--death!" he added, as he tried the handle, "it is locked--and I am unarmed. Madman that I am to be so!"

"Help!" shrieked Mrs. Sheppard.

"Be silent," said Jonathan, striding deliberately into the room; "these cries will avail you nothing. Whoever answers them must assist me to capture your son. Be silent, I say, if you value his safety."

Awed by Jonathan's manner, Mrs. Sheppard repressed the scream that rose to her lips, and both mother and son gazed with apprehension at the heavy figure of the thief-taker, which, viewed in the twilight, seemed dilated to twice its natural size, and appeared almost to block up the window. In addition to his customary arms, Jonathan carried a bludgeon with a large heavy knob, suspended from his wrist by a loop; a favourite weapon, which he always took with him on dangerous expeditions, and which, if any information had been requisite, would have told Sheppard that the present was one of them.

"Well, Jack," he said, after a pause, "are you disposed to go back quietly with me?"

"You'll ascertain that when you attempt to touch me," rejoined Sheppard, resolutely.

"My janizaries are within call," returned Wild. "I'm armed; you are not."

"It matters not. You shall not take me alive."

"Spare him! spare him!" cried Mrs. Sheppard, falling on her knees.

"Get up, mother," cried Jack; "do not kneel to him. I wouldn't accept my life from him. I've foiled him hitherto, and will foil him yet. And, come what will, I'll balk him of the satisfaction of hanging me."

Jonathan raised his bludgeon, but controlled himself by a powerful effort.

"Fool!" he cried, "do you think I wouldn't have secured you before this if I hadn't some motive for my forbearance?"

"And that motive is fear," replied Jack contemptuously.

"Fear!" echoed Wild, in a terrible tone,--"fear! Repeat that word again, and nothing shall save you."

"Don't anger him, my dear son," implored the poor widow, with a look of anguish at Jack. "Perhaps he means well."

"Mad as you are, you're the more sensible of the two, I must say," rejoined Jonathan.

"Spare him!" cried Mrs, Sheppard, who fancied she had made some impression on the obdurate breast of the thief-taker,--"spare him! and I will forgive you, will thank you, bless you. Spare him! spare him!"

"On one condition I *will* spare him," returned Wild; "on one condition only."

"What is it?" asked the poor woman.

"Either he or you must return with me," answered Jonathan.

"Take *me*, then," replied the widow. And she would have rushed to him, if she had not been forcibly withheld by her son.

"Do not go near him, mother," cried Jack; "do not believe him. There is some deep treachery hidden beneath his words."

"I *will* go," said Mrs. Sheppard, struggling to get free.

"Attend to me, Mrs. Sheppard," said Jonathan, looking calmly on at this distressing scene, "Attend to me, and do not heed him. I swear to you, solemnly swear to you, I will save your son's life, nay more, will befriend him, will place him out of the reach of his enemies, if you consent to become my wife."

"Execrable villain!" exclaimed Jack.

"You hear that," cried Mrs. Sheppard; "he swears to save you."

"Well," replied her son; "and you spurn the proposal."

"No; she accepts it," rejoined Jonathan, triumphantly. "Come along, Mrs. Sheppard. I've a carriage within call shall convey you swiftly to town. Come! come!"

"Hear me, mother," cried Jack, "and I will explain to you *why* the villain makes this strange and revolting proposal. He well knows that but two lives--those of Thames Darrell and Sir Rowland Trenchard,--stand between you and the vast possessions of the family. Those lives removed,--and Sir Rowland is completely in his power, the estates would be yours--HIS! if he were your husband. Now do you see his motive?"

"I see nothing but your danger," replied his mother, tenderly.

"Granted it were as you say, Jack," said Wild;--"and I sha'n't take the trouble to contradict you--the estates would be *yours* hereafter."

"Liar!" cried Jack. "Do you affect ignorance that I am a condemned felon, and can inherit nothing? But do not imagine that under any circumstances I would accept your terms. My mother shall never degrade herself by a connection with you."

"Degrade herself," rejoined Jonathan, brutally. "Do you think I would take a harlot to my bed, if it didn't suit my purposes to do so?"

"He says right," replied Mrs. Sheppard, distractedly. "I am only fit for such as him. Take me! take me!"

"Before an hour you shall be mine," said Jonathan advancing towards her.

"Back!" cried Jack fiercely: "lay a finger on her, and I will fell you to the ground. Mother! do you know what you do? Would you sell yourself to this fiend?"

"I would sell myself, body and soul, to save you," rejoined his mother, bursting from his grasp.

Jonathan caught her in his arms.

"Come away!" he cried, with the roar of a demon.

This laugh and his looks alarmed her.

"It *is* the fiend!" she exclaimed, recoiling. "Save me!--save me!"

"Damnation!" vociferated Jonathan, savagely. "We've no time for any Bedlam scenes now. Come along, you mad jade. I'll teach you submission in time."

With this, he endeavoured to force her off; but, before he could accomplish his purpose, he was arrested, and his throat seized by Jack. In the struggle, Mrs. Sheppard broke from him, and filled the room with her shrieks.

"I'll now pay the debt I owe you," cried Jack, tightening his grip till the thief-taker blackened in the face.

"Dog!" cried Wild, freeing himself by a powerful effort, and dealing Jack a violent blow with the heavy bludgeon, which knocked him backwards, "you are not yet a match for Jonathan Wild. Neither you nor your mother shall escape me. But I must summon my janizaries." So saying, he raised a whistle to his lips, and blew a loud call; and, as this was unanswered, another still louder. "Confusion!" he cried; "something has happened. But I won't be cheated of my prize."

"Help! help!" shrieked Mrs. Sheppard, fleeing from him to the farthest corner of the room.

But it was of no avail. Jonathan again seized her, when the door was thrown open, and Thames Darrell, followed by Mr. Wood and several serving-men, all well armed, rushed into the room. A glance sufficed to show the young man how matters stood. He flew to the window, and would have passed his sword through the thief-taker's body, if the latter had not quickly interposed the person of Mrs. Sheppard, so that if the blow had been stricken she must have received it.

"Quilt!--Mendez!--Where are you?" vociferated Wild, sounding his whistle for the third time.

"You call in vain," rejoined Thames. "Your assistants are in my power. Yield, villain!"

"Never!" replied Jonathan.

"Put down your burthen, monster!" shouted Wood, pointing an immense blunderbuss at him.

"Take her," cried Jonathan; and, flinging the now inanimate body of the poor widow, who had fainted in the struggle, into the arms of Thames, he leapt through the window, and by the time the latter could consign her to Wood, and dart after him, he had disappeared.

"Pursue him," cried Thames to the attendants, "and see that he does not escape."

The order was promptly obeyed.

"Jack," continued Thames, addressing Sheppard, who had only just recovered from the blow, and regained his feet, "I don't ask *how* you came here, nor do I blame your rashness in doing so. Fortunately, ever since Wild's late murderous attack, the household has all been well armed. A post-chaise seen in the road first alarmed us. On searching the grounds, we found two suspicious-looking fellows in the garden, and had scarcely secured them, when your mother's cries summoned us hither, just in time to preserve her."

"Your arrival was most providential," said Jack.

"You must not remain here another instant," replied Thames. "My horse is at the door, saddled, with pistols in the holsters,--mount him and fly."

"Thames, I have much to say," said Jack, "much that concerns your safety."

"Not now," returned Thames, impatiently. "I cannot--will not suffer you to remain here."

"I will go, if you will consent to meet me at midnight near the old house in Wych Street," replied Jack. "By that time, I shall have fully considered a plan which occurs to me for defeating the schemes of your enemies."

"Before that time you will be captured, if you expose yourself thus," rejoined Thames. "However, I will be there. Farewell."

"Till midnight," replied Jack.

And imprinting a kiss upon his mother's cold lips, he left the room. He found the horse where Thames told him he would find him, mounted, and rode off across the fields in the direction of town.

CHAPTER XII.
The Well Hole.

JONATHAN Wild's first object, as soon as he had made good his retreat, was to ascertain what had become of his janizaries, and, if possible, to release them. With this view, he hurried to the spot where he had left the post-chaise, and found it drawn up at the road-side, the postilion dismounted, and in charge of a couple of farming-men. Advancing towards them, sword in hand, Jonathan so terrified the hinds by his fierce looks and determined manner, that, after a slight show of resistance, they took to their heels, leaving him master of the field. He then threw open the door of the vehicle, in which he found his janizaries with their arms pinioned, and, leaping into it, ordered the man to drive off. The postilion obeyed, and dashed off as hard as his horses could gallop along the beautiful road leading to Neasdon and Willesden, just as the serving-men made their appearance. Arrived at the latter place, Jonathan, who, meanwhile, had contrived to liberate his attendants from their bonds, drew up at the Six Bells, and hiring a couple of horses, despatched his attendants in search of Jack Sheppard, while he proceeded to town. Dismissing the post-chaise at the Old Bailey, he walked to Newgate to ascertain what had occurred since the escape. It was just upon the stroke of nine as he entered the Lodge, and Mr. Austin was dismissing a host of inquirers who had been attracted thither by the news,--for it had already been extensively noised abroad. Some of these persons were examining the spot where the spike had been cut off; others the spike itself, now considered a remarkable object; and all were marvelling how Jack could have possibly squeezed himself through such a narrow aperture, until it was explained to them by Mr. Austin that the renowned housebreaker was of slender bodily conformation, and therefore able to achieve a feat, which he, Mr. Austin, or any man of similar dimensions, would have found wholly impossible. Affixed to the wall, in a conspicuous situation, was a large placard, which, after minutely describing Sheppard's appearance and attire, concluded thus:--"*Whoever will discover or apprehend the above* JOHN SHEPPARD, so that he be brought to justice, shall receive ONE HUNDRED GUINEAS REWARD, *to be paid by* MR. PITT, *the keeper of Newgate*."

This placard attracted universal attention. While Jonathan was conversing with Austin, from whom he took care to conceal the fact of his having seen Sheppard since his escape, Ireton entered the Lodge.

"Altogether unsuccessful, Sir," said the chief turnkey, with a look of disappointment, not unmixed with apprehension, as he approached Wild. "I've been to all the flash cases in town, and can hear nothing of him or his wives. First, I went to Country Tom's, the Goat, in Long Lane. Tom swore he hadn't set eyes on him since the trial. I next proceeded to Jenny Bunch's, the Ship, in Trig Lane--there I got the same answer. Then to the Feathers, in Drury Lane. Then to the Golden Ball, in the same street. Then to Martin's brandy-shop, in Fleet Street. Then to Dan Ware's, in Hanging Sword Court. Then to the Dean's Head, in St. Martin's Le Grand. And, lastly, to the Seven Cities o' Refuge, in the New Mint. And nowhere could I obtain the slightest information."

"Humph!" exclaimed Wild.

"Have you been more successful, Sir?" ventured Ireton.

Jonathan shook his head.

"Mr. Shotbolt thinks he has a scheme that can't fail," interposed Austin; "but he wishes to know whether you'll be as good as your word, in respect to the great reward you offered for Jack's capture."

"Have I ever broken my word in such matters, that he dares put the question?" rejoined Jonathan sternly. "Tell Mr. Shotbolt that if he, or any other person, takes Jack Sheppard before to-morrow morning, I'll double it. Do you hear?"

"I do, Sir," replied Austin respectfully.

"Two hundred pounds, if he's lodged in Newgate before to-morrow morning," continued Wild. "Make it known among your friends." And he strode out of the place.

"Two hundred pounds!" exclaimed Ireton, "besides the governor's offer--that's three hundred. I must go to work again. Keep a sharp look out, Austin, and see that we lose no one else. I should be sorry if Shotbolt got the reward."

"Devilish hard! I'm not allowed a chance," grumbled Austin, as he was left alone. "However, some one *must* look after the jail; and they're all gone but me. It's fortunate we've no more Jack Sheppards, or I should stand but a poor chance. Well, I don't think they'll any of 'em nab him, that's one comfort."

On quitting the Lodge, Wild repaired to his own habitation. Telling the porter that he would attend to the house himself, he bade him go in search of Jack Sheppard. There was something in Jonathan's manner, as he issued this command, that struck the man as singular, and he afterwards recalled it. He, however, made no remark at the time, but instantly prepared to set out. As soon as he was gone, Jonathan went up stairs to the audience-chamber; and, sitting down, appeared for some time buried in reflection. The dark and desperate thoughts that were passing through his mind at this time will presently be shown. After a while, he raised his eyes; and, if their glance could have been witnessed at the moment, it could not have been easily forgotten. Muttering something to himself, he appeared to be telling upon his fingers the advantages and disadvantages of some scheme he had in contemplation. That he had resolved upon its execution, whatever it might be, was evident from his saying aloud,--

"I will do it. So good an opportunity may never occur again."

Upon this he arose, and paced the room hastily backwards and forwards, as if further arranging his plans. He then unlocked a cabinet, opened a secret drawer, and, lifter ransacking its contents, discovered a paper he was in search of, and a glove. Laying these carefully aside, he restored the drawer to its place. His next occupation was to take out his pistols, examine the priming, and rub the flints. His sword then came in for his scrutiny: he felt at, and appeared satisfied with its edge. This employment seemed to afford him the highest satisfaction; for a diabolical grin--it cannot be called a smile--played upon his face all the time he was engaged in it. His sword done with, he took up the bludgeon; balanced it in his hand; upon the points of his fingers; and let it fall with a smash, intentionally, upon the table.

"After all," he said, "this is the safest weapon. No instrument I've ever used has done me such good service. It *shall* be the bludgeon." So saying, he slung it upon his wrist.

Taking up a link, which was blazing beside him, he walked across the room; and touching a spring in the wall, a secret door flew open. Beyond was a narrow bridge, crossing a circular building, at the bottom of which lay a deep well. It was a dark mysterious place, and what it was used for no one exactly knew; but it was called by those who had seen it the Well Hole. The bridge was protected on either side by a railing with bannisters placed at wide intervals. Steps to aid the descent, which was too steep to be safe without them, led to, a door on the opposite side. This door, which was open, Jonathan locked and took out the key. As he stood upon the bridge, he held down the light, and looked into the profound abyss. The red glare fell upon the slimy brick-work, and tinged the inky waters below. A slight cough uttered by Jonathan at the moment awakened the echoes of the place, and was returned in hollow reverberations. "There'll be a louder echo here presently," thought Jonathan. Before leaving the place he looked upwards, and could just discern the blue vault and pale stars of Heaven through an iron grating at the top.

On his return to the room, Jonathan purposely left the door of the Well Hole ajar. Unlocking a cupboard, he then took out some cold meat and other viands, with a flask of wine, and a bottle of brandy, and began to eat and drink voraciously. He had very nearly cleared the board, when a knock was heard below, and descending at the summons, he found his two janizaries. They had both been unsuccessful. As Jonathan scarcely expected a more satisfactory result, he made no comment; but, ordering Quilt to continue his search, and not to return until he had found the fugitive, called Abraham Mendez into the house, and shut the door.

"I want you for the job I spoke of a short time ago, Nab," he said. "I mean to have no one but yourself in it. Come up stairs, and take a glass of brandy."

Abraham grinned, and silently followed his master, who, as soon as they reached the audience-chamber, poured out a bumper of spirits, and presented it to him. The Jew swallowed it at a draught.

"By my shoul!" he exclaimed, smacking his lips, "dat ish goot--very goot."

"You shall finish the bottle when the job's done," replied Jonathan.

"Vat ish it, Mishter Vild?" inquired Mendez. "Shir Rowland Trenchard's affair--eh?"

"That's it," rejoined Jonathan; "I expect him here every minute. When you've admitted him, steal into the room, hide yourself, and don't move till I utter the words, 'You've a long journey before you.' That's your signal."

"And a famoush goot shignal it ish," laughed Abraham. "He hash a long journey before him--ha! ha!"

"Peace!" cried Jonathan. "There's his knock. Go, and let him in. And mind you don't arouse his suspicions."

"Never fear--never fear," rejoined Abraham, as he took up the link, and left the room.

Jonathan cast a hasty glance around, to see that all was properly arranged for his purpose; placed a chair with its back to the door; disposed the lights on the table so as to throw the entrance of the room more into shadow; and then flung himself into a seat to await Sir Rowland's arrival.

He had not to wait long. Enveloped in a large cloak, Sir Rowland stalked into the room, and took the seat assigned him; while the Jew, who received a private signal from Jonathan, set down the link near the entrance of the Well Hole, and, having made fast the door, crept behind one of the cases.

Fancying they were alone, Sir Rowland threw aside his cloak, and produced a heavy bag of money, which he flung upon the table; and, when Wild had feasted his greedy eyes sufficiently upon its golden contents, he handed him a pocket-book filled with notes.

"You have behaved like a man of honour, Sir Rowland," said Wild, after he had twice told over the money. "Right to a farthing."

"Give me an acquittance," said Trenchard.

"It's scarcely necessary," replied Wild; "however, if you require it, certainly. There it is. 'Received from Sir Rowland Trenchard, 15,000 L.--Jonathan Wild: August 31st, 1724.' Will that do?"

"It will," replied Trenchard. "This is our last transaction together."

"I hope not," replied Wild.

"It is the last," continued the knight, sternly; "and I trust we may never meet again, I have paid you this large sum--not because you are entitled to it, for you have failed in what you undertook to do, but because I desire to be troubled with you no further. I have now settled my affairs, and made every preparation for my departure to France, where I shall spend the remainder of my days. And I have made such arrangements that at my decease tardy justice will be done my injured nephew."

"You have made no such arrangements as will compromise me, I hope, Sir

Rowland?" said Wild, hastily.

"While I live you are safe," rejoined Trenchard; "after my death I can answer for nothing."

"'Sblood!" exclaimed Wild, uneasily. "This alters the case materially. When were you last confessed, Sir Rowland?" he added abruptly.

"Why do you ask?" rejoined the other haughtily.

"Because--because I'm always distrustful of a priest," rejoined Jonathan.

"I have just parted from one," said Trenchard.

"So much the worse," replied Jonathan, rising and taking a turn, as if uncertain what to do.

"So much the better," rejoined Sir Rowland. "He who stands on the verge of the grave, as I do, should never be unprepared."

"You're strangely superstitious, Sir Rowland," said Jonathan, halting, and looking steadfastly at him.

"If I were so, I should not be here," returned Trenchard.

"How so?" asked Wild, curiously.

"I had a terrible dream last night. I thought my sister and her murdered husband dragged me hither, to this very room, and commanded you to slay me."

"A terrible dream, indeed," said Jonathan thoughtfully. "But you mustn't indulge these gloomy thoughts. Let me recommend a glass of wine."

"My penance forbids it," said Trenchard, waving his hand. "I cannot remain here long."

"You will remain longer than you anticipate," muttered Wild.

"Before I go," continued Sir Rowland, "I must beg of you to disclose to me all you know relative to the parentage of Thames Darrell."

"Willingly," replied Wild. "Thinking it likely you might desire to have this information, I prepared accordingly. First, look at this glove. It belonged to his father, and was worn by him on the night he was murdered. You will observe that a coronet is embroidered on it."

"Ha!" exclaimed Trenchard, starting, "is he so highly born?"

"This letter will inform you," replied Wild, placing a document in his hand.

"What is this!" cried Sir Rowland. "I know the hand--ha! my friend! and I have murdered *him*! And my sister was thus nobly, thus illustriously wedded. O God! O

God!"

And he appeared convulsed with agony.

"Oh! if I had known this," he exclaimed, "what guilt, what remorse might have been spared me!"

"Repentance comes too late when the deed's done," returned Wild, bitterly.

"It is not too late to repair the wrong I have done my nephew," cried Trenchard. "I will set about it instantly. He shall have the estates. I will return to Manchester at once."

"You had better take some refreshment before you start," rejoined Wild. "'You've a long journey before you.'"

As the signal was given, the Jew, who had been some time in expectation of it, darted swiftly and silently behind Sir Rowland, and flung a cloth over his head, while Jonathan, rushing upon him in front, struck him several quick and violent blows in the face with the bludgeon. The white cloth was instantly dyed with crimson; but, regardless of this, Jonathan continued his murderous assault. The struggles of the wounded man were desperate--so desperate, that in his agony he overset the table, and, in the confusion, tore off the cloth, and disclosed a face horribly mutilated, and streaming with blood. So appalling was the sight, that even the murderers--familiar as they were with scenes of slaughter,--looked aghast at it.

During this dreadful pause the wretched man felt for his sword. It had been removed from the scabbard by the Jew. He uttered a deep groan, but said nothing.

"Despatch him!" roared Jonathan.

Having no means of defence, Sir Rowland cleared the blood from his vision; and, turning to see whether there was any means of escape, he descried the open door behind him leading to the Well Hole, and instantly darted through it.

"As I could wish!" cried Jonathan. "Bring the light, Nab."

The Jew snatched up the link, and followed him.

A struggle of the most terrific kind now ensued. The wounded man had descended the bridge, and dashed himself against the door beyond it; but, finding it impossible to force his way further, he turned to confront his assailants. Jonathan aimed a blow at him, which, if it had taken place, must have instantly terminated the strife; but, avoiding this, he sprang at the thief-taker, and grappled with him. Firmly built, as it was, the bridge creaked in such a manner with their contending efforts, that Abraham durst not venture beyond the door, where he stood, holding the light, a horrified spectator of the scene. The contest, however, though desperate, was brief. Disengaging his right arm, Jonathan struck his victim a tremendous blow on the head with the bludgeon, that fractured his skull; and, exerting all his strength, threw him over the rails, to which he clung with the tenacity of despair.

"Spare me!" he groaned, looking upwards. "Spare me!"

Jonathan, however, instead of answering him, searched for his knife, with the intention of severing his wrist. But not finding it, he had again recourse to the bludgeon, and began beating the hand fixed on the upper rail, until, by smashing the fingers, he forced it to relinquish its hold. He then stamped upon the hand on the lower bannister, until that also relaxed its gripe.

Sir Rowland then fell.

A hollow plunge, echoed and re-echoed by the walls, marked his descent into the water.

"Give me the link," cried Jonathan.

Holding down the light, he perceived that the wounded man had risen to the surface, and was trying to clamber up the slippery sides of the well.

"Shoot him! shoot him! Put him out of hish mishery," cried the Jew.

"What's the use of wasting a shot?" rejoined Jonathan, savagely. "He can't get out."

After making several ineffectual attempts to keep himself above water, Sir Rowland sunk, and his groans, which had become gradually fainter and fainter, were heard no more.

"All's over," muttered Jonathan.

"Shall ve go back to de other room?" asked the Jew. "I shall breathe more freely dere. Oh! Christ! de door's shut! It musht have schwung to during de schuffle!"

"Shut!" exclaimed Wild. "Then we're imprisoned. The spring can't be opened on this side."

"Dere's de other door!" cried Mendez, in alarm.

"It only leads to the fencing crib," replied Wild. "There's no outlet that way."

"Can't ve call for asshistanche?"

"And who'll find us, if we do?" rejoined Wild, fiercely. "But they *will* find the evidences of slaughter in the other room,--the table upset,--the bloody cloth,--the dead man's sword,--the money,--and my memorandum, which I forgot to remove. Hell's curses! that after all my precautions I should be thus entrapped. It's all your fault, you shaking coward! and, but that I feel sure you'll swing for your carelessness, I'd throw you into the well, too."

CHAPTER XIII.
The Supper at Mr. Kneebone's.

PERSUADED that Jack Sheppard would keep his appointment with Mr. Kneebone, and feeling certain of capturing him if he did so, Shotbolt, on quitting Newgate, hurried to the New Prison to prepare for the enterprise. After debating with himself for some time whether he should employ an assistant, or make the attempt alone, his love of gain overcame his fears, and he decided upon the latter plan. Accordingly, having armed himself with various weapons, including a stout oaken staff then ordinarily borne by the watch, and put a coil of rope and a gag in his pocket, to be ready in case of need, he set out, about ten o'clock, on the expedition.

Before proceeding to Wych Street, he called at the Lodge to see how matters were going on, and found Mrs. Spurling and Austin at their evening meal, with Caliban in attendance.

"Well, Mr. Shotbolt," cried the turnkey, "I've good news for you. Mr. Wild has doubled his offer, and the governor has likewise proclaimed a reward of one hundred guineas for Jack's apprehension."

"You don't say so!" exclaimed Shotbolt.

"Read that," rejoined Austin, pointing to the placard. "I ought to tell you that Mr. Wild's reward is conditional upon Jack's being taken before to-morrow morning. So I fear there's little chance of any one getting it."

"You think so, eh?" chuckled Shotbolt, who was eagerly perusing the reward, and congratulating himself upon his caution; "you think so--ha! ha! Well, don't go to bed, that's all."

"What for?" demanded the turnkey.

"Because the prisoner's arrival might disturb you--ha! ha!"

"I'll lay you twenty guineas you don't take him to-night," rejoined Austin.

"Done!" cried Shotbolt. "Mrs. Spurling, you're a witness to the bet. Twenty guineas, mind. I shan't let you off a farthing. Egad! I shall make a good thing of it."

"Never count your chickens till they're hatched," observed Mrs. Spurling, dri-ly.

"*My* chickens are hatched, or, at least, nearly so," replied Shotbolt, with increased merriment. "Get ready your heaviest irons, Austin. I'll send you word when I catch him."

"You'd better send *him*," jeered the turnkey.

"So I will," rejoined Shotbolt; "so I will. If I don't, you shall clap me in the Condemned Hold in his stead. Good-bye, for the pressent--ha! ha!" And, laughing loudly at his own facetiousness, he quitted the Lodge.

"I'll lay my life he's gone on a fox-and-goose-chase to Mr. Kneebone's," remarked Austin, rising to fasten the door.

"I shouldn't wonder," replied Mrs. Spurling, as if struck by a sudden idea. And, while the turnkey was busy with the keys, she whispered to the black, "Follow him, Caliban. Take care he don't see you,--and bring me word where he goes, and what he does."

"Iss, missis," grinned the black.

"Be so good as to let Caliban out, Mr. Austin," continued the tapstress; "he's only going on an errand."

Austin readily complied with her request. As he returned to the table, he put his finger to his nose; and, though he said nothing, he thought he had a much better chance of winning his wager.

Unconscious that his movements were watched, Shotbolt, meanwhile, hastened towards Wych Street. On the way, he hired a chair with a couple of stout porters, and ordered them to follow him. Arrived within a short distance of his destination, he came to a halt, and pointing out a dark court nearly opposite the woollen-draper's abode, told the chairmen to wait there till they were summoned.

"I'm a peace-officer," he added, "about to arrest a notorious criminal. He'll be brought out at this door, and may probably make some resistance. But you must get him into the chair as fast as you can, and hurry off to Newgate."

"And what'll we get for the job, yer hon'r?" asked the foremost chairman, who, like most of his tribe at the time, was an Irishman.

"Five guineas. Here's a couple in hand."

"Faix, then we'll do it in style," cried the fellow. "Once in this chair, yer hon'r, and I'll warrant he'll not get out so aisily as Jack Sheppard did from the New Pris'n."

"Hold your tongue, sirrah," rejoined Shotbolt, not over-pleased by the remark, "and mind what I tell you. Ah! what's that?" he exclaimed, as some one brushed hastily past him. "If I hadn't just left him, I could have sworn it was Mrs. Spurling's sooty imp, Caliban."

Having seen the chairmen concealed in the entry, Shotbolt proceeded to Mr. Kneebone's habitation, the shutters of which were closed, and knocked at the door. The summons was instantly answered by a shop-boy.

"Is your master at home?" inquired the jailer.

"He is," replied a portly personage, arrayed in a gorgeous yellow brocade dressing-gown, lined with cherry-coloured satin, and having a crimson velvet cap, surmounted by a gold tassel, on his head. "My name is Kneebone," added the portly personage, stepping forward. "What do you want with me?"

"A word in private," replied the other.

"Stand aside, Tom," commanded Kneebone. "Now Sir," he added, glancing suspiciously at the applicant "your business?"

"My business is to acquaint you that Jack Sheppard has escaped, Mr. Kneebone," returned Shotbolt.

"The deuce he has! Why, it's only a few hours since I beheld him chained down with half a hundred weight of iron, in the strongest ward at Newgate. It's almost incredible. Are you sure you're not misinformed, Sir?"

"I was in the Lodge at the time," replied the jailer.

"Then, of course, you must know. Well, it's scarcely credible. When I gave him an invitation to supper, I little thought he'd accept it. But, egad! I believe he *will*."

"I'm convinced of it," replied Shotbolt; "and it was on that very account I came here." And he proceeded to unfold his scheme to the woollen-draper.

"Well, Sir," said Kneebone, when the other concluded, "I shall certainly not oppose his capture, but, at the same time, I'll lend you no assistance. If he keeps *his* word, I'll keep *mine*. You must wait till supper's over."

"As you please, Sir,--provided you don't let him off."

"That I'll engage not to do. I've another reason for supposing he'll pay me a visit. I refused to sign a petition in his behalf to the Recorder; not from any ill-will to him, but because it was prepared by a person whom I particularly dislike--Captain Darrell."

"A very sufficient reason," answered the jailer.

"Tom," continued Kneebone, calling to the shop-boy, "don't go home. I may want you. Light the lantern. And, if you hear any odd noise in the parlour, don't mind it."

"Not in the least, Sir," replied Tom, in a drowsy tone, and with a look seeming to imply that he was too much accustomed to odd noises at night to heed them.

"Now, step this way, Mr. What's-your-name?"

"Shotbolt, Sir," replied the jailer.

"Very well, Mr. Slipshod; follow me." And he led the way to an inner room, in the middle of which stood a table, covered with a large white cloth.

"Jack Sheppard knows this house, I believe, Sir," observed Shotbolt.

"Every inch of it," replied the woollen-draper. "He *ought* to do, seeing that he served his apprenticeship in it to Mr. Wood, by whom it was formerly occupied. His name is carved upon a beam up stairs."

"Indeed!" said Shotbolt. "Where can I hide myself?" he added, glancing round the room in search of a closet.

"Under the table. The cloth nearly touches the floor. Give me your staff. It'll be in your way."

"Suppose he brings Blueskin, or some other ruffian with him," hesitated the jailer.

"Suppose he does. In that case I'll help you. We shall be equally matched. You're not afraid, Mr. Shoplatch."

"Not in the least," replied Shotbolt, creeping beneath the table; "there's my staff. Am I quite hidden?"

"Not quite;--keep your feet in. Mind you don't stir till supper's over. I'll stamp twice when we've done."

"I forgot to mention there's a trifling reward for his capture," cried Shotbolt, popping his head from under the cloth. "If we take him, I don't mind giving you a share--say a fourth--provided you lend a helping hand."

"Curse your reward!" exclaimed Kneebone, angrily. "Do you take me for a thief-catcher, like Jonathan Wild, that you dare to affront me by such a proposal?"

"No offence, Sir," rejoined the jailer, humbly. "I didn't imagine for a moment that you'd accept it, but I thought it right to make you the offer."

"Be silent, and conceal yourself. I'm about to ring for supper."

The woollen-draper's application to the bell was answered by a very pretty young woman, with dark Jewish features, roguish black eyes, sleek glossy hair, a trim waist, and a remarkably neat figure: the very model, in short, of a bachelor's housekeeper.

"Rachel," said Mr. Kneebone, addressing his comely attendant; "put a few more plates on the table, and bring up whatever there is in the larder. I expect company."

"Company!" echoed Rachel; "at this time of night?"

"Company, child," repeated Kneebone. "I shall want a bottle or two of sack, and a flask of usquebaugh."

"Anything else, Sir?"

"No:--stay! you'd better not bring up any silver forks or spoons."

"Why, surely you don't think your guests would steal them," observed Rachel, archly.

"They shan't have the opportunity," replied Kneebone. And, by way of checking his housekeeper's familiarity, he pointed significantly to the table.

"Who's there?" cried Rachel. "I'll see." And before she could be prevented, she lifted up the cloth, and disclosed Shotbolt. "Oh, Gemini!" she exclaimed. "A man!"

"At your service, my dear," replied the jailer.

"Now your curiosity's satisfied, child," continued Kneebone, "perhaps, you'll attend to my orders."

Not a little perplexed by the mysterious object she had seen, Rachel left the room, and, shortly afterwards returned with the materials of a tolerably good supper;--to wit, a couple of cold fowls, a tongue, the best part of a sirloin of beef, a jar of pickles, and two small dishes of pastry. To these she added the wine and spirits directed, and when all was arranged looked inquisitively at her master.

"I expect a very extraordinary person to supper, Rachel," he remarked.

"The gentleman under the table," she answered. "He *does* seem a very extraordinary person."

"No; another still more extraordinary."

"Indeed!--who is it?"

"Jack Sheppard."

"What! the famous housebreaker. I thought he was in Newgate."

"He's let out for a few hours," laughed Kneebone; "but he's going back again after supper."

"Oh, dear! how I should like to see him. I'm told he's so handsome."

"I'm sorry I can't indulge you," replied her master, a little piqued. "I shall want nothing more. You had better go to bed."

"It's no use going to bed," answered Rachel. "I shan't sleep a wink while Jack Sheppard's in the house."

"Keep in your own room, at all events," rejoined Kneebone.

"Very well," said Rachel, with a toss of her pretty head, "very well. I'll have a peep at him, if I die for it," she muttered, as she went out.

Mr. Kneebone, then, sat down to await the arrival of his expected guest. Half an hour passed, but Jack did not make his appearance. The woollen-draper looked at his watch. It was eleven o'clock. Another long interval elapsed. The watch was again consulted. It was now a quarter past twelve. Mr. Kneebone, who began to feel sleepy, wound it up, and snuffed the candles.

"I suspect our friend has thought better of it, and won't come," he remarked.

"Have a little patience, Sir," rejoined the jailer.

"How are you off there, Shoplatch?" inquired Kneebone. "Rather cramped, eh?"

"Rather so, Sir," replied the other, altering his position. "I shall be able to stretch my limbs presently--ha! ha!"

"Hush!" cried Kneebone, "I hear a noise without. He's coming."

The caution was scarcely uttered, when the door opened, and Jack Sheppard presented himself. He was wrapped in a laced roquelaure, which he threw off on his entrance into the room. It has been already intimated that Jack had an excessive passion for finery; and it might have been added, that the chief part of his ill-gotten gains was devoted to the embellishment of his person. On the present occasion, he appeared to have bestowed more than ordinary attention on his toilette. His apparel was sumptuous in the extreme, and such as was only worn by persons of the highest distinction. It consisted of a full-dress coat of brown flowered velvet, laced with silver; a waistcoat of white satin, likewise richly embroidered; shoes with red heels, and large diamond buckles; pearl-coloured silk stockings with gold clocks; a muslin cravat, or steen-kirk, as it was termed, edged with the fine point lace; ruffles of the same material, and so ample as almost to hide the tips of his fingers; and a silver-hilted sword. This costume, though somewhat extravagant, displayed his slight, but perfectly-proportioned figure to the greatest advantage. The only departure which he made from the fashion of the period, was in respect to the peruke--an article he could never be induced to wear. In lieu of it, he still adhered to the sleek black crop, which, throughout life, formed a distinguishing feature in his appearance. Ever since the discovery of his relationship to the Trenchard family, a marked change had taken place in Jack's demeanour and looks, which were so much refined and improved that he could scarcely be recognised as the same person. Having only seen him in the gloom of a dungeon, and loaded with fetters, Kneebone had not noticed this alteration: but he was now greatly struck by it. Advancing towards him, he made him a formal salutation, which was coldly returned.

"I am expected, I find," observed Jack, glancing at the well-covered board.

"You are," replied Kneebone. "When I heard of your escape, I felt sure I should see you."

"You judged rightly," rejoined Jack; "I never yet broke an engagement with friend or foe--and never will."

"A bold resolution," said the woollen-draper. "You must have made some exertion to keep your present appointment. Few men could have done as much."

"Perhaps not," replied Jack, carelessly. "I would have done more, if necessary."

"Well, take a chair," rejoined Kneebone. "I've waited supper, you perceive."

"First, let me introduce my friends," returned Jack, stepping to the door.

"Friends!" echoed Kneebone, with a look of dismay. "My invitation did not extend to them."

Further remonstrance, however, was cut short by the sudden entrance of Mrs. Maggot and Edgeworth Bess. Behind them stalked Blueskin, enveloped in a rough great-coat, called--appropriately enough in this instance,--a wrap-rascal. Folding his arms, he placed his back against the door, and burst into a loud laugh. The ladies were, as usual, very gaily dressed; and as usual, also, had resorted to art to heighten their attractions--

From patches, justly placed, they borrow'd graces,
And with vermilion lacquer'd o'er their faces.

Edgeworth Bess wore a scarlet tabby negligee,--a sort of undress, or sack, then much in vogue,--which suited her to admiration, and upon her head had what was called a fly-cap, with richly-laced lappets. Mrs. Maggot was equipped in a light blue riding-habit, trimmed with silver, a hunting-cap and a flaxen peruke, and, instead of a whip, carried a stout cudgel.

For a moment, Kneebone had hesitated about giving the signal to Shotbolt, but, thinking a more favourable opportunity might occur, he determined not to hazard matters by undue precipitation. Placing chairs, therefore, he invited the ladies to be seated, and, paying a similar attention to Jack, began to help to the various dishes, and otherwise fulfil the duties of a host. While this was going on, Blueskin, seeing no notice whatever taken of him, coughed loudly and repeatedly. But finding his hints totally disregarded, he, at length, swaggered up to the table, and thrust in a chair.

"Excuse me," he said, plunging his fork into a fowl, and transferring it to his plate. "This tongue looks remarkably nice," he added, slicing off an immense wedge, "excuse me--ho! ho!"

"You make yourself at home, I perceive," observed Kneebone, with a look of ineffable disgust.

"I generally do," replied Blueskin, pouring out a bumper of sack. "Your health, Kneebone."

"Allow me to offer you a glass of usquebaugh, my dear," said Kneebone, turning from him, and regarding Edgeworth Bess with a stare so impertinent, that even that not over-delicate young lady summoned up a blush.

"With pleasure, Sir," replied Edgeworth Bess. "Dear me!" she added, as she pledged the amorous woollen-draper, "what a beautiful ring that is."

"Do you think so?" replied Kneebone, taking it off, and placing it on her finger, which he took the opportunity of kissing at the same time; "wear it for my sake."

"Oh, dear!" simpered Edgeworth Bess, endeavouring to hide her confusion by looking steadfastly at her plate.

"You don't eat," continued Kneebone, addressing Jack, who had remained for some time thoughtful, and pre-occupied with his head upon his hand.

"The Captain has seldom much appetite," replied Blueskin, who, having disposed of the fowl, was commencing a vigorous attack upon the sirloin. "I eat for both."

"So it seems," observed the woollen-draper, "and for every one else, too."

"I say, Kneebone," rejoined Blueskin, as he washed down an immense mouthful with another bumper, "do you recollect how nearly Mr. Wild and I were nabbing you in this very room, some nine years ago?"

"I do," replied Kneebone; "and now," he added, aside, "the case is altered. I'm nearly nabbing *you*."

"A good deal has occurred since then, eh, Captain!" said Blueskin, nudging Jack.

"Much that I would willingly forget. Nothing that I desire to remember," replied Sheppard, sternly. "On that night,--in this room,--in your presence, Blueskin,--in yours Mr. Kneebone, Mrs. Wood struck me a blow which made me a robber."

"She has paid dearly for it," muttered Blueskin.

"She has," rejoined Sheppard. "But I wish her hand had been as deadly as yours. On that night,--that fatal night,--Winifred crushed all the hopes that were rising in my heart. On that night, I surrendered myself to Jonathan Wild, and became--what I am."

"On that night, you first met me, love," said Edgeworth Bess, endeavouring to take his hand, which he coldly withdrew.

"And me," added Mrs. Maggot tenderly.

"Would I had never seen either of you!" cried Jack, rising and pacing the apartment with a hurried step.

"Well, I'm sure Winifred could never have loved you as well as I do," said Mrs. Maggot.

"*You*!" cried Jack, scornfully. "Do you compare *your* love--a love which all may purchase--with *hers*? No one has ever loved me."

"Except me, dear," insinuated Edgeworth Bess. "I've been always true to you."

"Peace!" retorted Jack, with increased bitterness. "I'm your dupe no longer."

"What the devil's in the wind now, Captain?" cried Blueskin, in astonishment.

"I'll tell you," replied Jack, with forced calmness. "Within the last few minutes, all my guilty life has passed before me. Nine years ago, I was honest--was happy. Nine years ago, I worked in this very house--had a kind indulgent master, whom I robbed--twice robbed, at your instigation, villain; a mistress, whom you have murdered; a companion, whose friendship I have for ever forfeited; a mother, whose heart I have well-nigh broken. In this room was my ruin begun: in this room it should be ended."

"Come, come, don't take on thus, Captain," cried Blueskin, rising and walking towards him. "If any one's to blame, it's me. I'm ready to bear it all."

"Can you make me honest?" cried Jack. "Can you make me other than a condemned felon? Can you make me not Jack Sheppard?"

"No," replied Blueskin; "and I wouldn't if I could."

"Curse you!" cried Jack, furiously,--"curse you!--curse you!"

"Swear away, Captain," rejoined Blueskin, coolly. "It'll ease your mind."

"Do you mock me?" cried Jack, levelling a pistol at him.

"Not I," replied Blueskin. "Take my life, if you're so disposed. You're welcome to it. And let's see if either of these women, who prate of their love for you, will do as much."

"This is folly," cried Jack, controlling himself by a powerful effort.

"The worst of folly," replied Blueskin, returning to the table, and taking up a glass; "and, to put an end to it, I shall drink the health of Jack Sheppard, the housebreaker, and success to him in all his enterprises. And now, let's see who'll refuse the pledge."

"I will," replied Sheppard, dashing the glass from his hand. "Sit down, fool!"

"Jack," said Kneebone, who had been considerably interested by the foregoing scene, "are these regrets for your past life sincere?"

"Suppose them so," rejoined Jack, "what then?"

"Nothing--nothing," stammered Kneebone, his prudence getting the better of his sympathy. "I'm glad to hear it, that's all," he added, taking out his snuff-box, his never-failing resource in such emergencies. "It won't do to betray the officer," he muttered.

"O lud! what an exquisite box!" cried Edgeworth Bess. "Is it gold?"

"Pure gold," replied Kneebone. "It was given me by poor dear Mrs. Wood, whose loss I shall ever deplore."

"Pray, let me have a pinch!" said Edgeworth Bess, with a captivating glance. "I am so excessively fond of snuff."

The woollen-draper replied by gallantly handing her the box, which was instantly snatched from her by Blueskin, who, after helping himself to as much of its contents as he could conveniently squeeze between his thumb and finger, put it very coolly in his pocket.

The action did not pass unnoticed by Sheppard.

"Restore it," he cried, in an authoritative voice.

"O'ons! Captain," cried Blueskin, as he grumblingly obeyed the command; "if you've left off business yourself, you needn't interfere with other people."

"I should like a little of that plum-tart," said Mrs. Maggot; "but I don't see a spoon."

"I'll ring for one," replied Kneebone, rising accordingly; "but I fear my servants are gone to bed."

Blueskin, meanwhile, having drained and replenished his glass, commenced chaunting a snatch of a ballad:--

> Once on a time, as I've heard tell.
> In Wych Street Owen Wood did dwell;
> A carpenter he was by trade,
> And money, I believe, he made.
>   With his foodle doo!
>
> This carpenter he had a wife,
> The plague and torment of his life,
> Who, though she did her husband scold,
> Loved well a woollen-draper bold.

With her foodle doo!

"I've a toast to propose," cried Sheppard, filling a bumper. "You won't refuse it, Mr. Kneebone?"

"He'd better not," muttered Blueskin.

"What is it?" demanded the woollen-draper, as he returned to the table, and took up a glass.

"The speedy union of Thames Darrell with Winifred Wood," replied Jack.

Kneebone's cheeks glowed with rage, and he set down the wine untasted, while Blueskin resumed his song.

Now Owen Wood had one fair child,
Unlike her mother, meek and mild;
Her love the draper strove to gain,
But she repaid him with disdain.
    With his foodle doo!

"Peace!" cried Jack.

But Blueskin was not to be silenced. He continued his ditty, in spite of the angry glances of his leader.

In vain he fondly urged his suit,
And, all in vain, the question put;
She answered,--"Mr. William Kneebone,
Of me, Sir, you shall never be bone."
    With your foodle doo!

"Thames Darrell has my heart alone,

A noble youth, e'en you must own;
And, if from him my love could stir,
Jack Sheppard I should much prefer!"
    With his foodle doo!

"Do you refuse my toast?" cried Jack, impatiently.

"I do," replied Kneebone.

"Drink this, then," roared Blueskin. And pouring the contents of a small powder-flask into a bumper of brandy, he tendered him the mixture.

At this juncture, the door was opened by Rachel.

"What did you ring for, Sir?" she asked, eyeing the group with astonishment.

"Your master wants a few table-spoons, child," said Mrs. Maggot.

"Leave the room," interposed Kneebone, angrily.

"No, I shan't," replied Rachel, saucily. "I came to see Jack Sheppard, and I won't go till you point him out to me. You told me he was going back to Newgate after supper, so I mayn't have another opportunity."

"Oh! he told you that, did he?" said Blueskin, marching up to her, and chucking her under the chin. "I'll show you Captain Sheppard, my dear. There he stands. I'm his lieutenant,--Lieutenant Blueskin. We're two good-looking fellows, ain't we?"

"Very good-looking," replied Rachel. "But, where's the strange gentleman I saw under the table?"

"Under the table!" echoed Blueskin, winking at Jack. "When did you see him, my love?"

"A short time ago," replied the housekeeper, unsuspiciously.

"The plot's out!" cried Jack. And, without another word, he seized the table with both hands, and upset it; scattering plates, dishes, bottles, jugs, and glasses far and wide. The crash was tremendous. The lights rolled over, and were extinguished. And, if Rachel had not carried a candle, the room would have been plunged in total darkness. Amid the confusion, Shotbolt sprang to his feet, and levelling a pistol at Jack's head, commanded him to surrender; but, before any reply could be made, the jailer's arm was struck up by Blueskin, who, throwing himself upon him, dragged him to the ground. In the struggle the pistol went off, but without damage to either party. The conflict was of short duration; for Shotbolt was no match for his athletic antagonist. He was speedily disarmed; and the rope and gag being found upon him, were exultingly turned against him by his conqueror, who, after pinioning his arms tightly behind his back, forced open his mouth with the iron, and effectually prevented the utterance of any further outcries. While the strife was raging, Edgeworth Bess walked up to Rachel, and advised her, if she valued her life, not to scream or stir from the spot; a caution which the housekeeper, whose curiosity far outweighed her fears, received in very good part.

In the interim, Jack advanced to the woollen-draper, and regarding him sternly, thus addressed him:

"You have violated the laws of hospitality, Mr. Kneebone, I came hither as your guest. You have betrayed me."

"What faith is to be kept with a felon?" replied the woollen-draper, disdainfully.

"He who breaks faith with his benefactor may well justify himself thus," answered Jack. "I have not trusted you. Others who have done, have found you false."

"I don't understand you," replied Kneebone, in some confusion.

"You soon shall," rejoined Sheppard. "Where are the packets committed to your charge by Sir Rowland Trenchard?"

"The packets!" exclaimed Kneebone, in alarm.

"It is useless to deny it," replied Jack. "You were watched to-night by Blueskin. You met Sir Rowland at the house of a Romisch priest, Father Spencer. Two packets were committed to your charge, which you undertook to deliver,--one to another priest, Sir Rowland's chaplain, at Manchester, the other to Mr. Wood. Produce them!"

"Never!" replied Kneebone.

"Then, by Heaven! you are a dead man!" replied Jack, cocking a pistol, and pointing it deliberately at his head. "I give you one minute for reflection. After that time nothing shall save you."

There was a brief, breathless pause. Even Blueskin looked on with anxiety.

"It is past," said Jack, placing his finger on the trigger.

"Hold!" cried Kneebone, flinging down the packets; "they are nothing to me."

"But they are everything to me," cried Jack, stooping to pick them up. "These packets will establish Thames Darrell's birth, win him his inheritance, and procure him the hand of Winifred Wood."

"Don't be too sure of that," rejoined Kneebone, snatching up the staff, and aiming a blow at his head, which was fortunately warded off by Mrs. Maggot, who promptly interposed her cudgel.

"Defend yourself!" cried Jack, drawing his sword.

"Leave his punishment to me, Jack," said Mrs. Maggot. "I've the Bridewell account to settle."

"Be it so," replied Jack, putting up his blade. "I've a good deal to do. Show him no quarter, Poll. He deserves none."

"And shall find none," replied the Amazon. "Now, Mr. Kneebone," she added, drawing up her magnificent figure to its full height, and making the heavy cudgel whistle through the air, "look to yourself."

"Stand off, Poll," rejoined the woollen-draper; "I don't want to hurt you. It shall never be said that I raised my arm willingly against a woman."

"I'll forgive you all the harm you do me," rejoined the Amazon. "What! you still hesitate! Will that rouse you, coward?" And she gave him a smart rap on the head.

"Coward!" cried Kneebone. "Neither man nor woman shall apply that term to me. If you forget your sex, jade, I must forget mine."

With this, he attacked her vigorously in his turn.

It was a curious sight to see how this extraordinary woman, who, it has been said, was not less remarkable for the extreme delicacy of her features, and the faultless symmetry of her figure, than for her wonderful strength and agility, conducted herself in the present encounter; with what dexterity she parried every blow aimed against her by her adversary, whose head and face, already marked by various ruddy streams, showed how successfully her own hits had been made;--how she drew him hither and thither, now leading him on, now driving him suddenly back; harassing and exhausting him in every possible way, and making it apparent that she could at any moment put an end to the fight, and only delayed the finishing stroke to make his punishment the more severe.

Jack, meanwhile, with Blueskin's assistance, had set the table once more upon its legs, and placing writing materials, which he took from a shelf, upon it, made

Shotbolt, who was still gagged, but whose arms were for the moment unbound, sit down before them.

"Write as I dictate," he cried, placing a pen in the jailer's hand and a pistol to his ear.

Shotbolt nodded in token of acquiescence, and emitted an odd guttural sound.

"Write as follows," continued Jack. "'I have succeeded in capturing Jack Sheppard. The reward is mine. Get all ready for his reception. In a few minutes after the delivery of this note he will be in Newgate.' Sign it," he added, as, after some further threats, the letter was indited according to his dictation, "and direct it to Mr. Austin. That's well. And, now, to find a messenger."

"Mr. Kneebone's man is in the shop," said Rachel; "he'll take it."

"Can I trust him?" mused Jack. "Yes; he'll suspect nothing. Give him this letter, child, and bid him take it to the Lodge at Newgate without loss of time. Blueskin will go with you,--for fear of a mistake."

"You might trust me," said Rachel, in an offended tone; "but never mind."

And she left the room with Blueskin, who very politely offered her his arm.

Meanwhile, the combat between Kneebone and Mrs. Maggot had been brought to a termination. When the woollen-draper was nearly worn out, the Amazon watched her opportunity, and hitting him on the arm, disabled it.

"That's for Mrs. Wood," she cried, as the staff fell from his grasp.

"I'm at your mercy, Poll," rejoined Kneebone, abjectly.

"That's for Winifred," vociferated the Amazon, bringing the cudgel heavily upon his shoulder.

"Damnation!" cried Kneebone.

"That's for myself," rejoined Mrs. Maggot, dealing him a blow, which stretched him senseless on the floor.

"Bravo, Poll!" cried Jack, who having again pinioned Shotbolt, was now tracing a few hasty lines on a sheet of paper. "You've given him a broken head, I perceive."

"He'll scarcely need a plaister," replied Mrs. Maggot, laughing. "Here, Bess, give me the cord, and I'll tie him to this chest of drawers. I don't think he'll come to himself too soon. But it's best to be on the safe side."

"Decidedly so," replied Edgeworth Bess; "and I'll take this opportunity, while

Jack's back is turned,--for he's grown so strangely particular,--of easing him of his snuff-box. Perhaps," she added, in a whisper, as she appropriated the before-named article, "he has a pocket-book."

"Hush!" replied Mrs. Maggot; "Jack will hear you. We'll come back for that by and by, and the dressing-gown."

At this moment, Rachel and Blueskin returned. Their momentary absence seemed to have worked wonders; for now the most perfect understanding appeared to subsist between them.

"Have you sent off the note?" inquired Jack.

"We have, Captain," replied Blueskin. "I say *we*, because Miss Rachel and I have struck up a match. Shall I bring off anything?" he added, looking eagerly round.

"No," replied Jack, peremptorily.

Having now sealed his letter, Sheppard took a handkerchief, and tying it over Shotbolt's face, so as completely to conceal the features, clapped his hat upon his head, and pushed it over his brows. He, next, seized the unlucky jailer, and forced him along, while Blueskin expedited his movements by administering a few kicks behind.

When they got to the door, Jack opened it, and, mimicking the voice of the jailer, shouted, "Now, my lads, all's ready?"

"Here we are," cried the chairmen, hurrying out of the court with their swinging vehicle, "where is he?"

"Here," replied Sheppard, dragging out Shotbolt by the collar, while Blueskin pushed him behind, and Mrs. Maggot held up a lantern, which she found in the shop. "In with him!"

"Ay--ay, yer hon'r," cried the foremost chairman, lending a helping hand. "Get in wid ye, ye villin!"

And, despite his resistance, Shotbolt was thrust into the chair, which was instantly fastened upon him.

"There, he's as safe as Jack Sheppard in the Condemned Hould," laughed the man.

"Off with you to Newgate!" cried Jack, "and don't let him out till you get inside the Lodge. There's a letter for the head turnkey, Mr. Irreton. D'ye hear."

"Yes, yer hon'r," replied the chairman, taking the note.

"What are you waiting for?" asked Jack, impatiently.

"The gen'l'man as hired us," replied the chairman.

"Oh! he'll be after you directly. He's settling an account in the house. Lose no time. The letter will explain all."

The chair was then rapidly put in motion, and speedily disappeared.

"What's to be done next?" cried Blueskin, returning to Rachel, who was standing with Edgeworth Bess near the door.

"I shall go back and finish my supper," said Mrs. Maggot.

"And so shall I," replied Edgeworth Bess.

"Stop a minute," cried Jack, detaining his mistresses. "Here we part,--perhaps for ever. I've already told you I'm about to take a long journey, and it's more than probable I shall never return."

"Don't say so," cried Mrs. Maggot. "I should be perfectly miserable if I thought you in earnest."

"The very idea is dreadful," whimpered Edgeworth Bess.

"Farewell!" cried Jack, embracing them. "Take this key to Baptist Kettleby. On seeing it, he'll deliver you a box, which it will unlock, and in which you'll find a matter of fifty guineas and a few trinkets. Divide the money between you, and wear the ornaments for my sake. But, if you've a spark of love for me, don't meddle with anything in that house."

"Not for worlds!" exclaimed both ladies together.

"Farewell!" cried Jack, breaking from them, and rushing down the street.

"What shall we do, Poll?" hesitated Edgeworth Bess.

"Go in, to be sure, simpleton," replied Mrs. Maggot, "and bring off all we can. I know where everything valuable is kept. Since Jack has left us, what does it matter whether he's pleased or not?"

At this moment, a whistle was heard.

"Coming!" cried Blueskin, who was still lingering with Rachel. "The Captain's in such a desperate hurry, that there's no time for love-making. Adieu! my charmer. You'll find those young ladies extremely agreeable acquaintances. Adieu!"

And, snatching a hasty kiss, he darted after Jack.

The chair, meanwhile, with its unhappy load, was transported at a brisk pace to Newgate. Arrived there, the porter thundered at the massive door of the Lodge, which was instantly opened--Shotbolt's note having been received just before. All the turnkeys were assembled. Ireton and Langley had returned from a second unsuccessful search; Marvel had come thither to bid good-night to Mrs. Spurling; Austin had never quitted his post. The tapstress was full of curiosity; but she appeared more easy than the others. Behind her stood Caliban, chuckling to himself, and grinning from ear to ear.

"Well, who'd have thought of Shotbolt beating us all in this way!" said Ireton. "I'm sorry for old Newgate that another jail should have it. It's infernally provoking."

"Infernally provoking!" echoed Langley.

"Nobody has so much cause for complaint as me," growled Austin. "I've lost my wager."

"Twenty pounds," rejoined Mrs. Spurling. "I witnessed the bet."

"Here he is!" cried Ireton, as the knocking was heard without. "Get ready the irons, Caliban."

"Wait a bit, massa," replied the grinning negro,--"lilly bit--see all right fust."

By this time, the chair had been brought into the Lodge.

"You've got him?" demanded Ireton.

"Safe inside," replied the chairman, wiping the heat from his brow; "we've run all the way."

"Where's Mr. Shotbolt?" asked Austin.

"The gen'l'man'll be here directly. He was detained. T' other gen'l'man said the letter 'ud explain all."

"Detained!" echoed Marvel. "That's odd. But, let's see the prisoner."

The chair was then opened.

"Shotbolt! by--" cried Austin, as the captive was dragged forth. "I've won, after all."

Exclamations of wonder burst from all. Mrs. Spurling bit her lips to conceal her mirth. Caliban absolutely crowed with delight.

"Hear the letter," said Ireton, breaking the seal. "'*This is the way in which I will serve all who attempt to apprehend me*.' It is signed JACK SHEPPARD."

"And, so Jack Sheppard has sent back Shotbolt in this pickle," said Langley.

"So it appears," replied Marvel. "Untie his arms, and take off that handkerchief.

The poor fellow's half smothered."

"I guess what share you've had in this," whispered Austin to Mrs. Spurling.

"Never mind," replied the tapstress. "You've won your wager."

Half an hour after this occurrence, when it had been sufficiently laughed at and discussed; when the wager had been settled, and the chairman dismissed with the remaining three guineas, which Shotbolt was compelled to pay; Ireton arose, and signified his intention of stepping across the street to inform Mr. Wild of the circumstance.

"As it's getting late, and the porter may be gone to bed," he observed; "I'll take the pass-key, and let myself in. Mr. Wild is sure to be up. He never retires to rest till daybreak--if at all. Come with me, Langley, and bring the lantern."

CHAPTER XIV.
How Jack Sheppard was again captured.

JACK Sheppard, after whistling to Blueskin, hurried down a short thoroughfare leading from Wych Street to the back of Saint Clement's Church, where he found Thames Darrell, who advanced to meet him.

"I was just going," said Thames. "When I parted from you at Mr. Kneebone's door, you begged me to await your return here, assuring me you would not detain me five minutes. Instead of which, more than half an hour has elapsed."

"You won't complain of the delay when I tell you what I've done," answered Jack. "I've obtained two packets, containing letters from Sir Rowland Trenchard, which I've no doubt will establish your title to the estates. Take them, and may they prove as serviceable to you as I desire."

"Jack," replied Thames, greatly moved, "I wish I could devise any means of brightening your own dark prospects."

"That's impossible," replied Jack. "I am utterly lost."

"Not utterly," rejoined the other.

"Utterly," reiterated Jack, gloomily,--"as regards all I hold dear. Listen to me, Thames. I'm about to leave this country for ever. Having ascertained that a vessel sails for France from the river at daybreak to-morrow morning, I have secured a passage in her, and have already had the few effects I possess, conveyed on board. Blueskin goes with me. The faithful fellow will never leave me."

"Never, while I've breath in my body, Captain," rejoined Blueskin, who had joined them. "England or France, London or Paris, it's all one to me, so I've you to command me."

"Stand out of earshot," rejoined his leader. "I'll call you when you're wanted."

And Blueskin withdrew.

"I cannot but approve the course you are about to take, Jack," said Thames, "though on some accounts I regret it. In after years you can return to your own country--to your friends."

"Never," replied Sheppard bitterly. "My friends need not fear my return. They shall hear of me no more. Under another name,--not my own hateful one,--I will strive to distinguish myself in some foreign service, and win myself a reputation, or perish honourably. But I will never--never return."

"I will not attempt to combat your resolution, Jack," returned Thames, after a pause. "But I dread the effect your departure may have upon your poor mother. Her life hangs upon a thread, and this may snap it."

"I wish you hadn't mentioned her," said Jack, in a broken voice, while his whole frame shook with emotion. "What I do is for the best, and I can only hope she may have strength to bear the separation. You must say farewell to her, for I cannot. I don't ask you to supply my place--for that is, perhaps, impossible. But, be like a son to her."

"Do not doubt me," replied Thames, warmly pressing his hand.

"And now, I've one further request," faltered Jack; "though I scarcely know how to make it. It is to set me right with Winifred. Do not let her think worse of me than I deserve,--or even so ill. Tell her, that more than once, when about to commit some desperate offence, I have been restrained by her gentle image. If hopeless love for her made me a robber, it has also saved me many a crime. Will you tell her that?"

"I will," replied Thames, earnestly.

"Enough," said Jack, recovering his composure. "And now, to your own concerns. Blueskin, who has been on the watch all night, has dogged Sir Rowland Trenchard to Jonathan Wild's house; and, from the mysterious manner in which he was admitted by the thief-taker's confidential servant, Abraham Mendez, and not by the regular porter, there is little doubt but they are alone, and probably making some arrangements prior to our uncle's departure from England."

"Is he leaving England?" demanded Thames, in astonishment.

"He sails to-morrow morning in the very vessel by which I start," replied Jack. "Now, if as I suspect,--from the documents just placed in your possession,--Sir Rowland meditates doing you justice after his departure, it is possible his intentions may be frustrated by the machinations of Wild, whose interest is obviously to prevent such an occurrence, unless we can surprise them together, and, by proving to Sir Rowland that we possess the power of compelling a restitution of your rights, force the other treacherous villain into compliance. Jonathan, in all probability, knows nothing of these packets; and their production may serve to intimidate him. Will you venture?"

"It is a hazardous experiment," said Thames, after a moment's reflection; "but I will make it. You must not, however, accompany me, Jack. The risk I run is nothing to yours."

"I care for no risk, provided I can serve you," rejoined Sheppard. "Besides, you'll not be able to get in without me. It won't do to knock at the door, and Jonathan Wild's house is not quite so easy of entrance as Mr. Wood's."

"I understand," replied Thames; "be it as you will."

"Then, we'll lose no more time," returned Jack. "Come along, Blueskin."

Starting at a rapid pace in the direction of the Old Bailey, and crossing Fleet Bridge, "for oyster tubs renowned," the trio skirted the right bank of the muddy stream until they reached Fleet Lane, up which they hurried. Turning off again on the left, down Seacoal Lane, they arrived at the mouth of a dark, narrow alley, into which they plunged; and, at the farther extremity found a small yard, overlooked by the blank walls of a large gloomy habitation. A door in this house opened upon the yard. Jack tried it, and found it locked.

"If I had my old tools with me, we'd soon master this obstacle," he muttered. "We shall be obliged to force it."

"Try the cellar, Captain," said Blueskin, stamping upon a large board in the ground. "Here's the door. This is the way the old thief brings in all his heavy plunder, which he stows in out-of-the-way holes in his infernal dwelling. I've seen him often do it."

While making these remarks, Blueskin contrived, by means of a chisel which he chanced to have about him, to lift up the board, and, introducing his fingers beneath it, with Jack's assistance speedily opened it altogether, disclosing a dark hole, into which he leapt.

"Follow me, Thames," cried Jack, dropping into the chasm.

They were now in a sort of cellar, at one end of which was a door. It was fastened inside. But, taking the chisel from Blueskin, Jack quickly forced back the bolt.

As they entered the room beyond, a fierce growl was heard.

"Let me go first," said Blueskin; "the dogs know me. Soho! boys." And, walking up to the animals, which were chained to the wall, they instantly recognised him, and suffered the others to pass without barking.

Groping their way through one or two dark and mouldy-smelling vaults, the party ascended a flight of steps, which brought them to the hall. As Jack conjectured, no one was there, and, though a lamp was burning on a stand, they decided upon proceeding without it. They then swiftly mounted the stairs, and stopped before the audience-chamber. Applying his ear to the keyhole, Jack listened, but could detect no sound. He, next cautiously tried the door, but found it fastened inside.

"I fear we're too late," he whispered to Thames. "But, we'll soon see. Give me the chisel, Blueskin." And, dexterously applying the implement, he forced open the lock.

They then entered the room, which was perfectly dark.

"This is strange," said Jack, under his breath. "Sir Rowland must be gone. And, yet, I don't know. The key's in the lock, on the inner side. Be on your guard."

"I am so," replied Thames, who had followed him closely.

"Shall I fetch the light, Captain?" whispered Blueskin.

"Yes," replied Jack. "I don't know how it is," he added in a low voice to Thames, as they were left alone, "but I've a strange foreboding of ill. My heart fails me. I almost wish we hadn't come."

As he said this, he moved forward a few paces, when, finding his feet glued to the ground by some adhesive substance, he stooped to feel what it was, but instantly withdrew his hand, with an exclamation of horror.

"God in Heaven!" he cried, "the floor is covered with blood. Some foul murder has been committed. The light!--the light!"

Astounded at his cries, Thames sprang towards him. At this moment, Blueskin appeared with the lamp, and revealed a horrible spectacle,--the floor deluged with blood,--various articles of furniture upset,--papers scattered about,--the murdered man's cloak, trampled upon, and smeared with gore,--his hat, crushed and similarly stained,--his sword,--the ensanguined cloth,--with several other ghastly evidences of the slaughterous deed. Further on, there were impressions of bloody footsteps along the floor.

"Sir Rowland is murdered!" cried Jack, as soon as he could find a tongue.

"It is plain he has been destroyed by his perfidious accomplice," rejoined Thames. "Oh God! how fearfully my father is avenged!"

"True," replied Jack, sternly; "but we have our uncle to avenge. What's this?" he added, stooping to pick up a piece of paper lying at his feet--it was Jonathan's memorandum. "This is the explanation of the bloody deed."

"Here's a pocket-book full of notes, and a heavy bag of gold," said Blueskin, examining the articles on the floor.

"The sum which incited the villain to the murder," replied Jack. "But he can't be far off. He must be gone to dispose of the body. We shall have him on his return."

"I'll see where these footsteps lead to," said Blueskin, holding the light to the floor. "Here are some more papers, Captain."

"Give them to me," replied Jack. "Ah!" he exclaimed, "a letter, beginning 'dearest Aliva,'--that's your mother's name, Thames."

"Let me see it," cried Thames, snatching it from him. "It *is* addressed to my mother," he added, as his eye glanced rapidly over it, "and by my father. At length, I shall ascertain my name. Bring the light this way--quick! I cannot decipher the signature."

Jack was about to comply with the request, when an unlooked-for interruption occurred. Having traced the footsteps to the wall, and perceiving no outlet, Blueskin elevated the lamp, and discovered marks of bloody fingers on the boards.

"He must have gone this way," muttered Blueskin. "I've often heard of a secret door in this room, though I never saw it. It must be somewhere hereabouts. Ah!" he exclaimed, as his eye fell upon a small knob in the wall, "there's the spring!"

He touched it, and the door flew open.

The next moment, he was felled to the ground by Jonathan Wild, who sprang into the room, followed by Abraham bearing the link. A single glance served to show the thief-taker how matters stood. From the slight sounds that had reached him in his place of confinement, he was aware that some persons had found their way to the scene of slaughter, and in a state of the most intense anxiety awaited the result of their investigation, prepared for the worst. Hearing the spring touched, he dashed through on the instant, and struck down the person who presented himself, with his bludgeon. On beholding the intruders, his fears changed to exultation, and he uttered a roar of satisfaction as he glared at them, which could only be likened to the cry of some savage denizen of the plains.

On his appearance, Jack levelled a pistol at his head. But his hand was withheld by Thames.

"Don't fire," cried the latter. "It is important not to slay him. He shall expiate his offences on the gibbet. You are my prisoner, murderer."

"*Your* prisoner!" echoed Jonathan, derisively. "You mistake,--you are mine. And so is your companion,--the convict Sheppard."

"Waste not another word with him, Thames," cried Jack. "Upon him!"

"Yield, villain, or die!" shouted Thames, drawing his sword and springing to-wards him.

"There's my answer!" rejoined Wild, hurling the bludgeon at him, with such fatal effect, that striking him on the head it brought him instantly to the ground.

"Ah! traitor!" cried Jack, pulling the trigger of his pistol.

Anticipating this, Wild avoided the shot by suddenly, ducking his head. He had a narrow escape, however; for, passing within an inch of him, the bullet burried itself deeply in the wall.

Before he could fire a second shot, Jack had to defend himself from the thief-taker, who, with his drawn hanger, furiously assaulted him. Eluding the blow, Jack plucked his sword from the scabbard, and a desperate conflict began.

"Pick up that blade, Nab," vociferated Wild, finding himself hotly pressed, "and stab him. I won't give him a chance."

"Cowardly villain!" cried Jack, as the Jew, obeying the orders of his principal, snatched up the weapon of the murdered man, and assailed him. "But I'll yet disap-point you."

And springing backwards, he darted suddenly through the door.

"After him," cried Wild; "he mustn't escape. Dead or alive, I'll have him. Bring the link."

And, followed by Abraham, he rushed out of the room.

Just as Jack got half way down the stairs, and Wild and the Jew reached the upper landing, the street-door was opened by Langley and Ireton, the latter of whom carried a lantern.

"Stop him!" shouted Jonathan from the stair-head, "stop him! It's Jack Sheppard!"

"Give way!" cried Jack fiercely. "I'll cut down him who opposes me."

The head turnkey, in all probability, would have obeyed. But, being pushed forward by his subordinate officer, he was compelled to make a stand.

"You'd better surrender quietly, Jack," he cried; "you've no chance.'"

Instead of regarding him, Jack glanced over the iron bannisters, and measured the distance. But the fall was too great, and he abandoned the attempt.

"We have him!" cried Jonathan, hurrying down the steps. "He can't escape."

As this was said, Jack turned with the swiftness of thought, and shortening his sword, prepared to plunge it into the thief-taker's heart. Before he could make the thrust, however, he was seized behind by Ireton, who flung himself upon him.

"Caught!" shouted the head-turnkey. "I give you joy of the capture, Mr. Wild," he added, as Jonathan came up, and assisted him to secure and disarm the prisoner. "I was coming to give you intelligence of a comical trick played by this rascal, when I find him here--the last place, I own, where I should have expected to find him."

"You've arrived in the very nick of time," rejoined Jonathan; "and I'll take care your services are not overlooked."

"Mr. Ireton," cried Jack, in accents of the most urgent entreaty, "before you take me hence, I implore you--if you would further the ends of justice--search this house. One of the most barbarous murders ever committed has just been perpetrated by the monster Wild. You will find proofs of the bloody deed in his room. But go thither at once, I beseech you, before he has time to remove them."

"Mr. Ireton is welcome to search every room in my house if he pleases," said Jonathan, in a tone of bravado. "As soon as we've conveyed you to Newgate, I'll accompany him."

"Mr. Ireton will do no such thing," replied the head-turnkey. "Bless your soul! d'ye think I'm to be gammoned by such nonsense. Not I. I'm not quite such a greenhorn as Shotbolt, Jack, whatever you may think."

"For mercy's sake go up stairs," implored Sheppard. "I have not told you half. There's a man dying--Captain Darrell. Take me with you. Place a pistol at my ear, and shoot me, if I've told you false."

"And, what good would that do?" replied Ireton, sarcastically. "To shoot you would be to lose the reward. You act your part capitally, but it won't do."

"Won't you go?" cried Jack passionately. "Mr. Langley, I appeal to you. Murder, I say, has been done! Another murder will be committed if you don't prevent it. The blood will rest on your head. Do you hear me, Sir? Won't you stir!"

"Not a step," replied Langley, gruffly.

"Off with him to Newgate!" cried Jonathan. "Ireton, as you captured him, the reward is yours. But I request that a third may be given to Langley."

"It shall be, Sir," replied Ireton, bowing. "Now come along, Jack."

"Miscreants!" cried Sheppard, almost driven frantic by the violence of his emotions; "you're all in league with him."

"Away with him!" cried Jonathan. "I'll see him fettered myself. Remain at the door, Nab," he added, loitering for a moment behind the others, "and let no one in, or out."

Jack, meanwhile, was carried to Newgate. Austin could scarcely credit his senses when he beheld him. Shotbolt, who had in some degree recovered from the effects of his previous mortification, was thrown into an ecstacy of delight, and could not sufficiently exult over the prisoner. Mrs. Spurling had retired for the night. Jack appealed to the new auditors, and again detailed his story, but with no better success than heretofore. His statement was treated with derision. Having seen him heavily ironed, and placed in the Condemned Hold, Jonathan recrossed the street.

He found Abraham on guard as he had left him.

"Has any one been here?" he asked.

"No von," replied the Jew.

"That's well," replied Wild, entering the house, and fastening the door. "And now to dispose of our dead. Why, Nab, you shake as if you'd got an ague?" he added, turning to the Jew, whose teeth chattered audibly.

"I haven't quite recovered the fright I got in the Vell-Hole," replied Abraham.

On returning to the audience-chamber, Jonathan found the inanimate body of Thames Darrell lying where he had left it; but, on examining it, he remarked that the pockets were turned inside out, and had evidently been rifled. Startled by this circumstance, he looked around, and perceived that the trap-door,--which has been mentioned as communicating with a secret staircase,--was open. He, next, discovered that Blueskin was gone; and, pursuing his scrutiny, found that he had carried off all the banknotes, gold, and letters,--including, what Jonathan himself was not aware of,--the two packets which he had abstracted from the person of Thames. Uttering a terrible imprecation, Jonathan snatched up the link, and hastily descended the stairs, leaving the Jew behind him. After a careful search below, he could detect no trace of Blueskin. But, finding the cellar-door open, concluded he had got out that way.

Returning to the audience-chamber in a by-no-means enviable state of mind, he commanded the Jew to throw the body of Thames into the Well Hole.

"You musht do dat shob yourself, Mishter Vild," rejoined Abraham, shaking his head. "No prize shall indushe me to enter dat horrid plashe again."

"Fool!" cried Wild, taking up the body, "what are you afraid of? After all," he added, pausing, "he may be of more use to me alive than dead."

Adhering to this change of plan, he ordered Abraham to follow him, and, descending the secret stairs once more, carried the wounded man into the lower part of the premises. Unlocking several doors, he came to a dark vault, that would have rivalled the gloomiest cell in Newgate, into which he thrust Thames, and fastened the door.

"Go to the pump, Nab," he said, when this was done, "and fill a pail with water. We must wash out those stains up stairs, and burn the cloth. Blood, they say, won't come out. But I never found any truth in the saying. When I've had an hour's rest, I'll be after Blueskin."

CHAPTER XV.
How Blueskin underwent the Peine Forte et Dure.

AS soon as it became known, through the medium of the public prints on the following day, that Jack Sheppard had broken out of prison, and had been again captured during the night, fresh curiosity was excited, and larger crowds than ever flocked to Newgate, in the hope of obtaining admission to his cell; but by the governor's express commands, Wild having privately counselled the step, no one was allowed to see him. A question next arose whether the prisoner could be executed under the existing warrant,--some inclining to one opinion, some to another. To settle the point, the governor started to Windsor, delegating his trust in the interim to Wild, who took advantage of his brief rule to adopt the harshest measures towards the prisoner. He had him removed from the Condemned Hold, stripped of his fine apparel, clothed in the most sordid rags, loaded with additional fetters, and thrust into the Stone Hold,--already described as the most noisome cell in the whole prison. Here, without a glimpse of daylight; visited by no one except Austin at stated intervals, who neither answered a question nor addressed a word to him; fed upon the worst diet, literally mouldy bread and ditch-water; surrounded by stone walls; with a flagged floor for his pillow, and without so much as a blanket to protect him from the death-like cold that pierced his frame,--Jack's stout heart was subdued, and he fell into the deepest dejection, ardently longing for the time when even a violent death should terminate his sufferings. But it was not so ordered. Mr. Pitt returned with intelligence that the warrant was delayed, and, on taking the opinion of two eminent lawyers of the day, Sir William Thomson and Mr. Serjeant Raby, it was decided that it must be proved in a regular and judicial manner that Sheppard was the identical person who had been convicted and had escaped, before a fresh order could be made for his execution;

and that the matter must, therefore, stand over until the next sessions, to be held at the Old Bailey in October, when it could be brought before the court.

The unfortunate prisoner, meanwhile, who was not informed of the respite, languished in his horrible dungeon, and, at the expiration of three weeks, became so seriously indisposed that it was feared he could not long survive. He refused his food,--and even when better provisions were offered him, rejected them. As his death was by no means what Jonathan desired, he resolved to remove him to a more airy ward, and afford him such slight comforts as might tend to his restoration, or at least keep him alive until the period of execution. With this view, Jack was carried--for he was no longer able to move without assistance--to a ward called the Castle, situated over the gateway on the western side, in what was considered the strongest part of the jail. The walls were of immense thickness; the small windows double-grated and unglazed; the fire-place was without a grate; and a barrack-bed, divided into two compartments, occupied one corner. It was about twelve feet high, nine wide, and fourteen long; and was approached by double doors each six inches thick. As Jack appeared to be sinking fast, his fetters were removed, his own clothes were returned to him, and he was allowed a mattress and a scanty supply of bed-linen. Mrs. Spurling attended him as his nurse, and, under her care, he speedily revived. As soon as he became convalescent, and all fears of his premature dissolution were at an end, Wild recommenced his rigorous treatment. The bedding was removed; Mrs. Spurling was no longer allowed to visit him; he was again loaded with irons; fastened by an enormous horse-padlock to a staple in the floor; and only allowed to take repose in a chair. A single blanket constituted his sole covering at night. In spite of all this, he grew daily better and stronger, and his spirits revived. Hitherto, no visiters had been permitted to see him. As the time when his identity had to be proved approached, this rigour was, in a trifling degree, relaxed, and a few persons were occasionally admitted to the ward, but only in the presence of Austin. From none of these could Jack ascertain what had become of Thames, or learn any particulars concerning the family at Dollis Hill, or of his mother. Austin, who had been evidently schooled by Wild, maintained a profound silence on this head. In this way, more than a month passed over. October arrived; and in another week the court would be sitting at the Old Bailey.

One night, about this time, just as Austin was about to lock the great gate,

Jonathan Wild and his two janizaries entered the Lodge with a prisoner bound hand and foot. It was Blueskin. On the cords being removed, he made a desperate spring at Wild, bore him to the ground, clutched at his throat, and would, infallibly, have strangled him, if the keepers had not all thrown themselves upon him, and by main force torn him off. His struggles were so violent, that, being a man of tremendous strength, it was some time before they could master him, and it required the combined efforts of all the four partners to put him into irons. It appeared from what he said that he had been captured when asleep,--that his liquor had been drugged,--otherwise, he would never have allowed himself to be taken alive. Wild, he asserted, had robbed him of a large sum of money, and till it was restored he would never plead.

"We'll see that," replied Jonathan. "Take him to the bilbowes. Put him in the stocks, and there let him sleep off his drunken fit. Whether he pleads or not, he shall swing with his confederate, Jack Sheppard."

At this allusion to his leader, a shudder passed through Blueskin's athletic frame.

"Where is he?" he cried. "Let me see him. Let me have a word with him, and you may take all the money."

Jonathan made no answer, but motioned the partners to take him away.

As soon as Blueskin was removed, Wild intimated his intention of visiting the Castle. He was accompanied by Ireton and Austin. The massive door was unlocked, and they entered the cell. What was their surprise to find it vacant, and the prisoner gone! Jonathan, could scarcely believe his eyes. He looked fiercely and inquiringly from one to the other of his companions; but, though both of them were excessively frightened, neither appeared guilty. Before a word could be said, however, a slight noise was heard in the chimney, and Jack with his irons on descended from it. Without betraying the slightest confusion, or making a single remark, he quietly resumed his seat.

"Amazement!" cried Wild. "How has he unfastened his padlock? Austin, it must be owing to your negligence."

"My negligence, Mr. Wild," said the turnkey, trembling in every joint. "I assure you, Sir, when I left him an hour ago, it was locked. I tried it myself, Sir. I'm as much astonished as you. But I can't account for it!"

"At all events, you shall answer for it," thundered Wild, with a bitter imprecation.

"He's not to blame," said Jack, rising. "I opened the padlock with this crooked nail, which I found in the floor. If you had arrived ten minutes later, or if there hadn't been an iron bar in the chimney, that hindered my progress, I should have been beyond your reach."

"You talk boldly," replied Wild. "Go to the Iron Hold, Austin, and tell two of the partners to bring another padlock of the largest size, and the heaviest handcuffs they can find. We'll try whether he'll get loose again."

Sheppard said nothing, but a disdainful smile curled his lips.

Austin departed, and presently afterwards returned with the two subordinate officers, each of whom wore a leathern apron round his waist, and carried a large hammer. As soon as the manacles were slipped over the prisoner's wrists, and the new padlock secured to the staple, they withdrew.

"Leave me alone with him a moment," said Jonathan. And the jailers also retired.

"Jack," said Wild, with a glance of malignant triumph, "I will now tell you what I have done. All my plans have succeeded. Before a month has elapsed, your mother will be mine. The Trenchard estates will likewise be mine, for Sir Rowland is no more, and the youth, Thames, will never again see daylight. Blueskin, who had evaded me with the papers and the money, is a prisoner here, and will perish on the same gallows as yourself. My vengeance is completely gratified."

Without waiting for a reply, but darting a malevolent look at the prisoner, he quitted the cell, the door of which was instantly double-locked and bolted.

"I've not quite done yet," said Jonathan, as he joined the turnkeys. "I should like to see whether Blueskin is a little more composed. I've a question to ask him. Give me the keys and the light. I'll go alone."

So saying, he descended a short spiral staircase, and, entering a long stone gallery, from which several other passages branched, took one of them, and after various turnings--for he was familiar with all the intricacies of the prison--arrived at the cell of which he was in search. Selecting a key from the heavy bunch committed to him by Austin, he threw open the door, and beheld Blueskin seated at the back of the small chamber, handcuffed, and with his feet confined in a heavy pair of stocks.

He was asleep when Jonathan entered, and growled at being disturbed. But, as soon as he perceived who it was, he roused himself, and glared fiercely at the intruder from under his bent brows.

"What do you want?" he asked, in a gruff voice.

"I want to know what you've done with the rest of the notes--with the gold--and the papers you took away from my room!" rejoined Wild.

"Then you'll never know more than this," retorted Blueskin, with a grin of satisfaction;--"they're in a place of safety, where *you*'ll never find 'em, but where somebody else *will*, and that before long."

"Hear me, Blueskin," said Jonathan, restraining his choler. "If you'll tell me where to look for these things, and I *do* find them, I'll set you free. And you shall have a share of the gold for yourself."

"I'll tell you what I'll do," rejoined the other. "Set Captain Sheppard free, and when I hear he's safe,--not before,--I'll put the money and papers into your possession, and some other matters, too, that you know nothing about."

"Impracticable dolt!" exclaimed Jonathan, furiously. "Do you think I'd part with the sweetest morsel of revenge on those terms? No! But I'll have the secret out of you by other means."

So saying, he violently shut and locked the door.

About ten days after this interview, Blueskin, having been indicted by Wild for several robberies, and true bills found against him, was placed at the bar of the Old Bailey to be arraigned; when he declared that he would not plead to the indictment, unless the sum of five hundred pounds, taken from him by Jonathan Wild, was first restored to him. This sum, claimed by Wild under the statute 4th and 5th of William and Mary, entitled "*An act for encouraging the apprehending of Highwaymen*," was granted to him by the court.

As Blueskin still continued obstinate, the judgment appointed to be executed upon such prisoners as stood mute, was then read. It was as follows, and, when uttered, produced a strong effect upon all who heard it, except the prisoner, who, in no respect, altered his sullen and dogged demeanour.

"Prisoner at the bar," thus ran the sentence, "you shall be taken to the prison from whence you came, and put into a mean room, stopped from the light; and shall there be laid on the bare ground, without any litter, straw, or other covering, and without any garment. You shall lie upon your back; your head shall be covered; and your feet shall be bare. One of your arms shall be drawn to one side of the room, and the other arm to the other side, and your legs shall be served in the like manner. Then, there shall be laid upon your body as much iron, or stone as you can bear, and more. And the first day, you shall have three morsels of barley bread, without any drink; and the second day, you shall be allowed to drink as much as you can, at three times, of the water that is next to the prison-door, except running-water, without any bread. And this shall be your diet till you die."

"Prisoner at the bar," continued the clerk of the court, "he against whom this judgment is given, forfeits his goods to the king."

An awful silence prevailed throughout the court. Every eye was fixed upon the prisoner. But, as he made no answer, he was removed.

Before the full sentence was carried into execution, he was taken into a small room adjoining the court. Here Marvel, the executioner, who was in attendance, was commanded by Wild to tie his thumbs together, which he did with whipcord so tightly, that the string cut to the bone. But, as this produced no effect, and did not even elicit a groan, the prisoner was carried back to Newgate.

The Press Room, to which Blueskin was conveyed on his arrival at the jail, was a small square chamber, walled and paved with stone. In each corner stood a stout square post reaching to the ceiling. To these a heavy wooden apparatus was attached, which could be raised or lowered at pleasure by pullies. In the floor were set four ring-bolts, about nine feet apart. When the prisoner was brought into this room, he was again questioned; but, continuing contumacious, preparations were made for inflicting the torture. His great personal strength being so well known, it was deemed prudent by Marvel to have all the four partners, together with Caliban, in attendance. The prisoner, however, submitted more quietly than was anticipated. He allowed his irons and clothes to be taken off without resistance. But just as they were about to place him on the ground, he burst from their hold, and made a desperate spring at Jonathan, who was standing with his arms folded near the door watching the scene. The attempt was unsuccessful. He was instantly overpowered, and stretched upon the ground. The four men fell upon him, holding his arms and legs, while Caliban forced back his head. In this state, he contrived to get the poor black's hand into his mouth, and nearly bit off one of his fingers before the sufferer could be rescued. Meanwhile, the executioner had attached strong cords to his ankles and wrists, and fastened them tightly to the iron rings. This done, he unloosed the pulley, and the ponderous machine, which resembled a trough, slowly descended upon the prisoner's breast. Marvel, then, took two iron weights, each of a hundred pounds, and placed them in the press. As this seemed insufficient, after a lapse of five minutes, he added another hundred weight. The prisoner breathed with difficulty. Still, his robust frame enabled him to hold out. After he had endured this torture for an hour, at a sign from Wild another hundred weight was added. In a few minutes, an appalling change was perceptible. The veins in his throat and forehead swelled and blackened; his eyes protruded from their sockets, and stared wildly; a thick damp gathered on his brow: and blood gushed from his mouth, nostrils, and ears.

"Water!" he gasped.

The executioner shook his head.

"Do you submit?" interrogated Wild.

Blueskin answered by dashing his head violently against the flagged floor. His efforts at self-destruction were, however, prevented.

"Try fifty pounds more," said Jonathan.

"Stop!" groaned Blueskin.

"Will you plead?" demanded Wild, harshly.

"I will," answered the prisoner.

"Release him," said Jonathan. "We have cured his obstinacy, you perceive," he added to Marvel.

"I *will* live," cried Blueskin, with a look of the deadliest hatred at Wild, "to be revenged on you."

And, as the weights were removed, he fainted.

CHAPTER XVI.
How Jack Sheppard's Portrait was painted.

EARLY in the morning of Thursday, the 15th of October, 1724, the door of the Castle was opened by Austin, who, with a look of unusual importance, announced to the prisoner that four gentlemen were shortly coming up with the governor to see him,--"four *such* gentlemen," he added, in a tone meant to impress his auditor with a due sense of the honour intended him, "as you don't meet every day."

"Is Mr. Wood among them?" asked Jack, eagerly.

"Mr. Wood!--no," replied the turnkey. "Do you think I'd take the trouble to announce *him*? These are persons of consequence, I tell you."

"Who are they?" inquired Sheppard.

"Why, first," rejoined Austin, "there's Sir James Thornhill, historical painter to his Majesty, and the greatest artist of the day. Those grand designs in the dome of St. Paul's are his work. So is the roof of the state-room at Hampton Court Palace, occupied by Queen Anne, and the Prince of Denmark. So is the chapel of All Souls at Oxford, and the great hall at Blenheim, and I don't know how many halls and chapels besides. He's now engaged on the hall at Greenwich Hospital."

"I've heard of him," replied Jack, impatiently. "Who are the others?"

"Let me see. There's a friend of Sir James--a young man, an engraver of masquerade tickets and caricatures,--his name I believe is Hogarth. Then, there's Mr. Gay, the poet, who wrote the 'Captives,' which was lately acted at Drury Lane, and was so much admired by the Princess of Wales. And, lastly, there's Mr. Figg, the noted prize-fighter, from the New Amphitheatre in Marylebone Fields."

"Figg's an old friend of mine," rejoined Jack; "he was my instructor in the small sword and back sword exercise. I'm glad he's come to see me."

"You don't inquire what brings Sir James Thornhill here?" said Austin.

"Curiosity, I suppose," returned Jack, carelessly.

"No such thing," rejoined the jailer; "he's coming on business."

"On what business, in the name of wonder?" asked Sheppard.

"To paint your portrait," answered the jailer.

"My portrait!" echoed Jack.

"By desire of his Majesty," said the jailer, consequentially. "He has heard of your wonderful escapes, and wishes to see what you're like. There's a feather in your cap! No house-breaker was ever so highly honoured before."

"And have my escapes really made so much noise as to reach the ear of royalty?" mused Jack. "I have done nothing--nothing to what I *could* do--to what I *will* do!"

"You've done quite enough," rejoined Austin; "more than you'll ever do again."

"And then to be taken thus, in these disgraceful bonds!" continued Jack, "to be held up as a sight for ever!"

"Why, how else would you be taken?" exclaimed the jailer, with a coarse laugh. "It's very well Mr. Wild allowed you to have your fine clothes again, or you might have been taken in a still more disgraceful garb. For my part, I think those shackles extremely becoming. But, here they are."

Voices being heard at the door, Austin flew to open it, and admitted Mr. Pitt, the governor, a tall pompous personage, who, in his turn, ushered in four other individuals. The first of these, whom he addressed as Mr. Gay, was a stout, good-looking, good-humoured man, about thirty-six, with a dark complexion, an oval face, fine black eyes, full of fire and sensibility, and twinkling with roguish humour--an expression fully borne out by the mouth, which had a very shrewd and sarcastic curl. The poet's appearance altogether was highly prepossessing. With a strong tendency to satire, but without a particle of malice or ill-nature in its display. Gay, by his strokes of pleasantry, whether in his writings or conversation, never lost a friend. On the contrary, he was a universal favourite, and numbered amongst his intimate acquaintances the choicest spirits of the time,--Pope, Swift, Arbuthnot, and "all the better brothers." His demeanour was polished; his manners singularly affable and gentle; and he was remarkable, for the generosity of his temper. In worldly matters Gay was not fortunate. Possessed, at one time, of a share in the South Sea stock, he conceived himself worth twenty thousand pounds. But, on the bursting of that bubble, his hopes vanished with it. Neither did his interest,--which was by no means inconsiderable,--nor his general popularity, procure him the preferment he desired. A constant attendant at court, he had the mortification to see every one promoted but himself, and thus bewails his ill-luck.

     Places, I found, were daily given away,   And yet no friendly gazette mentioned Gay.

The prodigious success of the "Beggars' Opera," which was produced about four years after the date of this history, rewarded him for all his previous disappointments, though it did not fully justify the well-known epigram, alluding to himself and the manager, and "make Gay *rich*, and Rich *gay*." At the time of his present introduction, his play of "The Captives," had just been produced at Drury Lane, and he was meditating his "Fables," which were published two years afterwards.

Behind the poet came Sir James Thornhill. The eminent painter had handsome, expressive features, an aquiline nose, and a good deal of dignity in his manner. His age was not far from fifty. He was accompanied by a young man of about seven-and-twenty, who carried his easel, set it in its place, laid the canvass upon it, opened the paint box, took out the brushes and palette, and, in short, paid him the most assiduous attention. This young man, whose features, though rather plain and coarse, bore the strongest impress of genius, and who had a dark gray, penetrating eye, so quick in its glances that it seemed to survey twenty objects at once, and yet only to fasten upon one, bore the honoured name of William Hogarth. Why he paid so much attention to Sir James Thornhill may be explained anon.

The rear of the party was brought up by a large, powerfully-built man, with a bluff, honest, but rugged countenance, slashed with many a cut and scar, and stamped with that surly, sturdy, bull-dog-like look, which an Englishman always delights to contemplate, because he conceives it to be characteristic of his countrymen. This formidable person, who was no other than the renowned Figg, the "Atlas of the sword," as he is termed by Captain Godfrey, had removed his hat and "skull covering," and was wiping the heat from his bepatched and close-shaven pate. His shirt also was unbuttoned, and disclosed a neck like that of an ox, and a chest which might have served as a model for a Hercules. He had a flattish, perhaps, it should be called, a *flattened* nose, and a brown, leathern-looking hide, that seemed as if it had not unfrequently undergone the process of tanning. Under his arm he carried a thick, knotted crab-stick. The above description of

     --the great Figg, by the prize-fighting swains   Sole monarch acknowledged of Mary'bone plains--

may sound somewhat tame by the side of the glowing account given of him by his gallant biographer, who asserts that "there was a majesty shone in his countenance, and blazed in his actions, beyond all I ever saw;" but it may, possibly, convey a more accurate notion of his personal appearance. James Figg was the most perfect master of self-defence of his day. Seconded by his strength and temper, his skill rendered him invincible and he is reputed never to have lost a battle. His imperturbable demeanour in the fight has been well portrayed by Captain Godfrey, who here condescends to lay aside his stilts. "His right leg bold and firm, and his left, which could hardly ever be disturbed, gave him a surprising advantage, and struck his adversary with despair and panic. He had a peculiar way of stepping in, in a parry; knew his arm, and its just time of moving; put a firm faith in that, and never let his opponent escape. He was just as much a greater master than any other I ever saw, as he was a greater judge of time and measure." Figg's prowess in a combat with Button has been celebrated by Dr. Byrom,--a poet of whom his native town, Manchester, may be justly proud; and his features and figure have been preserved by the most illustrious of his companions on the present occasion,--Hogarth,--in the levee in the "Rake's Progress," and in "Southwark Fair."

On the appearance of his visitors, Sheppard arose,--his gyves clanking heavily as he made the movement,--and folding his arms, so far as his manacles would permit him, upon his breast, steadily returned the glances fixed upon him.

"This is the noted house-breaker and prison-breaker, gentlemen," said Mr. Pitt, pointing to the prisoner.

"Odd's life!" cried Gay, in astonishment; "is this slight-made stripling Jack Sheppard? Why, I expected to see a man six foot high at the least, and as broad across the shoulders as our friend Figg. This is a mere boy. Are you sure you haven't mistaken the ward, Mr. Pitt?"

"There is no mistake, Sir," rejoined the prisoner, drawing himself up, "I am Jack Sheppard."

"Well, I never was more surprised in my life," said the poet,--"never!"

"He's just the man I expected to see," observed Hogarth, who, having arranged everything to Thornhill's satisfaction, had turned to look at the prisoner, and was now with his chin upon his wrist, and his elbow supported by the other hand, bending his keen gray eyes upon him, "just the man! Look at that light, lithe figure,--all muscle and activity, with not an ounce of superfluous flesh upon it. In my search after strange characters, Mr. Gay, I've been in many odd quarters of our city--have visited haunts frequented only by thieves--the Old Mint, the New Mint, the worst part of St. Giles's, and other places--but I've nowhere seen any one who came up so completely to my notion of a first-rate housebreaker as the individual before us. Wherever I saw him, I should pick him out as a man designed by nature to plan and accomplish the wonderful escapes he has effected."

As he spoke, a smile crossed Sheppard's countenance.

"He understands me, you perceive," said Hogarth.

"Well, I won't dispute your judgment in such matters, Mr. Hogarth," replied Gay. "But I appeal to you, Sir James, whether it isn't extraordinary that so very slight a person should be such a desperate robber as he is represented--so young, too, for such an *old* offender. Why, he can scarcely be twenty."

"I am one-and-twenty," observed Jack.

"One-and-twenty, ah!" repeated Gay. "Well, I'm not far from the mark."

"He is certainly extremely youthful-looking and very slightly made," said Thornhill, who had been attentively studying Sheppard's countenance. "But I agree with Hogarth, that he is precisely the person to do what he has done. Like a thorough-bred racer, he would sustain twice as much fatigue as a person of heavier mould. Can I be accommodated with a seat, Mr. Pitt?"

"Certainly, Sir James, certainly," replied the governor. "Get a chair, Austin."

While this order was obeyed, Figg, who had been standing near the door, made his way to the prisoner, and offered him his huge hand, which Jack warmly grasped.

"Well, Jack," said the prize-fighter, in a rough, but friendly voice, and with a cut-and-thrust abrupt manner peculiar to himself; "how are you, lad, eh? Sorry to see you here. Wouldn't take my advice. Told you how it would be. One mistress enough to ruin a man,--two, the devil. Laughed at me, then. Laugh on the wrong side of your mouth, now."

"You're not come here to insult me, Mr. Figg?" said Jack, peevishly.

"Insult you! not I;" returned Figg. "Heard of your escapes. Everybody talking of you. Wished to see you. Old pupil. Capital swordsman. Shortly to be executed. Come to take leave. Trifle useful?" he added, slipping a few gold pieces into Jack's hand.

"You are very kind," said Jack, returning the money; "but I don't require assistance."

"Too proud, eh?" rejoined the prize-fighter. "Won't be under an obligation."

"There you're wrong, Mr. Figg," replied Jack, smiling; "for, before I'm taken to Tyburn, I mean to borrow a shirt for the occasion from you."

"Have it, and welcome," rejoined Figg. "Always plenty to spare. Never bought a shirt in my life, Mr. Gay," he added, turning to the poet. "Sold a good many, though."

"How do you manage that, Mr. Figg?" asked Gay.

"Thus," replied the prize-fighter. "Proclaim a public fight. Challenge accepted. Fifty pupils. Day before, send round to each to borrow a shirt. Fifty sent home. All superfine holland. Wear one on the stage on the following day. Cut to pieces-- slashed--bloodied. Each of my scholars thinks it his own shirt. Offer to return it to each in private. All make the same answer--'d--n you, keep it.'"

"An ingenious device," laughed Gay.

Sir James Thornhill's preparations being completed, Mr. Pitt desired to know if he wanted anything further, and being answered in the negative, he excused himself on the plea that his attendance was required in the court at the Old Bailey, which was then sitting, and withdrew.

"Do me the favour to seat yourself, Jack," said Sir James. "Gentlemen, a little further off, if you please."

Sheppard immediately complied with the painter's request; while Gay and Figg drew back on one side, and Hogarth on the other. The latter took from his pocket a small note-book and pencil.

"I'll make a sketch, too," he said. "Jack Sheppard's face is well worth preserving."

After narrowly examining the countenance of the sitter, and motioning him with his pencil into a particular attitude, Sir James Thornhill commenced operations; and, while he rapidly transferred his lineaments to the canvass, engaged him in conversation, in the course of which he artfully contrived to draw him into a recital of his adventures. The *ruse* succeeded almost beyond his expectation. During the narration Jack's features lighted up, and an expression, which would have been in vain looked for in repose, was instantly caught and depicted by the skilful artist. All the party were greatly interested by Sheppard's history--especially Figg, who laughed loud and long at the escape from the Condemned Hold. When Jack came to speak of Jonathan Wild, his countenance fell.

"We must change the subject," remarked Thornhill, pausing in his task; "this will never do."

"Quite right, Sir James," said Austin. "We never suffer him to mention Mr. Wild's name. He never appears to so little advantage as when speaking of him."

"I don't wonder at it," rejoined Gay.

Here Hogarth received a private signal from Thornhill to attract Sheppard's attention.

"And so you've given up all hope of escaping, eh, Jack?" remarked Hogarth.

"That's scarcely a fair question, Mr. Hogarth, before the jailer," replied Jack. "But I tell you frankly, and Mr. Austin, may repeat it if he pleases to his master, Jonathan Wild,--I have *not*."

"Well said, Jack," cried Figg. "Never give in."

"Well," observed Hogarth, "if, fettered as you are, you contrive to break out of this dungeon, you'll do what no man ever did before."

A peculiar smile illuminated Jack's features.

"There it is!" cried Sir James, eagerly. "There's the exact expression I want. For the love of Heaven, Jack, don't move!--Don't alter a muscle, if you can help it."

And, with a few magical touches, he stamped the fleeting expression on the canvass.

"I have it too!" exclaimed Hogarth, busily plying his pencil. "Gad! it's a devilish fine face when lit up."

"As like as life, Sir," observed Austin, peeping over Thornhill's shoulder at the portrait. "As like as life."

"The very face," exclaimed Gay, advancing to look at it;--"with all the escapes written in it."

"You flatter me," smiled Sir James. "But, I own, I think it *is* like."

"What do you think of *my* sketch, Jack?" said Hogarth, handing him the drawing.

"It's like enough, I dare say," rejoined Sheppard. "But it wants something *here*." And he pointed significantly to the hand.

"I see," rejoined Hogarth, rapidly sketching a file, which he placed in the hands of the picture. "Will that do?" he added, returning it.

"It's better," observed Sheppard, meaningly. "But you've given me what I don't possess."

"Hum!" said Hogarth, looking fixedly at him. "I don't see how I can improve it."

"May I look at it, Sir!" said Austin, stepping towards him.

"No," replied Hogarth, hastily effacing the sketch. "I'm never satisfied with a first attempt."

"Egad, Jack," said Gay, "you should write your adventures. They would be quite as entertaining as the histories of Guzman D'Alfarache, Lazarillo de Tormes, Estevanillo Gonzalez, Meriton Latroon, or any of my favourite rogues,--and far more instructive."

"You had better write them for me, Mr. Gay," rejoined Jack.

"If you'll write them, I'll illustrate them," observed Hogarth.

"An idea has just occurred to me," said Gay, "which Jack's narrative has suggested. I'll write an opera the scene of which shall be laid altogether in Newgate, and the principal character shall be a highmaywan. I'll not forget your two mistresses, Jack."

"Nor Jonathan Wild, I hope," interposed Sheppard.

"Certainly not," replied Gay. "I'll gibbet the rascal. But I forget," he added, glancing at Austin; "it's high treason to speak disrespectfully of Mr. Wild in his own domain."

"I hear nothing, Sir," laughed Austin.

"I was about to add," continued Gay, "that my opera shall have no music except the good old ballad tunes. And we'll see whether it won't put the Italian opera out of fashion, with Cutzoni, Senesino, and the 'divine' Farinelli at its head."

"You'll do a national service, then," said Hogarth. "The sums lavished upon those people are perfectly disgraceful, and I should be enchanted to see them hooted from the stage. But I've an idea as well as you, grounded in some measure upon Sheppard's story. I'll take two apprentices, and depict their career. One, by perseverance and industry shall obtain fortune, credit, and the highest honours; while the other by an opposite course, and dissolute habits, shall eventually arrive at Tyburn."

"Your's will be nearer the truth, and have a deeper moral, Mr. Hogarth," remarked Jack, dejectedly. "But if my career were truly exhibited, it must be as one long struggle against destiny in the shape of--"

"Jonathan Wild," interposed Gay. "I knew it. By the by, Mr. Hogarth, didn't I see you last night at the ridotto with Lady Thornhill and her pretty daughter?"

"Me!--no, Sir," stammered Hogarth, colouring. And he hazarded a wink at the poet over the paper on which he was sketching. Luckily, Sir James was so much engrossed by his own task, that both the remark and gesture escaped him.

"I suppose I was mistaken," returned Gay. "You've been quizzing my friend Kent, I perceive, in your Burlington Gate."

"A capital caricature that," remarked Thornhill, laughing. "What does Mr. Kent say to it?"

"He thinks so highly of it, that he says if he had a daughter he would give her to the artist," answered Gay, a little maliciously.

"Ah!" exclaimed Sir James.

"'Sdeath!" cried Hogarth, aside to the poet. "You've ruined my hopes."

"Advanced them rather," replied Gay, in the same tone. "Miss Thornhill's a charming girl. I think a wife a needless incumbrance, and mean to die a bachelor. But, if I were in your place, I know what I'd do--"

"What--what would you do?" asked Hogarth, eagerly.

"Run away with her," replied Gay.

"Pish!" exclaimed Hogarth. But he afterwards acted upon the suggestion.

"Good-b'ye, Jack," said Figg, putting on his hat. "Rather in the way. Send you the shirt. Here, turnkey. Couple of guineas to drink Captain Sheppard's speedy escape. Thank him, not me, man. Give this fellow the slip, if you can, Jack. If not, keep up your spirits. Die game."

"Never fear," replied Jack. "If I get free, I'll have a bout with you at all weapons. If not, I'll take a cheerful glass with you at the City of Oxford, on my way to Tyburn."

"Give you the best I have in either case," replied Figg. "Good-b'ye!" And with a cordial shake of the hand he took his departure.

Sir James Thornhill, then, rose.

"I won't trouble you further, Jack," he remarked. "I've done all I can to the portrait here. I must finish it at home."

"Permit me to see it, Sir James!" requested Jack. "Ah!" he exclaimed, as the painting was turned towards him. "What would my poor mother say to it?"

"I was sorry to see that about your mother, Jack," observed Hogarth.

"What of her?" exclaimed Jack, starting up. "Is she dead?"

"No--no," answered Hogarth. "Don't alarm yourself. I saw it this morning in the Daily Journal--an advertisement, offering a reward--"

"A reward!" echoed Jack. "For what?"

"I had the paper with me. 'Sdeath! what can I have done with it? Oh! here it is," cried Hogarth, picking it from the ground. "I must have dropped it when I took out my note-book. There's the paragraph. 'Mrs. Sheppard left Mr. Wood's house at Dollis Hill on Tuesday'--that's two days ago,--'hasn't been heard of since.'"

"Let me see," cried Jack, snatching the paper, and eagerly perusing the advertisement. "Ah!" he exclaimed, in a tone of anguish. "She has fallen into the villain's hands."

"What villain?" cried Hogarth.

"Jonathan Wild, I'll be sworn," said Gay.

"Right!--right!" cried Jack, striking his fettered hands against his breast. "She is in his power, and I am here, chained hand and foot, unable to assist her."

"I could make a fine sketch of him now," whispered Hogarth to Gay.

"I told you how it was, Sir James," said Austin, addressing the knight, who was preparing for his departure, "he attributes every misfortune that befals him to Mr. Wild."

"And with some justice," replied Thornhill, drily.

"Allow me to assist you, Sir James," said Hogarth.

"Many thanks, Sir," replied Thornhill, with freezing politeness; "but Id not require assistance."

"I tell you what, Jack," said Gay, "I've several urgent engagements this morning; but I'll return to-morrow, and hear the rest of your story. And, if I can render you any service, you may command me."

"To-morrow will be too late," said Sheppard, moodily.

The easel and palette having been packed up, and the canvass carefully removed by Austin, the party took leave of the prisoner, who was so much abstracted that he scarcely noticed their departure. Just as Hogarth got to the door, the turnkey stopped him.

"You have forgotten your knife, Mr. Hogarth," he observed, significantly.

"So I have," replied Hogarth, glancing at Sheppard.

"I can do without it," muttered Jack.

The door was then locked, and he was left alone.

At three o'clock, on the same day, Austin brought up Jack's provisions, and, after carefully examining his fetters, and finding all secure, told him if he wanted anything further he must mention it, as he should not be able to return in the evening, his presence being required elsewhere. Jack replied in the negative, and it required all his mastery over himself to prevent the satisfaction which this announcement afforded him from being noticed by the jailer.

With the usual precautions, Austin then departed.

"And now," cried Jack, leaping up, "for an achievement, compared with which all I have yet done shall be as nothing!"

CHAPTER XVII.
The Iron Bar.

JACK Sheppard's first object was to free himself from his handcuffs. This he accomplished by holding the chain that connected them firmly between his teeth, and squeezing his fingers as closely together as possible, succeeded in drawing his wrists through the manacles. He next twisted the heavy gyves round and round, and partly by main strength, partly by a dexterous and well-applied jerk, sapped asunder the central link by which they were attached to the padlock. Taking off his stockings, he then drew up the basils as far as he was able, and tied the fragments of the broken chain to his legs, to prevent them from clanking, and impeding his future exertions.

Jack's former attempt to pass up the chimney, it may be remembered, was obstructed by an iron bar. To remove this obstacle it was necessary make an extensive breach in the wall. With the broken links of the chain, which served him in lieu of more efficient implements, he commenced operations just above the chimney-piece, and soon contrived to pick a hole in the plaster.

He found the wall, as he suspected, solidly constructed of brick and stone; and with the slight and inadequate tools which he possessed, it was a work of infinite labour and skill to get out a single brick. That done, however, he was well aware the rest would be comparatively easy, and as he threw the brick to the ground, he exclaimed triumphantly, "The first step is taken--the main difficulty is overcome."

Animated by this trifling success, he proceeded with fresh ardour, and the rapidity of his progress was proclaimed by the heap of bricks, stones, and mortar which before long covered the floor. At the expiration of an hour, by dint of unremitting exertion, he had made so large a breach in the chimney, that he could stand upright in it. He was now within a foot of the bar, and introducing himself into the hole, speedily worked his way to it.

Regardless of the risk he incurred from some heavy stone dropping on his head or feet,--regardless also of the noise made by the falling rubbish, and of the imminent danger which he consequently ran of being interrupted by some of the jailers, should the sound reach their ears, he continued to pull down large masses of the wall, which he flung upon the floor of the cell.

Having worked thus for another quarter of an hour without being sensible of fatigue, though he was half stifled by the clouds of dust which his exertions raised, he had made a hole about three feet wide, and six high, and uncovered the iron bar. Grasping it firmly with both hands, he quickly wrenched if from the stones in which it was mortised, and leapt to the ground. On examination it proved to be a flat bar of iron, nearly a yard in length, and more than an inch square. "A capital instrument for my purpose," thought Jack, shouldering it, "and worth all the trouble I have had in procuring it."

While he was thus musing, he fancied he heard the lock tried. A chill ran through his frame, and, grasping the heavy weapon with which chance had provided him, prepared to strike down the first person who should enter the cell. After listening attentively for a short time without drawing breath, he became convinced that his apprehensions were groundless, and, greatly relieved, sat down upon the chair to rest himself and prepare for further efforts.

Acquainted with every part of the jail, Jack well knew that his only chance of effecting an escape must be by the roof. To reach it would be a most difficult undertaking. Still it was possible, and the difficulty was only a fresh incitement.

The mere enumeration of the obstacles that existed would have deterred any spirit less daring than Sheppard's from even hazarding the attempt. Independently of other risks, and of the chance of breaking his neck in the descent, he was aware that to reach the leads he should have to break open six of the strongest doors of the prison. Armed, however, with the implement he had so fortunately obtained, he did not despair of success.

"My name will only be remembered as that of a robber," he mused; "but it shall be remembered as that of a bold one: and this night's achievement, if it does nothing else, shall prevent me from being classed with the common herd of depredators."

Roused by this reflection, filled with the deepest anxiety for his mother, and burning to be avenged upon Jonathan Wild, he grasped the iron bar, which, when he sat down, he had laid upon his knees, and stepped quickly across the room. In doing so, he had to clamber up the immense heap of bricks and rubbish which now littered the floor, amounting almost to a car-load, and reaching up nearly to the top of the chimney-piece.

"Austin will stare," thought Jack, "when he comes here in the morning. It will cost them something to repair their stronghold, and take them more time to build it up again than I have taken to pull it down."

Before proceeding with his task, he considered whether it would be possible to barricade the door; but, reflecting that the bar would be an indispensable assistant in his further efforts, he abandoned the idea, and determined to rely implicitly on that good fortune which had hitherto attended him on similar occasions.

Having once more got into the chimney, he climbed to a level with the ward above, and recommenced operations as vigorously as before. He was now aided with a powerful implement, with which he soon contrived to make a hole in the wall.

"Every brick I take out," cried Jack, as fresh rubbish clattered down the chimney, "brings me nearer my mother."

CHAPTER XVIII.
The Red Room.

THE ward into which Jack was endeavouring to break was called the Red Room, from the circumstance of its walls having once been painted in that colour; all traces of which had, however, long since disappeared. Like the Castle, which it resembled in all respects except that it was destitute even of a barrack-bedstead, the Red Room was reserved for state-prisoners, and had not been occupied since the year 1716, when the jail, as has before been mentioned, was crowded by the Preston rebels.

Having made a hole in the wall sufficiently large to pass through, Jack first tossed the bar into the room and then crept after it. As soon as he had gained his feet, he glanced round the bare blank walls of the cell, and, oppressed by the musty, close atmosphere, exclaimed, "I'll let a little fresh air into this dungeon. They say it hasn't been opened for eight years--but I won't be eight years in getting out of it."

In stepping across the room, some sharp point in the floor pierced his foot, and stooping to examine it, he found that the wound had been inflicted by a long rusty nail, which projected from the boards. Totally disregarding the pain, he picked up the nail, and reserved it for future use. Nor was he long in making it available.

On examining the door, he found it secured by a large rusty lock, which he endeavoured to pick with the nail he had just acquired; but all his efforts proving ineffectual, he removed the plate that covered it with the bar, and with his fingers contrived to draw back the bolt.

Opening the door he then stepped into a dark narrow passage leading, as he was well aware, to the chapel. On the left there were doors communicating with the King's Bench Ward and the Stone Ward, two large holds on the Master Debtors' side. But Jack was too well versed in the geography of the place to attempt either of them. Indeed, if he had been ignorant of it, the sound of voices which he could faintly distinguish, would have served as a caution to him.

Hurrying on, his progress was soon checked by a strong door, several inches in thickness, and nearly as wide as the passage. Running his hand carefully over it in search of the lock, he perceived to his dismay that it was fastened on the other side. After several vain attempts to burst it open, he resolved, as a last alternative, to break through the wall in the part nearest to the lock. This was a much more serious task than he anticipated. The wall was of considerable thickness, and built altogether of stone; and the noise he was compelled to make in using the heavy bar, which brought sparks with every splinter he struck off, was so great, that he feared it must be heard by the prisoners on the Debtors' side. Heedless, however, of the consequences, he pursued his task.

Half an hour's labour, during which he was obliged more than once to pause to regain breath, sufficed to make a hole wide enough to allow a passage for his arm up to the elbow. In this way he was able to force back a ponderous bolt from its socket; and to his unspeakable joy, found that the door instantly yielded.

Once more cheered by daylight, he hastened forward, and entered the chapel.

CHAPTER XIX.
The Chapel.

SITUATED at the upper part of the south-east angle of the jail, the chapel of Old Newgate was divided on the north side into three grated compartments, or pens as they were termed, allotted to the common debtors and felons. In the north-west angle, there was a small pen for female offenders, and, on the south, a more commodious enclosure appropriated to the master-debtors and strangers. Immediately beneath the pulpit stood a large circular pew where malefactors under sentence of death sat to hear the condemned sermon delivered to them, and where they formed a public spectacle to the crowds, which curiosity generally attracted on those occasions.

To return. Jack had got into one of the pens at the north side of the chapel. The enclosure by which it was surrounded was about twelve feet high; the under part being composed of taken planks, the upper of a strong iron grating, surmounted by sharp iron spikes. In the middle there was a gate. It was locked. But Jack speedily burst it open with the iron bar.

Clearing the few impediments in his way, he soon reached the condemned pew, where it had once been his fate to sit; and extending himself on the seat endeavoured to snatch a moment's repose. It was denied him, for as he closed his eyes--though but for an instant--the whole scene of his former visit to the place rose before him. There he sat as before, with the heavy fetters on his limbs, and beside him sat his three companions, who had since expiated their offences on the gibbet. The chapel was again crowded with visitors, and every eye--even that of Jonathan Wild who had come thither to deride him,--was fixed upon him. So perfect was the illusion, that he could almost fancy he heard the solemn voice of the ordinary warning him that his race was nearly run, and imploring him to prepare for eternity. From this perturbed state he was roused by thoughts of his mother, and fancying he heard her gentle voice urging him on to fresh exertion, he started up.

On one side of the chapel there was a large grated window, but, as it looked upon the interior of the jail, Jack preferred following the course he had originally decided upon to making any attempt in this quarter.

Accordingly, he proceeded to a gate which stood upon the south, and guarded the passage communicating with the leads. It was grated and crested with spikes, like that he had just burst open, and thinking it a needless waste of time to force it, he broke off one of the spikes, which he carried with him for further purposes, and then climbed over it.

A short flight of steps brought him to a dark passage, into which he plunged. Here he found another strong door, making the fifth he had encountered. Well aware that the doors in this passage were much stronger than those in the entry he had just quitted he was neither surprised nor dismayed to find it fastened by a lock of unusual size. After repeatedly trying to remove the plate, which was so firmly screwed down that it resisted all his efforts, and vainly attempting to pick it with the spike and nail; he, at length, after half an hour's ineffectual labour, wrenched off the box by means of the iron bar, and the door, as he laughingly expressed it, "became his humble servant."

But this difficulty was only overcome to be succeeded by one still greater. Hastening along the passage he came to the sixth door. For this he was prepared; but he was not prepared for the almost insurmountable obstacles which it presented. Running his hand hastily over it, he was startled to find it one complicated mass of bolts and bars. It seemed as if all the precautions previously taken were here accumulated. Any one less courageous than himself would have abandoned the attempt from a conviction of its utter hopelessness; but, though it might for a moment damp his ardour, it could not deter him.

Once again, he passed his hand over the surface and carefully noted all the obstacles. There was a lock, apparently more than a foot wide, strongly plated, and girded to the door with thick iron hoops. Below it a prodigiously large bolt was shot into the socket, and, in order to keep it there, was fastened by a hasp, and further protected by an immense padlock. Besides this, the door was crossed and recrossed by iron bars, clenched by broad-headed nails. An iron fillet secured the socket of the bolt and the box of the lock to the main post of the doorway.

Nothing disheartened by this survey, Jack set to work upon the lock, which he attacked with all his implements;--now attempting to pick it with the nail;--now to wrench it off with the bar: but all without effect. He not only failed in making any impression, but seemed to increase the difficulties, for after an hour's toil he had broken the nail and slightly bent the iron bar.

Completely overcome by fatigue, with strained muscles, and bruised hands; streaming with perspiration, and with lips so parched that he would gladly have parted with a treasure if he had possessed it for a draught of water; he sank against the wall, and while in this state was seized with, a sudden and strange alarm. He fancied that the turnkeys had discovered his flight and were in pursuit of him,--that they had climbed up the chimney,--entered the Red Room,--tracked him from door to door, and were now only detained by the gate which he had left unbroken in the chapel. He even thought he could detect the voice of Jonathan, urging and directing them.

So strongly was he impressed with this idea, that grasping the iron bar with both hands, he dashed it furiously against the door, making the passage echo with the blows.

By degrees, his fears vanished, and hearing nothing, he grew calmer. His spirits revived, and encouraging himself with the idea that the present impediment, though the greatest, was the last, he set himself seriously to consider how it might best be overcome.

On reflection, it occurred to him that he might, perhaps, be able to loosen the iron fillet; a notion no sooner conceived than executed. With incredible labour, and by the aid of both spike and nail, he succeeded in getting the point of the bar beneath the fillet. Exerting all his energies, and using the bar as a lever, he forced off the iron band, which was full seven feet high, seven inches wide, and two thick, and which brought with it in its fall the box of the lock and the socket of the bolt, leaving no further hinderance.

Overjoyed beyond measure at having vanquished this apparently-insurmountable obstacle, Jack darted through the door.

CHAPTER XX.
The Leads.

ASCENDING a short flight of steps, Jack found at the summit a door, which being bolted in the inside he speedily opened.

The fresh air, which blew in his face, greatly revived him. He had now reached what was called the Lower Leads,--a flat, covering a part of the prison contiguous to the gateway, and surrounded on all sides by walls about fourteen feet high. On the north stood the battlements of one of the towers of the gate. On this side a flight of wooden steps, protected by a hand-rail, led to a door opening upon the summit of the prison. This door was crested with spikes, and guarded on the right by a bristling semicircle of spikes. Hastily ascending these steps, Jack found the door, as he anticipated, locked. He could have easily forced it, but preferred a more expeditious mode of reaching the roof which suggested itself to him. Mounting the door he had last opened, he placed his hands on the wall above, and quickly drew himself up.

Just as he got on the roof of the prison, St. Sepulchre's clock struck eight. It was instantly answered by the deep note of St. Paul's; and the concert was prolonged by other neighbouring churches. Jack had thus been six hours in accomplishing his arduous task.

Though nearly dark, there was still light enough left to enable him to discern surrounding objects. Through the gloom he distinctly perceived the dome of St. Paul's, hanging like a black cloud in the air; and nearer to him he remarked the golden ball on the summit of the College of Physicians, compared by Garth to a "gilded pill." Other towers and spires--St. Martin's on Ludgate-hill, and Christchurch in Newgate Street, were also distinguishable. As he gazed down into the courts of the prison, he could not help shuddering, lest a false step might precipitate him below.

To prevent the recurrence of any such escape as that just described, it was deemed expedient, in more recent times, to keep a watchman at the top of Newgate. Not many years ago, two men, employed on this duty, quarrelled during the night, and in the morning their bodies were found stretched upon the pavement of the yard beneath.

Proceeding along the wall, Jack reached the southern tower, over the battlements of which he clambered, and crossing it, dropped upon the roof of the gate. He then scaled the northern tower, and made his way to the summit of that part of the prison which fronted Giltspur Street. Arrived at the extremity of the building, he found that it overlooked the flat-roof of a house which, as far as he could judge in the darkness, lay at a depth of about twenty feet below.

Not choosing to hazard so great a fall, Jack turned to examine the building, to see whether any more favourable point of descent presented itself, but could discover nothing but steep walls, without a single available projection. As he looked around, he beheld an incessant stream of passengers hurrying on below. Lights glimmered in the windows of the different houses; and a lamp-lighter was running from post to post on his way to Snow Hill.

Finding it impossible to descend on any side, without incurring serious risk, Jack resolved to return for his blanket, by the help of which he felt certain of accomplishing a safe landing on the roof of the house in Giltspur Street.

Accordingly, he began to retrace his steps, and pursuing the course he had recently taken, scaling the two towers, and passing along the wall of the prison, he descended by means of the door upon the Lower Leads. Before he re-entered the prison, he hesitated from a doubt whether he was not fearfully increasing his risk of capture; but, convinced that he had no other alternative, he went on.

During all this time, he had never quitted the iron bar, and he now grasped it with the firm determination of selling his life dearly, if he met with any opposition. A few seconds sufficed to clear the passage, through which it had previously cost him more than two hours to force his way. The floor was strewn with screws, nails, fragments of wood and stone, and across the passage lay the heavy iron fillet. He did not disturb any of this litter, but left it as a mark of his prowess.

He was now at the entrance of the chapel, and striking the door over which he had previously climbed a violent blow with the bar, it flew open. To vault over the pews was the work of a moment; and having gained the entry leading to the Red Room he passed through the first door; his progress being only impeded by the pile of broken stones, which he himself had raised.

Listening at one of the doors leading to the Master Debtors' side, he heard a loud voice chanting a Bacchanalian melody, and the boisterous laughter that accompanied the song, convinced him that no suspicion was entertained in this quarter. Entering the Red Room, he crept through the hole in the wall, descended the chimney, and arrived once more in his old place of captivity.

How different were his present feelings compared with those he had experienced on quitting it. *Then*, though full of confidence, he half doubted his power of accomplishing his designs. *Now*, he *had* achieved them, and felt assured of success. The vast heap of rubbish on the floor had been so materially increased by the bricks and plaster thrown down in his attack upon the wall of the Red Room, that it was with some difficulty he could find the blanket which was almost buried beneath the pile. He next searched for his stockings and shoes, and when found, put them on.

While he was thus employed, his nerves underwent a severe shock. A few bricks, dislodged probably by his last descent, came clattering down the chimney, and as it was perfectly dark, gave him the notion that some one was endeavouring to force an entrance into the room.

But these fears, like those he had recently experienced, speedily vanished, and he prepared to return to the roof, congratulating himself that owing to the opportune falling of the bricks, he had in all probability escaped serious injury.

Throwing the blanket over his left arm and shouldering the iron bar, he again clambered up the chimney; regained the Red Room; hurried along the first passage; crossed the Chapel; threaded the entry to the Lower Leads; and, in less than ten minutes after quitting the Castle, had reached the northern extremity of the prison.

Previously to his descent he had left the nail and spike on the wall, and with these he fastened the blanket to the stone coping. This done, he let himself carefully down by it, and having only a few feet to drop, alighted in safety.

Having now fairly got out of Newgate for the second time, with a heart throbbing with exultation, he hastened to make good his escape. To his great joy he found a small garret-door in the roof of the opposite house open. He entered it; crossed the room, in which there was only a small truckle-bed, over which he stumbled; opened another door and gained the stair-head. As he was about to descend his chains slightly rattled. "Oh, lud! what's that?" exclaimed a female voice, from an adjoining room. "Only the dog," replied the rough tones of a man.

Securing the chain in the best way he could, Jack then hurried down two pair of stairs, and had nearly reached the lobby, when a door suddenly opened, and two persons appeared, one of whom held a light. Retreating as quickly as he could, Jack opened the first door he came to, entered a room, and searching in the dark for some place of concealment, fortunately discovered a skreen, behind which he crept.

CHAPTER XXI.
What befell Jack Sheppard in the Turner's House.

JACK was scarcely concealed when the door opened, and the two persons of whom he had caught a glimpse below entered the room. What was his astonishment to recognise in the few words they uttered the voices of Kneebone and Winifred! The latter was apparently in great distress, and the former seemed to be using his best efforts to relieve her anxiety.

"How very fortunate it is," he observed, "that I happened to call upon Mr. Bird, the turner, to give him an order this evening. It was quite an unexpected pleasure to meet you and your worthy father."

"Pray cease these compliments," returned Winifred, "and, if you have any communication to make, do not delay it. You told me just now that you wished to speak a few words to me in private, concerning Thames Darrell, and for that purpose I have left my father below with Mr. Bird and have come hither. What have you got to say?"

"Too much," replied Kneebone, shaking his head; "sadly too much."

"Do not needlessly alarm me, I beseech you," replied Winifred. "Whatever your intelligence may be I will strive to bear it. But do not awaken my apprehension, unless you have good cause for so doing.--What do you know of Thames?--Where is he?"

"Don't agitate yourself, dearest girl," rejoined the woollen-draper; "or I shall never be able to commence my relation."

"I am calm--perfectly calm," replied Winifred. "Pray, make no further mystery; but tell me all without reserve."

"Since you require it, I must obey," replied Kneebone; "but prepare yourself for a terrible shock."

"For mercy's sake, go on!" cried Winifred.

"At all hazards then then you shall know the truth," replied the woollen-draper, in a tone of affected solicitude,--"but are you really prepared?"

"Quite--quite!" replied Winifred. "This suspense is worse than torture."

"I am almost afraid to utter it," said Kneebone; "but Thames Darrell is murdered."

"Murdered!" ejaculated Winifred.

"Basely and inhumanly murdered, by Jack Sheppard and Blueskin," continued Kneebone.

"Oh! no--no--no," cried Winifred, "I cannot believe it. You must be misinformed, Mr. Kneebone. Jack may be capable of much that is wicked, but he would never lift his hand against his friend,--of that I am assured."

"Generous girl!" cried Jack from behind the skreen.

"I have proofs to the contrary," replied Kneebone. "The murder was committed after the robbery of my house by Sheppard and his accomplices. I did not choose to mention my knowledge of this fact to your worthy father; but you may rely on its correctness."

"You were right not to mention it to him," rejoined Winifred, "for he is in such a state of distress at the mysterious disappearance of Mrs. Sheppard, that I fear any further anxiety might prove fatal to him. And yet I know not--for the object of his visit here to-night was to serve Jack, who, if your statement is correct, which I cannot however for a moment believe, does not deserve his assistance."

"You may rest assured he does not," rejoined Kneebone, emphatically, "but I am at a loss to understand in what way your father proposes to assist him."

"Mr. Bird, the turner, who is an old friend of our's, has some acquaintance with the turnkeys of Newgate," replied Winifred, "and by his means my father hoped to convey some implements to Jack, by which he might effect another escape."

"I see," remarked Kneebone. "This must be prevented," he added to himself.

"Heaven grant you may have been wrongly informed with respect to Thames!" exclaimed Winifred; "but, I beseech you, on no account to mention what you have told me to my poor father. He is not in a state of mind to bear it."

"Rely on me," rejoined Kneebone. "One word before we part, adorable girl--only one," he continued, detaining her. "I would not venture to renew my suit while Thames lived, because I well knew your affections were fixed upon him. But now that this bar is removed, I trust I may, without impropriety, urge it."

"No more of this," said Winifred, angrily. "Is this a season to speak on such a subject?"

"Perhaps not," rejoined the woollen-draper; "but the uncontrollable violence of my passion must plead my excuse. My whole life shall be devoted to you, beloved girl. And when you reflect how much at heart your poor mother, whose loss we must ever deplore, had our union, you will, I am persuaded, no longer refuse me."

"Sir!" exclaimed Winifred.

"You will make me the happiest of mankind," cried the woollen-draper, falling on his knees, and seizing her hand, which he devoured with kisses.

"Let me go," cried Winifred. "I disbelieve the whole story you have told me."

"By Heaven!" cried Kneebone, with increasing fervour, "it is true--as true as my affection for you."

"I do not doubt it," retorted Winifred, scornfully; "because I attach credit neither to one nor the other. If Thames *is* murdered, you are his assassin. Let me go, Sir."

The woollen-draper made no answer, but hastily starting up, bolted the door.

"What do you mean?" cried Winifred in alarm.

"Nothing more than to obtain a favourable answer to my suit," replied Kneebone.

"This is not the way to obtain it," said Winifred, endeavouring to reach the door.

"You shall not go, adorable girl," cried Kneebone, catching her in his arms, "till you have answered me. You must--you shall be mine."

"Never," replied Winifred. "Release me instantly, or I will call my father."

"Do so," replied Kneebone; "but remember the door is locked."

"Monster!" cried Winifred. "Help! help!"

"You call in vain," returned Kneebone.

"Not so," replied Jack, throwing down the skreen. "Release her instantly, villain!"

Both Winifred and her suitor started at this sudden apparition. Jack, whose clothes were covered with dust, and whose face was deathly pale from his recent exertion, looked more like a phantom than a living person.

"In the devil's name, is that you, Jack!" ejaculated Kneebone.

"It is," replied Sheppard. "You have uttered a wilful and deliberate falsehood in asserting that I have murdered Thames, for whom you well know I would lay down my life. Retract your words instantly, or take the consequences."

"What should I retract, villain?" cried the woollen-draper, who at the sound of Jack's voice had regained his confidence. "To the best of my belief, Thames Darrell has been murdered by you."

"A lie!" exclaimed Jack in a terrible tone. And before Kneebone could draw his sword, he felled him to the ground with the iron bar.

"You have killed him," cried Winifred in alarm.

"No," answered Jack, approaching her, "though, if I had done so, he would have merited his fate. You do not believe his statement?"

"I do not," replied Winifred. "I could not believe you capable of so foul a deed. But oh! by what wonderful chance have you come hither so seasonably?"

"I have just escaped from Newgate," replied Jack; "and am more than repaid for the severe toil I have undergone, in being able to save you. But tell me," he added with much anxiety, "has nothing been heard of Thames since the night of my former escape?"

"Nothing whatever," answered Winifred. "He left Dollis Hill at ten o'clock on that night, and has not since returned. My father has made every possible inquiry, and offered large rewards; but has not been able to discover the slightest trace of him. His suspicions at first fell upon you. But he has since acquitted you of any share in it."

"Oh, Heaven!" exclaimed Jack.

"He has been indefatigable in his search," continued Winifred, "and has even journeyed to Manchester. But though he visited Sir Rowland Trenchard's seat, Ashton Hall, he could gain no tidings of him, or of his uncle, Sir Rowland, who, it seems, has left the country."

"Never to return," remarked Jack, gloomily. "Before to-morrow morning I will ascertain what has become of Thames, or perish in the attempt. And now tell me what has happened to my poor mother?"

"Ever since your last capture, and Thames's mysterious disappearance, she has been dreadfully ill," replied Winifred; "so ill, that each day was expected to be her last. She has also been afflicted with occasional returns of her terrible malady. On Tuesday night, she was rather better, and I had left her for a short time, as I thought, asleep on the sofa in the little parlour of which she is so fond--"

"Well," exclaimed Jack.

"On my return, I found the window open, and the room vacant. She was gone."

"Did you discover any trace of footsteps?" inquired Jack eagerly.

"There were some marks near the window; but whether recently made or not could not be ascertained," replied Winifred.

"Oh God!" exclaimed Jack, in a tone of the bitterest anguish. "My worst fears are realized. She is in Wild's power."

"I ought to add," continued Winifred, "that one of her shoes was picked up in the garden, and that prints of her feet were discovered along the soft mould; whether made in flying from any one, or from rushing forth in distracted terror, it is impossible to say. My father thought the latter. He has had the whole country searched; but hitherto without success."

"I know *where* she will be found, and *how*," rejoined Jack with a shudder.

"I have something further to tell you," pursued Winifred. "Shortly after your last visit to Dollis Hill, my father was one evening waylaid by a man, who informed him that he had something to communicate respecting Thames, and had a large sum of money, and some important documents to deliver to him, which would be given up, provided he would undertake to procure your liberation."

"It was Blueskin," observed Jack.

"So my father thought," replied Winifred; "and he therefore instantly fired upon him. But though the shot took effect, as was evident from the stains on the ground, the villain escaped."

"Your father did right," replied Jack, with some bitterness. "But if he had not fired that shot, he might have saved Thames, and possessed himself of papers which would have established his birth, and his right to the estates of the Trenchard family."

"Would you have had him spare my mother's murderer?" cried Winifred.

"Ho, no," replied Jack. "And yet--but it is only part of the chain of ill-luck that seems wound around me. Listen to me, Winifred."

And he hastily related the occurrences in Jonathan Wild's house.

The account of the discovery of Sir Rowland's murder filled Winifred with alarm; but when she learnt what had befallen Thames--how he had been stricken down by the thief-taker's bludgeon, and left for dead, she uttered a piercing scream, fainted, and would have fallen, if Jack had not caught her in his arms.

Jack had well-nigh fallen too. The idea that he held in his arms the girl whom he had once so passionately loved, and for whom he still retained an ardent but hopeless attachment, almost overcame him. Gazing at her with eyes blinded with tears, he imprinted one brotherly kiss upon her lips. It was the first--and the last!

At this juncture, the handle of the door was tried, and the voice of Mr. Wood was heard without, angrily demanding admittance.

"What's the matter?" he cried. "I thought I heard a scream. Why is the door fastened? Open it directly!"

"Are you alone?" asked Jack, mimicking the voice of Kneebone.

"What for?" demanded Wood. "Open the door, I say, or I'll burst it open."

Carefully depositing Winifred on a sofa, Jack then extinguished the light, and, as he unfastened the door, crept behind it. In rushed Mr. Wood, with a candle in his hand, which Jack instantly blew out, and darted down stairs. He upset some one--probably Mr. Bird,--who was rushing up stairs, alarmed by Mr. Wood's cries: but, regardless of this, he darted along a passage, gained the shop, and passed through an open door into the street.

And thus he was once more free, having effected one of the most wonderful escapes ever planned or accomplished.

CHAPTER XXII.
Fast and Loose.

ABOUT seven o'clock on the same night, Jonathan Wild's two janizaries, who had been for some time in attendance in the hall of his dwelling at the Old Bailey, were summoned to the audience-chamber. A long and secret conference then took place between the thief-taker and his myrmidons, after which they were severally dismissed.

Left alone, Jonathan lighted a lamp, and, opening the trap-door, descended the secret stairs. Taking the opposite course from that which he had hitherto pursued when it has been necessary to attend him in his visits to the lower part of his premises, he struck into a narrow passage on the right, which he tracked till he came to a small door, like the approach to a vault. Unlocking it, he entered the chamber, which by no means belied its external appearance.

On a pallet in one corner lay a pale emaciated female. Holding the lamp over her rigid but beautiful features, Jonathan, with some anxiety, placed his hand upon her breast to ascertain whether the heart still beat. Satisfied with his scrutiny, he produced a pocket-flask, and taking off the silver cup with which it was mounted, filled it with the contents of the flask, and then seizing the thin arm of the sleeper, rudely shook it. Opening her large black eyes, she fixed them upon him for a moment with a mixture of terror and loathing, and then averted her gaze.

"Drink this," cried Jonathan, handing her the cup. "You'll feel better after it."

Mechanically raising the potion to her lips, the poor creature swallowed it without hesitation.

"Is it poison?" she asked.

"No," replied Jonathan, with a brutal laugh. "I'm not going to get rid of you just yet. It's gin--a liquor you used to like. You'll find the benefit of it by and by. You've a good deal to go through to-night."

"Ah!" exclaimed Mrs. Sheppard, "are you come to renew your terrible proposals?"

"I'm come to execute my threats," replied Wild. "To-night you shall be my wedded wife."

"I will die first," replied Mrs. Sheppard.

"You may die *afterwards* as soon as you please," retorted Jonathan; "but live till then you *shall*. I've sent for the priest."

"Mercy!" cried Mrs. Sheppard, vainly trying to discover a gleam of compassion in the thief-taker's inexorable countenance,--"Mercy! mercy!"

"Pshaw!" rejoined Jonathan. "You should be glad to be made an honest woman."

"Oh! let me die," groaned the widow. "I have not many days,--perhaps, not many hours to live. But kill me rather than commit this outrage."

"That wouldn't answer my purpose," replied Jonathan, savagely. "I didn't carry you off from old Wood to kill you, but to wed you."

"What motive can you have for so vile a deed?" asked Mrs. Sheppard.

"You know my motive well enough," answered Jonathan. "However, I'll refresh your memory. I once might have married you for your beauty,--now I marry you for your wealth."

"My wealth," replied Mrs. Sheppard. "I have nothing."

"You are heiress to the Trenchard property," rejoined Jonathan, "one of the largest estates in Lancashire."

"Not while Thames Darrell and Sir Rowland live."

"Sir Rowland is dead," replied Jonathan, gloomily. "Thames Darrell only waits my mandate to follow him. Before our marriage there will be no life between you and the estates."

"Ah!" exclaimed Mrs. Sheppard.

"Look here," cried Jonathan, stooping down and taking hold of a ring in the floor, with which by a great effort he raised up a flag. "In this pit," he added, pointing to the chasm below, "your brother is buried. Here your nephew will speedily be thrown."

"Horrible!" cried Mrs. Sheppard, shuddering violently. "But your dreadful projects will recoil on your own head. Heaven will not permit the continuance of such wickedness as you practise."

"I'll take my chance," replied Jonathan, with a sinister smile. "My schemes have succeeded tolerably well hitherto."

"A day of retribution will assuredly arrive," rejoined Mrs. Sheppard.

"Till then, I shall remain content," returned Wild. "And now, Mrs. Sheppard, attend to what I'm about to say to you. Years ago, when you were a girl and in the bloom of your beauty, I loved you."

"Loved me! *You*!"

"I loved you," continued Jonathan, "and struck by your appearance, which seemed above your station, inquired your history, and found you had been stolen by a gipsy in Lancashire. I proceeded to Manchester, to investigate the matter further, and when there ascertained, beyond a doubt, that you were the eldest daughter of Sir Montacute Trenchard. This discovery made, I hastened back to London to offer you my hand, but found you had married in the mean time a smock-faced, smooth-tongued carpenter named Sheppard. The important secret remained locked in my breast, but I resolved to be avenged. I swore I would bring your husband to the gallows,--would plunge you in such want, such distress, that you should have no alternative but the last frightful resource of misery,--and I also swore, that if you had a son he should share the same fate as his father."

"And terribly you have kept your vow," replied Mrs. Sheppard.

"I have," replied Jonathan. "But I am now coming to the point which most concerns you. Consent to become my wife, and do not compel me to have recourse to violence to effect my purpose, and I will spare your son."

Mrs. Sheppard looked fixedly at him, as if she would penetrate the gloomy depth of his soul.

"Swear that you will do this," she cried.

"I swear it," rejoined Jonathan, readily.

"But what is an oath to you!" cried the widow, distrustfully. "You will not hesitate to break it, if it suits your purpose. I have suffered too much from your treachery. I will not trust you."

"As you please," replied Jonathan, sternly. "Recollect you are in my power. Jack's life hangs on your determination."

"What shall I do?" cried Mrs. Sheppard, in a voice of agony.

"Save him," replied Jonathan. "You *can* do so."

"Bring him here,--let me see him--let me embrace him--let me be assured that he is safe, and I am yours. I swear it."

"Hum!" exclaimed Jonathan.

"You hesitate--you are deceiving me."

"By my soul, no," replied Jonathan, with affected sincerity. "You shall see him to-morrow."

"Delay the marriage till then. I will never consent till I see him."

"Yon ask impossibilities," replied Jonathan, sullenly. "All is prepared. The marriage cannot--shall not be delayed. Yon must be mine to-night."

"Force shall not make me yours till Jack is free," replied the widow, resolutely.

"An hour hence, I shall return with the priest," replied Jonathan, striding towards the door.

And, with a glance of malignant exultation, he quitted the vault, and locked the door.

"An hour hence, I shall be beyond your malice," said Mrs. Sheppard, sinking backwards upon the pallet.

CHAPTER XXIII.
The last Meeting between Jack Sheppard and his Mother.

AFTER escaping from the turner's house, Jack Sheppard skirted St. Sepulchre's church, and hurrying down Snow Hill, darted into the first turning on the left. Traversing Angel Court, and Green Arbour Court,--celebrated as one of Goldsmith's retreats,--he speedily reached Seacoal Lane, and pursuing the same course, which he and Thames had formerly taken, arrived at the yard at the back of Jonathan's habitation.

A door, it may be remembered, opened from Wild's dwelling into this yard. Before he forced an entrance, Jack tried it, and, to his great surprise and delight, found it unfastened. Entering the house, he found himself in a narrow passage leading to the back stairs. He had not taken many steps when he perceived Quilt Arnold in the upper gallery, with a lamp in his hand. Hearing a noise below, Quilt called out, supposing it occasioned by the Jew. Jack hastily retreated, and taking the first means of concealment that occurred to him, descended the cellar steps.

Quilt, meanwhile, came down, examined the door, and finding it unfastened, locked it with a bitter imprecation on his brother-janizary's carelessness. This done, he followed the course which Jack had just taken. As he crossed the cellar, he passed so near to Jack who had concealed himself behind a piece of furniture that he almost touched him. It was Jack's intention to have knocked him down with the iron bar; but he was so struck with the janizary's looks, that he determined to spare him till he had ascertained his purpose. With this view, he suffered him to pass on.

Quilt's manner, indeed, was that of a man endeavouring to muster up sufficient resolution for the commission of some desperate crime. He halted,--looked fearfully around,--stopped again, and exclaimed aloud, "I don't like the job; and yet it must be done, or Mr. Wild will hang me." With this, he appeared to pluck up his courage, and stepped forward more boldly.

"Some dreadful deed is about to be committed, which I may perhaps prevent," muttered Jack to himself. "Heaven grant I may not be too late!"

Followed by Jack Sheppard, who kept sufficiently near him to watch his proceedings, and yet not expose himself, Quilt unlocked one or two doors which he left open, and after winding his way along a gloomy passage, arrived at the door of a vault. Here he set down the lamp, and took out a key, and as he did so the expression of his countenance was so atrocious, that Jack felt assured he was not wrong in his suspicions.

By this time, the door was unlocked, and drawing his sword, Quilt entered the cell. The next moment, an exclamation was heard in the voice of Thames. Darting forward at this sound, Jack threw open the door, and beheld Quilt kneeling over Thames, who'se hands and feet were bound with cords, and about to plunge his sword into his breast. A blow from the iron bar instantly stretched the ruffian on the floor. Jack then proceeded to liberate the captive from his bondage.

"Jack!" exclaimed Thames. "Is it you?"

"It is," replied Sheppard, as he untied the cords. "I might return the question. Were it not for your voice, I don't think I should know you. You are greatly altered."

Captivity had, indeed, produced a striking alteration in Thames. He looked like the shadow of himself--thin, feeble, hollow-eyed--his beard unshorn--nothing could be more miserable.

"I have never been out of this horrible dungeon since we last met," he said; "though how long ago that is, I scarcely know. Night and day have been alike to me."

"Six weeks have elapsed since that fatal night," replied Jack. "During the whole of that time I have been a close prisoner in Newgate, whence I have only just escaped."

"Six weeks!" exclaimed Thames, in a melancholy tone. "It seems like six long months to me."

"I do not doubt it," returned Jack; "none but those who have experienced it can understand the miseries of imprisonment."

"Do not speak of it," rejoined Thames, with a look of horror. "Let us fly from this frightful place."

"I will conduct you to the outlet," replied Jack; "but I cannot leave it till I have ascertained whether my mother also is a prisoner here."

"I can answer that," replied Thames. "She is. The monster, Wild, when he visited my dungeon last night, told me, to add to my misery, that she occupied a cell near me."

"Arm yourself with that ruffian's weapons," replied Jack, "and let us search for her."

Thames complied. But he was so feeble, that it seemed scarcely possible he could offer any effectual resistance in case of an attack.

"Lean on me," said Jack.

Taking the light, they then proceeded along the passage. There was no other door in it, and Jack therefore struck into another entry which branched off to the right. They had not proceeded far when a low moan was heard.

"She is here," cried Jack, darting forward.

A few steps brought him to the door of the vault in which his mother was immured. It was locked. Jack had brought away the bunch of keys which he had taken from Quilt Arnold, but, none of them would open it. He was therefore obliged to use the iron bar, which he did with as much caution as circumstances would permit. At the first blow, Mrs. Sheppard uttered a piercing scream.

"Wretch!" she cried, "you shall not force me to your hateful purpose. I will never wed you. I have a weapon--a knife--and if you attempt to open the door, will plunge it to my heart."

"Oh God!" exclaimed Jack, paralysed by her cries. "What shall I do? If I persist, I shall destroy her."

"Get hence," continued Mrs. Sheppard, with a frenzied laugh. "You shall never behold me alive."

"Mother!" cried Jack, in a broken voice. "It is your son."

"It is false," cried Mrs. Sheppard. "Think not to deceive me, monster. I know my son's voice too well. He is in Newgate. Hence!"

"Mother! dear mother!" cried Jack, in a voice, the tones of which were altered by his very anxiety to make them distinct, "listen to me. I have broken from prison, and am come to save you."

"It is *not* Jack's voice," rejoined Mrs. Sheppard. "I am not to be deceived. The knife is at my breast. Stir a foot, and I strike."

"Oh Heavens!" cried Jack, driven to his wits' end. "Mother--dear mother! Once again, I beseech you to listen to me. I am come to rescue you from Wild's violence. I must break open the door. Hold your hand for a moment."

"You have heard my fixed determination, villain," cried Mrs. Sheppard. "I know my life is valuable to you, or you would not spare it. But I will disappoint you. Get you gone. Your purposes are defeated."

"Footsteps are approaching," cried Thames. "Heed her not. It is but a wild threat."

"I know not how to act," exclaimed Jack, almost driven to desperation.

"I hear you plotting with your wicked associates," cried Mrs. Sheppard. "I have baffled you."

"Force the door," said Thames, "or you will be too late."

"Better she die by her own hand, than by that monster's," cried Jack, brandishing the bar. "Mother, I come to you."

With this, he struck the door a heavy blow.

He listened. There was a deep groan, and the sound of a fall within.

"I have killed her," exclaimed Jack, dropping the bar,--"by your advice, Thames. Oh God! pardon me."

"Do not delay," cried Thames. "She may yet be saved. I am too weak to aid you."

Jack again seized the bar, and, dashing it furiously against the door, speedily burst it open.

The unfortunate woman was stretched upon the floor, with a bloody knife in her hand.

"Mother!" cried Jack, springing towards her.

"Jack!" she cried, raising her head. "Is it you?"

"It is," replied her son, "Oh! why would you not listen to me?"

"I was distracted," replied Mrs. Sheppard, faintly.

"I have killed you," cried Jack, endeavouring to staunch the effusion of blood from her breast. "Forgive--forgive me!"

"I have nothing to forgive," replied Mrs. Sheppard. "I alone am to blame."

"Can I not carry you where you can obtain help?" cried Jack in a agony of distress.

"It is useless," replied Mrs. Sheppard: "nothing can save me. I die happy--quite happy in beholding you. Do not remain with me. You may fall into the hands of your enemy. Fly! fly!"

"Do not think of me, mother, but of yourself," cried Jack, in an agony of tears.

"You have always been, far dearer to me than myself," replied Mrs. Sheppard. "But I have one last request to make. Let me lie in Willesden churchyard."

"You shall--you shall," answered Jack.

"We shall meet again ere long, my son," cried Mrs. Sheppard, fixing her glazing eyes upon him.

"Oh God! she is dying," exclaimed Jack in a voice suffocated by emotion. "Forgive me--oh, forgive me!"

"Forgive you--bless you!" she gasped.

A cold shiver ran through her frame, and her gentle spirit passed away for ever.

"Oh, God! that I might die too," cried Jack, falling on his knees beside her.

After the first violent outbreak of grief had in some degree subsided, Thames addressed him.

"You must not remain here," he said. "You can render no further service to your poor mother."

"I can avenge her," cried Jack in a terrible tone.

"Be ruled by me," returned Thames. "You will act most in accordance with her wishes, could she dictate them, by compliance. Do not waste time in vain regrets, but let us remove the body, that we may fulfil her last injunctions."

After some further arguments, Jack assented to this proposal.

"Go on first with the light," he said. "I will bear the body." And he raised it in his arms.

Just as they reached the end of the passage, they heard the voices of Jonathan and the Jew in Thames's late place of confinement. Wild had evidently discovered the body of Quilt Arnold, and was loudly expressing his anger and astonishment.

"Extinguish the light," cried Jack; "turn to the left. Quick! Quick!"

The order was only just given in time. They had scarcely gained the adjoining cellar when Jonathan and the Jew rushed past in the direction of the vault.

"Not a moment is to be lost," cried Jack: "follow me."

So saying, he hurried up stairs, opened the back door, and was quickly in the yard. Having ascertained that Thames was at his heels, he hurried with his ghastly burthen down Seacoal Lane.

"Where are you going?" cried Thames, who, though wholly disencumbered, was scarcely able to keep up with him.

"I know not--and care not," replied Jack.

At this moment, a coach passed them, and was instantly hailed by Thames.

"You had better let me convey her to Dollis Hill," he said.

"Be it so," replied Jack.

Luckily it was so dark, and there was no lamp near, that the man did not notice the condition of the body, which was placed in the vehicle by the two young men.

"What will you do?" asked Thames.

"Leave me to my fate," rejoined Jack. "Take care of your charge."

"Doubt me not," replied Thames.

"Bury her in Willesden churchyard, as she requested, on Sunday," said Jack. "I will be there at the time."

So saying, he closed the door.

The coachman having received his order, and being offered an extra fare if he drove quickly, set off at full speed.

As Jack departed, a dark figure, emerging from behind a wall, rushed after him.

CHAPTER XXIV.
The Pursuit.

AFTER running to some distance down Seacoal Lane, Jack stopped to give a last look at the vehicle which was bearing away the remains of his beloved and ill-fated mother. It was scarcely out of sight, when two persons, whom, he instantly recognised as Jonathan and Abraham Mendez, turned the corner of the street, and made it evident from their shouts, that they likewise perceived him.

Starting off at a rapid pace, Jack dashed down Turnagain-lane, skirted the eastern bank of Fleet-ditch, crossed Holborn Bridge, and began to ascend the neighbouring hill. By the time he had reached St. Andrew's Church, his pursuers had gained the bridge, and the attention of such passengers as crowded the streets was attracted towards him by their vociferations. Amongst others, the watchman whose box was placed against the churchyard wall, near the entrance to Shoe-lane, rushed out and sprung his rattle, which was immediately answered by another rattle from Holborn-bars.

Darting down Field-lane, Jack struck into a labyrinth of streets on the left; but though he ran as swiftly as he could, he was not unperceived. His course had been observed by the watchman, who directed Wild which way to take.

"It is Jack Sheppard, the noted housebreaker," cried Jonathan, at the top of his sonorous voice. "He has just broken out of Newgate. After him! A hundred pounds to the man who takes him."

Sheppard's name operated like magic on the crowd. The cry was echoed by twenty different voices. People ran out of their shops to join the pursuit; and, by the time Wild had got into Field-lane, he had a troop of fifty persons at his heels--all eager to assist in the capture.

"Stop thief!" roared Jonathan, who perceived the fugitive hurrying along a street towards Hatton Garden. "It is Sheppard--Jack Sheppard--stop him!" And his shouts were reiterated by the pack of bloodhounds at his heels.

Jack, meanwhile, heard, the shouts, and, though alarmed by them, held on a steady course. By various twistings and turnings, during all which time his pursuers, who were greatly increased in numbers, kept him in view, he reached Gray's-Inn-lane. Here he was hotly pursued. Fatigued by his previous exertions, and incumbered by his fetters, he was by no means--though ordinarily remarkably swift of foot--a match for his foes, who were fast gaining upon him.

At the corner of Liquorpond Street stood the old Hampstead coach-office; and, on the night in question, a knot of hostlers, waggoners, drivers, and stable-boys was collected in the yard. Hearing the distant shouts, these fellows rushed down to the entrance of the court, and arrived there just as Jack passed it. "Stop thief!" roared Jonathan. "Stop thief!" clamoured the rabble behind.

At no loss to comprehend that Jack was the individual pointed out by these outcries, two of the nearest of the group made a dash at him. But Jack eluded their grasp. A large dog was then set at him by a stable-boy; but, striking the animal with his faithful iron-bar, he speedily sent him yelping back. The two hostlers, however, kept close at his heels; and Jack, whose strength began to flag, feared he could not hold much longer. Determined, however, not be taken with life, he held on.

Still keeping ahead of his pursuers, he ran along the direct road, till the houses disappeared and he got into the open country. Here he was preparing to leap over the hedge into the fields on the left, when he was intercepted by two horsemen, who, hearing the shouts, rode up and struck at him with the butt-ends of their heavy riding-whips. Warding off the blows as well as he could with the bar, Jack struck both the horses on the head, and the animals plunged so violently, that they not only prevented their riders from assailing him, but also kept off the hostlers; and, in the confusion that ensued, Jack managed to spring over the fence, and shaped his course across the field in the direction of Sir John Oldcastle's.

The stoppage had materially lessened the distance between him and his pursuers, who now amounted to more than a hundred persons, many of whom carried lanterns and links. Ascertaining that it was Sheppard of whom this concourse was in pursuit, the two horsemen leapt the hedge, and were presently close upon him.

Like a hare closely pressed, Jack attempted to double, but the device only brought him nearer his foes, who were crossing the field in every direction, and rending the air with their shouts. The uproar was tremendous--men yelling--dogs barking,--but above all was heard the stentorian voice of Jonathan, urging them on. Jack was so harrassed that he felt half inclined to stand at bay.

While he was straining every sinew, his foot slipped, and he fell, head foremost, into a deep trench, which he had not observed in the dark. This fall saved him, for the horsemen passed over him. Creeping along quickly on his hands and knees, he found the entrance to a covered drain, into which he crept. He was scarcely concealed when he heard the horsemen, who perceived they had overshot their mark, ride back.

By this time, Jonathan and the vast mob attending him, had come up, and the place was rendered almost as light as day by the links.

"He must be somewhere hereabouts," cried one of the horsemen, dismounting. "We were close upon him when he suddenly disappeared."

Jonathan made no answer, but snatching a torch from a bystander, jumped into the trench and commenced a diligent search. Just as he had arrived at the mouth of the drain, and Jack felt certain he must be discovered, a loud shout was raised from the further end of the field that the fugitive was caught. All the assemblage, accompanied by Jonathan, set off in this direction, when it turned out that the supposed housebreaker was a harmless beggar, who had been found asleep under a hedge.

Jonathan's vexation at the disappointment was expressed in the bitterest imprecations, and he returned as speedily as he could to the trench. But he had now lost the precise spot; and thinking he had examined the drain, turned his attention to another quarter.

Meanwhile, the excitement of the chase had in some degree subsided. The crowd dispersed in different directions, and most fortunately a heavy shower coming on, put them altogether to flight. Jonathan, however, still lingered. He seemed wholly insensible to the rain, though it presently descended in torrents, and continued his search as ardently as before.

After occupying himself thus for the best part of an hour, he thought Jack must have given him the slip. Still, his suspicions were so strong, that he ordered Mendez to remain on guard near the spot all night, and, by the promise of a large reward induced two other men to keep him company.

As he took his departure, he whispered to the Jew: "Take him dead or alive; but if we fail now, and you heard him aright in Seacoal Lane, we are sure of him at his mother's funeral on Sunday."

CHAPTER XXV.
How Jack Sheppard got rid of his Irons.

ABOUT an hour after this, Jack ventured to emerge from his place of concealment. It was still raining heavily, and profoundly dark. Drenched to the skin,--in fact, he had been lying in a bed of muddy water,--and chilled to the very bone, he felt so stiff, that he could scarcely move.

Listening attentively, he fancied he heard the breathing of some one near him, and moved cautiously in the opposite direction. In spite of his care, he came in contact with a man, who, endeavouring to grasp him, cried, in the voice of Mendez, "Who goes dere? Shpeak! or I fire!"

No answer being returned, the Jew instantly discharged his pistol, and though the shot did no damage, the flash discovered Sheppard. But as the next moment all was profound darkness, Jack easily managed to break away from them.

Without an idea where he was going, Jack pursued his way through the fields; and, as he proceeded, the numbness of his limbs in some degree wore off, and his confidence returned. He had need of all the inexhaustible energy of his character to support him through his toilsome walk over the wet grass, or along the slippery ploughed land. At last, he got into a lane, but had not proceeded far when he was again alarmed by the sound of a horse's tread.

Once more breaking through the hedge he took to the fields. He was now almost driven to despair. Wet as he was, he felt if he lay down in the grass, he should perish with cold; while, if he sought a night's lodging in any asylum, his dress, stained with blood and covered with dirt, would infallibly cause him to be secured and delivered into the hands of justice. And then the fetters, which were still upon his legs:--how was he to get rid of them?

Tired and dispirited, he still wandered on. Again returning to the main road, he passed through Clapton; and turning off on the left, arrived at the foot of Stamford Hill. He walked on for an hour longer, till he could scarcely drag one leg after another. At length, he fell down on the road, fully expecting each moment would prove his last.

How long he continued thus he scarcely knew; but just before dawn, he managed to regain his legs, and, crawling up a bank, perceived he was within a quarter of a mile of Tottenham. A short way off in the fields he descried a sort of shed or cow-house, and thither he contrived to drag his weary limbs. Opening the door, he found it littered with straw, on which he threw himself, and instantly fell asleep.

When he awoke it was late in the day, and raining heavily. For some time he could not stir, but felt sick and exhausted. His legs were dreadfully swelled; his hands bruised; and his fetters occasioned him intolerable pain. His bodily suffering, however, was nothing compared with his mental anguish. All the events of the previous day rushed to his recollection; and though he had been unintentionally the cause of his mother's death, he reproached himself as severely as if he had been her actual murderer.

"Had I not been the guilty wretch I am," he cried, bursting into an agony of tears, "she would never have died thus."

This strong feeling of remorse having found a natural vent, in some degree subsided, and he addressed himself to his present situation. Rousing himself, he went to the door. It had ceased raining, but the atmosphere was moist and chill, and the ground deluged by the recent showers. Taking up a couple of large stones which lay near, Jack tried to beat the round basils of the fetters into an oval form, so as to enable him to slip his heels through them.

While he was thus employed a farming man came into the barn. Jack instantly started to his feet, and the man, alarmed at his appearance, ran off to a neighbouring house. Before he could return, Jack had made good his retreat; and, wandering about the lanes and hedges, kept out of sight as much as possible.

On examining his pockets, he found about twenty guineas in gold, and some silver. But how to avail himself of it was the question, for in his present garb he was sure to be recognised. When night fell, he crept into the town of Tottenham. As he passed along the main thoroughfare, he heard his own name pronounced, and found that it was a hawker, crying a penny history of his escapes. A crowd was collected round the fellow, who was rapidly disposing of his stock.

"Here's the full, true, and particular account of Jack Sheppard's last astonishing and never-to-be-forgotten escape from the Castle of Newgate," bawled the hawker, "with a print of him taken from the life, showing the manner, how he was shackled and handcuffed. Only one penny--two copies--two pence--thank you, Sir. Here's the----"

"Let me have one," cried a servant maid, running across the street, and in her haste forgetting to shut the door,--"here's the money. Master and missis have been talking all day long about Jack Sheppard, and I'm dying to read his life."

"Here you have it, my dear," returned the hawker. "Sold again!"

"If you don't get back quickly, Lucy," observed a bystander, "Jack Sheppard will be in the house before you."

This sally occasioned a general laugh.

"If Jack would come to my house, I'd contrive to hide him," remarked a buxom dame. "Poor fellow! I'm glad he has escaped."

"Jack seems to be a great favourite with the fair sex," observed a smirking grocer's apprentice.

"Of course," rejoined the bystander, who had just spoken, and who was of a cynical turn,--"the greater the rascal, the better they like him."

"Here's a particular account of Jack's many robberies and escapes," roared the hawker,--"how he broke into the house of his master, Mr. Wood, at Dollis Hill--"

"Let me have one," said a carpenter, who was passing by at the moment,--"Mr. Wood was an old friend of mine--and I recollect seeing Jack when he was bound 'prentice to him."

"A penny, if you please, Sir," said the hawker.--"Sold again! Here you have the full, true, and particular account of the barbarous murder committed by Jack Sheppard and his associate, Joseph Blake, *alias* Blueskin, upon the body of Mrs. Wood--"

"That's false!" cried a voice behind him.

The man turned at the exclamation, and so did several of the bystanders; but they could not make out who had uttered it.

Jack, who had been lingering near the group, now walked on.

In the middle of the little town stood the shop of a Jew dealer in old clothes.

The owner was at the door unhooking a few articles of wearing apparel which he had exposed outside for sale. Amongst other things, he had just brought down an old laced bavaroy, a species of surtout much worn at the period.

"What do you want fot that coat, friend?" asked Jack, as he came up.

"More than you'll pay for it, friend," snuffled the Jew.

"How do you know that?" rejoined Jack. "Will you take a guinea for it?"

"Double that sum might tempt me," replied the Jew; "it's a nobleman's coat, upon my shoul!"

"Here's the money," replied Jack, taking the coat.

"Shall I help you on with it, Sir?" replied the Jew, becoming suddenly respectful.

"No," replied Jack.

"I half suspect this is a highwayman," thought the Jew; "he's so ready with his cash. I've some other things inside, Sir, which you might wish to buy,--some pistols."

Jack was about to comply; but not liking the man's manner, he walked on.

Further on, there was a small chandler's shop, where Jack observed an old woman seated at the counter, attended by a little girl. Seeing provisions in the window, Jack ventured in and bought a loaf. Having secured this,--for he was almost famished,--he said that he had lost a hammer and wished to purchase one. The old woman told him she had no such article to dispose of, but recommended him to a neighbouring blacksmith.

Guided by the glare of the forge, which threw a stream of ruddy light across the road, Jack soon found the place of which he was in search. Entering the workshop, he found the blacksmith occupied in heating the tire of a cart wheel. Suspending his labour on Jack's appearance, the man demanded his business. Making up a similar story to that which he had told the old woman, he said he wanted to purchase a hammer and a file.

The man looked hard at him.

"Answer me one question first?" he said; "I half suspect you're Jack Sheppard."

"I am," replied Jack, without hesitation; for he felt assured from the man's manner that he might confide in him.

"You're a bold fellow, Jack," rejoined the blacksmith. "But you've done well to trust me. I'll take off your irons--for I guess that's the reason why you want the hammer and file--on one condition."

"What is it?"

"That you give 'em to me."

"Readily."

Taking Jack into a shed behind the workshop the smith in a short time freed him from his fetters. He not only did this, but supplied him with an ointment which allayed the swelling of his limbs, and crowned all by furnishing him with a jug of excellent ale.

"I'm afraid, Jack, you'll come to the gallows," observed the smith; "buth if you do, I'll go to Tyburn to see you. But I'll never part with your irons."

Noticing the draggled condition Jack was in, he then fetched him a bucket of water, with which Jack cleansed himself as well as he could, and thanking the honest smith, who would take nothing for his trouble, left the shop.

Having made a tolerably good meal upon the loaf, overcome by fatigue, Jack turned into a barn in Stoke Newington, and slept till late in the day, when he awakened much refreshed. The swelling in his limbs had also subsided. It rained heavily all day, so he did not stir forth.

Towards night, however, he ventured out, and walked on towards London. When he arrived at Hoxton, he found the walls covered with placards offering a reward for his apprehension, and he everywhere appeared to be the general subject of conversation. Prom a knot of idlers at a public-house, he learnt that Jonathan Wild had just ridden past, and that his setters were scouring the country in every direction.

Entering London, he bent his way towards the west-end; and having some knowledge of a secondhand tailor's shop in Rupert Street, proceeded thither, and looked out a handsome suit of mourning, with a sword, cloak, and hat, and demanded the price. The man asked twelve guineas, but after a little bargaining, he came down to ten.

Taking his new purchase under his arm, Jack proceeded to a small tavern in the same street, where, having ordered dinner, he went to a bed-room to attire himself. He had scarcely completed his toilet, when he was startled by a noise at the door, and heard his own name pronounced in no friendly accents. Fortunately, the window was not far from the ground; so opening it gently, he dropped into a backyard, and from thence got into the street.

Hurrying down the Haymarket, he was arrested by a crowd who were collected round a street-singer. Jack paused for a moment, and found that his own adventures formed the subject of the ballad. Not daring, however, to listen to it, he ran on.

CHAPTER XXVI.
How Jack Sheppard attended his Mother's Funeral.

THAT night Jack walked to Paddington, and took up his quarters at a small tavern, called the Wheat-sheaf, near the green. On the next morning--Sunday--the day on which he expected his mother's funeral to take place, he set out along the Harrow Road.

It was a clear, lovely, October morning. The air was sharp and bracing, and the leaves which had taken their autumnal tints were falling from the trees. The road which wound by Westbourne Green, gave him a full view of the hill of Hampstead with its church, its crest of houses, and its villas peeping from out the trees.

Jack's heart was too full to allow him to derive any pleasure from this scene; so he strolled on without raising his eyes till he arrived at Kensal Green. Here he obtained some breakfast, and mounting the hill turned off into the fields on the right. Crossing them, he ascended an eminence, which, from its singular shape, seems to have been the site of a Roman encampment, and which commands a magnificent prospect.

Leaning upon a gate he looked down into the valley. It was the very spot from which his poor mother had gazed after her vain attempt to rescue him at the Mint; but, though he was ignorant of this, her image was alone present to him. He beheld the grey tower of Willesden Church, embosomed in its grove of trees, now clothed, in all the glowing livery of autumn. There was the cottage she had inhabited for so many years,--in those fields she had rambled,--at that church she had prayed. And he had destroyed all this. But for him she might have been alive and happy. The recollection was too painful, and he burst into an agony of tears.

Aroused by the sound of the church bells, he resolved, at whatever risk, to attend Divine service. With this view, he descended the hill and presently found a footpath leading to the church. But he was destined to have every tide of feeling awakened--every wound opened. The path he had selected conducted him to his mother's humble dwelling. When she occupied, it, it was neatness itself; the little porch was overrun with creepers--the garden trim and exquisitely kept. Now, it was a wilderness of weeds. The glass in the windows was broken--the roof unthatched-- the walls dilapidated. Jack turned away with an aching heart. It seemed an emblem of the ruin he had caused.

As he proceeded, other painful reminiscences were aroused. At every step he seemed to be haunted by the ghost of the past. There was the stile on which Jonathan had sat, and he recollected distinctly the effect of his mocking glance--how it had hardened his heart against his mother's prayer. "O God!" he exclaimed, "I am severely punished."

He had now gained the high road. The villagers were thronging to church. Bounding the corner of a garden wall, he came upon his former place of imprisonment. Some rustic hand had written upon the door "JACK SHEPPARD'S CAGE;" and upon the wall was affixed a large placard describing his person, and offering a reward for his capture. Muffling up his face, Jack turned away; but he had not proceeded many steps when he heard a man reading aloud an account of his escapes from a newspaper.

Hastening to the church, he entered it by the very door near which his first crime had been committed. His mother's scream seemed again to ring in his ears, and he was so deeply affected that, fearful of exciting attention, he was about to quit the sacred edifice, when he was stopped by the entrance of Thames, who looked pale as death, with Winifred leaning on his arm. They were followed by Mr. Wood in the deepest mourning.

Shrinking involuntarily back into the farthest corner of the seat, Jack buried his face in his hands. The service began. Jack who had not been in a place of worship for many years was powerfully affected. Accidentally raising his eyes, he saw that he was perceived by the family from Dollis Hill, and that he was an object of the deepest interest to them.

As soon as the service was over, Thames contrived to approach him, and whispered, "Be cautious,--the funeral will take place after evening service."

Jack would not hazard a glance at Winifred; but, quitting the church, got into an adjoining meadow, and watched the party slowly ascending the road leading to Dollis Hill. At a turn in the road, he perceived Winifred looking anxiously towards him, and when she discovered him, she waved her hand.

Returning to the churchyard, he walked round it; and on the western side, near a small yew-tree discovered a new-made grave.

"Whose grave is this?" he inquired of a man who was standing near it.

"I can't say," answered the fellow; "but I'll inquire from the sexton, William Morgan. Here, Peter," he added to a curly-headed lad, who was playing on one of the grassy tombs, "ask your father to step this way."

The little urchin set off, and presently returned with the sexton.

"It's Mrs. Sheppard's grave,--the mother of the famous housebreaker," said Morgan, in answer to Jack's inquiry;--"and it's well they let her have Christian burial after all--for they say she destroyed herself for her son. The crowner's 'quest sat on her yesterday--and if she hadn't been proved out of her mind, she would have been buried at four lane-ends."

Jack could stand no more. Placing a piece of money in Morgan's hands, he hurried out of the churchyard.

"By my soul," said the sexton, "that's as like Jack Sheppard as any one I ever seed i' my born days."

Hastening to the Six Bells, Jack ordered some refreshment, and engaged a private room, where he remained till the afternoon absorbed in grief.

Meantime, a change had taken place in the weather. The day had become suddenly overcast. The wind blew in fitful gusts, and scattered the yellow leaves from the elms and horse-chestnuts. Roused by the bell tolling for evening service, Jack left the house. On reaching the churchyard, he perceived the melancholy procession descending the hill. Just then, a carriage drawn by four horses, drove furiously up to the Six Bells; but Jack was too much absorbed to take any notice of it.

At this moment, the bell began to toll in a peculiar manner, announcing the approach of the corpse. The gate was opened; the coffin brought into the churchyard; and Jack, whose eyes were filled with tears, saw Mr. Wood and Thames pass him, and followed at a foot's pace behind them.

Meanwhile, the clergyman, bare-headed and in his surplice, advanced to meet them. Having read the three first verses of the impressive service appointed for the burial of the dead, he returned to the church, whither the coffin was carried through the south-western door, and placed in the centre of the aisle--Mr. Wood and Thames taking their places on either side of it, and Jack at a little distance behind.

Jack had been touched in the morning, but he was now completely prostrated. In the midst of the holy place, which he had formerly profaned, lay the body of his unfortunate mother, and he could not help looking upon her untimely end as the retributive vengeance of Heaven for the crime he had committed. His grief was so audible, that it attracted the notice of some of the bystanders, and Thames was obliged to beg him to control it. In doing this, he chanced to raise his eyes and half fancied he beheld, shaded by a pillar at the extremity of the western aisle, the horrible countenance of the thief-taker.

Before the congregation separated, the clergyman descended from the pulpit; and, followed by the coffin-bearers and mourners, and by Jack at a respectful distance, entered the churchyard.

The carriage, which it has been mentioned drove up to the Six Bells, contained four persons,--Jonathan Wild, his two janizaries, and his porter, Obadiah Lemon. As soon as they had got out, the vehicle was drawn up at the back of a tree near the cage. Having watched the funeral at some distance, Jonathan fancied he could discern the figure of Jack; but not being quite sure, he entered the church. He was daring enough to have seized and carried him off before the whole congregation, but he preferred waiting.

Satisfied with his scrutiny, he returned, despatched Abraham and Obadiah to the northwest corner of the church, placed Quilt behind a buttress near the porch, and sheltered himself behind one of the mighty elms.

The funeral procession had now approached the grave, around which many of the congregation, who were deeply interested by the sad ceremonial, had gathered. A slight rain fell at the time; and a few leaves, caught by the eddies, whirled around. Jonathan mixed with the group, and, sure of his prey, abided his time.

The clergyman, meanwhile, proceeded with the service, while the coffin was deposited at the brink of the grave.

Just as the attendants were preparing to lower the corpse into the earth, Jack fell on his knees beside the coffin, uttering the wildest exclamations of grief, reproaching himself with the murder of his mother, and invoking the vengeance of Heaven on his own head.

A murmur ran through the assemblage, by several of whom Jack was recognised. But such was the violence of his grief,--such the compunction he exhibited, that all but one looked on with an eye of compassion. That person advanced towards him.

"I have killed her," cried Jack.

"You have," rejoined Jonathan, laying a forcible grasp on his shoulder. "You are my prisoner."

Jack started to his feet; but before he could defend himself, his right arm was grasped by the Jew who had silently approached him.

"Hell-hounds!" he cried; "release me!"

At the same moment, Quilt Arnold rushed forward with such haste, that, stumbling over William Morgan, he precipitated him into the grave.

"Wretch!" cried Jack. "Are you not content with the crimes you have committed,--but you must carry your villany to this point. Look at the poor victim at your feet."

Jonathan made no reply, but ordered his myrmidons to drag the prisoner along.

Thames, meanwhile, had drawn his sword, and was about to rush upon Jonathan; but he was withheld by Wood.

"Do not shed more blood," cried the carpenter.

Groans and hoots were now raised by the crowd, and there was an evident disposition to rescue. A small brickbat was thrown, which struck Jonathan in the face.

"You shall not pass," cried several of the crowd.

"I knew his poor mother, and for her sake I'll not see this done," cried John Dump.

"Slip on the handcuffs," cried the thief-taker. "And now let's see who'll dare to oppose me. I am Jonathan Wild. I have arrested him in the King's name."

A deep indignant groan followed.

"Let me see the earth thrown over her," implored Jack; "and take me where you please."

"No," thundered Wild.

"Allow him that small grace," cried Wood.

"No, I tell you," rejoined Jonathan, shouldering his way out of the crowd.

"My mother,--my poor mother!" exclaimed Jack.

But, in spite of his outcries and resistance, he was dragged along by Jonathan and his janizaries.

At the eastern gate of the churchyard stood the carriage with the steps lowered. The mob pursued the thief-taker and his party all the way, and such missiles as could be collected were hurled at them. They even threatened to cut the traces and take off the wheels from the carriage. The Jew got in first. The prisoner was then thrust in by Quilt. Before Jonathan followed he turned to face his assailants.

"Back!" he cried fiercely. "I am an officer in the execution of my duty. And he who opposes me in it shall feel the weight of my hand."

He then sprung into the coach, the door of which was closed by Obadiah, who mounted the box.

"To Newgate," cried Jonathan, putting his head out of the window.

A deep roar followed this order, and several missiles were launched at the vehicle, which was driven off at a furious pace.

And while her son was reconveyed to prison the body of the unfortunate Mrs. Sheppard was committed to the earth.

CHAPTER XXVII.
How Jack Sheppard was brought back to Newgate.

JACK Sheppard's escape from Newgate on the night of the 15th of October was not discovered till the following morning; for although the intelligence was brought by several parties to the Lodge in the course of the night, Austin, who was the officer in attendance, paid no attention to them.

After pursuing the fugitive as before related, Jonathan Wild returned to his own habitation, where he was occupied during the remainder of the night with Quilt Arnold and Obadiah Lemon in removing everything which, in case of a search, might tend to criminate him. Satisfied in this respect, he flung himself into a chair, for his iron frame seldom required the indulgence of a bed, and sought an hour's repose before he began the villanies of another day.

He was aroused from his slumber, about six o'clock, by the return of Abraham Mendez, who not choosing to confess that Jack had eluded his vigilance, contended himself with stating that he had kept watch till daybreak, when he had carefully searched the field, and, finding no trace of him, had thought it better to return.

This information was received by Jonathan with a lowering brow. He comforted himself, however, with the certainty which he felt of capturing his prey on the Sunday. His breakfast despatched, which he ate with a wolfish appetite, he walked over to Newgate, chuckling as he went at the consternation which his appearance would create amongst the turnkeys.

Entering the Lodge, the first person he beheld was Austin, who was only just up, and whose toilette appeared scarcely completed. A glance satisfied Jonathan that the turnkey was not aware of the prisoner's escape; and he resolved not to destroy what he considered a good jest, by a premature disclosure of it.

"You are out betimes this morning, Mr. Wild," observed Austin, as he put on his coat, and adjusted his minor bob. "Something fresh on hand, I suppose?"

"I'm come to inquire after Jack Sheppard," returned Jonathan.

"Don't alarm yourself about him, Sir," replied Austin. "He's safe enough, I assure you."

"I should like to satisfy myself on that score," rejoined Wild, drily.

"So you shall, Sir," replied Austin, who at this moment recollected, with some uneasiness, the applications at the lodge-door during the night. "I hope you don't imagine anything has gone wrong, Sir."

"It matters not what I think," replied Wild. "Come with me to the Castle."

"Instantly, Sir," replied Austin; "instantly. Here, Caliban, attend to the door, and keep the wicket locked till I return. D'ye hear. Now, Sir."

Taking the keys, he led the way, followed by Jonathan, who chuckled internally at the shock that awaited the poor fellow.

The door was opened, and Austin entered the cell, when he absolutely recoiled before the spectacle he beheld, and could scarcely have looked more alarmed if the prison had tumbled about his ears. Petrified and speechless, he turned an imploring look at Wild, who was himself filled with astonishment at the pile of rubbish lying before him.

"'Sdeath!" cried Jonathan, staring at the breach in the wall. "Some one *must* have assisted him. Unless he has dealings with the devil, he could never have done this alone."

"I firmly believe he *has* dealings with the devil," replied Austin, trembling from head to foot. "But, perhaps, he has not got beyond the room above. It's as strong, if not stronger, than this. I'll see."

So saying, he scrambled over the rubbish, and got into the chimney. But though the breach was large enough to admit him below, he could not squeeze his bulky person through the aperture into the Red Room.

"I believe he's gone," he said, returning to Jonathan. "The door's open, and the room empty."

"You believe--you *know* it," replied Jonathan, fixing one of his sternest and most searching glances upon him. "Nothing you can say to the contrary will convince me that you have not been accessory to his flight."

"I, Sir!--I swear----"

"Tush!" interrupted Jonathan, harshly. "I shall state my suspicions to the governor. Come down with me to the Lodge directly. All further examinations must be conducted in the presence of proper witnesses."

With these words, he strode out of the room, darted down the stone stairs, and, on his arrival at the Lodge, seized the rope of the great bell communicating with the interior of the prison, which he rang violently. As this was never done, except in some case of great emergency, the application was instantly answered by all the other turnkeys, by Marvel, the four partners, and Mrs. Spurling. Nothing could exceed the dismay of these personages when they learnt why they had been summoned. All seemed infected with Austin's terrors except Mrs. Spurling, who did not dare to exhibit her satisfaction otherwise than by privately pinching the arm of her expected husband.

Headed by Jonathan, all the turnkeys then repaired to the upper part of the jail, and, approaching the Red Room by a circuitous route, several doors were unlocked, and they came upon the scene of Jack's exploits. Stopping before each door, they took up the plates of the locks, examined the ponderous bolts, and were struck with the utmost astonishment at what they beheld.

Arriving at the chapel, their wonder increased. All the jailers declared it utterly impossible he could have accomplished his astonishing task unaided; but who had lent him assistance was a question they were unable to answer. Proceeding to the entry to the Lower Leads, they came to the two strong doors, and their surprise was so great at Jack's marvellous performance, that they could scarcely persuade themselves that human ingenuity could have accomplished it.

"Here's a door," remarked Ireton, when he got to that nearest the leads, "which I could have sworn would have resisted anything. I shall have no faith in future in bolts and bars."

Mounting the roof of the prison, they traced the fugitive's course to the further extremity of the building, where they found his blanket attached to the spike proving that he escaped in that direction.

After severely examining Austin, and finding it proved, on the testimony of his fellow-jailers, that he could not have aided Jack in his flight, Jonathan retracted his harsh sentence, and even went so far as to say that he would act as mediator between him and the governor.

This was some satisfaction to the poor fellow, who was dreadfully frightened, as indeed he might well be, it being the opinion of the jailers and others who afterwards examined the place, that Jack had accomplished, single-handed, in a few hours, and, as far as it could be ascertained, with imperfect implements, what it would have taken half a dozen men several days, provided with proper tools, to effect. In their opinion a hundred pounds would not repair the damage done to the prison.

As soon as Jack's escape became known, thousands of persons flocked to Newgate to behold his workmanship; and the jailers reaped am abundant harvest from their curiosity.

Jonathan, meanwhile, maintained profound secrecy as to his hopes of capturing the fugitive; and when Jack was brought back to Newgate on the Sunday evening, his arrival was wholly unexpected.

At a little after five, on that day, four horses dashed round the corner of the Old Bailey, and drew up before the door of the Lodge. Hearing the stoppage, Austin rushed out, and could scarcely believe his eyes when he beheld Jack Sheppard in the custody of Quilt Arnold and Abraham Mendez.

Jack's recapture was speedily made known to all the officers of the jail, and the Lodge was instantly crowded. The delight of the turnkeys was beyond all bounds; but poor Mrs. Spurling was in a state of distraction and began to abuse Jonathan so violently that her future husband was obliged to lay forcible hands upon her and drag her away.

By Wild's command the prisoner was taken to the Condemned Hold, whither he was followed by the whole posse of officers and by the partners; two of whom carried large hammers and two the fetters. There was only one prisoner in the ward. He was chained to the ground, but started up at their approach. It was Blueskin. When he beheld Jack he uttered a deep groan.

"Captain," he cried, in a voice of the bitterest anguish, "have these dogs again hunted you down? If you hadn't been so unlucky, I should have been with you before to-morrow night."

Jack made no answer, nor did he even cast his eyes upon his follower. But Jonathan, fixing a terrible look upon him, cried.

"Ha! say you so? You must be looked to. My lads," he continued, addressing the partners; "when you've finished this job give that fellow a fresh set of darbies. I suspect he has been at work upon those he has on."

"The link of the chain next the staple is sawn through," said Ireton, stooping to examine Blueskin's fetters.

"Search him and iron him afresh;" commanded Jonathan. "But first let us secure Sheppard. We'll then remove them both to the Middle Stone Hold, where a watch shall be kept over them night and day till they're taken to Tyburn. As they're so fond of each other's society they shan't part company even on that occasion, but shall swing from the same tree."

"You'll never live to see that day," cried Blueskin, fixing a menacing look upon him.

"What weight are these irons?" asked Jonathan, coolly addressing one of the partners.

"More than three hundred weight, Sir," replied the man. "They're the heaviest set we have,--and were forged expressly for Captain Sheppard."

"They're not half heavy enough," replied Wild. "Let him be handcuffed, and doubly ironed on both legs; and when we get him into the Stone Ward, he shall not only be chained down to the ground, but shall have two additional fetters running through the main links, fastened on each side of him. We'll see whether he'll get rid of his new bonds?" he added with a brutal laugh, which was echoed by the bystanders.

"Mark me," said Jack, sternly; "I have twice broken out of this prison in spite of all your precautions. And were you to load me with thrice the weight of iron you have ordered you should not prevent my escaping a third time."

"That's right, Captain," cried Blueskin. "We'll give them the slip yet, and hang that butcherly thief-taker upon his own gibbet."

"Be silent dog," cried Jonathan. And with his clenched hand he struck him a violent blow in the face.

For the first time, perhaps, in his life, he repented of his brutality. The blow was scarcely dealt, when, with a bound like that of a tiger, Blueskin sprang upon him. The chain, which had been partially cut through, snapped near the staple. Before any assistance could be rendered by the jailers, who stood astounded, Blueskin had got Wild in his clutches. His strength has been described as prodigious; but now, heightened by his desire for vengeance, it was irresistible. Jonathan, though a very powerful man, was like an infant in his gripe. Catching hold of his chin, he bent back the neck, while with his left hand he pulled out a clasp knife, which he opened with his teeth, and grasping Wild's head with his arm, notwithstanding his resistance, cut deeply into his throat. The folds of a thick muslin neckcloth in some degree protected him, but the gash was desperate. Blueskin drew the knife across his throat a second time, widening and deepening the wound; and wrenching back the head to get it into a more favourable position, would infallibly have severed it from the trunk, if the officers, who by this time had recovered from their terror, had not thrown themselves upon him, and withheld him.

"Now's your time," cried Blueskin, struggling desperately with his assailants and inflicting severe cuts with his knife. "Fly, Captain--fly!"

Aroused to a sense of the possibility of escape, Jack, who had viewed the deadly assault with savage satisfaction, burst from his captors and made for the door. Blueskin fought his way towards it, and exerting all his strength, cutting right and left as he proceeded, reached it at the same time. Jack in all probability, would have escaped, if Langley, who was left in the Lodge, had not been alarmed at the noise and rushed thither. Seeing Jack at liberty, he instantly seized him, and a struggle commenced.

At this moment, Blueskin came up, and kept off the officers with his knife. He used his utmost efforts to liberate Jack from Langley, but closely pressed on all sides, he was not able to render any effectual assistance.

"Fly!" cried Jack; "escape if you can; don't mind me."

Casting one look of anguish at his leader, Blueskin then darted down the passage.

The only persons in the Lodge were Mrs. Spurling and Marvel. Hearing the noise of the scuffle, the tapstress, fancying it was Jack making an effort to escape, in spite of the remonstrances of the executioner, threw open the wicket. Blueskin therefore had nothing to stop him. Dashing through the open door, he crossed the Old Bailey, plunged into a narrow court on the opposite side of the way, and was out of sight in a minute, baffling all pursuit.

On their return, the jailers raised up Jonathan, who was weltering in his blood, and who appeared to be dying. Efforts were made to staunch his wounds and surgical assistance sent for.

"Has he escaped?" asked the thief-taker, faintly.

"Blueskin," said Ireton.

"No--Sheppard?" rejoined Wild.

"No, no, Sir," replied Ireton. "He's here."

"That's right," replied Wild, with a ghastly smile. "Remove him to the Middle Stone Hold,--watch over him night and day, do you mind?"

"I do, Sir."

"Irons--heavy irons--night and day."

"Depend upon it, Sir."

"Go with him to Tyburn,--never lose sight of him till the noose is tied. Where's Marvel?"

"Here, Sir," replied the executioner.

"A hundred guineas if you hang Jack Sheppard. I have it about me. Take it, if I die."

"Never fear, Sir," replied Marvel.

"Oh! that I could live to see it," gasped Jonathan. And with a hideous expression of pain, he fainted.

"He's dead," exclaimed Austin.

"I am content," said Jack. "My mother is avenged. Take me to the Stone Room. Blueskin, you are a true friend."

The body of Jonathan was then conveyed to his own habitation, while Jack was taken to the Middle Stone Room, and ironed in the manner Wild had directed.

CHAPTER XXVIII.
What happened at Dollis Hill.

At length this tragedy is at an end," said Mr. Wood, as, having seen the earth thrown over the remains of the unfortunate Mrs. Sheppard, he turned to quit the churchyard. "Let us hope that, like her who 'loved much,' her sins are forgiven her."

Without another word, and accompanied by Thames, he then took his way to Dollis Hill in a state of the deepest depression. Thames did not attempt to offer him any consolation, for he was almost as much dejected. The weather harmonized with their feelings. It rained slightly, and a thick mist gathered in the air, and obscured the beautiful prospect.

On his arrival at Dollis Hill, Mr. Wood was so much exhausted that he was obliged to retire to his own room, where he continued for some hours overpowered by grief. The two lovers sat together, and their sole discourse turned upon Jack and his ill-fated mother.

As the night advanced, Mr. Wood again made his appearance in a more composed frame of mind, and, at his daughter's earnest solicitation, was induced to partake of some refreshment. An hour was then passed in conversation as to the possibility of rendering any assistance to Jack; in deploring his unhappy destiny; and in the consideration of the course to be pursued in reference to Jonathan Wild.

While they were thus occupied, a maid-servant entered the room, and stated that a person was without who had a packet for Captain Darrell, which must be delivered into his own hands. Notwithstanding the remonstrances of Wood and Winifred, Thames instantly followed the domestic, and found a man, with his face muffled up, at the door, as she had described. Somewhat alarmed at his appearance, Thames laid his hand upon his sword.

"Fear nothing, Sir," said the man, in a voice which Thames instantly recognised as that of Blueskin. "I am come to render you a service. There are the packets which my Captain hazarded his life to procure for you, and which he said would establish your right to the estates of the Trenchard family. There are also the letters which were scattered about Wild's room after the murder of Sir Rowland. And there," he added, placing in his hands a heavy bag of money, and a pocket-book, "is a sum little short of fifteen thousand pounds."

"How have you procured these things?" asked Thames, in the utmost astonishment.

"I carried them off on the fatal night when we got into Wild's house, and you were struck down," replied Blueskin. "They have ever since been deposited in a place of safety. You have nothing more to fear from Wild."

"How so?" asked Thames.

"I have saved the executioner a labour, by cutting his throat," replied Blueskin. "And, may I be cursed if I ever did anything in my whole life which gave me so much satisfaction."

"Almighty God! is this possible?" exclaimed Thames.

"You will find it true," replied Blueskin. "All I regret is, that I failed in liberating the Captain. If he had got off, they might have hanged me, and welcome."

"What can be done for him?" cried Thames.

"That's not an easy question to answer," rejoined Blueskin. "But I shall watch night and day about Newgate, in the hope of getting him out. He wouldn't require my aid, but before I stopped Jonathan's mouth, he had ordered him to be doubly-ironed, and constantly watched. And, though the villain can't see his orders executed, I've no doubt some one else will."

"Poor Jack!" exclaimed Thames. "I would sacrifice all my fortune--all my hopes--to liberate him."

"If you're in earnest," rejoined Blueskin, "give me that bag of gold. It contains a thousand pounds; and, if all other schemes fail, I'll engage to free him on the way to Tyburn."

"May I trust you?" hesitated Thames.

"Why did I not keep the money when I had it?" returned Blueskin, angrily. "Not a farthing of it shall be expended except in the Captain's service."

"Take it," replied Thames.

"You have saved his life," replied Blueskin. "And now, mark me. You owe what I have done for you, to him, not to me. Had I not known that you and your affianced bride are dearer to him than life I should have used this money to secure my own safety. Take it, and take the estates, in Captain Sheppard's name. Promise me one thing before I leave you."

"What is it?" asked Thames.

"If the Captain *is* taken to Tyburn, be near the place of execution--at the end of the Edgeware Road."

"I will."

"In case of need you will lend a helping hand?"

"Yes--yes."

"Swear it!"

"I do."

"Enough!" rejoined Blueskin. And he departed, just as Wood, who had become alarmed by Thames's long absence, made his appearance with a blunderbuss in his hand.

Hastily acquainting him with the treasures he had unexpectedly obtained, Thames returned to the room to apprize Winifred of his good fortune. The packets were hastily broken open; and, while Wood was absorbed in the perusal of the despatch addressed to him by Sir Rowland, Thames sought out, and found the letter which he had been prevented from finishing on the fatal night at Jonathan Wild's. As soon as he had read it, he let it fall from his grasp.

Winifred instantly picked it up.

"You are no longer Thames Darrell," she said, casting her eyes rapidly over it; "but the Marquis de Chatillon."

"My father was of the blood-royal of France," exclaimed Thames.

"Eh-day! what's this?" cried Wood, looking up from beneath his spectacles. "Who--who is the Marquis de Chatillon?"

"Your adopted son, Thames Darrell," answered Winifred.

"And the Marchioness is your daughter," added Thames.

"O, Lord!" ejaculated Wood. "My head fairly turns round. So many distresses--so many joys coming at the same time are too much for me. Read that letter,

Thames--my lord marquis, I mean. Read it, and you'll find that your unfortunate uncle, Sir Rowland, surrenders to you all the estates in Lancashire. You've nothing to do but to take possession."

"What a strange history is mine!" said Thames. "Kidnapped, and sent to France by one uncle, it was my lot to fall into the hands of another,--my father's own brother, the Marshal Gaucher de Chatillon; to whom, and to the Cardinal Dubois, I owed all my good fortune."

"The ways of Providence are inscrutable," observed Wood.

"When in France, I heard from the Marshal that his brother had perished in London on the night of the Great Storm. It was supposed he was drowned in crossing the river, as his body had never been found. Little did I imagine at the time that it was my own father to whom he referred."

"I think I remember reading something about your father in the papers," observed Wood. "Wasn't he in some way connected with the Jacobite plots?"

"He was," replied Thames. "He had been many years in this country before his assassination took place. In this letter, which is addressed to my ill-fated mother, he speaks of his friendship for Sir Rowland, whom it seems he had known abroad; but entreats her to keep the marriage secret for a time, for reasons which are not fully developed."

"And so Sir Rowland murdered his friend," remarked Wood. "Crime upon crime."

"Unconsciously, perhaps," replied Thames. "But be it as it may, he is now beyond the reach of earthly punishment."

"But Wild still lives," cried Wood.

"He; also, has paid the penalty of his offences," returned Thames. "He has fallen by the hand of Blueskin, who brought me these packets."

"Thank God for that!" cried Wood, heartily. "I could almost forgive the wretch the injury he did me in depriving me of my poor dear wife--No, not quite *that*," he added, a little confused.

"And now," said Thames, (for we must still preserve the name,) "you will no longer defer my happiness."

"Hold!" interposed Winifred, gravely. "I release you from your promise. A carpenter's daughter is no fit match for a peer of France."

"If my dignity must be purchased by the loss of you, I renounce it," cried Thames. "You will not make it valueless in my eyes," he added, catching her in his arms, and pressing her to his breast.

"Be it as you please," replied Winifred. "My lips would belie my heart were I to refuse you."

"And now, father, your blessing--your consent!" cried Thames.

"You have both," replied Wood, fervently. "I am too much honoured--too happy in the union. Oh! that I should live to be father-in-law to a peer of France! What would my poor wife say to it, if she could come to life again? Oh, Thames!--my lord marquis, I mean--you have made me the happiest--the proudest of mankind."

Not many days after this event, on a bright October morning, the bells rang a merry peal from the old gray tower of Willesden church. All the village was assembled in the churchyard. Young and old were dressed in their gayest apparel; and it was evident from the smiles that lighted up every countenance, from the roguish looks of the younger swains, and the demure expression of several pretty rustic maidens, that a ceremony, which never fails to interest all classes,--a wedding,--was about to take place.

At the gate opening upon the road leading to Dollis Hill were stationed William Morgan and John Dump. Presently, two carriages dashed down the hill, and drew up before it. From the first of these alighted Thames, or, as he must now be styled, the Marquis de Chatillon. From the second descended Mr. Wood--and after him came his daughter.

The sun never shone upon a lovelier couple than now approached the altar. The church was crowded to excess by the numbers eager to witness the ceremony; and as soon as it was over the wedded pair were followed to the carriage, and the loudest benedictions uttered for their happiness.

In spite of the tumultuous joy which agitated him, the bridegroom could not prevent the intrusion of some saddening thoughts, as he reflected upon the melancholy scene which he had so recently witnessed in the same place.

The youthful couple had been seated in the carriage a few minutes when they were joined by Mr. Wood, who had merely absented himself to see that a public breakfast, which he had ordered at the Six Bells for all who chose to partake of it, was in readiness. He likewise gave directions that in the after part of the day a whole bullock should be roasted on the green and distributed, together with a bar-rel of the strongest ale.

In the evening, a band of village musicians, accompanied by most of the young inhabitants of Willesden, strolled out to Dollis Hill, where they formed a rustic concert under the great elm before the door. Here they were regaled with another plentiful meal by the hospitable carpenter, who personally superintended the re-past.

These festivities, however, were not witnessed by the newly-married pair, who had departed immediately after the ceremony for Manchester.

CHAPTER XXIX.
How Jack Sheppard was taken to Westminster Hall.

L OADED with the heaviest fetters, and constantly watched by two of the jailers' assistants, who neither quitted him for a single moment, nor suffered any visitor to approach him, Jack Sheppard found all attempts to escape impracticable.

He was confined in the Middle Stone Ward, a spacious apartment, with good light and air, situated over the gateway on the western side, and allotted to him, not for his own convenience, but for that of the keepers, who, if he had been placed in a gloomier or more incommodious dungeon, would have necessarily had to share it with him.

Through this, his last trial, Jack's spirits never deserted him. He seemed resigned but cheerful, and held frequent and serious discourses with the ordinary, who felt satisfied of his sincere penitence. The only circumstance which served to awaken a darker feeling in his breast was, that his implacable foe Jonathan Wild had survived the wound inflicted by Blueskin, and was slowly recovering.

As soon as he could be moved with safety, Jonathan had himself transported to Newgate, where he was carried into the Middle Ward, that he might feast his eyes upon his victim. Having seen every precaution taken to ensure his safe custody, he departed, muttering to himself, "I shall yet live to see him hanged--I shall live to see him hanged."

Animated by his insatiate desire of vengeance, he seemed to gain strength daily,--so much so, that within a fortnight after receiving his wound he was able to stir abroad.

On Thursday, the 12th of November, after having endured nearly a month's imprisonment, Jack Sheppard was conveyed from Newgate to Westminster Hall.

He was placed in a coach, handcuffed, and heavily fettered, and guarded by a vast posse of officers to Temple Bar, where a fresh relay of constables escorted him to Westminster.

By this time, Jack's reputation had risen to such a height with the populace,--his exploits having become the universal theme of discourse, that the streets were almost impassable for the crowds collected to obtain a view of him. The vast area in front of Westminster Hall was thronged with people, and it was only by a vigorous application of their staves that the constables could force a passage for the vehicle. At length, however, the prisoner was got out, when such was the rush of the multitude that several persons were trampled down, and received severe injuries.

Arrived in the Hall, the prisoner's handcuffs were removed, and he was taken before the Court of King's Bench. The record of his conviction at the Old Bailey sessions was then read; and as no objection was offered to it, the Attorney-General moved that his execution might take place on Monday next. Upon this, Jack earnestly and eloquently addressed himself to the bench, and besought that a petition which he had prepared to be laid before the King might be read. This request, however, was refused; and he was told that the only way in which he could entitle himself to his Majesty's clemency would be by discovering who had abetted him in his last escape; the strongest suspicions being entertained that he had not affected it alone.

Sheppard replied by a solemn assertion, "that he had received no assistance except from Heaven."--An answer for which he was immediately reprimanded by the court. It having been stated that it was wholly impossible he could have removed his irons in the way he represented, he offered, if his handcuffs were replaced, to take them off in the presence of the court. The proposal, however, was not acceded to; and the Chief Justice Powis, after enumerating his various offences and commenting upon their heinousness, awarded sentence of death against him for the following Monday.

As Jack was removed, he noticed Jonathan Wild at a little distance from him, eyeing him with a look of the most savage satisfaction. The thief-taker's throat was bound up with thick folds of linen, and his face had a ghastly and cadaverous look, which communicated an undefinable and horrible expression to his glances.

Meanwhile, the mob outside had prodigiously increased, and had begun to exhibit some disposition to riot. The coach in which the prisoner had been conveyed was already broken to pieces, and the driver was glad to escape with life. Terrific shouts were raised by the rabble, who threatened to tear Wild in pieces if he showed himself.

Amid this tumult, several men armed with tremendous bludgeons, with their faces besmeared with grease and soot, and otherwise disguised, were observed to be urging the populace to attempt a rescue. They were headed by an athletic-looking, swarthy-featured man, who was armed with a cutlass, which he waved over his head to cheer on his companions.

These desperadoes had been the most active in demolishing the coach, and now, being supported by the rabble, they audaciously approached the very portals of the ancient Hall. The shouts, yells, and groans which they uttered, and which were echoed by the concourse in the rear, were perfectly frightful.

Jonathan, who with the other constables had reconnoitred this band, and recognised in its ring-leader, Blueskin, commanded the constables to follow him, and made a sally for the purpose of seizing him. Enfeebled by his wound, Wild had lost much of his strength, though nothing of his ferocity and energy,--and fiercely assailing Blueskin, he made a desperate but unsuccessful attempt to apprehend him.

He was, however, instantly beaten back; and the fury of the mob was so great that it was with difficulty he could effect a retreat. The whole force of the constables, jailers and others was required to keep the crowd out of the Hall. The doors were closed and barricaded, and the mob threatened to burst them open if Jack was not delivered to them.

Things now began to wear so serious a aspect that a messenger was secretly despatched to the Savoy for troops, and in half an hour a regiment of the guards arrived, who by dint of great exertion succeeded in partially dispersing the tumultuous assemblage. Another coach was then procured, in which the prisoner was placed.

Jack's appearance was hailed with the loudest cheers, but when Jonathan followed and took a place beside him in the vehicle, determined, he said, never to lose sight of him, the abhorrence of the multitude was expressed by execrations, hoots, and yells of the most terrific kind. So dreadful were these shouts as to produce an effect upon the hardened feelings of Jonathan, who shrank out of sight.

It was well for him that he had taken his place by Sheppard, as regard for the latter alone prevented the deadliest missiles being hurled at him. As it was, the mob went on alternately hooting and huzzaing as the names of Wild and Sheppard were pronounced, while some individuals, bolder than the rest, thrust their faces into the coach-window, and assured Jack that he should never be taken to Tyburn.

"We'll see that, you yelping hounds!" rejoined Jonathan, glaring fiercely at them.

In this way, Jack was brought back to Newgate, and again chained down in the Middle Ward.

It was late before Jonathan ventured to his own house, where he remained up all night, and kept his janizaries and other assistants well armed.

CHAPTER XXX.
How Jonathan Wild's House was burnt down.

THE day appointed for the execution was now close at hand, and the prisoner, who seemed to have abandoned all hopes of escape, turned his thoughts entirely from worldly considerations.

On Sunday, he was conveyed to the chapel, through which he had passed on the occasion of his great escape, and once more took his seat in the Condemned Pew. The Rev. Mr. Purney, the ordinary, who had latterly conceived a great regard for Jack, addressed him in a discourse, which, while it tended to keep alive his feelings of penitence, was calculated to afford him much consolation. The chapel was crowded to excess. But here,--even here, the demon was suffered to intrude, and Jack's thoughts were distracted by Jonathan Wild, who stood at a little distance from him, and kept his bloodthirsty eyes fixed on him during the whole of the service.

On that night, an extraordinary event occurred, which convinced the authorities that every precaution must be taken in conducting Jack to Tyburn,--a fact of which they had been previously made aware, though scarcely to the same extent, by the riotous proceedings near Westminster Hall. About nine o'clock, an immense mob collected before the Lodge at Newgate. It was quite dark; but as some of the assemblage carried links, it was soon ascertained to be headed by the same party who had mainly incited the former disturbance. Amongst the ring-leaders was Blueskin, whose swarthy features and athletic figure were easily distinguished. Another was Baptist Kettleby, and a third, in a Dutch dress, was recognised by his grizzled beard as the skipper, Van Galgebrok.

Before an hour had elapsed, the concourse was fearfully increased. The area in front of the jail was completely filled. Attempts were made upon the door of the

Lodge; but it was too strong to be forced. A cry was then raised by the leaders to attack Wild's house, and the fury of the mob was instantly directed to that quarter. Wrenched from their holds, the iron palisades in front of the thief-taker's dwelling were used as weapons to burst open the door.

While this was passing, Jonathan opened one of the upper windows, and fired several shots upon the assailants. But though he made Blueskin and Kettleby his chief marks, he missed both. The sight of the thief-taker increased the fury of the mob to a fearful degree. Terrific yells rent the air. The heavy weapon thundered against the door; and it speedily yielded to their efforts.

"Come on, my lads!" vociferated Blueskin, "we'll unkennel the old fox."

As he spoke, several shots were fired from the upper part of the house, and two men fell mortally wounded. But this only incensed the assailing party the more. With a drawn cutlass in one hand and a cocked pistol in the other, Blueskin rushed up stairs. The landing was defended by Quilt Arnold and the Jew. The former was shot by Blueskin through the head, and his body fell over the bannisters. The Jew, who was paralysed by his companion's fate, offered no resistance, and was instantly seized.

"Where is your accursed master?" demanded Blueskin, holding the sword to his throat.

The Jew did not speak, but pointed to the audience-chamber. Committing him to the custody of the others, Blueskin, followed by a numerous band, darted in that direction. The door was locked; but, with the bars of iron, it was speedily burst open. Several of the assailants carried links, so that the room was a blaze of light. Jonathan, however, was nowhere to be seen.

Rushing towards the entrance of the well-hole, Blueskin touched the secret spring. He was not there. Opening the trap-door, he then descended to the vaults-- searched each cell, and every nook and corner separately. Wild had escaped.

Robbed of their prey, the fury of the mob became ungovernable. At length, at the end of a passage, next to the cell where Mrs. Sheppard had been confined, Blue-skin discovered a trap-door which he had not previously noticed. It was instantly burst open, when the horrible stench that issued from it convinced them that it must be a receptacle for the murdered victims of the thief-taker.

Holding a link into the place, which had the appearance of a deep pit, Blueskin noticed a body richly dressed. He dragged it out, and perceiving, in spite of the decayed frame, that it was the body of Sir Rowland Trenchard, commanded his attendants to convey it up stairs--an order which was promptly obeyed.

Returning to the audience-chamber, Blueskin had the Jew brought before him. The body of Sir Rowland was then laid on the large table. Opposite to it was placed the Jew. Seeing from the threatening looks of his captors, that they were about to wreak their vengeance upon him, the miserable wretch besought mercy in abject terms, and charged his master with the most atrocious crimes. His relation of the murder of Sir Rowland petrified even his fierce auditors.

One of the cases in Jonathan's museum was now burst open, and a rope taken from it. In spite of his shrieks, the miserable Jew was then dragged into the well-hole, and the rope being tied round his neck, he was launched from the bridge.

The vengeance of the assailants did not stop here. They broke open the entrance into Jonathan's store-room--plundered it of everything valuable--ransacked every closet, drawer, and secret hiding-place, and stripped them of their contents. Large hoards of money were discovered, gold and silver plate, cases of watches, and various precious articles. Nothing, in short, portable or valuable was left. Old implements of housebreaking were discovered; and the thief-taker's most hidden depositories were laid bare.

The work of plunder over, that of destruction commenced. Straw and other combustibles being collected, were placed in the middle of the audience-chamber. On these were thrown all the horrible contents of Jonathan's museum, together with the body of Sir Rowland Trenchard. The whole was then fired, and in a few minutes the room was a blaze. Not content with this, the assailants set fire to the house in half-a-dozen other places; and the progress of the flames was rapid and destructive.

Meanwhile, the object of all this fearful disturbance had made his escape to Newgate, from the roof of which he witnessed the destruction of his premises. He saw the flames burst from the windows, and perhaps in that maddening spectacle suffered torture equivalent to some of the crimes he had committed.

While he was thus standing, the flames of his house, which made the whole street as light as day, and ruddily illumined the faces of the mob below, betrayed him to them, and he was speedily driven from his position by a shower of stones and other missiles.

The mob now directed their attention to Newgate; and, from their threats, appeared determined to fire it. Ladders, paviour's rams, sledge-hammers, and other destructive implements were procured, and, in all probability, their purpose would have been effected, but for the opportune arrival of a detachment of the guards, who dispersed them, not without some loss of life.

Several prisoners were taken, but the ring-leaders escaped. Engines were brought to play upon Wild's premises, and upon the adjoining houses. The latter were saved; but of the former nothing but the blackened stone walls were found standing on the morrow.

CHAPTER XXXI.
The Procession to Tyburn.

THE noise of this disturbance did not fail to reach the interior of the prison. In fact, the reflection of the flames lighted up the ward in which Jack Sheppard was confined.

The night his execution was therefore passed in a most anxious state of mind; nor was his uneasiness allayed by the appearance of Jonathan Wild, who, after he had been driven from the roof of the jail, repaired to the Middle Stone Ward in a fit of ungovernable passion, to vent his rage upon the prisoner, whom he looked upon as the cause of the present calamity. Such was his fury, that if he had not been restrained by the presence of the two turnkeys, he might perhaps have anticipated the course of justice, by laying violent hands upon his victim.

After venting his wrath in the wildest manner, and uttering the most dreadful execrations, Jonathan retired to another part of the prison, where he passed the night in consultation with the governor, as to the best means of conveying the prisoner securely to Tyburn. Mr. Pitt endeavoured to dissuade him from attending in person, representing the great risk he would incur from the mob, which was certain to be assembled. But Jonathan was not to be deterred.

"I have sworn to see him hanged," he said, "and nothing shall keep me away-- nothing, by----."

By Wild's advice, the usual constabulary force was greatly augmented. Messengers were despatched to all the constables and head-boroughs to be in attendance,-- to the sheriffs to have an extraordinary number of their officers in attendance,--and to the Savoy, to obtain the escort of a troop of grenadier-guards. In short, more preparations were made than if a state criminal was about to be executed.

The morning of Monday the 16th of November 1724 at length dawned. It was a dull, foggy day, and the atmosphere was so thick and heavy, that, at eight o'clock, the curious who arrived near the prison could scarcely discern the tower of St. Sepulchre's church.

By and by the tramp of horses' feet was heard slowly ascending Snow Hill, and presently a troop of grenadier guards rode into the area facing Newgate. These were presently joined by a regiment of foot. A large body of the constables of Westminster next made their appearance, the chief of whom entered the Lodge, where they were speedily joined by the civic authorities. At nine o'clock, the sheriffs arrived, followed by their officers and javelin-men.

Meantime, the Stone Hall was crowded by all the inmates of the jail, debtors, felons, turnkeys, and officers who could obtain permission to witness the ceremony of the prisoner's irons being struck off. Caliban, who, through the interest of Mr. Ireton, was appointed to the office, stood with a hammer in one hand, and a punch in the other, near the great stone block, ready to fulfil his duty. Close behind him stood the tall gaunt figure of Marvel, with his large bony hands, his scraggy neck, and ill-favoured countenance. Next to the executioner stood his wife--the former Mrs. Spurling. Mrs. Marvel held her handkerchief to her eyes, and appeared in great distress. But her husband, whose deportment to her was considerably changed since the fatal knot had been tied, paid no attention whatever to her grief.

At this moment, the bell of Newgate began to toll, and was answered by another bell from St. Sepulchre's. The great door of the Stone Hall was thrown open, and the sheriffs, preceded by the javelin-men, entered the room. They were followed by Jonathan, who carried a stout stick under his arm, and planted himself near the stone. Not a word was uttered by the assemblage; but a hush of expectation reigned throughout.

Another door was next opened, and, preceded by the ordinary, with the sacred volume in his hand, the prisoner entered the room. Though encumbered by his irons, his step was firm, and his demeanour dignified. His countenance was pale as death, but not a muscle quivered; nor did he betray the slightest appearance of fear. On the contrary, it was impossible to look at him without perceiving that his resolution was unshaken.

Advancing with a slow firm step to the stone-block he placed his left foot upon it, drew himself up to his full height, and fixed a look so stern upon Jonathan, that the thief-taker quailed before it.

The black, meantime, began to ply his hammer, and speedily unriveted the chains. The first stroke appeared to arouse all the vindictive passions of Jonathan. Fixing a ferocious and exulting look upon Jack Sheppard, he exclaimed.

"At length, my vengeance is complete."

"Wretch!" cried Jack, raising his hand in a menacing manner, "your triumph will be short-lived. Before a year has expired, you will share the same fate."

"If I do, I care not," rejoined Wild; "I shall have lived to see you hanged."

"O Jack, dear, dear Jack!" cried Mrs. Marvel, who was now quite dissolved in tears, "I shall never survive this scene."

"Hold your tongue, hussy!" cried her husband gruffly. "Women ought never to show themselves on these occasions, unless they can behave themselves properly."

"Farewell, Jack," cried twenty voices.

Sheppard looked round, and exchanged kindly glances with several of those who addressed him.

"My limbs feel so light, now that my irons are removed," he observed with a smile, "that I am half inclined to dance."

"You'll dance upon nothing, presently," rejoined Jonathan, brutally.

"Farewell for ever," said Jack, extending his hand to Mrs. Marvel.

"Farewell!" blubbered the executioner's wife, pressing his hand to her lips. "Here are a pair of gloves and a nosegay for you. Oh dear!--oh dear! Be careful of him," she added to her husband, "and get it over quickly, or never expect to see me again."

"Peace, fool!" cried Marvel, angrily. "Do you think I don't know my own business?"

Austin and Langley then advanced to the prisoner, and, twinning their arms round his, led him down to the Lodge, whither he was followed by the sheriffs, the ordinary, Wild, and the other officials.

Meantime, every preparation had been made outside for his departure. At the end of two long lines of foot-guards stood the cart with a powerful black horse harnessed to it. At the head of the cart was placed the coffin. On the right were several mounted grenadiers: on the left, some half dozen javelin-men. Soldiers were stationed at different points of the street to keep off the mob, and others were riding backwards and forwards to maintain an open space for the passage of the procession.

The assemblage which was gathered together was almost countless. Every house-top, every window, every wall, every projection, had its occupants. The wall of St. Sepulchre's church was covered--so was the tower. The concourse extended along Giltspur Street as far as Smithfield. No one was allowed to pass along Newgate Street, which was barricaded and protected by a strong constabulary force.

The first person who issued from the Lodge was Mr. Marvel, who proceeded to the cart, and took his seat upon the coffin. The hangman is always an object of peculiar detestation to the mob, a tremendous hooting hailed his appearance, and both staves and swords were required to preserve order.

A deep silence, however, now prevailed, broken only by the tolling of the bells of Newgate and St. Sepulchre's. The mighty concourse became for a moment still. Suddenly, such a shout as has seldom smitten human ears rent the air. "He comes!" cried a thousand voices, and the shout ascended to Smithfield, descended to Snow Hill, and told those who were assembled on Holborn Hill that Sheppard had left the prison.

Between the two officers, with their arms linked in his, Jack Sheppard was conducted to the cart. He looked around, and as he heard that deafening shout,--as he felt the influence of those thousand eyes fixed upon him,--as he listened to the cheers, all his misgivings--if he had any--vanished, and he felt more as if he were marching to a triumph, than proceeding to a shameful death.

Jack had no sooner taken his place in the cart, than he was followed by the ordinary, who seated himself beside him, and, opening the book of prayer, began to read aloud. Excited by the scene, Jack, however, could pay little attention to the good man's discourse, and was lost in a whirl of tumultuous emotions.

The calvacade was now put slowly in motion. The horse-soldiers wheeled round and cleared a path: the foot closed in upon the cart. Then came the javelin-men, walking four abreast, and lastly, a long line of constables, marching in the same order.

The procession had just got into line of march, when a dreadful groan, mixed with yells, hootings, and execrations, was heard. This was occasioned by Jonathan Wild, who was seen to mount his horse and join the train. Jonathan, however, paid no sort of attention to this demonstration of hatred. He had buckled on his hanger, and had two brace of pistols in his belt, as well as others in this holsters.

By this time, the procession had reached the west end of the wall of St. Sepulchre's church, where, in compliance with an old custom, it halted. By the will of Mr. Robert Dow, merchant tailor, it was appointed that the sexton of St. Sepulchre's should pronounce a solemn exhortation upon every criminal on his way to Tyburn, for which office he was to receive a small stipend. As soon as the cavalcade stopped, the sexton advanced, and, ringing a handbell, pronounced the following admonition.

"All good people pray heartily unto God for this poor sinner, who is now going to take his death, for whom this great bell doth toll.

"You who are condemned to die, repent with lamentable tears. Ask mercy of the Lord for the salvation of your own soul, through the merits of the death and passion of Jesus Christ, who now sits at the right hand of God, to make intercession for you, if you penitently return to him. The Lord have mercy upon you!"

This ceremony concluded, the calvacade was again put in motion.

Slowly descending Snow Hill, the train passed on its way, attended by the same stunning vociferations, cheers, yells, and outcries, which had accompanied it on starting from Newgate. The guards had great difficulty in preserving a clear passage without resorting to severe measures, for the tide, which poured upon them behind, around, in front, and at all sides, was almost irresistible. The houses on Snow Hill were thronged, like those in Old Bailey. Every window, from the groundfloor to the garret had its occupant, and the roofs were covered with spectators. Words of encouragement and sympathy were addressed to Jack, who, as he looked around, beheld many a friendly glance fixed upon him.

In this way, they reached Holborn Bridge. Here a little delay occurred. The passage was so narrow that there was only sufficient room for the cart to pass, with a single line of foot-soldiers on one side; and, as the walls of the bridge were covered with spectators, it was not deemed prudent to cross it till these persons were dislodged.

While this was effected, intelligence was brought that a formidable mob was pouring down Field Lane, the end of which was barricaded. The advanced guard rode on to drive away any opposition, while the main body of the procession crossed the bridge, and slowly toiled up Holborn Hill.

The entrance of Shoe Lane, and the whole line of the wall of St. Andrew's church, the bell of which was tolling, was covered with spectators. Upon the steps leading to the gates of the church stood two persons whom Jack instantly recognised. These were his mistresses, Poll Maggot and Edgeworth Bess. As soon as the latter beheld him, she uttered a loud scream, and fainted. She was caught by some of the bystanders, who offered by her every assistance in their power. As to Mrs. Maggot, whose nerves were more firmly strung, she contented herself with waving her hand affectionately to her lover, and encouraging him by her gestures.

While this was taking place, another and more serious interruption occurred. The advanced guard had endeavoured to disperse the mob in Field Lane, but were not prepared to meet with the resistance they encountered. The pavement had been hastily picked up, and heaped across the end of the street, upon which planks, barrels, and other barricades, were laid. Most of the mob were armed with pikes, staves, swords, muskets, and other weapons, and offered a most desperate resistance to the soldiery, whom they drove back with a shower of paving-stones.

The arrival of the cart at the end of Field Lane, appeared the signal for an attempt at rescue. With a loud shout, and headed by a powerfully-built man, with a face as black as that of a mulatto, and armed with a cutlass, the rabble leapt over the barricades, and rushed towards the vehicle. An immediate halt took place. The soldiers surrounded the cart, drew their swords, and by striking the rioters first with the blunt edge of their blades, and afterwards with the sharp points, succeeded in driving them back.

Amid this skirmish Jonathan greatly distinguished himself. Drawing his hanger he rode amongst the crowd, trampled upon those most in advance, and made an attempt to seize their leader, in whom he recognised Blueskin.

Baffled in their attempt, the mob uttered a roar, such as only a thousand angry voices can utter, and discharged a volley of missiles at the soldiery. Stones and brickbats were showered on all sides, and Mr. Marvel was almost dislodged from his seat on the coffin by a dead dog, which was hurled against him, and struck him in the face.

At length, however, by dealing blows right and left with their swords, and even inflicting severe cuts on the foremost of the rabble, the soldiers managed to gain a clear course, and to drive back the assailants; who, as they retreated behind the barricades, shouted in tones of defiance, "To Tyburn! to Tyburn!"

The object of all this tumult, meanwhile, never altered his position, but sat back in the cart, as if resolved not to make even a struggle to regain his liberty.

The procession now wound its way, without further interruption, along Holborn. Like a river swollen by many currents, it gathered force from the various avenues that poured their streams into it. Fetter Lane, on the left, Gray's Inn, on the right, added their supplies. On all hands Jack was cheered, and Jonathan hooted.

At length, the train approached St. Giles's. Here, according to another old custom, already alluded to, a criminal taken to execution was allowed to halt at a tavern, called the Crown, and take a draught from St. Giles's bowl, "as his last refreshment on earth." At the door of this tavern, which was situated on the left of the street, not more than a hundred yards distant from the church, the bell of which began to toll as soon as the procession came in sight, the cart drew up, and the whole cavalcade halted. A wooden balcony in one of the adjoining houses was thronged with ladies, all of whom appeared to take a lively interest in the scene, and to be full of commiseration for the criminal, not, perhaps, unmixed with admiration of his appearance. Every window in the public house was filled with guests; and, as in the case of St. Andrew's, the churchyard wall of St. Giles's was lined with spectators.

A scene now ensued, highly characteristic of the age, and the occasion. The doleful procession at once assumed a festive character. Many of the soldiers dismounted, and called for drink. Their example was immediately imitated by the officers, constables, javelin men, and other attendants; and nothing was to be heard but shouts of laughter and jesting,--nothing seen but the passing of glasses, and the emptying of foaming jugs. Mr. Marvel, who had been a little discomposed by the treatment he had experienced on Holborn Hill, very composedly filled and lighted his pipe.

One group at the door attracted Jack's attention, inasmuch as it was composed of several of his old acquaintances--Mr. Kneebone, Van Galgebrok, and Baptist Kettleby--all of whom greeted him cordially. Besides these, there was a sturdy-looking fellow, whom he instantly recognised as the honest blacksmith who had freed him from his irons at Tottenham.

"I am here, you see," said the smith.

"So I perceive," replied Jack.

At this moment, the landlord of the Crown, a jovial-looking stout personage, with a white apron round his waist, issued from the house, bearing a large wooden bowl filled with ale, which he offered to Jack, who instantly rose to receive it. Raising the bowl in his right hand, Jack glanced towards the balcony, in which the group of ladies were seated, and begged to drink their healths; he then turned to Kneebone and the others, who extended their hands towards him, and raised it to his lips. Just as he was about to drain it, he encountered the basilisk glance of Jonathan Wild, and paused.

"I leave this bowl for you," he cried, returning it to the landlord untasted.

"Your father said so before you," replied Jonathan, malignantly; "and yet it has tarried thus long."

"You will call for it before six months are passed," rejoined Jack, sternly.

Once again the cavalcade was in motion, and winding its way by St. Giles's church, the bell of which continued tolling all the time, passed the pound, and entered Oxford Road, or, as it was then not unfrequently termed, Tyburn Road. After passing Tottenham Court Road, very few houses were to be seen on the right hand, opposite Wardour Street it was open country.

The crowd now dispersed amongst the fields, and thousands of persons were seen hurrying towards Tyburn as fast as their legs could carry them, leaping over hedges, and breaking down every impediment in their course.

Besides those who conducted themselves more peaceably, the conductors of the procession noticed with considerable uneasiness, large bands of men armed with staves, bludgeons, and other weapons, who were flying across the field in the same direction. As it was feared that some mischief would ensue, Wild volunteered, if he were allowed a small body of men, to ride forward to Tyburn, and keep the ground clear until the arrival of the prisoner.

This suggestion being approved, was instantly acted upon, and the thief-taker, accompanied by a body of the grenadiers, rode forward.

The train, meantime, had passed Marylebone Lane, when it again paused for a moment, at Jack's request, near the door of a public-house called the City of Oxford.

Scarcely had it come to a halt, when a stalwart man shouldered his way, in spite of their opposition, through the lines of soldiery to the cart, and offered his large horny hand to the prisoner.

"I told you I would call to bid you farewell, Mr. Figg," said Jack.

"So you did," replied the prize-fighter. "Sorry you're obliged to keep your word. Heard of your last escape. Hoped you'd not be retaken. Never sent for the shirt."

"I didn't want it," replied Jack; "but who are those gentlemen?"

"Friends of yours," replied Figg; "come to see you;--Sir James Thornhill, Mr. Hogarth, and Mr. Gay. They send you every good wish."

"Offer them my hearty thanks," replied Jack, waving his hand to the group, all of whom returned the salutation. "And now, farewell, Mr. Figg! In a few minutes, all will be over."

Figg turned aside to hide the tears that started to his eyes,--for the stout prize-fighter, with a man's courage, had a woman's heart,--and the procession again set forward.

CHAPTER XXXII.
The Closing Scene.

TYBURN was now at hand. Over the sea of heads arose a black and dismal object. It was the gallows. Jack, whose back was towards it, did not see it; but he heard, from the pitying exclamations of the crowd, that it was in view. This circumstance produced no further alteration in his demeanour except that he endeavoured to abstract himself from the surrounding scene, and bend his attention to the prayers which the ordinary was reciting.

Just as he had succeeded in fixing his attention, it was again shaken, and he was almost unnerved by the sight of Mr. Wood, who was standing at the edge of a raised platform, anxiously waving his hand to him.

Jack instantly sprang to his feet, and as his guards construed the motion into an attempt to escape, several of them drew their swords and motioned to him to sit down. But Jack did not heed them. His looks were fixed on his old benefactor.

"God in Heaven bless you, unhappy boy!" cried. Wood, bursting into tears, "God bless you!"

Jack extended his hand towards him, and looked anxiously for Thames; but he was nowhere to be seen. A severe pang shot through Jack's heart, and he would have given worlds if he possessed them to have seen his friend once more. The wish was vain: and, endeavouring to banish every earthly thought, he addressed himself deeply and sincerely to prayer.

While this was passing, Jonathan had ridden back to Marvel to tell him that all was ready, and to give him his last instructions.

"You'll lose no time," said the thief-taker. "A hundred pounds if you do it quickly."

"Rely on me," rejoined the executioner, throwing away his pipe, which was just finished.

A deep dread calm, like that which precedes a thunderstorm, now prevailed amongst the assemblage. The thousand voices which a few moments before had been so clamorous were now hushed. Not a breath was drawn. The troops had kept a large space clear around the gallows. The galleries adjoining it were crowded with spectators,--so was the roof of a large tavern, then the only house standing at the end of the Edgeware Road,--so were the trees,--the walls of Hyde Park,--a neighbouring barn, a shed,--in short, every available position.

The cart, meantime, had approached the fatal tree. The guards, horse and foot, and constables formed a wide circle round it to keep off the mob. It was an awful moment--so awful, that every other feeling except deep interest in the scene seemed suspended.

At this terrible juncture, Jack maintained his composure,--a smile played upon his face before the cap was drawn over it,--and the last words he uttered were, "My poor mother! I shall soon join her!" The rope was then adjusted, and the cart began to move.

The next instant, he was launched into eternity!

Scarcely had he been turned off a moment, when a man with swarthy features leapt into the cart with an open clasp-knife in his hand, and, before he could be prevented, severed the rope, and cut down the body. It was Blueskin. His assistance came too late. A ball from Wild's pistol passed through his heart, and a volley of musketry poured from the guards lodged several balls in the yet breathing body of his leader.

Blueskin, however, was not unattended. A thousand eager assistants pressed behind him. Jack's body was caught, and passed from hand to hand over a thousand heads, till it was far from the fatal tree.

The shouts of indignation--the frightful yells now raised baffle description. A furious attack was made on Jonathan, who, though he defended himself like a lion, was desperately wounded, and would inevitably have perished if he had not been protected by the guards, who were obliged to use both swords and fire-arms upon the mob in his defence. He was at length rescued from his assailants,--rescued to perish, seven months afterwards, with every ignominy, at the very gibbet to which he had brought his victim.

The body of Jack Sheppard, meanwhile, was borne along by that tremendous host, which rose and fell like the waves of the ocean, until it approached the termination of the Edgeware Road.

At this point a carriage with servants in sumptuous liveries was stationed. At the open door stood a young man in a rich garb with a mask on his face, who was encouraging the mob by words and gestures. At length, the body was brought towards him. Instantly seizing it, the young man placed it in the carriage, shut the door, and commanded his servants to drive off. The order was promptly obeyed, and the horses proceeded at a furious pace along the Edgeware Road.

Half an hour afterwards the body of Jack was carefully examined. It had been cut down before life was extinct, but a ball from one of the soldiers had pierced his heart.

Thus died Jack Sheppard.

That night a grave was dug in Willesden churchyard, next to that in which Mrs. Sheppard had been interred. Two persons, besides the clergyman and sexton, alone attended the ceremony. They were a young man and an old one, and both appeared deeply affected. The coffin was lowered into the grave, and the mourners departed. A simple wooden monument was placed over the grave, but without any name or date. In after years, some pitying hand supplied the inscription, which ran thus--

THE END.

The Codes Of Hammurabi And Moses
W. W. Davies

QTY

The discovery of the Hammurabi Code is one of the greatest achievements of archaeology, and is of paramount interest, not only to the student of the Bible, but also to all those interested in ancient history...

Religion   ISBN: *1-59462-338-4*   **Pages:132**
MSRP $12.95

The Theory of Moral Sentiments
Adam Smith

QTY

This work from 1749. contains original theories of conscience amd moral judgment and it is the foundation for systemof morals.

Philosophy ISBN: *1-59462-777-0*   **Pages:536**
MSRP $19.95

Jessica's First Prayer
Hesba Stretton

QTY

In a screened and secluded corner of one of the many railway-bridges which span the streets of London there could be seen a few years ago, from five o'clock every morning until half past eight, a tidily set-out coffee-stall, consisting of a trestle and board, upon which stood two large tin cans, with a small fire of charcoal burning under each so as to keep the coffee boiling during the early hours of the morning when the work-people were thronging into the city on their way to their daily toil...

Pages:84

Childrens   ISBN: *1-59462-373-2*   **MSRP $9.95**

My Life and Work
Henry Ford

QTY

Henry Ford revolutionized the world with his implementation of mass production for the Model T automobile. Gain valuable business insight into his life and work with his own auto-biography... "We have only started on our development of our country we have not as yet, with all our talk of wonderful progress, done more than scratch the surface. The progress has been wonderful enough but..."

Pages:300

Biographies/   ISBN: *1-59462-198-5*   **MSRP $21.95**

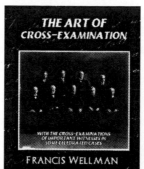

The Art of Cross-Examination
Francis Wellman

QTY

I presume it is the experience of every author, after his first book is published upon an important subject, to be almost overwhelmed with a wealth of ideas and illustrations which could readily have been included in his book, and which to his own mind, at least, seem to make a second edition inevitable. Such certainly was the case with me; and when the first edition had reached its sixth impression in five months, I rejoiced to learn that it seemed to my publishers that the book had met with a sufficiently favorable reception to justify a second and considerably enlarged edition. ..

Pages:412

Reference   **ISBN:** *1-59462-647-2*   *MSRP $19.95*

On the Duty of Civil Disobedience
Henry David Thoreau

QTY

Thoreau wrote his famous essay, On the Duty of Civil Disobedience, as a protest against an unjust but popular war and the immoral but popular institution of slave-owning. He did more than write—he declined to pay his taxes, and was hauled off to gaol in consequence. Who can say how much this refusal of his hastened the end of the war and of slavery ?

Law   **ISBN:** *1-59462-747-9*   **Pages:48**
MSRP $7.45

Dream Psychology Psychoanalysis for Beginners
Sigmund Freud

QTY

Sigmund Freud, born Sigismund Schlomo Freud (May 6, 1856 - September 23, 1939), was a Jewish-Austrian neurologist and psychiatrist who co-founded the psychoanalytic school of psychology. Freud is best known for his theories of the unconscious mind, especially involving the mechanism of repression; his redefinition of sexual desire as mobile and directed towards a wide variety of objects; and his therapeutic techniques, especially his understanding of transference in the therapeutic relationship and the presumed value of dreams as sources of insight into unconscious desires.

Pages:196

Psychology   **ISBN:** *1-59462-905-6*   *MSRP $15.45*

The Miracle of Right Thought
Orison Swett Marden

QTY

Believe with all of your heart that you will do what you were made to do. When the mind has once formed the habit of holding cheerful, happy, prosperous pictures, it will not be easy to form the opposite habit. It does not matter how improbable or how far away this realization may see, or how dark the prospects may be, if we visualize them as best we can, as vividly as possible, hold tenaciously to them and vigorously struggle to attain them, they will gradually become actualized, realized in the life. But a desire, a longing without endeavor, a yearning abandoned or held indifferently will vanish without realization.

Pages:360

Self Help   **ISBN:** *1-59462-644-8*   *MSRP $25.45*

www.bookjungle.com *email: sales@bookjungle.com fax: 630-214-0564 mail: Book Jungle PO Box 2226 Champaign, IL 61825*

QTY

The Rosicrucian Cosmo-Conception Mystic Christianity *by Max Heindel*   ISBN: *1-59462-188-8*   **$38.95**
The Rosicrucian Cosmo-conception is not dogmatic, neither does it appeal to any other authority than the reason of the student. It is: not controversial, but is: sent forth in the, hope that it may help to clear...   *New Age/Religion Pages 646*

Abandonment To Divine Providence *by Jean-Pierre de Caussade*   ISBN: *1-59462-228-0*   **$25.95**
"The Rev. Jean Pierre de Caussade was one of the most remarkable spiritual writers of the Society of Jesus in France in the 18th Century. His death took place at Toulouse in 1751. His works have gone through many editions and have been republished...   *Inspirational/Religion Pages 400*

Mental Chemistry *by Charles Haanel*   ISBN: *1-59462-192-6*   **$23.95**
Mental Chemistry allows the change of material conditions by combining and appropriately utilizing the power of the mind. Much like applied chemistry creates something new and unique out of careful combinations of chemicals the mastery of mental chemistry...   *New Age Pages 354*

The Letters of Robert Browning and Elizabeth Barret Barrett 1845-1846 vol II   ISBN: *1-59462-193-4*   **$35.95**
by Robert Browning and Elizabeth Barrett   *Biographies Pages 596*

Gleanings In Genesis (volume I) *by Arthur W. Pink*   ISBN: *1-59462-130-6*   **$27.45**
Appropriately has Genesis been termed "the seed plot of the Bible" for in it we have, in germ form, almost all of the great doctrines which are afterwards fully developed in the books of Scripture which follow...   *Religion/Inspirational Pages 420*

The Master Key *by L. W. de Laurence*   ISBN: *1-59462-001-6*   **$30.95**
In no branch of human knowledge has there been a more lively increase of the spirit of research during the past few years than in the study of Psychology, Concentration and Mental Discipline. The requests for authentic lessons in Thought Control, Mental Discipline and...   *New Age/Business Pages 422*

The Lesser Key Of Solomon Goetia *by L. W. de Laurence*   ISBN: *1-59462-092-X*   **$9.95**
This translation of the first book of the "Lernegton" which is now for the first time made accessible to students of Talismanic Magic was done, after careful collation and edition, from numerous Ancient Manuscripts in Hebrew, Latin, and French...   *New Age/Occult Pages 92*

Rubaiyat Of Omar Khayyam *by Edward Fitzgerald*   ISBN: *1-59462-332-5*   **$13.95**
Edward Fitzgerald, whom the world has already learned, in spite of his own efforts to remain within the shadow of anonymity, to look upon as one of the rarest poets of the century, was born at Bredfield, in Suffolk, on the 31st of March, 1809. He was the third son of John Purcell...   *Music Pages 172*

Ancient Law *by Henry Maine*   ISBN: *1-59462-128-4*   **$29.95**
The chief object of the following pages is to indicate some of the earliest ideas of mankind, as they are reflected in Ancient Law, and to point out the relation of those ideas to modern thought.   *Religion/History Pages 452*

Far-Away Stories *by William J. Locke*   ISBN: *1-59462-129-2*   **$19.45**
"Good wine needs no bush, but a collection of mixed vintages does. And this book is just such a collection. Some of the stories I do not want to remain buried for ever in the museum files of dead magazine-numbers an author's not unpardonable vanity..."   *Fiction Pages 272*

Life of David Crockett *by David Crockett*   ISBN: *1-59462-250-7*   **$27.45**
"Colonel David Crockett was one of the most remarkable men of the times in which he lived. Born in humble life, but gifted with a strong will, an indomitable courage, and unremitting perseverance...   *Biographies/New Age Pages 424*

Lip-Reading *by Edward Nitchie*   ISBN: *1-59462-206-X*   **$25.95**
Edward B. Nitchie, founder of the New York School for the Hard of Hearing, now the Nitchie School of Lip-Reading, Inc, wrote "LIP-READING Principles and Practice". The development and perfecting of this meritorious work on lip-reading was an undertaking...   *How-to Pages 400*

A Handbook of Suggestive Therapeutics, Applied Hypnotism, Psychic Science   ISBN: *1-59462-214-0*   **$24.95**
by Henry Munro   *Health/New Age/Health/Self-help Pages 376*

A Doll's House: and Two Other Plays *by Henrik Ibsen*   ISBN: *1-59462-112-8*   **$19.95**
Henrik Ibsen created this classic when in revolutionary 1848 Rome. Introducing some striking concepts in playwriting for the realist genre, this play has been studied the world over.   *Fiction/Classics/Plays 308*

The Light of Asia *by sir Edwin Arnold*   ISBN: *1-59462-204-3*   **$13.95**
In this poetic masterpiece, Edwin Arnold describes the life and teachings of Buddha. The man who was to become known as Buddha to the world was born as Prince Gautama of India but he rejected the worldly riches and abandoned the reigns of power when...   *Religion/History/Biographies Pages 170*

The Complete Works of Guy de Maupassant *by Guy de Maupassant*   ISBN: *1-59462-157-8*   **$16.95**
"For days and days, nights and nights, I had dreamed of that first kiss which was to consecrate our engagement, and I knew not on what spot I should put my lips..."   *Fiction/Classics Pages 240*

The Art of Cross-Examination *by Francis L. Wellman*   ISBN: *1-59462-309-0*   **$26.95**
Written by a renowned trial lawyer, Wellman imparts his experience and uses case studies to explain how to use psychology to extract desired information through questioning.   *How-to/Science/Reference Pages 408*

Answered or Unanswered? *by Louisa Vaughan*   ISBN: *1-59462-248-5*   **$10.95**
Miracles of Faith in China   *Religion Pages 112*

The Edinburgh Lectures on Mental Science (1909) *by Thomas*   ISBN: *1-59462-008-3*   **$11.95**
This book contains the substance of a course of lectures recently given by the writer in the Queen Street Hall, Edinburgh. Its purpose is to indicate the Natural Principles governing the relation between Mental Action and Material Conditions..   *New Age/Psychology Pages 148*

Ayesha *by H. Rider Haggard*   ISBN: *1-59462-301-5*   **$24.95**
Verily and indeed it is the unexpected that happens! Probably if there was one person upon the earth from whom the Editor of this, and of a certain previous history, did not expect to hear again...   *Classics Pages 380*

Ayala's Angel *by Anthony Trollope*   ISBN: *1-59462-352-X*   **$29.95**
The two girls were both pretty, but Lucy who was twenty-one who supposed to be simple and comparatively unattractive, whereas Ayala was credited, as her Bombwhat romantic name might show, with poetic charm and a taste for romance. Ayala when her father died was nineteen...   *Fiction Pages 484*

The American Commonwealth *by James Bryce*   ISBN: *1-59462-286-8*   **$34.45**
An interpretation of American democratic political theory. It examines political mechanics and society from the perspective of Scotsman James Bryce   *Politics Pages 572*

Stories of the Pilgrims *by Margaret P. Pumphrey*   ISBN: *1-59462-116-0*   **$17.95**
This book explores pilgrims religious oppression in England as well as their escape to Holland and eventual crossing to America on the Mayflower, and their early days in New England...   *History Pages 268*

www.bookjungle.com *email: sales@bookjungle.com fax: 630-214-0564 mail: Book Jungle PO Box 2226 Champaign, IL 61825*

QTY

The Fasting Cure *by Sinclair Upton*   ISBN: *1-59462-222-1* **$13.95**
In the Cosmopolitan Magazine for May, 1910, and in the Contemporary Review (London) for April, 1910, I published an article dealing with my experiences in fasting. I have written a great many magazine articles, but never one which attracted so much attention... New Age/Self Help/Health Pages 164

Hebrew Astrology *by Sepharial*   ISBN: *1-59462-308-2* **$13.45**
In these days of advanced thinking it is a matter of common observation that we have left many of the old landmarks behind and that we are now pressing forward to greater heights and to a wider horizon than that which represented the mind-content of our progenitors... Astrology Pages 144

Thought Vibration or The Law of Attraction in the Thought World   ISBN: *1-59462-127-6* **$12.95**
by William Walker Atkinson   *Psychology/Religion Pages 144*

Optimism *by Helen Keller*   ISBN: *1-59462-108-X* **$15.95**
Helen Keller was blind, deaf, and mute since 19 months old, yet famously learned how to overcome these handicaps, communicate with the world, and spread her lectures promoting optimism. An inspiring read for everyone... Biographies/Inspirational Pages 84

Sara Crewe *by Frances Burnett*   ISBN: *1-59462-360-0* **$9.45**
In the first place, Miss Minchin lived in London. Her home was a large, dull, tall one, in a large, dull square, where all the houses were alike, and all the sparrows were alike, and where all the door-knockers made the same heavy sound... Childrens/Classic Pages 88

The Autobiography of Benjamin Franklin *by Benjamin Franklin*   ISBN: *1-59462-135-7* **$24.95**
The Autobiography of Benjamin Franklin has probably been more extensively read than any other American historical work, and no other book of its kind has had such ups and downs of fortune. Franklin lived for many years in England, where he was agent... Biographies/History Pages 332

Name	
Email	
Telephone	
Address	
City, State ZIP	

☐ Credit Card   ☐ Check / Money Order

Credit Card Number	
Expiration Date	
Signature	

Please Mail to: Book Jungle
PO Box 2226
Champaign, IL 61825
or Fax to: 630-214-0564

ORDERING INFORMATION
web: *www.bookjungle.com*
email: *sales@bookjungle.com*
fax: *630-214-0564*
mail: *Book Jungle PO Box 2226 Champaign, IL 61825*
or PayPal *to sales@bookjungle.com*

Please contact us for bulk discounts

DIRECT-ORDER TERMS

20% Discount if You Order Two or More Books
Free Domestic Shipping!
Accepted: Master Card, Visa, Discover, American Express

9 781604 241037

Only copy in system— ~~2013~~ /2015